LATIN AMERICA

AND THE

ASIAN GIANTS

LATIN AMERICA

—— AND THE ——

ASIAN GIANTS

EVOLVING TIES WITH CHINA AND INDIA

Edited by

RIORDAN ROETT AND GUADALUPE PAZ

BROOKINGS INSTITUTION PRESS

Washington, D.C.

Library of Congress Cataloging-in-Publication data are available.
ISBN 978-0-8157-2696-8 (pbk. : alk. paper)
ISBN 978-0-8157-2697-5 (epub)

9 8 7 6 5 4 3 2 1

Typeset in Sabon

Composition by Westchester Publishing Services

CONTENTS

Part II
CRITICAL POLICY ISSUES FOR LATIN AMERICA, CHINA, AND INDIA

ACKNOWLEDGMENTS

We are indebted to numerous individuals and institutions that played a role in the completion of this volume. It would be impossible to name them all, but we would like to highlight those whose contributions were indispensable. We owe our greatest debt of gratitude to the Zemurray Foundation, whose generous support was instrumental in launching this book project. We would also like to thank Stephanie and Ludovico Feoli for their unfailing support and interest in our various academic endeavors. To our fellow authors we owe thanks not only for their valuable contributions but also for their patience during the lengthy editing process. A number of other experts provided input during the planning phase, as did the manuscript reviewers: we are grateful for their thoughtful efforts. Bill Finan and his team at the Brookings Institution Press were a pleasure to work with. We also thank Charles and Julian Roberts for their superb translation work. The research assistance provided by Ge "Pepe" Zhang was particularly helpful, as was the general support provided by the Johns Hopkins-SAIS Latin American Studies Program team, especially John McGeoch and Anne McKenzie. Finally, a very special thank you is owed to Theodore Kahn, a contributing author, for his additional assistance in finalizing the manuscript.

CHAPTER 1

Introduction

ASSESSING LATIN AMERICA'S RELATIONS
WITH THE ASIAN GIANTS

Guadalupe Paz

Since China adopted a "going global" strategy at the start of the twenty-first century, much has been written about its rapidly growing international presence, particularly in developing regions such as Southeast Asia, Africa, and Latin America. Sino–Latin American relations deepened considerably in recent years, to the point that we can refer to the first decade of the twenty-first century as "Latin America's China decade" (as Kevin Gallagher and Rebecca Ray do in chapter 4). In fact, while China was barely present on the region's radar screen in the previous decades, today it is difficult to imagine any discussion of Latin America's economic future without mentioning China as an important player.[1] However, as predicted early on, Latin America's trade relationship with China has been characterized by commodity-based exports from the region and manufactured imports from China that compete with local economic growth sectors. Although the China-driven commodity boom clearly helped the region weather the global financial crisis that erupted in 2008–09, Latin America's policymakers are increasingly preoccupied with the unbalanced nature of their trade relationship with China, particularly as the Asian giant faces an economic slowdown and global commodity prices are on a downward trend.

India, on the other hand, is only just beginning to emerge as a potentially important player in Latin America. Whether or not it will become

1

"Latin America's next big thing" remains an open question, but, as noted by the Inter-American Development Bank, "any cursory analysis of the complementarity between the two economies shows that the potential for massive bilateral trade is there; not unlike that which the region has been experiencing with China."[2] While India offers some interesting parallels to China's engagement with Latin America in terms of the size of its market, similar complementarities, and south-south diplomatic cooperation opportunities, some contrasts stand out, such as its strong democratic traditions and its service-driven insertion into the global economy. The main impediment to deeper relations between India and Latin America has thus far been the high cost of trade stemming from tariffs, nontariff barriers, and transportation costs. New diplomatic overtures on both sides have shown encouraging signs that these challenges can be overcome. If so, the prospects of a virtuous circle, in which more trade leads to greater cooperation and greater cooperation in turn leads to more trade, are promising.[3] The question for Latin American policymakers is how to build a balanced partnership by applying some of the lessons learned from the region's relationship with China.

This volume explores key policy concerns with respect to Latin America's evolving relationship with the Asian giants. In part I, the authors offer various perspectives on the expanding role that China and India are playing in Latin America, including an assessment of Latin America's changing global and geopolitical priorities (chapter 2), a south-south analysis of Indo–Latin American relations (chapter 3), and a compilation of short commentaries by leading experts and practitioners on Sino–Latin American relations, the growing ties between India and Latin America, and the opportunities and risks the region faces going forward (chapter 4). Part II takes a closer look at critical policy questions, including energy (chapter 5), food security (chapter 6), trade (chapter 7), migration (chapter 8), and broad security considerations (chapter 9). In part III, the authors offer diverse regional perspectives on key case studies: Chile as a bridge to Asia (chapter 10), Mexico as a case of weak institutional capacity in dealing with the Asian giants (chapter 11), and Argentina and Brazil as key regional players that have bet on Mercosur as a potential vehicle for greater international insertion (chapter 12). Part IV (chapter 13) offers a set of possible future scenarios for Latin America's relations with China and India. This introductory chapter presents an overview of the main questions explored in more detail in subsequent chapters, with the objective of providing a general basis for coherent analysis of the volume as a whole.

LATIN AMERICA'S ASIA STRATEGY: CHANGING DYNAMICS

In chapter 2, Riordan Roett provides a brief historical analysis leading up to Latin America's recent interest in trade and investment with Asia, portraying it as a hallmark of the present century and a manifestation of an emerging economic development model in the region. An important historical reference is the so-called resource curse that plagued the region in the post-independence era (1820s to 1940s). The newly independent states opted for insertion into the global free trade system, relying on commodity exports and capital goods imports for their economic development. However, Latin America soon fell victim to external shocks that are part and parcel of global cyclical patterns. World War I, the Great Depression, and World War II were particularly difficult periods for the region.

By the 1940s, most countries in Latin America had turned away from an export-led growth model and had instead adopted an inward-looking development strategy known as import substitution industrialization, which eventually proved inadequate in the face of globalization and the region's inability to compete in the international trading system with locally produced higher-priced, lower-quality products. Following the debt crisis and the "lost decade" of the 1980s, the region adopted a new model of economic and political liberalization known as the Washington Consensus, with different levels of success. By the late 1990s, a number of countries in the region had begun to vocally condemn the liberalization trend and revert to state-led—and heavily populist—economic development strategies, epitomized by the rise of Hugo Chávez in Venezuela. It is against this backdrop that China's emergence in the region changed Latin America's development outlook.

Roett describes the region's pivot to Asia as a redirection of trade and investment as well as a recognition of geopolitical opportunities, underscoring the importance of the Trans-Pacific Partnership (TPP) and the Pacific Alliance as historical shifts redefining global priorities. As concerns about overreliance on the Chinese market grow, India is becoming an interesting trade and investment alternative for Latin America. According to Roett, it is imperative that the region maintain an outward-looking posture; as he writes, "The TPP and the Pacific Alliance offer, selectively, an exit from failed or moribund regional groupings that remain highly exclusive and inward-looking."

Chapter 3 offers an overview of Latin America's incipient economic engagement with India. After a brief history of Indo–Latin American relations, Jorge Heine and Hari Seshasayee focus on the current state of the relationship, taking the 1990s, when both sides adopted neoliberal policies, as a turning point. India's impressive growth in the 2000s, coupled with its enormous market and demand for commodities, set in motion a growing momentum for deeper commercial and other ties. To date, the main areas of Indo–Latin American economic interaction have been energy, mining, information and communications technology (ICT), pharmaceuticals, and motor vehicles. As the authors note, these relationships are maturing from being merely transactional to developing into deeper engagement through investment and joint ventures. Among the gaps that need to be addressed through enhanced political efforts on both sides are tariffs and other market access barriers, distance-related connectivity, and general knowledge and information access.

India's engagement with Latin America has occurred primarily through bilateral channels. The authors note that there is room to strengthen collaboration in areas of mutual interest, particularly in international forums such as the United Nations. They also argue that India needs to adopt a more nuanced approach to Latin America by differentiating among three different regional subgroupings, each of which offers different opportunities. Although it is still early to gauge whether India's government will invest in deepening Indo–Latin American relations or will instead follow an "India-first" strategy focused on addressing domestic challenges, it is expected that closer ties between the two regions will continue to develop.

REGIONAL POLICY PERSPECTIVES

In chapter 4, various leading specialists provide short opinion pieces on Sino–Latin American relations and the growing importance of India in the region. As Sun Hongbo argues in his commentary on Sino–Latin American relations from the Chinese perspective, a number of hurdles will need to be addressed in the coming years. Uncertainty regarding the implications of China's economic slowdown and the structural reforms under way, coupled with the uncertainty derived from Latin American political cycles, will undoubtedly influence how policymakers think about the future of the relationship. Mutual trust also needs to be strengthened. As Sun notes, skepticism about China's activities and incentives in the region remains an issue, as fears regarding "financial imperialism" and deindustrialization persist. Expanded Chinese financing in infrastructure and other areas could open the door to diversification into noncommodity sectors, greater Chinese development aid, and technology transfer.

Xiang Lanxin offers another perspective on China's diplomatic strategy in the twenty-first century, which he characterizes as one focused on managing its very different bilateral relations across the globe while at the same time promoting the country's "peaceful rise" and a "harmonious world" in light of the perceived decline of the United States in a multipolar world. In this context, China has established a set of "strategic partnerships" with Latin American countries, increasingly displaying a more comprehensive approach to Latin America that includes a geopolitical calculation.

Xiang posits that there are three main reasons China now views Latin America as an important geopolitical asset: (1) China's deepening ties with Latin America will put pressure on the United States, distracting it from the proposed "pivot to Asia" diplomatic initiative; (2) the Chinese policy establishment believes Latin American countries will consider China a viable counterweight to U.S. hegemony in the region; and (3) as a member of the BRICS bloc—Brazil, Russia, India, China, and South Africa—which China envisions as a major vehicle for collective south-south leadership in reshaping global economic policymaking, Brazil is viewed as China's anchor in the region. He argues that while Chinese investment in the region is not helping local industry as much as it could, the threat of deindustrialization is overblown. In addition, China has a long-term interest in Latin American prosperity and stability, and as Chinese wages rise, Latin America will be better able to implement a more effective set of policies to make its manufacturing sectors more competitive. Although China has applied a consistent strategy across the region, the future of Sino–Latin American relations hinges on a set of diverse responses from the Latin American countries facing different challenges associated with the bilateral relationship.

Jorge Guajardo presents a Latin American perspective on China's growing presence in the region. He argues that the commonly accepted narrative that China offers important economic opportunities for Latin America as well as a geopolitical counterpoint to U.S. influence is too simplistic. To better understand Sino–Latin American relations, he proposes three considerations: (1) China is driven almost entirely by economic self-interest; (2) Latin American economies are diverse, and hence generalizations at the regional level are not appropriate; and (3) a number of policy options are available to Latin American policymakers to maximize the benefits and minimize the costs of engagement with China.

Several problems with the current dynamics in Sino–Latin American relations stand out. Chinese loans to the region are often made on less favorable terms than those by Western creditors and often include requirements to purchase Chinese equipment or hire Chinese labor, limiting the benefits of investment. Trade patterns are making Latin America overly dependent on extractive industries and restricting competitive growth in manufacturing sectors. Also, Chinese state-owned enterprises (SOEs) tend to operate in a nontransparent fashion, sometimes leading to misunderstandings in democratic environments where public support for projects is essential.

So what can be done to address these issues? In line with the approach offered by Robert Devlin and Theodore Kahn in chapter 7, Guajardo outlines how policy options vary according to the different economic profiles of Latin American countries. Major manufacturers such as Mexico compete head-to-head with China and hence have less to gain and more to lose from increased Chinese influence in the region. In these cases, priority should be given to blocking anticompetitive practices such as unfair domestic subsidies and dumping policies, while also taking advantage of areas where there are clear benefits (such as participating in the TPP) and complementarities (Mexico could gain from promoting tourism and expanding agricultural trade with China). Major commodity producers such as Brazil and Chile should focus on diversifying away from a China-centric export strategy through trade agreements with countries outside the region (for example, through the TPP) or by incorporating industry and services provisions in bilateral agreements with China. Further developing tourism industry opportunities and taking a more cautious approach to infrastructure investments are other mechanisms at their disposal. Central American countries have limited natural resources and small manufacturing sectors (with the exception of Costa Rica). These countries may benefit from Chinese foreign direct investment (FDI) in apparel and other low-tech manufacturing, areas where they may have a labor cost advantage. They may also benefit from increased agricultural trade and infrastructure development deals with China. Finally, countries lacking access to global financial markets, such as pre-Macri Argentina and Venezuela, should carefully weigh their options, particularly if Chinese financial deals are worse than default in the long run.

Kevin P. Gallagher and Rebecca Ray outline both the benefits and risks associated with linking Latin America's development strategy with China's recent economic boom. Latin American exports to China grew faster than exports to the rest of the world, but they were mostly limited to primary commodity sectors. Chinese finance in the region also grew significantly in the first decade of the twenty-first century—to the point that it rivaled financing from the World Bank and the Inter-American Development Bank—although FDI remained relatively low, as noted by Anthony Boadle in chapter 4.

Gallagher and Ray highlight some of the risks associated with Latin America's economic ties with China. On the one hand, both exports from the region and finance from China—which have predominantly focused on the extraction, mining, and agricultural sectors—have created incentives for deindustrialization (and related low job growth), environmental degradation, and social conflict. On the other hand, overreliance on commodity exports without sound countercyclical measures—such as investing a portion of the high returns associated with the commodity boom in economic upgrading and diversification, environmental protection measures, and savings for future downturns—left the region vulnerable to China's economic slowdown and a return to volatile global commodity prices. As various authors in this volume point out, demand for commodities from China and other growing economies, particularly India, is likely to remain high. The key will be for Latin America to think more strategically going forward in order to mitigate the above-mentioned risks.

Regarding India's perspective on Latin America, in chapter 4 Deepak Bhojwani argues that the country's foreign policy priorities have shifted along with its impressive economic growth in the past decades. But only recently has India focused on the potential that Latin America has to offer, particularly that emanating from significant economic complementarities. As noted by various authors, Indo–Latin American trade grew significantly in the 2003–2013 decade, but it is highly skewed toward hydrocarbon imports from India. However, excess Indian refining capacity has led to Latin American imports of petroleum products from India. According to Bhojwani, the main hurdle for greater Indian investment in the region's energy sector is financial; in his words, India "does not have pockets as deep as the Chinese and is far more stringent on the bottom line."

Politically, Bhojwani notes, some Latin American countries also fail to inspire sufficient investor confidence. Food security is another area of complementarity—India has the second-largest population in the world and, in contrast to Latin America, its land-population ratio is poor, as are its agricultural output and water resources. However, lack of familiarity with local conditions, coupled with unfavorable land tenure laws, has discouraged Indian investment in the agricultural sector. Cooperation in security and technology has been limited, and though trade and investment have yielded better results, tariffs and nontariff barriers, transportation costs, and poor connectivity all remain significant obstacles. Bhojwani argues that "India needs to take the initiative to establish better connectivity, and above all, it needs to realize the importance of political approximation as the catalyst for economic partnership."

Furthermore, he states, "India must make up for lost time. Its foreign policy establishment has suffered from insufficient political acknowledgment of the partnership that is on offer with Latin America."

Rengaraj Viswanathan provides a perspective on India's ties with the four countries analyzed as case studies in Part III of this volume—Argentina, Brazil, Chile, and Mexico—which account for about half of India's trade with the entire Latin American region ($20.43 billion in 2013), with Brazil and Mexico accounting for the bulk of this share (trade with Brazil was about $10 billion and trade with Mexico was about $6 billion that same year).[4] However, as he points out, India is not likely to follow in China's footsteps and become a major trading partner of these countries in the near future (in 2013, China's trade with these four countries was ten times that of India's). Nonetheless, India will remain a top destination for certain exports, such as crude oil from Brazil and Mexico, soy oil from Argentina, and copper from Chile.

Viswanathan argues that, in general, Indian companies enjoy a more positive image in Latin America than their Chinese counterparts, which can only help deepen bilateral ties as governments on both sides increasingly work toward achieving shared goals, both at the global level and in terms of bilateral relations. He states that Modi's government is likely to be more proactive on foreign policy initiatives and predicts that trade between India and the four case study countries will likely continue to grow at a pace of 15–20 percent annually.

Anthony Boadle reiterates how China's economic slowdown has highlighted Latin America's overreliance on commodity exports to China and how the region is facing the possibility of deindustrialization as a result of competition from Chinese manufactured imports. In addition, he argues, Latin American countries face structural difficulties in their trade relationship with China, such as physical distance and the lack of a level playing field regarding state regulations. In terms of investment, similar patterns have emerged. Most of China's investment in Latin America has gone into extractive industries, and promised Chinese investment in infrastructure projects has in many cases stalled. As Boadle notes, Chinese investment in the region is very small in proportion to the volume of Sino–Latin American trade. A good portion of financial flows into the region has come in the form of "loans-for-oil" deals with countries such as Venezuela, and in 2010, Chinese loans to Latin America exceeded those of the World Bank, the Inter-American Development Bank, and the U.S. Export-Import Bank combined. While these loans generally come with higher interest rates than loans from the international financial institutions, they have less restrictive conditions attached to them. Investment in China by Latin American companies has been very limited.

Boadle also looks into the role that India, an emerging player in Latin America, might have in the region's future. As various contributors to this volume point out, India presents an opportunity for Latin America to diversify away from China, although trade with India thus far has been much more modest and has followed a similar commodities-for-manufactures pattern. However, India may have more to offer, given its share of services in its exports and more sophisticated, private sector-led investments. Like other contributors, Boadle notes that Indo–Latin American trade is expected to continue growing, and India is seen as a new potential source of technology transfer in the region.

KEY POLICY ISSUES

The main areas driving relations between Latin America and the Asian giants are energy resources, food security, and overall trade complementarities. New policy considerations are also rapidly emerging, such as migration trends and changing security and geopolitical realities. Part II of this volume takes a closer look at the latest developments in these key areas and explores policy options for the future.

In chapter 5, Francisco González offers an overview of Latin America's energy landscape, focusing on the strategies and policies of the region's main hydrocarbon producers to maximize the benefits—and also minimize the costs—of their growing energy ties with China and India. In the first decade of the twenty-first century, China significantly increased its presence in Latin America's energy sectors, particularly in hydrocarbon exploration, production, and refining, as well as in storage and transportation. Although India is only just emerging as a potentially important player, more than half of its overall trade with Latin America in 2013 was in crude oil ($22 billion out of $42 billion).

Also since the start of the twenty-first century, Latin America's energy markets have been hit by several external shocks. The first was a positive demand shock resulting from the rapid consumption growth in China and the United States. The second was a negative supply shock caused by disruptions in conflict areas where there is significant oil production (such as Iraq, Libya, and Nigeria). The third was the shale revolution, which since the mid-2000s has caused a positive supply shock to fossil fuel markets across the globe. González posits that the shale industry will likely be a game changer in Latin America, where traditional oil exporters to the United States (Mexico and Venezuela) are being displaced by domestic U.S. shale oil producers.

He also notes that the international energy landscape has led to two main approaches to energy policy in Latin America: a statist one (in Bolivia, Ecuador, and Venezuela, and to a lesser extent in Argentina and Brazil) and a more business-friendly one (in Colombia and Mexico—since its recent and historic energy sector opening—and Peru). Such diversity makes it difficult to generalize how China and India will engage the region's energy sector in the future, but it is clear that energy security concerns will continue to drive the Asian giants' energy ties with Latin America. González points to the possibility that the twenty-first century will indeed turn out to be the "Asian century" as a sound business proposition for Latin American hydrocarbon producers; in this context, he provides a set of rational scenarios for Chinese investment in the region, and for Latin American energy policy in the coming years.

On the issue of food security, Mariano Turzi (chapter 6) explains how more intense competition for food resources, in particular agricultural goods, is increasingly linking Latin America and Asia and framing an important part of the broader international relations discourse. He lists four main factors affecting the growing demand for food commodities. First, global population growth, a greater concentration of urban population, and longer life spans have resulted in a structural upward shift in food demand. Feed for livestock is another important driver of agricultural demand. Biofuels production has, to some extent, affected demand for certain food crops when high oil prices have made it an economically rational alternative. Finally, the so-called financialization of food commodities has also had an impact on food prices—the commodities futures market grew from \$13 billion in 2003 to an impressive \$412 billion in 2012.

With regard to China, where food supply is limited by land and water constraints and demand exceeds supply, Turzi notes the following: "As relative food scarcities continue to deepen and move the world into a new age of geopolitical and geoeconomic competition, securing agricultural resources in Latin America is fast becoming a priority of Chinese foreign policy and a key element in guaranteeing food security. For Beijing, the strategic aim of securing supplies is directly linked with guaranteeing social stability and regime preservation." Deeming free trade an insufficient source of food, China has pursued its food security interests in Latin America primarily through SOEs to build its own "state-owned international food supply chain."

Like China, India is also drawn to Latin America by food security interests. However, India's engagement with the region has been driven primarily by private agribusiness actors. As such, the Indian government's food security interests align with those of profit-seeking enterprises, and rather than "crowding out" local participation in food value chains as the Chinese SOEs do, Indian investments allow for "synergistic integration" between local and foreign actors at different stages of the value chain.

On the supply side, Latin American countries face a number of challenges beyond those related to commodity-based trade patterns and economic structures, including climate change, decreasing water resources as a result of mismanagement and pollution, and land degradation. Turzi contends that the region lacks adequate policy responses to many of these issues and that too often, short-sighted political cycles drive government priorities. Overall, it is clear that food security is an increasingly important issue, with global characteristics and implications, and that China and India are playing a key role in reshaping agricultural structures, international networks, and trade patterns simply by virtue of their market size. Turzi argues that, as suppliers of much-needed agricultural resources, Latin American countries have some leverage to negotiate better trade and investment deals with the Asian giants and other interested parties. Looking ahead, the countries in the region have a unique opportunity to capitalize on their agricultural comparative advantage to better serve their development needs by taking a more proactive approach to defining the changing dynamics of global food security networks.

In chapter 7, Robert Devlin and Theodore Kahn offer an interesting analysis of the role of trade in Latin America's growth and economic development. They posit that the region needs an effective "business plan" or policy strategy for trade to be a driver of sustained growth and productivity. Any such business plan would inevitably include China and India because of the size of their economies, but it must also consider how to better leverage existing opportunities both in Asia and other regions—particularly close to home, within the Western Hemisphere.

Devlin and Kahn differentiate between two subregions in Latin America when analyzing the effects of increased trade with China in the 2003–2013 decade. South America's exports are dominated by commodities and its imports by manufactured products, whereas in the Mexico–Central America–Dominican Republic (DR) subregion both exports and imports are dominated by manufactured goods. These different profiles have led to different outcomes vis-à-vis trade with China. South American countries have registered trade surpluses, even if in some cases (Argentina and Brazil, in particular) the manufacturing sector has suffered owing to competition from cheap manufactured imports from China. In the Mexico–Central America–DR subregion there has been a clear displacement of domestic producers of manufactured goods, while there has been little or no gain from Chinese demand for commodities, resulting in considerable trade deficits with the Asian giant. Trade with India, on the other hand, has been quite small in comparison, with only a few countries considered significant trade partners (Venezuela and Colombia). However, volume aside, the patterns are similar to those of China's trade with the region: natural resource–rich South America has registered trade surpluses with India while the northern countries of the region have registered trade deficits.

Although reversing the commodities-for-manufactures pattern of trade between Latin America and the Asian giants may not be feasible in light of resource endowments and complementarities, Devlin and Kahn argue that there is still room to use Asian-driven demand for commodities to finance upgrading strategies. At the core of these strategies should be promoting competitiveness and productivity through enhanced industrial policies aimed at research and development, diversification of exports and production, and participation in global value chains to upgrade into higher-value-added activities. The authors also suggest taking a closer look at regional markets—Latin America and North America—as part of their strategies to diversify and upgrade, in light of the advantages of intraregional trade in terms of greater value-added and diversity of products.

Migration is becoming an increasingly important issue in Latin America's relations with China and, to a lesser degree, India. As Jacqueline Mazza explains in chapter 8, the changing migration trend lines are cause for new tensions and also opportunities as Chinese and Indian investments in the region reach new heights. Although existing data most likely fail to capture the true extent of migration flows, clear patterns emerge when one examines the trend lines: Chinese migration to the region is concentrated in South America, while Indian migration, seven times smaller than China's, is mainly to Central America and the Caribbean. Chinese migration is most notable after 2005, and Mazza distinguishes three main types: (1) workforce migrants (mostly low- and medium-skilled male workers), tied to investments or donations, (2) independent diaspora-linked migrants, and (3) transit migrants whose final destination is the United States or another country in the region. In recent years, a fourth category—human trafficking and criminal migration related to Chinese gangs—has become a notorious issue in some countries. Indian migration to the region since 2000 has shown a steady increase, but it remains relatively small and quite limited geographically.

The main source of tension stemming from Chinese migration is related to local employment, namely, the secrecy surrounding Chinese labor flows—particularly in areas where there is high unemployment—and the compound living conditions of labor migrants, which prevents them from integrating into the local communities. Mazza posits that Latin American policymakers will need to think more strategically with regard to Chinese and Indian investments in the region and aim for better integration with the local labor markets and greater gains for local workers, noting that "migration in a more mobile and global world economy is, or could be, a more integrated feature and player in the future economic advances of Latin America, China, and India."

The security dimension of China's and India's engagement with Latin America is addressed by R. Evan Ellis in chapter 9. As in other areas of bilateral relations, China has developed a much greater presence in the region than India, but in both cases, military activities by the Asian giants in Latin America are more significant than most people realize, particularly in recent years. From arms sales to military-to-military ties, coupled with broader issues linked to commercial ties, reduced U.S. influence in the region, and the survival of populist regimes in Latin America, Ellis argues, such military engagement is fundamentally changing the security dynamics of the Western Hemisphere.

Chinese arms companies have sold sophisticated military systems to Venezuela and other politically sympathetic members of the Bolivarian Alliance for the Peoples of Our America (ALBA), namely, Bolivia and Ecuador. Sales have included radar systems, fighter aircraft, military transport aircraft, amphibious assault vehicles, rocket launchers, and self-propelled grenade launchers, along with less sophisticated nonlethal products. Attempts to expand sales to other countries, such as Argentina and Peru, have been less successful owing to various setbacks and last-minute cancellations, but expanded sales in the region appear to be moving forward. In this regard, not only has China expanded arms procurement options for rogue states like Venezuela, which cannot purchase arms from the United States, but it has done so offering generally lower prices than competitors, along with financing from Chinese banks.

Indian military sales to the region have been modest in comparison, and they have been limited primarily to light helicopters and light military trucks. However, joint efforts between India's Defense Research and Development Organization (DRDO) and Brazil's Ministry of Defense and the aircraft company Embraer have led to the production of an airborne radar platform. Also, in early 2014, the Indian Ministry of Defense authorized the sale of hypersonic missiles, in which Venezuela has expressed an interest.

Among the concerns generated by arms sales in the region is the fear that sophisticated weapons could make their way into the hands of organized crime and terrorist organizations. Furthermore, as commercial interests drive efforts to improve transport and other infrastructure networks within Latin America, illegal activities will also find easier access to previously isolated areas. A more established physical presence of Asian companies and other actors in Latin America could also translate into greater economic and other "soft power" leverage in the region. Trans-Pacific organized crime is also of growing concern. A higher incidence of human trafficking, drug trafficking, sales of contraband goods and precursor chemicals, money laundering, and illegal trade in minerals is evident, and governments on both sides of the Pacific have proven ill-equipped to deal with these challenges. Finally, Ellis argues that the growing influence of the Asian giants in the region could not only indirectly help prolong the life of anti-U.S. populist regimes (particularly in the case of China's engagement with Venezuela and Ecuador) but also reshape future military scenarios should there be, for example, a confrontation between the United States and China, as some Latin American governments could opt to side against the United States and allow China access to strategic ports, airfields, and other infrastructure.

CASE STUDIES: CHINA, INDIA, AND KEY ACTORS IN LATIN AMERICA

Looking ahead, it is important to consider the role of certain key countries in the context of Latin America's pivot to Asia. Part III focuses on the case studies of Argentina, Brazil, Chile, and Mexico. The three South American countries account for the bulk of the region's exports to China—in fact, they are among a handful of countries in the region that can boast an accumulated trade surplus with China throughout the first decade of the twenty-first century and the early 2010s. Mexico, in contrast, competes directly with China, both in terms of export products (composed primarily of manufactured goods) and U.S. market share. Compared to its aforementioned South American neighbors, Mexico's exports to China are rather limited, but it is the largest recipient of Chinese exports to the region. Hence, several authors differentiate between the South American commodity exporters and countries such as Mexico, whose experiences with China differ considerably. India's engagement with these countries has thus far shown some similar patterns, although important differences are also highlighted by various authors.

Also of relevance when considering the four case studies is the notion that there are two distinct blocs in Latin America that differ considerably in their regional and cross-regional economic and diplomatic strategies. The first bloc is integrated by Pacific-facing nations—in particular the members of the Pacific Alliance, Chile, Colombia, Mexico, and Peru—whose preferred development models are based on liberal principles, free trade, and closer ties to the United States. The second bloc is composed of Atlantic-facing nations—in particular Mercosur members Argentina, Brazil, and Venezuela—whose preferred strategy is to give the state a leading role in economic development and whose general tendency is to be wary of U.S. influence in the region.[5] These different approaches have influenced the way individual countries in each bloc view the opportunities and risks associated with greater engagement with the Asian giants.

Alicia Frohmann and Manfred Wilhelmy (chapter 10) explore Chile's position as a possible bridge between Latin America and Asia. They argue that the idea of a bridge country is a misguided self-perception by Chile with a fundamentally unilateral character, and that neighboring countries have developed their own strategies to deal with the Asian giants. The authors note, however, that a central challenge for most Latin American countries is scale: compared to the much larger Asian economies, South American economies (except Brazil) have limited leverage over Asian countries in bilateral negotiations. Hence, subregional blocs—in particular the Pacific Alliance and Mercosur—are critical when seeking to deepen trade relations. Although a number of formal integration efforts within Latin America have suffered serious setbacks, de facto regional integration through investment, trade, and migration has raised Chile's profile regionally and globally (for example, Chilean "multilatinas" have successfully established operations in several Latin American countries). Chile is thus well positioned to play a relevant role in strengthening regional ties with Asia through its growing economic presence in the region and its participation in key groups such as the Pacific Alliance and Mercosur.

In chapter 11, Enrique Dussel Peters explains how Mexico has been slow to place Asia in focus in terms of policy planning, noting that the government's 2013 national strategic plan, the Plan Nacional de Desarrollo 2013–2018 (PND), is the first to offer specific goals with regard to Asia. Over the course of the first decade of the twenty-first century, China became Mexico's second-largest trading partner, but Mexico faces important competition in key manufacturing sectors and a considerable trade deficit with the Asian giant. Much like its Latin American neighbors, Mexico risks increasing the "primarization" of its export basket. In addition, Chinese investment in Mexico has been scarce. In recent years, government efforts on both sides have emphasized the importance of increasing Chinese investment in Mexico. India, on the other hand, appears to be ahead on the investment front. India does not make the list of Mexico's top ten trading partners but has, since the 1990s, significantly increased its investment presence in the steel, manufacturing, and software sectors. Dussel Peters writes that "there is an increasing gap between [Mexico's] growing economic ties [with China and India] and the [country's] institutional capacity to address this new reality." He proposes strengthening Mexico's bilateral ties with the two Asian giants, rather than relying on multilateral forums such as the TPP and the Pacific Alliance, by investing in existing and new institutions.

In chapter 12, Henrique Altemani de Oliveira offers a perspective on Mercosur's leading members, Argentina and Brazil. He argues that rather than an "Atlantic" strategy, Mercosur was a gamble on Southern Cone regionalism as an alternative to broader integration schemes, and at the core of its political agenda was the notion that the United States has never had a genuine interest in regional integration with Latin America. Further, Altemani perceives Mercosur as an effort to bolster regional cooperation, noting that "the fact that the region now features different models of economic development and different political regimes does not represent the rise of antagonistic blocs." In this regard, he considers cooperation between the Pacific Alliance and Mercosur as likely, especially in light of recent signs of interest on both sides to engage in dialogue.

The emergence of China and India as commercial partners in the region has positioned them to be strategic partners for both Brazil and Argentina, an arrangement that would open up new opportunities for diplomatic engagement, most often characterized as south-south cooperation. To date, however (as noted by various authors), the trend has been to deepen relations at the bilateral, national level rather than at the regional level, although China and India have pursued different multilateral strategies as well, the former through participation in regional institutions such as the Organization of American States (OAS), the Inter-American Development Bank, and the Caribbean Development Bank, and the latter through trade and dialogue initiatives with Mercosur, the Andean Community, the Caribbean Community and Common Market (CARICOM), and others.

Altemani argues that China's more substantial interests in Latin America have led to a gradual deepening of economic ties, to the point that FDI from China is moving toward more productive manufacturing sectors; indeed, there are promising signs that the relationship is maturing and diversifying away from commodities-based trade. For India, on the other hand, Latin America seems to be of lesser priority. However, partnerships in sectors where India has a clear comparative advantage—in particular ICT and pharmaceuticals—have become increasingly common in Argentina, Brazil, and other countries in the region. He concludes that "in the context of a nonexclusionary Mercosur, Argentina and Brazil have turned to Asia as another priority in their international insertion efforts. . . . Among the main considerations are (1) their economic and commercial capacity, (2) the availability of resources as a source of FDI, (3) the potential for scientific-technological cooperation, and (4) Asia's coinciding interest in reevaluating the current international order."

PREPARING FOR THE NEXT DECADE

A common theme throughout this volume is the heightened awareness of Latin American governments of the risks associated with the pattern of commodities-for-manufactures trade established between Latin America and China since the late 1990s, and increasingly between Latin America and India. One of the region's most important long-term priorities is to develop effective strategies to diversify trade and upgrade to higher-value-added production chains to be more competitive in the increasingly complex global economy. Significant new investment in research and development, human capital, and infrastructure will be required. It is also clear that, as Latin American ties with the Asian giants deepen, new challenges and opportunities in areas such as migration and security are emerging. Latin American governments should devise more comprehensive long-term policy plans to address areas of increasing strategic importance and to better leverage their comparative advantage sectors to more effectively channel resources toward key growth sectors.

In the concluding chapter, Mauricio Mesquita Moreira and Theodore Kahn present a set of policy options for the region to maximize the benefits and minimize the risks of the countries' growing ties with China and India. To illustrate how possible future scenarios regarding Latin America's engagement with China and India might unfold, they offer a "dream" scenario and "nightmare" scenario for the region's relations with each of the two Asian giants. The Sino–Latin American worst-case scenario would be one in which China applied its economic and geopolitical power to dictate the terms of its relationships with Latin American countries, further subordinating them to its interests. The dream Sino–Latin American scenario would be one in which diplomatic and economic cooperation supported a set of policies aimed at increasing opportunities to diversify trade toward more value-added exports and attract Chinese investment in areas that support sustained growth and increased competitiveness. For Indo–Latin American relations, the nightmare scenario would not look much different from the present situation—protectionism on both sides would continue to limit trade and investment opportunities. The dream scenario would instead consist of steadily increasing trade and investment, and governments working together to eliminate high tariffs and connectivity issues, with the private sector playing an important role.

As this volume illustrates, the new dynamics shaping the future of Latin America's relations with the Asian giants are primarily related to the question of how to expand trade and investment in such a way that the region can embark on a path of sustained growth by strengthening its competitiveness at the global level while also addressing ongoing environmental and social concerns. In the case of Latin America's relations with China, the direction that the fifth generation of leadership, currently led by Xi Jinping, decides to take in terms of the country's economic strategy will be a defining factor. The future of Indo–Latin American relations will be greatly affected by whether Narendra Modi's government succeeds in implementing important reforms, such as removing high tariffs and other obstacles to trade and investment, as a way to raise India's international profile. However, as Mesquita Moreira and Kahn note, perhaps a more important first step would be for the governments of Latin America to make the necessary reforms at home so that they can participate at the negotiating table from a position of greater strength.

NOTES

1. See, for example, Inter-American Development Bank (IDB), "Ten Years after the Take-off: Taking Stock of China–Latin America and the Caribbean Economic Relations" (Washington, DC: IDB, Integration and Trade Sector, October 2010).

2. Mauricio Mesquita Moreira, coordinator, *India: Latin America's Next Big Thing?* (Washington, DC: IDB, 2010), p. ix.

3. Ibid., p. 138.

4. Rengaraj Viswanathan, "Regional View on Prospects for the Future: India's Interaction with Argentina, Brazil, Chile, and Mexico," Gateway House, Mumbai, October 13, 2014, unpublished paper (preliminary version of contribution to this volume).

5. For a more detailed analysis of this two-bloc notion, see David Luhnow, "The Two Latin Americas," *Wall Street Journal*, January 3, 2014.

Part I

THE EXPANDING ROLE OF CHINA AND INDIA IN LATIN AMERICA

CHAPTER 2

Latin America Looks to Asia

Integration, Cooperation, and Geopolitical Goals

Riordan Roett

Latin America's role in the global economy has undergone numerous changes since independence in the early nineteenth century. But the current policy goal of expanding into Asian markets is a hallmark of the early twenty-first century. Undertakings such as the Pacific Alliance and the Trans-Pacific Partnership (TPP), as well as new bilateral trade arrangements and Latin American investment in Asia, indicate that a majority of the countries of the region have begun to opt for a new trade and development model. A few decades ago we would not have discussed investment from Latin America and the Caribbean (LAC) in countries like China, but today it is a growing reality. This chapter briefly traces the off-again, on-again relationship between LAC and the global economy. It also offers an assessment of the emerging scenarios for integration and cooperation between LAC and Asia, as well as the region's changing geopolitical interests vis-à-vis the Asian giants.

HISTORICAL BACKGROUND

Since independence, LAC linkages to the world economy have gone through significant changes. Beginning in the 1820s, the countries opted for free trade and access to international capital markets. But, as Victor

Bulmer-Thomas has written, these were a mixed blessing.[1] The availability of global financing, while attractive, was poorly managed by the new republics, and all were in default by the end of the 1820s. And though the issue of free trade, in theory, was viable, it soon became a debate over levels of taxation to support national budgets. Customs duties were the principal driver of trade policy for the next few decades. As the new republics began to stabilize politically, the ruling elites decided that the future development of the region was inexorably linked to an expansion of commodity and raw material exports and the import of needed capital goods. But governments soon discovered that they were dependent on a number of factors beyond their control. The cyclical patterns of international trade were a reality over which they had little, if any, control. External shocks often had an impact on market access—the U.S. Civil War, for example. And, not unlike today's dependence on one or a few commodity exports (the so-called resource curse), the countries entered into commodity dependence with limited opportunities for export diversification.

World War I ended the first phase of the region's insertion into the international free trade regime. International capital availability disappeared as Europe went to war and many countries recalled outstanding loans and were unable or unwilling to issue new loans. The European market had become increasingly important before the war for managing the financing of the balance of payments, usually in deficit, but exports to Europe dropped dramatically. As Europe began the traumatic process of rebuilding after the devastation of the war, the United States emerged as a new player in LAC and soon replaced Europe as a major trading partner for the region. The 1920s were a period of instability in trade patterns. Commodity prices fluctuated, creating instability in export earnings. By 1929 and the beginning of the worldwide depression, it was clear that LAC would need to identify a new trade strategy. As the 1930s opened, all of the countries suffered a sharp drop in export volumes and prices. The decade also saw the rise of strong and persistent pressures for protection in the developed countries. The most famous and draconian measure was probably the Smoot-Hawley Tariff Act, passed by the U.S. Congress in 1930, which sharply increased tariffs on more than 20,000 imported goods. The region suddenly faced a sharp reduction in its access to the U.S. market.

But in general, across the region, national leaders sought to transition from export-led growth to inward-looking development. With the onset of World War II in 1939, the region witnessed the third global downturn in less than twenty years, after the 1914 war and the Great Depression of 1929. Now, with another major disruption in international trade options, the decision was made across LAC countries to turn inward and to emphasize industrialization as the correct path to development. The British blockade had closed European ports, and the relatively easy access in the 1930s to European markets ended. In the larger republics, the state began to intervene directly in the economy to support industrial policies. Another option, relatively unimportant before the crisis of the 1930s, was intraregional trade, but it did not substitute for overseas exports.

As World War II ended in 1945, import substitution industrialization (ISI) was widely adopted as a development strategy. That policy decision was accompanied by the theoretical support for ISI by the newly created Economic Commission for Latin America (ECLA), located in Santiago, Chile.[2] The principal proponent of ISI would become the second director of ECLA, Raúl Prebisch. ECLA reflected the region's growing pessimism, after the war, with export-led growth. Foreign exchange shortages were rampant across the region and imports had to be sharply reduced. While different countries adopted different versions of ISI (and a few resisted), it became the preferred postwar development model for the region.

During the twenty years following the end of World War II, Latin America became increasingly disengaged from world trade. Both imports and exports declined. Once again, a number of externalities explained the decline in trade. The demand for and the prices of the region's commodity exports dropped after the war. Protectionism in the developed countries increased. Other countries began to compete with similar products for world market share. LAC remained highly dependent on a small number of export commodities, and demand for primary products was actually growing more slowly than world trade. In this context, it was becoming increasingly clear that ISI was not a panacea for the region. LAC's industrial products could not compete in the global marketplace—higher wages at home and the low quality of the goods produced were among the principal reasons. Ironically, the region remained dependent on commodity exports for its foreign exchange earnings. The ISI model led to a rapid expansion of the public sector; at the same time, it led to widespread corruption as many producers sought special access to the government for support.

As the European countries began to rebuild after the war, regional integration was adopted as the preferred strategy going forward. With the 1957 Treaty of Rome, they created the European Economic Community (EEC). Similarly, when ISI stalled in the 1960s, regional integration emerged as the new development option for Latin America. The pessimism that had existed in the war years over export-led growth now reversed course, and national leaders began to express pessimism about inward-looking development. Was export-led growth the appropriate choice for the times? A number of studies began to look at the experience—and success—of the countries in Southeast Asia. Export-led growth was impressive throughout the region. Those in favor of returning to an export-led model were well-served by a commodity price boom in the 1970s. But the region's outward turn was not particularly successful, and to support the chronic balance-of-payments dilemma, governments turned to foreign borrowing.

After the Yom Kippur War in 1973 in the Middle East, vast amounts of petrodollars were available at low interest rates from global commercial banks. It was generally overlooked that the interest rates, while low, were variable. With the second oil crisis, in 1979, countries that imported petroleum (Brazil imported about 80 percent of its needs) were in dire straits because of the rapid increase in the price of gasoline they purchased abroad. Oil exporters, of course, were the winners but were not particularly savvy guardians of their new national wealth. The government of Mexico defaulted on its foreign debt obligations in August 1982, and the "lost decade" of debt began. Because LAC countries were under severe international pressure to service their debt obligations—primarily to safeguard the solvency of the commercial banks in the United States and Europe—the region turned again to exports and the creation of trade surpluses to earn the foreign exchange needed to finance debt payments. This also required a severe reduction in support for social services in most countries.

As the 1980s ended and some debt relief was provided under the leadership of President George H. W. Bush and the Brady Plan for debt restructuring, discussions in the region turned to the search for a new model of development. This time they were guided by what came to be known as the Washington Consensus, a list of ten reforms the countries were urged to adopt to hasten the modernization of national economies and to further their integration into the global economy. Priority was given to macroeconomic reforms, privatization of state assets, a reduction in the size and the role of the state, and flexible exchange rates, among other reforms. Formulated in 1989, the Washington Consensus was quickly adopted by many of the governments in the region. Starting in 1983 in Argentina, and ending with the transition to democracy in Chile in 1990, military governments ceded power to civilian authorities. The Washington Consensus was an attractive agenda for the new governments that were dealing with the lasting effects of the lost debt decade.

The implementation of the Washington Consensus varied widely across the region, but its shelf life was limited to the early and mid-1990s. The policies adopted did not create many new jobs. Growth rates remained low. The call by the Washington Consensus for government investment in social services was ignored, and the expectations of judicial reform and a level playing field for all citizens went unmet. With the onset of the global financial crisis in the summer of 1997 in Thailand (and the contagion that spread the crisis across Asia), the collapse of the Russian currency in mid-1998, and the Brazilian government's decision to float the currency in January 1999, the short-lived era of the Washington Consensus faded. It was buried with the election of Hugo Chávez as president of Venezuela in late 1998 and by the succeeding elections of Rafael Correa in Ecuador and Evo Morales in Bolivia, who denounced the Washington Consensus as a Washington conspiracy driven by nefarious capitalist-imperialist interests.

REGIONAL ECONOMIC INTEGRATION EFFORTS

In the midst of the move back and forth from inward-looking development to export-led development, the region did explore regional integration, with varying degrees of success. The first tentative effort was the Latin American Free Trade Association (LAFTA), created by the Treaty of Montevideo in 1960. Ten South American republics and Mexico were members. LAFTA aimed at abolishing tariffs on intraregional trade by 1971. Frequent negotiations attempted to agree on common schedules for tariff reductions. Talks appeared to be making progress but were viewed as a failure by the late 1960s. The next step was the establishment of the Latin American Integration Association (Asociación Latinoamericana de Integración, ALADI) with the signing of the Treaty of Montevideo (which substituted for the previous treaty) in August 1980; ALADI absorbed LAFTA. The long-term goal of the entity was the creation of a Latin American common market.

A group of Andean countries—Bolivia, Chile, Colombia, Ecuador, and Peru—created the Andean Pact in 1969. Venezuela became a member in 1973; Chile withdrew during the Pinochet dictatorship in 1976, and Venezuela withdrew in 2006. In an effort to jump-start the organization, it transitioned into the Andean Community in the 1990s but with little visible success. Created in 1991, the Common Market of the South (Mercosur—in Spanish, Mercado Común del Sur; in Portuguese, Mercado Comum do Sul) brought together Argentina, Brazil, Paraguay, and Uruguay, with Venezuela becoming the fifth member in July 2012. To date, its goal of creating a common market has not been achieved. Frequent conflicts between Argentina and Brazil have impeded a deepening of Mercosur, and with the addition of Venezuela, many observers see the entity as more of a political than a trade organization. The Workers' Party in Brazil has maintained that Mercosur is critical to that government's pursuit of a south-south trade and development strategy. However, the financial and political crises that erupted following President Dilma Rousseff's reelection in October 2014 mean that trade policy will have little priority in Brasília and the status quo will be maintained into the foreseeable future.

The Andean Community and Mercosur agreed in 2004 to create a new organization that would develop a common currency, a tariff-free common market, and a regional parliament: the South American Community of Nations (SACN), which in 2007 became known as the Union of South American Nations (USAN) or Unión de Naciones Suramericanas (UNASUR). More recently, there has been some speculation that Mercosur and the Pacific Alliance would seek to collaborate. However, as one former Mexican ambassador to the United States has commented, "As one of the most innovative, and so far effective, inter-American groupings, the [Pacific] Alliance is a coalition of free-trade willing nations committed to economic growth and trade facilitation under the aegis of a rules-based 21st century international free and fair trading system,"[3] and Mercosur has shown little disposition to follow those guidelines. Diplomatically, it may be prudent to hold consultation meetings, but there appears to be little chance of a deepening relationship at this time.

Other integration initiatives have included the Central American Common Market (CACM) and the Community of Latin American and Caribbean States (in Spanish, Comunidad de Estados Latinoamericanos y Caribeños, or CELAC). Formed in 1960, the CACM countries set out to create a customs union, and negotiations led to a Common External Tariff (CET) in 1965. The CACM established the Central American Bank for Economic Integration (CABEI), which was relatively successful in supporting regional infrastructure projects. However, the CACM was weakened by a war between Honduras and El Salvador in 1969 over migration issues. CELAC, created in 2011, merged the Latin American and Caribbean Summit for Integration and Development (CALC), which in 2008 had convened the leaders of the thirty-three LAC states, and the Rio Group, an older diplomatic initiative that was created after the end of the conflict in Central America in the 1980s. At the fourth summit, held in Quito, Ecuador, in January 2016, the central theme appeared to be anti–United States. Outgoing chairman President Rafael Correa of Ecuador explicitly called for CELAC to replace the Organization of American States (OAS) as the principal forum in which to discuss hemispheric policy issues. There was a great deal of discussion about reducing poverty, the need for a strategy to address climate change, the development of science, technology, and innovation, and the need for financing to support development initiatives. But funds were not committed to implement these goals, and it is not clear that CELAC has the personnel or other resources to advance the agenda. It is noteworthy that none of these initiatives reached out to include Canada, the United States, or the European Union.

Three other initiatives were briefly significant. The first was the Free Trade Area of the Americas (FTAA), launched in Miami in December 1994 at the initiative of the U.S. government. Negotiations quickly ran into opposition from some of the major trading nations in the region, and in less than a decade the prospects for a hemisphere-wide trade agreement were dead. Brazil was particularly adamant that the FTAA would favor the United States and prejudice the trading goals of the developing countries. It also feared opening its economy to global competition.

The second was the 2001 Doha Round of the World Trade Organization (WTO), but it collapsed in a meeting in Geneva, Switzerland, in July 2008 over issues of agricultural trade between India, the United States, and China. The Ninth Ministerial Conference of the WTO, an effort to resuscitate the Doha talks, was held in Bali, Indonesia, in December 2013. Four major areas were approved: trade facilitation, agriculture, cotton, and development and LDC (less-developed countries) issues. While the conference represented an important breakthrough, a good deal of negotiating remains to reach full implementation of the four policy clusters.

The third was an initiative of President Hugo Chávez of Venezuela, the Bolivarian Alliance for the Peoples of Our America (Alianza Bolivariana para los Pueblos de Nuestra América, or ALBA), established in 2004 to challenge the FTAA. It included the left-of-center, anti-U.S. governments in the region. It had hopes of establishing a bank of the south and to challenge institutions such as the World Bank and the International Monetary Fund, which were seen as controlled by the United States and the developed nations of the north. To date it has not prospered, and since the death of President Chávez, its future remains uncertain, particularly in light of the precarious state of the Venezuelan economy.

There are many reasons for the inability of LAC countries to establish a successful economic integration agenda. Ideology often interferes with the search for pragmatic solutions to real problems. ALBA's "veto" of the FTAA is a good example. There is a growing sense that the future of the region should be less linked to the United States. Regional rivalries are always a reality. Often, overly ambitious schemes of integration are stymied by issues such as preferential treatment for some products over others. And the very different levels of economic and social development across the region have made it difficult to find a level playing field for all of the countries.

THE PIVOT TO ASIA

Beginning in 2002–03, the LAC region started looking to Asia for new export markets. The driver was China's insatiable need for raw materials and commodities, where LAC held a comparative advantage. As a recent study of Latin America's economic development observed:

> This trade activity has had widely varying impacts on the region. Its most positive effect has been that it has provided a market for South America's natural-resource-intensive exports, although the range of products is quite limited (oil, soybeans, copper and copper products, and iron ore and scrap iron). On the other hand, the robust increase in China's exports, mainly manufactures, to Latin America has saddled the region with a hefty trade deficit with the Asian Giant.[4]

In line with the discussion of other authors in this volume, the study goes on to say that the benefits of the new trade pattern are ambivalent. Specifically, it states that trade with China "has also been a contributing factor in the re-commoditization of Latin America's export and production structure."[5]

The pivot to the East has also resulted in a redirection of not only trade and investment but also geopolitical options. The two most important are the Trans-Pacific Partnership and the Pacific Alliance. Both represent a historical shift of some of the LAC countries to redefine their global trade and investment priorities. These initiatives also indicate a diversification of the region's political and diplomatic interests away from what had been seen by many as an overreliance on the United States. As the president of the Inter-American Development Bank recently commented, "In 2013 Asia accounted for an unprecedented 21 percent of Latin America's trade, and if current trends continue, in four years Asia will be the region's most important trade partner. China is already the top trade partner for Brazil, Chile, and Peru, and the second-biggest partner for Colombia."[6] He went on to say that Asia and Latin America are two of the fastest-growing regions in the world, with dynamic, outward-looking economies. And the reality today is that trade between the two regions is highly concentrated in a small number of countries:

China, India, Japan, and South Korea account for nearly 90 percent of Asia's trade with LAC, while Argentina, Brazil, Chile, and Mexico are LAC's principal trading nations with Asia. But this will change as more countries look to Asia to increase their trade options.

Trans-Pacific Partnership

With the failure of the latest Doha Development Agenda and the steady emergence of Asia as a growing market for developing-country products, a series of new trade initiatives has materialized. The Chilean government has been a pioneer in its outreach to the Asian market. The TPP began as an agreement in July 2005 among Brunei, New Zealand, Singapore, and Chile (originally called the Trans-Pacific Strategic Economic Partnership). In March 2010, Australia, Peru, Vietnam, and the United States joined the negotiations. Two years later Mexico and Canada indicated their interest in participating in the TPP, and President Barack Obama, in his State of the Union address in January 2013, indicated that concluding the treaty was a high priority for the United States. It was noted that the participants represented approximately 40 percent of global GDP and 40 percent of U.S. trade. Colombia and Costa Rica have also indicated strong interest in entering the process but are not members of the Asia-Pacific Economic Cooperation (APEC) group, which is a prerequisite for participation.

In April 2015, during a state visit to the United States, Prime Minister Shinzo Abe gave a historic address to a joint session of the U.S. Congress. He urged Congress to support the TPP, as negotiations to pass a measure for Trade Promotion Authority (TPA)—also known as the "fast-track" bill, TPA allows the president to submit a treaty to the legislature without the possibility of amendments—continued to stall. After heated debate in Congress, the fast-track bill was approved on June 29, 2015. Just one month later the U.S. trade representative brokered an unanticipated side deal with Japan, on behalf of the United States, Canada, and Mexico, that lowered the TPP local content threshold for automobiles in order to avoid tariffs when entering North America.[7] This arrangement allowed for a final round of discussions, and the trade agreement was signed on February 4, 2016, in Auckland, New Zealand, after seven years of intense negotiations. Ratification of the treaty requires that at least six of the signatories, representing 85 percent of the combined GDP of the TPP membership, successfully complete the domestic ratification process within a two-year window. The agreement enters into force within sixty days of ratification.

Chile and Mexico also have robust trade ties with Japan. The TPP should provide an avenue for stronger ties in both trade and investment. As important, the TPP would introduce those countries, and their neighbors, into a broader Asian geopolitical context that emphasizes democracy and fair trade, all in the interests of the Latin American members of the TPP. A report issued by the Washington, D.C.–based Peterson Institute indicated that Japan would gain more than any other participant in the TPP, and even more so if China or South Korea (or both) were to join the grouping.[8] An important consideration of the TPP is whether or not it will be seen by China as an effort by the United States to limit China's freedom in expanding its trade strategy. It is important for the Latin American countries that this does not happen. The LAC countries are increasingly dependent on China for expanded market access for their products. A geopolitical stand-off between Beijing and Washington is not in the interests of the region under any circumstances.

Another issue is whether or not there is "space" for Brazil in the TPP. Brazil is not a Pacific Ocean actor but it has important trade ties with Asia. As one commentator has written:

> Brazil also needs to forge a more coherent path in trade policy because the playing field is changing rapidly. One of the last major trade-related decisions that Brazil made was to reject the Free Trade Area of the Americas out of fear that an agreement that included the United States would prove a destructive force for its own industry. As a result, Brazil bet heavily on the WTO and the Doha Round of multilateral trade negotiations, as well as on the political coherence and economic potential of Mercosur.[9]

Unfortunately, as mentioned earlier in this chapter, the Doha Round is stalled and Mercosur has lost its impetus. There appears to be growing pressure from the private sector in Brazil for the government to recognize that the playing field is quickly changing.[10] The victory of the Workers' Party in the November 2014 national elections probably means that Brasília will continue to emphasize south-south relations and insist that Mercosur is a very relevant part of the country's trade policy as well as its diplomatic strategy in the region. However, many observers believe this is a short-sighted view of global trade dynamics in this century.

Pacific Alliance

Besides the TPP, a new option for deepening ties between Latin America and Asia is the recently created Pacific Alliance. The founding members are Chile, Colombia, Mexico, and Peru; Costa Rica and Panama have begun the process of joining the alliance, and some thirty additional countries have observer status. Chile, Peru, and Mexico are also members of the TPP negotiations. The Pacific Alliance is the by-product of a meeting organized by former Peruvian president Alan García in April 2011 (the alliance was formally approved in June 2012). The group issued the Declaration of Lima, which said that the principal goal of the alliance was to advance free trade and economic integration among the member states. It also stated that the alliance would have a strong orientation toward the markets of Asia. Taken together, the grouping represents the sixth-largest economy in the world.[11] As one recent study observed:

> While global attention has been trained on Brazil, the "Pacific Pumas" on Latin America's figurative and literal periphery have quietly become economic overachievers. This anonymity will be short lived. The four countries have already spearheaded a regional free trade and cooperation pact, the Pacific Alliance, which has captured global attention. Given the rise of China and the U.S. pivot to the East, the Pumas are poised to play a significant role in an emerging Pacific century.[12]

In sharp contrast to other efforts at economic integration, which have been internally oriented, the Pacific Alliance is explicitly outward-looking. It is also an entity that does not seek ideological confrontation with either the United States or other nations in the region or beyond. It seeks to create export platforms for international markets. Concrete steps have resulted in the elimination of 92 percent of tariffs on goods traded between them. That decision was taken at the eighth summit of the alliance in February 2014. The remaining 8 percent of tariffs—mostly on agricultural goods that require special treatment and must go through specific screening—will be phased in. The group will have joint embassies overseas, and a business council has been formed to include the perspective of the private sector in the four countries. Police and customs office cooperation to track cross-border criminal activity has begun. Export promotion agencies have agreed to share offices, information, experience, and sector projects, and to collectively offer products and services at international fairs. Joint market research and trade missions will be organized.

Perhaps the most progressive policy decision was to create, in 2010, the Integrated Latin American Market (Mercado Integrado Latinoamericano, or MILA). The goal of MILA is to integrate the stock markets of Colombia, Chile, and Peru. Mexico has expressed a strong interest in becoming a member. The MILA has evolved carefully, but the long-term hope is to provide a mechanism for deepening capital markets. There has been strong support within the business communities of the four Pacific Alliance states to develop a business networking process to encourage economic development and technological advances with the aim of strengthening regional integration.

The finance ministers of the Pacific Alliance met in October 2014 with U.S. Secretary of the Treasury Jacob L. Lew to discuss deepening the relationship between the group and the United States. In the same month, attending the fall session of the UN General Assembly, the four presidents encouraged the international business community to invest in their countries. These are all positive steps in the consolidation of the alliance. As was recently commented:

> United in the Pacific Alliance, the Pumas have the opportunity to emerge as regional leaders and flag bearers for Latin American integration; they have the opportunity to join a 21st century trans-Atlantic community that combines the experience and know-how of the U.S. and the EU with the growth potential of emerging markets. In a world that could see increasing regionalism, the Pumas have the opportunity to be strategic partners to the United States, Europe, and Asia.[13]

INDIA: THE EMERGING STRATEGIC ASIAN PLAYER

India has begun to emerge as a new alternative for trade and investment in LAC as the region's trade with China levels off with the slowdown of the Chinese economy and as concerns grow over the "resource curse," aggravated by overreliance on the Chinese market. In the last decade, India's trade with LAC has grown at a rate of approximately 25 percent annually, reaching a bilateral total of nearly $45 billion in 2015.[14] However, more can be done on the investment front—LAC has received only 4 percent of India's outward foreign direct investment (FDI) over the past two decades, amounting to about $16 billion, and LAC investment in India has also remained low.[15] To help address this issue, an India-LAC Investment Conclave was held in New Delhi in October 2014 with the objectives of enhancing understanding of investment opportunities on both sides and promoting economic engagement.

Prime Minister Narendra Modi's 2014 visit to Brazil to attend the BRICS (Brazil, Russia, India, China, and South Africa) summit may have represented a sense of renewed optimism in relations between LAC and New Delhi. The prime minister announced that the government of

India would establish centers of excellence in IT in a number of countries. India and Brazil signed three bilateral agreements in the fields of environment, consular, and mobility issues, and also agreed to set up a Brazilian Earth station that will receive data from Indian satellites. Modi recognized the growing importance of the region to India's energy and food security.

The ties between the region and India began slowly, with the creation by the Ministry of Commerce and Industry in New Delhi of the special trade promotion initiative "Focus: LAC" in 1997. The goal was to encourage the Indian private sector and state entities to deepen trade and investment ties with LAC and to enhance India's export of certain products—textiles, engineering products, computer software, chemicals, and pharmaceuticals—to the region.[16] Collaboration has also expanded to regional groupings such as the G-20, IBSA (India, Brazil, and South Africa), and the BRICS. The first meeting of the IBSA Trilateral Commission of foreign ministers took place in New Delhi in March 2004. The commission was an outcome of the IBSA Dialogue Forum, created in June 2003. The three foreign ministers signed the New Delhi Agenda for Cooperation and Plan of Action, which aims to boost bilateral trade and promote south-south cooperation. The Plan of Action calls for cooperation in such fields as health, IT, civil aviation, and defense. India has also negotiated a preferential trade agreement with Mercosur and a similar arrangement with Chile. In addition, the country has been granted observer status in the Pacific Alliance.

The Export-Import Bank of India works closely with "Focus: LAC" to facilitate Indian investment in Latin America. The Exim Bank has created a broad network of alliances with multilateral agencies, export credit agencies, and investment and trade promotion agencies to create an enabling environment for the two-way transfer of technology, trade, and investment. The Exim Bank has signed memoranda of cooperation with banks in a number of countries in the region. One recent initiative was a conference organized by the Confederation of Indian Industry and the Exim Bank in New Delhi in December 2013. Titled "Explore, Experience, Engage," the conference had the principal goal of deepening investment and trade ties.

Exports are also concentrated in a small group of countries—the major LAC exporters to India are Argentina, Brazil, Chile, Colombia, Mexico, and Venezuela. The increase in trade between India and LAC is impressive. According to India's Ministry of Commerce, in 2000, exports from India to LAC were about $660 million; by 2015 they had reached more than $14 billion. Similarly, LAC exports to India grew dramatically, from just below $1 billion in 2000 to more than $30 billion in 2015.[17] But as one commentator has noted, "Of course the geographical distribution is skewed toward Brazil and Venezuela, and much of the rise in trade is linked to petroleum products."[18] This raises again the issue of the resource curse phenomenon in LAC. In a review of the composition of trade between India and LAC, a challenge similar to that in trade relations with China has emerged, with India exporting manufactured products and LAC exporting primary products. Mauricio Mesquita Moreira clearly explains the challenge for LAC in its trade and investment relationship with India:

> Governments in the region would be wise to acknowledge a scenario in which India joins China as a major exporter of manufactured goods. Such a scenario will only add to predicaments Latin America already faces with China. It has become abundantly clear that the manufacturing "road" to development has become highly congested and particularly hazardous for countries that cannot count on an abundant supply of skilled workers.[19]

As Mesquita Moreira points out, LAC needs to address the outstanding policy challenges to productivity and competitiveness: infrastructure, education, access to credit, and science and technology if it wants to compete in global markets.

CONCLUSION

The engagement of LAC in global economic affairs has begun to focus on new opportunities in the twenty-first century. The TPP, which offers an opportunity for broad engagement with Asia for a limited number of countries, could be a major turning point in global trade trends. The caveat, as argued earlier in this chapter, is that LAC must avoid any impression that it views the TPP as a geopolitical effort, driven by the United States, to isolate China. Another interesting initiative is the Pacific Alliance. It brings together four democratic nation-states that are demonstrating impressive economic growth and the ability to compromise and focus on key trade and investment strategies. The four countries will likely soon be joined by Costa Rica and Panama. The key to the probable success of the Pacific Alliance is that it is "for" and not "against" any other existing agreements. It confirms the growing importance of the Pacific for LAC, a point of no return. An important aspect of the alliance is that it brings Mexico into South America in a meaningful way. For too long some governments have sought to argue that there is—or was—a South American-North American divide. With the success of the Pacific Alliance, that is no longer a tenable position. Mexico should prove to be a dynamic and positive addition to its three partners in a renewed South America.

The outlier in the changing trade and investment dynamics is Brazil. It is not a member of either the TPP or the Pacific Alliance. It stubbornly maintains that Mercosur is its principal mechanism for regional trade engagement when it is clear to most observers that the early success of the Common Market of the South has yielded to frustration and unmet expectations. China has been, and will continue to be, an essential trade partner for Brazil. India is becoming an important one as well. But Brazil continues to avoid commitments beyond South America, limiting its ability to influence overall global trade and investment options in the twenty-first century. The reelection of President Dilma Rousseff in October 2014 may confirm Brazil's unwillingness to "go abroad," to the detriment of the people of Brazil and its economy.

A significant number of LAC countries have finally understood the severe limitations of regional trade and investment arrangements. The economic and social disparities among the countries are too large and the politics are too contentious. The TPP and the Pacific Alliance offer, selectively, an exit from failed or moribund regional groupings that remain highly exclusive and inward-looking. The appropriate arena for LAC is outward-looking in a global sense. It can only be hoped that those countries that have insisted on remaining inwardly focused will understand the need to reconsider that policy.

NOTES

1. The chapter's historical background reflects the excellent analysis of Victor Bulmer-Thomas, *The Economic History of Latin America since Independence* (Cambridge University Press, 2014), and Luis Bértola and José Antonio Ocampo, *The Economic Development of Latin America since Independence* (Oxford University Press, 2012).

2. The organization changed its name to the Economic Commission for Latin America and the Caribbean (ECLAC) in 1984.

3. Arturo Sarukhan, comment in "Will Mercosur and the Pacific Alliance Strengthen Ties?," Inter-American Dialogue, *Latin America Advisor*, October 2, 2014, p. 4.

4. Bértola and Ocampo, *The Economic Development of Latin America*, p. 231.

5. Ibid.

6. Luis Alberto Moreno, preface to *Reaching across the Pacific: Latin America and Asia in the New Century*, edited by Cynthia J. Arnson and

Jorge Heine, with Christine Zaino (Washington, DC: Woodrow Wilson International Center for Scholars, 2014), p. 2.

7. Steven Chase, "Conservatives Were Sure Trans-Pacific Partnership Deal Would Be Signed," *Globe and Mail* (Ottawa, ON), August 5, 2015.

8. Peter A. Petri, Michael G. Plummer, and Fan Zhai, *The Trans-Pacific Partnership and Asia-Pacific Integration: A Quantitative Assessment*, Policy Analyses in International Economics 98 (Washington, DC: Peterson Institute for International Economics, 2012).

9. Adriana Erthal Abdenur, "Brazil-Asia Trade: Emerging Configurations," in Arnson and Heine, eds., *Reaching across the Pacific*, p. 150.

10. Ibid.

11. BBVA [Banco Bilbao Vizcaya Argentaria], "Economic Watch: Pacific Alliance" (Santiago, Chile: BBVA, October 16, 2013).

12. Samuel George, "The Pacific Pumas: An Emerging Model for Emerging Markets" (Washington, DC: Bertelsmann Foundation, 2014), p. 7.

13. Ibid., p. 45.

14. India-LAC Investment Conclave, "The Conclave" (Government of India, Ministry of Commerce and Industry) (www.indialacconclave.com); Government of India, Department of Commerce and Industry, Export Import Data Bank, Exports and Imports for Latin America (including Mexico) (http://commerce.nic.in/eidb/).

15. India-LAC Investment Conclave, "The Conclave."

16. Huma Siddiqui, "India, LAC Countries Can Together Become a Formidable Global Economic Force," *In Focus*, August 18, 2014 (Government of India, Ministry of External Affairs).

17. Government of India, Department of Commerce and Industry, Export Import Data Bank, Exports and Imports for Latin America (including Mexico) (http://commerce.nic.in/eidb/).

18. Jahangir Aziz, comment in "What Is Driving Latin America–India Energy Relations?," Inter-American Dialogue, *Latin America Advisor—Energy Advisor*, October 14–18, 2013, p. 3.

19. Mauricio Mesquita Moreira, "India: Latin America's Next Big Thing?," *Latin Trade*, July 29, 2010 (http://latintrade.com/india-latin-americas-next-big-thing/).

CHAPTER 3

Recasting South-South Links

INDO–LATIN AMERICAN RELATIONS

Jorge Heine and Hari Seshasayee

The sixth summit of the BRICS group—Brazil, Russia, India, China, and South Africa—held in Fortaleza, Brazil, on July 14–16, 2014, was a milestone in the gradual but perceptible shift toward a new global order. Held in the wake of the FIFA World Cup competition, it brought together key leaders from Asia, Africa, and Latin America and gave a fresh impetus to south-south cooperation.[1] Moreover, it did so not just by means of words but also through deeds. On the occasion, the launch of the BRICS Development Bank, or New Development Bank (NDB), was announced. With a capitalization of $50 billion and reserves of $100 billion, the Shanghai-based bank, run by an Indian CEO, was to focus first on infrastructure projects in the BRICS countries.[2] Lending to nonmember countries from the global south would be considered down the road. On July 10, 2014, Chinese president Xi Jinping met with a dozen Latin American leaders in Brasília, announcing a $25 billion cooperation fund for Latin American projects and the establishment of a China–Latin America Forum (the first ministerial meeting took place in Beijing in January 2015). For Indian prime minister Narendra Modi, the Fortaleza meeting was his first multilateral summit after taking office in May 2014.

For many, Mr. Modi's participation in this summit and his visit to Brazil and extensive discussions with Brazilian president Dilma Rousseff signaled an auspicious fresh start for Indo–Latin American and Caribbean (LAC) relations under India's new majority government.[3] That some 60 percent of Indo-LAC trade goes through Gujarat (the state Modi ran as chief minister from 2001 to 2014), his unprecedented two meetings with Latin American delegations in 2013, and the great verve with which he took up India's foreign policy challenges seemed to some observers to point toward a new period in the hitherto rather low-profile field of Indo–Latin American relations. This chapter examines the state of play of these linkages, where they came from, their possible future trajectories, and the degree to which, in the words of a 2010 Inter-American Development Bank report, India is indeed "Latin America's next big thing."[4]

Latin America's relations with India are part and parcel of the broader picture of the region's growing links with Asia in the twenty-first century, representing perhaps the most significant shift in the region's international insertion since independence.[5] Trade flows between Latin America and Asia grew at an annual rate of 20.5 percent between 2000 and 2011, reaching $442 billion in the latter year. As a result, Asia now accounts for 21 percent of Latin America's international trade, compared with a share of 34 percent for the United States. At this pace, it will not be long before Asia becomes Latin America's main trading partner. About half of this trade is with China. But trade with India has also been growing at a fast clip, reaching $49 billion in 2014, and links with India have their own specificities, as described in this chapter.[6]

The first section of the chapter looks at the background and history of Indo-LAC relations and how far they have come. The next section parses the current state of affairs on the commercial and political fronts, breaking them down into their various components and analyzing the gaps that remain to be filled. The following section maps out the way forward, addressing the issue of whether the Bharatiya Janata Party (BJP)-majority government in New Delhi should indeed be a cause for optimism about Indo-LAC links. The chapter then offers some final conclusions and forecasts for the future of Indo-LAC ties.

INDO-LAC LINKS IN PERSPECTIVE: HOW FAR HAVE THEY COME?

India has established ties with such regional organizations as Mercosur, the Community of Latin American and Caribbean Countries (CELAC), the Union of South American Nations (UNASUR), the Caribbean Community and Common Market (CARICOM), the Andean Community, and the Pacific Alliance, but there is still no unified regional mechanism that binds Latin America on the order of, say, the European Union or the Association of Southeast Asian Nations (ASEAN). India's association with LAC is thus determined by its bilateral relationships with Latin American nations. There are instances where bilateral and regional cooperation mechanisms intersect, as in the case of the BRICS and IBSA (India, Brazil, and South Africa), but the emphasis largely remains on bilateral ties.[7]

The most significant links are with Brazil and Mexico—a "strategic partnership" was forged with Brazil during Luiz Inácio Lula da Silva's presidency, and a "privileged partnership" was established with Mexico during President Felipe Calderón's visit to India. South American countries enjoy a growing commercial relationship with India centered on Latin American exports of crude oil, minerals, and agricultural products, imports of motor vehicles and pharmaceutical products, and significant Indian investments in the region. The English-speaking Caribbean nations are home to many people of Indian origin, most of whom arrived generations ago (primarily in the nineteenth century). The Central American and Caribbean republics are large recipients of aid from India, including medicines, humanitarian aid, and lines of credit for development projects, amounting in total to $300 million.[8]

Although the dominant links were forged in the past few decades, there are a few historical connections between India and LAC, restricted mostly to the migration of Indian indentured laborers to the Caribbean and the Portuguese colonial linkages between Goa, a state in western India, and Brazil. As discussed by Jacqueline Mazza in chapter 8, people of Indian origin make up a large portion of the population in the Caribbean, especially in Guyana, Suriname, Trinidad and Tobago, and Jamaica. In total, 1.08 million people of Indian origin reside in the Caribbean, Suriname, and Guyana, but only 23,000 people of Indian origin reside in South America, Central America, and Mexico.[9]

Goa and Brazil were both Portuguese colonies and thus share a part of their history. Some even traveled between the two territories: for example, the first bishop of Brazil, in 1551, Pedro Fernandes Sardinha, was previously the vicar-general of Goa.[10] Trade between Goa and Brazil soared in the early nineteenth century: Rio de Janeiro alone accounted for 77 percent of Goa's total exports in 1819.[11]

However, these linkages faded over time, and although there are more than 1 million people of Indian origin in the Caribbean, this demographic share has not translated into substantial economic or political gains for India.

Mexico was the first LAC country that independent India's first prime minister, Jawaharlal Nehru, visited in 1961. Nehru's trip to Mexico on November 14, 1961, came on the heels of the founding of the Non-Aligned Movement at a conference in Belgrade only a month earlier. Despite the fanfare with which the Mexican president, Adolfo López Mateos, greeted him, Nehru failed to convince Mexico to join the new entity. Mexico's stance was inexorable: as the *Milwaukee Sentinel* reported a week after Nehru's visit, "Living as they [Mexicans] do next to the U.S., they know that if the U.S. loses a global war between freedom and communist tyranny they also lose."[12] Mexico's position was reiterated with confidence less than a year later on October 7, 1962, when President López Mateos stated during a visit to New Delhi that "in the case of Mexico, the expression 'independent international policy' does neither mean 'neutralism' nor the will or aspiration of constituting a third block or being associated with it."[13]

Although some Latin American leaders visited India in the years following Nehru's trip, the next significant visit from an Indian leader came seven years later when Prime Minister Indira Gandhi traveled to eight Latin American countries in succession, from September 23 to October 13, 1968. She began her trip in Brazil, then continued on to Uruguay, Argentina, Chile, Colombia, Venezuela, Trinidad and Tobago, and Guyana. The three-week visit yielded some results and initiatives: India and Brazil agreed to cooperate in the field of atomic energy; India agreed to set up a diplomatic mission in Venezuela and Peru; a trade delegation would travel to LAC to advance commercial ties; and a gamut of cultural, technical, and educational agreements were signed. One of Gandhi's observations—which remains true to this day—was that the people of India "knew less about South America than the people of South America know of us."[14] Following the visit, however, neither India nor the countries of Latin America managed to capitalize on the experience in the form of lasting gains, and momentum was lost. India's attention shifted to the Indo-Pakistan war of 1971 and the subsequent creation of Bangladesh, and shortly after, India spiraled into a state of emergency imposed by Indira Gandhi. In turn, Latin America became caught up in a wave of military coups and rapidly rising inflation, which would lead to the "lost decade" of the 1980s.

Although Indira Gandhi did not include Mexico in her 1968 visit to Latin America, Mexico and India shared a close bond. Mexico was the first Latin American country to recognize India after its independence, and the role of Mexican semi-dwarf varieties of wheat in India's Green Revolution is well documented. During his visit to Mexico on August 7, 1986, India's prime minister, Rajiv Gandhi, stated:

It is no mere coincidence but a reflection of how similarly we are placed that the hybrid strain of wheat developed in Mexico brought about the germination of the Green Revolution in India. As a result, within two decades we have transformed our economy from one dependent on food imports to one which is self-sufficient in food, self-reliant on all fronts, and self-confident in the future.[15]

But he added that India and Mexico "have hardly tapped the potential for trade and industrial exchanges."[16] Thirty years later, there is still truth to that statement.

THE CURRENT STATE OF PLAY

Things changed in the 1990s, once Latin America had completed its transition to democracy and started to open up, implementing the Washington Consensus and embracing export-led development. India in turn went through its own economic transformation, enacting liberal reforms in 1991, inviting foreign investment, reducing trade tariffs, and deregulating markets. It is in this context that, at the turn of the twenty-first century, India and Latin America slowly began to rediscover each other.[17]

From India, a multitude of players led the way: pharmaceutical companies, which exported generic drug formulations and bulk drugs; oil companies, which invested in the upstream oil sector and also imported large amounts of crude oil; motor vehicle manufacturers, which exported auto parts, two-wheelers, cars, trucks, and tractors; and information and communications technology (ICT) companies, which opened offices in Latin America for their business and knowledge process outsourcing operations.[18]

There was equal interest from Latin America, which wanted to capitalize on India's boom in the twenty-first century—after all, India's GDP growth peaked at an average of 8.8 percent between 2003 and 2007.[19] Indian and Chinese demand for raw materials invigorated global commodities markets, and LAC was keen to be a new partner in this venture. The most essential demand from India was oil, and the oil-rich nations of LAC quickly increased their supply of crude oil to India. Besides oil, India also needed minerals for its growing industries. While many LAC countries began exporting minerals to India, the most significant supplier became Chile, which exports mostly copper ores. In the span of a decade, Chile's exports of copper to India grew from $148 million in 2002–03 to $2.7 billion in 2012–13.[20] India has now displaced the United States to become Chile's fifth-largest destination of

TABLE 3-1

India's Imports from Latin America, Various Years, 2000–14
($ million)

Country	2000	2005	2010	2014
Argentina	380.76	754.04	1,022.73	1,992.25
Bolivia	14.36	0.94	6.69	3.56
Brazil	145.17	893.06	3,548.88	5,400.91
Chile	57.14	434.50	1,550.25	3,080.63
Colombia	9.74	9.36	856.31	2,134.94
Costa Rica	0.88	37.86	95.33	155.30
Cuba	5.00	3.32	1.12	1.57
Dominican Republic	0.10	5.34	15.77	290.66
Ecuador	7.70	20.33	169.11	1,065.74
El Salvador	0.00	2.06	5.40	10.27
Guatemala	0.07	1.83	40.18	17.12
Honduras	0.06	0.31	1.43	25.31
Mexico	53.83	97.61	1,163.45	3,393.15
Nicaragua	0.02	5.49	0.91	2.19
Panama	9.50	247.44	188.47	30.46
Paraguay	0.54	4.21	5.31	88.12
Peru	9.13	23.06	187.36	590.40
Trinidad and Tobago	0.00	1.82	80.18	68.42
Uruguay	2.89	4.04	17.32	20.35
Venezuela	14.44	9.55	5,209.96	11,729.89

Source: Government of India, Ministry of Commerce and Industry. All data are for financial years.

mineral exports, behind China, the EU, Japan, and South Korea.[21] Another area of trade that has developed over the past decade is that of vegetable oils, including soybean and sunflower oils. Argentina and Brazil, among the world's largest exporters of soybean and soybean oil, now supply India with roughly $2 billion worth of soybean oil.[22] The volume (in dollars) of India's imports from and exports to Latin America at various years in the early twenty-first century is shown in tables 3-1 and 3-2.

Indo-LAC links, which gained much momentum in the 2000s, are now in a new phase. The aim now is to increase investment, diversify, identify new areas of cooperation, and work together in joint ventures. This momentum is most evident in economic links, and while some headway in diplomacy has also been made, obstacles remain. The social and

TABLE 3-2
India's Exports to Latin America, Various Years, 2000–13
($ million)

Country	2000	2005	2010	2014
Argentina	98.50	199.50	404.36	460.19
Bahamas	2.33	9.35	2,173.18	123.50
Bolivia	1.98	6.55	15.71	70.84
Brazil	226.05	1,090.61	4,024.16	5,963.82
Chile	108.45	152.15	507.55	565.82
Colombia	49.18	455.02	561.31	1,105.15
Costa Rica	6.85	16.06	61.47	95.84
Cuba	4.82	11.91	25.51	37.32
Dominican Republic	11.39	31.79	82.75	140.91
Ecuador	9.43	26.20	121.46	225.04
El Salvador	2.44	12.00	24.06	61.48
Guatemala	18.69	45.94	112.68	229.01
Honduras	15.29	34.60	63.07	187.56
Mexico	208.51	443.07	912.77	2,861.55
Nicaragua	4.06	10.63	30.01	65.51
Panama	65.65	63.05	124.16	302.40
Paraguay	8.27	16.38	41.53	106.48
Peru	26.32	84.26	417.60	819.86
Trinidad and Tobago	8.69	66.64	62.96	165.48
Uruguay	35.71	27.93	85.34	208.32
Venezuela	42.29	94.41	176.00	258.07

Source: Government of India, Ministry of Commerce and Industry. All data are for financial years.

cultural relationship has also seen some progress, but most of the activity can be viewed through two broad lenses, commercial and political.

Commercial Relations

Trade and investment have been the strongest elements of the India-LAC relationship and have increased multifold since 2001. The increase in commercial activity is palpable: Indo-LAC trade increased from roughly $2 billion in 2001–02 to $45 billion in 2014–15, and the total investments between India and LAC now amount to $20 billion.[23] While some of these commercial exchanges are still in the early stages, others stand out as potential areas of strategic cooperation. The main areas of interaction, which are evolving from transactional relationships to investment and joint-project relationships, are mining, energy, motor vehicles, ICT, and pharmaceuticals.

Mining

Many LAC countries have taken advantage of the commodities boom by increasing exports to emerging market countries, such as India and China. The mining industry is a significant one for most of Latin America—only some Central American and Caribbean countries are exceptions. The world's largest producers of copper, silver, iodine, lithium (used in batteries), niobium (used in the construction of gas pipelines and jet and rocket engines), and rhenium (used in constructing jet engines) are in Latin America. Mining exports constitute either the largest or second-largest group of total merchandise exports for Chile (65 percent), Peru (50 percent), Bolivia (36 percent), and Brazil (19 percent).[24]

India imports copper, silver, gold, phosphates, zinc, lead, iodine, and ferroalloys from Latin America, and its total imports of minerals and ores from LAC amounted to roughly $4.7 billion in the 2014–15 fiscal year.[25] Copper from Chile is the biggest component, amounting to $2.6 billion in 2014–15. The newest addition is gold from Latin America, imports of which began only in 2012, amounting to $1.8 billion in 2015.[26] Take Peru, for example: in 2015, gold made up more than half of the country's total exports to India, but there remains tremendous potential since this is only 6.2 percent of Peru's global gold exports.[27] However, traders in Switzerland determine much of the global trade in gold, so it is difficult to project how much gold Peru or other Latin American countries can export to India.

Besides importing minerals, Indian companies are also part of joint ventures in mining projects in Argentina, Brazil, Chile, Mexico, and Peru. One of the biggest corporate investments in mining was made by India's Jindal Group, in Bolivia's El Mutún iron ore mine, but because of various issues, the Jindals withdrew from the venture. Yet many other Indian companies are doing well. The most concentrated investments by Indian mining companies are in Brazil. These include the Aditya Birla Group's joint ventures and investments in Brazil's aluminum plants, carbon black plants, and a bauxite mine; Essar's prospecting license for an iron ore reserve in northern Brazil; and Rashtriya Ispat Nigam, NMDC, and MOIL, all three state-owned companies, which are in talks with the Brazilian government to acquire iron ore assets in Amapá, Brazil's northernmost state.[28] There are two investments in Chile, one by the Kolkata-based Tega Industries, which purchased Acotec, a local company providing products and solutions to the mining industry,[29] and one by the Jindal Group, which owns a 70 percent stake in a joint venture with Minera Santa Fe for mining iron ore in Chile.[30] According to India's Ministry of External Affairs, five Indian companies have invested in Peru's mining sector, including IFFCO and Zuari Agro Chemicals, which have stakes in phosphate mines in Peru.[31] The joint ventures of IFFCO and Zuari are strategic ones, where phosphate rock mined in Peru can be exported to India to use as fertilizers—this is significant since India imports roughly 85 percent of all its phosphate fertilizers. In 2015, 20 percent of Peru's total phosphate exports went to India, worth $71 million of a total of $349 million in global exports.[32] In the long run, the demand for some minerals, such as copper and phosphates, will remain high in India owing to insufficient domestic reserves; and for these, Latin America can be a reliable supplier and partner.

Energy

A number of countries in Latin America are major global producers of petroleum products and crude oil. The U.S. Energy Information Administration estimates that Latin America has roughly 339 billion barrels of proven oil reserves—but Venezuela alone accounts for a disproportionate 298 billion barrels. Brazil, Mexico, and Venezuela are among the world's top twelve oil producers. On the other hand, India is among the world's biggest oil consumers, behind only the United States, China, and Japan. Although Mexico (2.81 million barrels per day [bpd]) and Brazil (2.95 million bpd) produce more oil than Venezuela (2.68 million bpd), Venezuela is the biggest exporter since its domestic consumption is much lower than that of Brazil and Mexico.[33] In the past few years, Venezuela has decreased its oil exports to the United States while increasing exports to Asia. In 2014, it exported 21.59 million tons of oil to India. The other major oil exporters to India are Brazil (5 million tons), Mexico (4.34 million tons), Colombia (5.26 million tons), and Ecuador (1.31 million tons)—in total, India's crude oil imports from Latin America amounted to $24 billion in 2014.[34]

The demand for oil in India will remain high for the next few years—even if India diversifies to renewable sources, such as solar and wind power—and Latin America provides India with an opportunity to diversify its oil imports. At present, about 60 percent of India's oil imports come from West Asia. Between 2003 and 2014, Latin America's share of India's total oil imports rose from 4.5 percent to 19 percent.[35] Now, crude oil imports account for roughly half of total India–Latin America trade in goods, and Venezuela, the biggest supplier, is India's third-largest source of oil imports, after only Saudi Arabia and Iraq. Two developments in Latin America add to this strategic space: first is Mexico's energy reforms, which allow foreign companies to play a larger role in Mexico's oil industry; the second is the discovery of offshore oil reserves by a number of Latin American countries, including Brazil, Mexico, and Colombia.

There is another side to the story: India also exports petroleum products, such as diesel, to Latin America. According to India's Ministry of External Affairs, "Diesel exports by Reliance itself account for more than 52 percent of India's exports to Brazil, up from the forty one percent of India's exports in 2012." India's role in this sector has also evolved: Indian companies are increasingly part of joint ventures in exploration and production (upstream) activities. The biggest player is India's state-owned ONGC Videsh Ltd. (OVL), which has invested in oil blocks in Brazil, Colombia, Cuba, and Venezuela. In Colombia, OVL has a 50:50 joint venture with China's Sinopec, forming a new company called Mansarovar Energy Colombia Ltd.[36] OVL has also signed a memorandum of understanding with Mexico's state-owned Petróleos Mexicanos (Pemex) to cooperate in Mexico's upstream sector, and has set up an office in Mexico.[37] Private players such as Reliance, Assam Company, and Videocon Industries also have investments in Brazil and Colombia. Some of these investments are in offshore exploration blocks in Colombia, Peru, Cuba, and Brazil; exploration in such blocks can be costly, and if firms don't strike sufficient oil early, they can divest or relinquish their stake in the project. Reliance has done so in two blocks in Colombia[38] and one in Peru but is now looking to invest in Mexico.[39]

A new avenue for cooperation within the energy sector is through biofuels. Brazil is one of the world's largest producers of biofuels—second only to the United States—and Argentina, Colombia, Peru, and Paraguay are also producers of ethanol fuel, some of which is derived from sugarcane molasses and some from grain feedstock such as wheat and corn.[40] Indian companies such as Praj Industries and Renuka Sugars have sizable investments in ethanol and biofuel projects in Brazil, Colombia, Peru, Mexico, Argentina, Bolivia, and even some Central American countries.[41] There is a lot to be learned from these experiences, and it would be a prudent move to apply those lessons in India, where the demand for biofuels is increasing; it is also a way to combat India's energy security woes.

Motor Vehicles

Latin America has been a source of exports for Indian motor vehicle manufacturers for many decades. Bajaj Auto, Mahindra & Mahindra, and Tata Motors were among the early exporters, and their vehicles dot the landscapes of practically every country in South and Central America. Such companies as Sonalika International, Escorts Group, and Mahindra also sell their tractors to farmers in the Pampas region in Uruguay, Argentina, and Brazil. Car manufacturers from India also target Latin America: Mexico overtook South Africa as the largest destination of Indian car exports, totaling $787 million in 2014–15. India exported $1.3 billion worth of cars to Latin America in 2014–15. Some, such as TVS Motors and Bajaj, sell two-wheelers, and Bajaj is the market leader in Colombia and Central America, and is looking to enter new markets, including Paraguay. But their success there has invited more competition from India: Hero MotoCorp is targeting Latin America as a key growth area for its global business. Hero has inaugurated its first international manufacturing plant in Villa Rica, a small town in the western province of Colombia. The plant is expected to generate 2,200 jobs—a large number, insofar as the population of Villa Rica is only 15,000—and to manufacture up to 150,000 units per year. As Pawan Munjal, the chief executive officer of Hero, told India's *Economic Times,*

There is no country that is as strategically located than Colombia. If we want to sell in the Andean countries, it makes sense to use this base. We are also exploring the possibility of making Colombia the base for sending our products to markets in North America. We are simultaneously aiming to launch in Brazil by 2016, and an early launch in Argentina.[42]

Hero is not the only Indian motor vehicle manufacturer looking to set up a plant in Latin America. Tata's Jaguar Land Rover announced in December 2013 that it intends to build a manufacturing plant in Itatiaia, located in the state of Rio de Janeiro in Brazil, which will eventually produce up to 24,000 cars annually.[43] Ultimately, however, it may be more difficult for motor vehicle manufacturers to wade through the multifarious laws and regulations in Brazil, and some, like Hero, may find more success operating in Central America and the Andean region.

Information and Communications Technology

The presence of Indian ICT companies in Latin America provides perhaps the biggest value-added proposition in the India–Latin America commercial relationship. Unlike the commodity-based trade and investments in minerals and oil, this is where India's role is most visible. Indian ICT companies employ more than 25,000 people in Latin America. They provide solutions to a whole gamut of sectors, including retail, mining, manufacturing, banking, and finance. Tata Consultancy Services (TCS) has the largest presence, employing more than 14,000 locals in the region, with offices in nine Latin American countries—and it is still expanding. There are more than thirty Indian ICT companies present in Latin America; some are big players, such as Wipro, Infosys, and Tech Mahindra, and others are smaller enterprises, such as Mann India Technologies and Cellent.[44] These investments are a win-win proposition: Indian companies benefit from the near-shoring model of providing services to North American markets while also operating in India (thus working full-time in each time zone), and Latin America gains a much-needed value-added service, increased employment opportunities, and overall development of the ICT sector. Ankur Prakash, vice president of TCS's Latin America division, said in an interview with *Gestión*, a business and economics journal in Peru, that the company plans to double its 600 local employees in two years. He added that the IT market in Peru would continue its double-digit growth.[45]

We can expect more investments by Indian ICT companies, and the existing investors in Latin America are likely to expand and consolidate their business presence. These companies also play a part in shoring up India's image as a heavyweight in the global technology industry, which is in contrast to the image of India as the land of spiritual gurus and yoga.

Pharmaceuticals

Indian pharmaceutical companies are major players in the global pharmaceutical sector, and their exports to Latin America form a significant part of the trade basket. India began exporting pharmaceuticals to nearly all the countries in Latin America toward the end of the twentieth century, aided by a push from Brazil, which opened the doors to pharmaceutical majors from India, China, and Canada in 1997 in a bid to invite foreign investment and technology sharing in the sector. High-quality, low-cost generic drugs from India changed the market in Brazil, which allowed the import of generic drugs only in 2000. Brazil and Mexico became the most important partners in this venture, and the supply of active pharmaceutical ingredients (APIs) as well as finished formulations changed the nature of the pharmaceutical market in those countries. Indian majors such as Glenmark, Torrent Pharma, Dr. Reddy's, and also a handful of small and medium-sized pharmaceutical companies now operate in Latin America through local subsidiaries.[46] There is also a healthy mix of exports of finished formulations and APIs, with the former accounting for 55 percent of pharmaceutical exports and the latter accounting for 44 percent (with the remaining 1 percent constituting herbal and ayurvedic products).

Political Relations

There has been a noted increase in political will between the countries of Latin America and India. This has been highlighted by the increase in high-level political visits in the past five years and also by the meetings between India and the troika of CELAC in 2012 and in September 2014. In the past decade, the number of Indian embassies in Latin America has increased from seven to fourteen, and Latin American embassies in India have increased from twelve to twenty. Apart from the politicians, the main actors are the ministries of foreign affairs and commerce and diplomats in India and Latin America.[47]

The Ministry of Commerce and Industry in India has taken some steps to improve India's relationship with Latin American countries. The most notable step taken recently by the ministry is to review India's ten free trade agreements (FTAs) and five preferential trade agreements (PTAs) and to upgrade existing agreements with the region.[48] Emerging markets were identified as a new area of focus in 2014, and then Commerce Secretary Rajeev Kher said that the priority was to "negotiate FTAs with countries with which we feel India has a strong exporting interest. For us those regions are Latin America, Africa, West Asia, CIS where we will look for partners." He added that exports would be used as a means of "pulling up the economy."[49] In less than two years, the BJP-led government has begun negotiations on an FTA with Peru, and the Union Cabinet has approved the expansion of India's PTA with Chile.

India's Ministry of External Affairs has expressed an interest in deepening its relationship with LAC through efforts being made to improve ties with existing regional mechanisms such as the Pacific Alliance (of which India is an observer member) and Mercosur. Negotiations and dialogues to expand the PTA with Mercosur have already begun, and new trade agreements are planned with some LAC countries. From a trade policy perspective, India's exports to Latin America are already at a disadvantage when compared with those of China, the United States, Europe, and Japan, all of which have FTAs with Latin American countries. If India intends to increase exports to Latin America and reduce its large trade deficit, FTAs will be a key determinant. Many analysts in India as well as in Latin America share this sentiment. Patricia Campos de Mello, editor-at-large with the newspaper *Folha de São Paulo,* remarks that "there is a modest trade agreement between India and Mercosur, which is narrow and should be expanded. But Brazil exports only a few products to India (mainly commodities) and the relationship has a lot of room to improve."[50]

Peru has been particularly interested in signing an FTA with India, a stance reiterated by Peruvian president Ollanta Humala at the BRICS-UNASUR meeting in 2014. Humala spoke of a "mutual" interest for Peru and India to sign an FTA and also of a possible state visit to India.[51] According to a high-level Peruvian diplomat, "Peru has great expectations from the new government in India, to increase commerce, tourism, and investments between both countries. One of the measures could be through the signing of an FTA."[52] Negotiations have begun in 2016, after a short joint feasibility study was conducted. Nonetheless, signing an FTA—be it with Peru or any other Latin American country—is a lengthy process, and the effectiveness of such an FTA in improving economic relations will depend on how it is implemented by actors on both sides.

While there is increased political will from most Latin American countries, the same cannot be said of Brazil, which has become more inward-looking in the past few years. This was anticipated, owing to the economic slump and internal political issues. In a personal interview, Oliver Stuenkel, coordinator of Fundação Getúlio Vargas's School of History and Social Science, observed that "Brazil is undergoing a systemic foreign policy retreat. The budget of the Ministry of External Affairs has been cut by roughly 30 percent and there has been a massive reduction of activities. It is unfortunate that when the economy deteriorates, foreign policy is the first to suffer." He added that the intake of diplomats has also decreased to only eighteen recently, from a high of 100 during Lula's presidency.[53]

Thus, on the Latin American side, a key question is whether Brazil will remain at the forefront of the region's ties to Asia in general and to India in particular. President Lula visited India three times in his eight years in office, and his government played a key role in launching and supporting the IBSA initiative. Yet during President Rousseff's first term in office there was a palpable decline in Brazil's global south agenda, and during the 2014 presidential campaign a key foreign policy issue was whether Brazil should return to its more traditional pro-Western stances in global affairs. This was underscored especially by the center-right Brazilian Social Democratic Party candidate Aécio Neves, but also (perhaps less predictably) by the Socialist Party candidate Marina Silva. If Brazil drops its leadership role in moving forward the Indo-LAC agenda, it is not obvious which country is ready to pick it up. A first victim of this could be the otherwise commendable IBSA initiative, already under severe strain as a result of the competition and close overlap with the much better funded BRICS group. An obvious candidate is Argentina, but some would argue the country is still caught up in its domestic economic and political challenges to do any such thing. The same could be said of Venezuela.

Gaps to Be Filled

Like any other relationship, the Indo-LAC relationship has its share of gaps. India and Latin America must take certain measures to address issues of significance to both. What are these issues, and what kind of forward movement can we expect?

There are three main issues: high tariff barriers and restricted market access, lack of knowledge, and a lack of connectivity. The first issue is one of relevance not only to Latin America but to all of India's trading partners. The same problems can also be attributed to some Latin American countries, such as Brazil. In August 2014, Colombian diplomats in India were reported to have said that "market access is a challenge" and that import duties on some products, such as coffee, apparel, and flowers, could be as high as 100 percent.[54] Greater access to markets should also help lift trade from its current stagnancy. India's announcement of working toward a national goods and services tax—which would replace taxes levied by states—should also ease the task of doing business in India.[55]

The lack of knowledge is a problem, but it can also be viewed as an opportunity. Soraya Caro, director of the Center for Research on India and South Asia (CESICAM) at the Universidad Externado in Colombia, in a personal interview said that "the lack of knowledge about the opportunities generated by India's growth puts Colombians at a disadvantage when investing and partnering with India in strategic areas like infrastructure, management, and development of public services, specialty cafés, and mining services." She added that it created an opportunity for academia, to fill the knowledge gap by providing contemporary research on India and Latin America within the context of geopolitics, geoeconomics, and changing social dynamics.[56]

Lack of connectivity can be a major problem for commerce as well as social interactions. Owing to a lack of well-established maritime routes between India and Latin America, some carriers take between forty-five and sixty days to arrive. Some countries, among them Chile (which is the country most distant from India in the world), have demonstrated that this need not be a barrier if integrated trade routes exist. After all, trade between India and South Asia amounts to only half of the trade between India and Latin America.[57] The lack of air connectivity hinders social contact, but an effort is being made to improve this situation and also to make air travel more affordable for tourism. For example, Emirates, the UAE-based airline, has expressed interest in beginning a route between India and Panama City.[58]

DOES INDIA'S MODI GOVERNMENT PROVIDE A TURNING POINT IN INDO-LAC RELATIONS?

Much has been written about the Modi-led government in India. Political analysts in India tend to focus on Modi's role in the Gujarat riots in 2002 and on his personalized style of management during four terms as chief minister of that state, as well as on the implications of Hindutva ideology for India's foreign policy.[59] Economic analysts focus on the probability of replicating the growth in Gujarat on a national scale, and on the prospects of reviving India's economic growth.[60]

The media in LAC have followed the new administration right from Modi's electoral campaign. As the results of the elections were announced in May 2014, Peru's *El Comercio* and Brazil's *O Globo* carried reports on the BJP's massive electoral victory and the imminent rise of Modi to the office of prime minister. *El Comercio*'s article was titled "Narendra Modi, from Tea Vendor to Ruler of India."[61] An editorial that appeared later in *O Globo* articulated it succinctly: "Modi, who as a young child sold tea along with his father, has an open view of the market. This can translate into more trade and mutual investments."[62] The columnist Andrés Oppenheimer looked at the results from a global perspective. Besides suggesting that the landslide election victory could revive India's economy, he went further to suggest that "if he succeeds, his government could also have a great impact on the global economy, especially in emerging markets."[63]

Such optimism is expected when the stakes are so high in India, but what does the Modi-led government bring into the India-LAC equation? The initial outlook is positive, and there are two broad reasons why. First, for the first time in thirty years, India has elected a majority government. This has brought about many changes: it cuts out coalition politics and gives more room to implement reforms. The Modi government has not made any major changes in foreign policy, but there appear to be fewer obstacles in the domestic arena. If his government is able to return India to higher growth, this will likely encourage global commodity markets, which in turn will benefit commodity exporters in LAC.

Second, Modi already has ties to Latin America, which were established well before he took office as prime minister. As the chief minister of Gujarat, a coastal state in western India, he met with a delegation of

Latin American diplomats and businesspersons—a meeting organized by GRULAC (Group of Latin American and Caribbean Countries)—not once but twice. This may seem strange insofar as Latin America has rarely, if ever, been on the priority list for Indian politicians. In this case, however, there was a clear convergence in Gujarat's large share of Indo-LAC trade and Modi's keen interest in Gujarat's international undertakings. The extent of Gujarat's commercial role must not be understated: it accounts for more than half of overall Indo-LAC trade. A large proportion consists of trade in petroleum products, whereby Indian conglomerates import crude oil from Latin America and some oil refiners, such as Reliance Industries, export diesel to Brazil. The exports of pharmaceuticals and agrochemicals are also part of this trade basket.[64]

As mentioned above, a start has been made with Modi's visit to Brazil for the BRICS summit in July 2014. Besides meeting with Brazil's president Dilma Rousseff—where Modi was welcomed with military honors at the Presidential Palace—Modi met the leaders of South America at the BRICS-UNASUR meeting in Brasília. At the meeting, Modi offered to expand cooperation to areas such as telemedicine, weather forecasting, e-governance, resource mapping, and disaster management, but, more important, he stated that India would work more closely with South America than ever before. Insofar as these statements were made shortly after he took office, they must be taken with a grain of salt—but they stand on their own.

The biggest concern for the India of 2015 is the state of its economy and the millions still living in poverty (estimated to be 21.9 percent of the population in 2014, according to the poverty line set by the Tendulkar Committee).[65] Despite being a global player in many industries, the government in New Delhi often follows an India-first policy, prioritizing domestic objectives such as the revival of GDP growth. India will also continue to focus on narrowing the current account deficit, infrastructure projects, poverty alleviation, increasing manufacturing and agricultural output, and modernizing its defense capabilities.[66]

Many initiatives on increasing investment, manufacturing, exports, and infrastructure projects have been announced and overtures have been made to key foreign partners, such as the United States, China, Japan, and Brazil. The prospects for growth seem positive, and this sentiment has been echoed by the financial and capital markets. On September 26, 2014, Standard & Poor's revised the outlook for India from "negative" to "stable." The credit-ratings agency attributed the revision to the changing political scenario, saying in a statement that "India's improved political setting offers an environment conducive to reforms, which could boost growth prospects and improve fiscal management." It further elaborated that the "current government's strong mandate will enable it to implement many of its administrative, fiscal, and economic reforms."[67] In February 2016 these forecasts were reaffirmed by the news that India's economy grew faster than China's in 2015, and would continue to grow at an average of 7.5 percent, according to the IMF.

India's growth story is an important one for Latin America too, which hopes to increase its commercial engagement with India through investments in ICT, infrastructure, energy, defense, and mining projects. Also relevant are the measures taken by India's Ministry of Commerce and Industry and the Ministry of External Affairs. Both have expressed an interest in Latin America: the "Focus: LAC" program initiated by the Ministry of Commerce and Industry, the opening of new diplomatic missions between India and Latin America, and the rising number of high-level political visits are only some examples.[68]

CONCLUSION

Indo-LAC links have come a long way. They have been driven by the commercial sector, but there has been a palpable increase in diplomatic and political will since the beginning of the twenty-first century. While the majority of the dealings are bilateral, a more concerted effort should be made to collaborate on mutual areas of interest in international forums, such as the United Nations, and in multilateral ones, such as IBSA. India's growth story is far from over, and Latin America's share of the global market is also expected to increase in years to come.

India must not be dampened by the news that Latin America's growth is slowing. According to an April 2016 report, the UN Economic Commission for Latin America and the Caribbean forecasts a contraction of 0.6 percent for the Latin American and Caribbean region in 2016. In assessing overall macroeconomic vulnerability, a September 2014 report by the Brookings Institution, a U.S.-based think tank, coined the expression "one region, three Latin Americas." The first group comprises Chile, Colombia, Peru, and Mexico; the second includes only Brazil; and Argentina and Venezuela make up the third group.[69] The lesson for India here is to maintain and diversify its growing commodity-based relationship with the third group, expand its trade and investment with Brazil, and focus more on areas of investment, trade agreements, and joint projects with the first group—Chile, Colombia, Peru, and Mexico. The last set of recommendations has already been initiated by way of trade negotiations with Peru, and an expansion of the existing PTA with Chile.

If both India and LAC work together on bridging some of the gaps mentioned above, they may achieve the momentum needed to elevate the relationship into more strategic areas of cooperation. As a rule, conservative governments in the region are less interested in Asia than progressive ones, and are keener to work with the region's traditional diplomatic partners in North America and Western Europe than with the Chinas and Indias of this world. The underlying question is how long it will take the word to penetrate to all political sectors in Latin America that the action in the new century has shifted from the North Atlantic to the Asia Pacific.

NOTES

1. Oliver Stuenkel, *The BRICS and the Future of Global Order* (Lanham, MD: Lexington Books, 2015).

2. All currency amounts are in U.S. dollars unless otherwise noted. On the BRICS Bank and other initiatives of the group, see Gregory Chin and Jorge Heine, "Consultative Forums: State Power and Multilateral Institutions," in *International Development: Ideas, Experience, and Prospects,* edited by Bruce Carrie-Alder and others (Oxford University Press, 2014), pp. 866–80.

3. On the results of the 2014 general elections in India, see E. Sridharan, "India's Watershed Vote: Behind Modi's Victory," *Journal of Democracy* 25, no. 4 (October 2014), pp. 20–33; and, by the same author, "Class Voting in India's 2014 Election: The Growing Size and Importance of the Middle Classes," *Economic and Political Weekly* 49, no. 39 (September 27, 2014).

4. Mauricio Mesquita Moreira, *India: Latin America's Next Big Thing?* (Washington, DC: Inter-American Development Bank, 2010).

5. See Cynthia Arnson and Jorge Heine, eds., *Reaching Across the Pacific: Latin America and Asia in the New Century* (Washington, DC: Woodrow Wilson International Center for Scholars, 2014).

6. On the evolution of Indo-LAC trade, see Economic Commission for Latin America and the Caribbean (ECLAC), "La India y América Latina y el Caribe: Oportunidades y desafíos en las relaciones comerciales y de inversión" (Santiago, Chile: International Trade and Regional Integration Division, ECLAC, February 2012).

7. On IBSA, see Oliver Stuenkel, *IBSA: The Rise of the Global South* (Oxford: Routledge, 2014). To place these initiatives within the broader setting of Indian foreign policy, see David Malone, *Does the Elephant Dance? Contemporary Indian Foreign Policy* (Oxford University Press, 2010).

8. Government of India, Ministry of External Affairs, "Central American Integration System (SICA)" (New Delhi, February 2013); and "Joint Communiqué of the Ministerial Meeting between India and SICA Member

Countries" (New Delhi, May 29, 2015) (www.mea.gov.in). Another Indian contribution to Central American republics is the setting up of IT training centers.

9. According to the former Ministry of Overseas Indian Affairs (MOIA), which is now part of the Ministry of External Affairs, in 2012 the total number of people of Indian origin in LAC was 1,110,195. Of the roughly 23,000 people of Indian origin in South America, Central America, and Mexico, two-thirds reside in Panama. (http://moia.gov.in/writereaddata /pdf/NRISPIOS-Data(15-06-12)new.pdf [accessed November 16, 2014]).

10. Philomena S. Antony, "Missionary Expansion: Cultural and Agricultural Contacts between Colonial Goa and Brazil," in *Discoveries, Missionary Expansion, and Asian Cultures*, edited by Teotonio R. De Souza (New Delhi: Concept Publishing Co., 1994), p. 160.

11. Rudy Bauss, "Textiles, Bullion and Other Trades of Goa: Commerce with Surat, Other Areas of India, Luso-Brazilian Ports, Macau and Mozambique, 1816–1819," *Indian Economic Social History Review* 3 (1997), p. 276 (http://ier.sagepub.com/content/34/3/275.short).

12. Daniel James, "Nehru Fails to Win Mexico," *Milwaukee Sentinel*, November 20, 1961.

13. Government of India, Ministry of External Affairs, *Foreign Affairs Record* (New Delhi, 1962), p. 580 (http://mealib.nic.in/?pdf2550?000).

14. Government of India, Ministry of External Affairs, *Foreign Affairs Record* (New Delhi, 1968), p. 684 (http://mealib.nic.in/?pdf2556?000).

15. Government of India, Ministry of External Affairs, *Foreign Affairs Record* (New Delhi, 1986), p. 369 (http://mealib.nic.in/?pdf2574?000).

16. Ibid.

17. On this rapprochement between India and Latin America, see Jorge Heine, *La Nueva India* (Santiago, Chile: El Mercurio/Aguilar, 2012), esp. pp. 61–65, as well as Jorge Heine and R. Viswanathan, "The Other BRIC in Latin America: India," *Americas Quarterly* (Spring 2011) (www.americas quarterly.org).

18. On Indian trade and investment with Latin America, see R. Viswanathan, "India and Latin America: A New Perception and a New Partnership," *Analyses of the Elcano Royal Institute* 37 (2014).

19. Data on India's GDP came from the World Bank, Washington, DC.

20. Government of India, Ministry of Commerce and Industry, Export Import Data Bank (http://commerce.nic.in/eidb/).

21. Victor Petersen, "Envíos de cobre a India suben 96% en primer semestre y se espera siga tendencia al alza," *Pulso*, August 26, 2014 (http://static .pulso.cl/20140825/1995094.pdf).

22. Government of India, Ministry of Commerce and Industry, Export Import Data Bank (http://commerce.nic.in/eidb/).

23. Government of India, Ministry of External Affairs, *Annual Report 2014–2015* (New Delhi), p. xiii (http://mea.gov.in/Uploads/PublicationDocs /25009_External_Affairs_2014-2015__English_.pdf).

24. Steven T. Anderson and others, "The Mineral Industries of Latin America and Canada," in U.S. Department of the Interior and U.S. Geological Survey, *2011 Minerals Yearbook: Latin America and Canada* [Advance Release] (U.S. Geological Survey, 2013) (http://minerals.usgs.gov/minerals/pubs/country/2011/myb3-sum-2011-latin-canada.pdf).

25. Government of India, Ministry of Commerce and Industry, Export Import Data Bank (http://commerce.nic.in/eidb/).

26. UN Comtrade Database (http://comtrade.un.org/data/).

27. Ibid.

28. Ajoy K. Das, "Indian Companies Hunt for Iron-Ore in Brazil," *Mining Weekly*, January 9, 2013.

29. Tega Industries, "Group Profile," TegaIndustries.com (http://www.tegaindustries.com/webpage.php?title=Group Profile&p_type=1&parent=12&catid=16).

30. John Satish Kumar, "JSW Steel Faces Concerns over Iron Ore Supplies," *Mint*, September 5, 2011.

31. Government of India, Ministry of External Affairs, "Foreign Relations: India-Peru Relations" (New Delhi, 2016) (http://mea.gov.in/Portal/ForeignRelation/India-Peru_January_2016.pdf).

32. UN Comtrade Database (http://comtrade.un.org/data/).

33. Data from the U.S. Energy Information Administration (http://www.eia.gov/countries/index.cfm).

34. U.S. Department of Energy, "Liquid Fuels and Natural Gas in the Americas" (U.S. Energy Information Administration, January 2014) (http://www.eia.gov/countries/americas/pdf/americas.pdf).

35. Hari Seshasayee, "Tapping into Latin America's Oil" (Mumbai: Gateway House, November 1, 2013) (http://www.gatewayhouse.in/tapping-into-latin-americas-oil/).

36. ONGC Videsh Ltd., "Assets: Latin America" (http://www.ongcvidesh.com/Assets.aspx?tab=3).

37. PTI [Press Trust of India], "ONGC Videsh Signs Agreement with Petróleos Mexicanos," *Hindu Business Line*, September 27, 2014.

38. Platts–McGraw Hill Financial, "Colombia to Build $400 Million LNG Regasification Plant: Official," Platts.com, December 6, 2013.

39. PTI, "Reliance Industries Divests Peru Oil Block Stake," *Economic Times (India)*, April 20, 2014.

40. Erin Voegele, "Reports Highlight Ethanol Production in 3 South American Nations," *Ethanol Producer Magazine*, July 25, 2013.

41. Christopher Lenton, "India's Growing Appetite for Latin American Resources," *BN Americas*, September 8, 2011.

42. Chanchal Pal Chauhan, "Hero MotorCorp Commences Construction of $70-Million Colombian Unit," *Economic Times (India)*, July 8, 2014.

43. Siddharth Philip, "Jaguar Land Rover Plans $392 Million Car Plant in Brazil," Bloomberg.com, December 5, 2013 (http://www.bloomberg.com/news/articles/2013-12-05/jaguar-land-rover-plans-392-million-car-plant-in-brazil).

44. Data on Indian IT in Latin America were obtained directly from Indian companies and through a personal interview with R. Viswanathan, former Indian diplomat and Distinguished Fellow, Latin American Studies, Gateway House (Indian Council on Global Relations), Mumbai.

45. "Tata Consultancy Services planea atender a sus clientes globales desde el Perú," *Gestión*, July 27, 2014.

46. Hari Seshasayee, "Indian Pharma in Latin America: A Strategic Investment," *Revista Zero* 1 (2014), pp. 48–54 (http://zero.uexternado.edu.co /?p=343).

47. For a fascinating, close-up perspective on this evolution from one of its key players, see R. Viswanathan, *From Malgudi to Macondo: The Journey of an Innocent Indian through the Seductive Latin America* (Chennai: Indo–Latin American Chamber of Commerce, 2012).

48. Government of India, Ministry of Commerce and Industry, "Free Trade Agreements," press release, December 9, 2013 (http://pib.nic.in/newsite /PrintRelease.aspx?relid=101156).

49. Asit Ranjan Mishra, "India to Negotiate FTAs with Emerging Market Nations," *Mint*, September 11, 2014.

50. Patricia Campos de Mello, personal interview, October 2014.

51. "Gobierno evalúa ingreso de bienes al mercado chino," *RPP Noticias*, July 17, 2014.

52. Peruvian diplomat, personal interview, October 2014.

53. Oliver Stuenkel, personal interview, October 2014.

54. PTI, "Colombia Keen to Have Talks on Trade Tariff with India," *Business Standard*, August 20, 2014.

55. Kartikay Mehrotra, "Narendra Modi's GST U-Turn Set to Make India Single Market for First Time," *Mint*, August 6, 2014.

56. Soraya Caro, personal interview, October 2014.

57. Government of India, Ministry of Commerce and Industry, Export Import Data Bank (http://commerce.nic.in/eidb/).

58. Emirates, "Emirates Announces Service to Panama City," press release, August 13, 2015 (http://www.emirates.com/english/about/media -centre/2569902/emirates-announces-service-to-panama-city).

59. See Pankaj Mishra, "Modi's Idea of India," *New York Times*, October 25, 2014.

60. On the economic and foreign policy expectations of the Modi government, see Shyam Saran, "India's External Relations: What the Modi Factor Promises," *RSIS Commentaries*, May 23, 2014.

61. "Narendra Modi, de vendedor de té a gobernante de la India," *El Comercio*, May 16, 2014.

62. Eliane Oliveira, "Brasil e Índia: Continuamos firmes?," *O Globo*, June 26, 2014. Authors' translation.

63. Andrés Oppenheimer, "El impacto global del cambio en India," *El Nuevo Herald*, May 21, 2014. Authors' translation.

64. On Gujarat–Latin America ties, see R. Viswanathan, "Gujarat-Latin America: Friends & Benefits" (Mumbai: Gateway House [Indian Council on Global Relations], May 12, 2014).

65. Government of India, Ministry of Statistics and Programme Implementation, "SAARC Social Charter India Country Report 2014" (Mumbai, 2014).

66. On India's economic situation and challenges, see Government of India, Ministry of Finance, *Union Budget of India 2014–15*; "Key Features of the Budget 2014–15" (Mumbai, 2014) (http://indiabudget.nic.in/ub2014 -15/bh/bh1.pdf).

67. "Research Update: India Outlook Revised to Stable from Negative; Ratings Affirmed at 'BBB–/A-3,'" *Standard & Poor's*, September 26, 2014.

68. On measures taken by the Indian government to boost Indo-LAC ties, see Deepak Bhojwani, "India and Latin America: Forging Deeper Ties," *Economic and Political Weekly* 48, no. 30 (July 27, 2013).

69. Ernesto Talvi, "Latin America Macroeconomic Outlook: A Global Perspective," Brookings Global-CERES Economic and Social Policy in Latin America Initiative (September 2014).

CHAPTER 4

Regional Policy Perspectives

This chapter offers a compilation of short commentaries by leading experts that complement the material in the preceding chapters through a variety of broad regional policy perspectives.[1] These commentaries also help frame the discussion for the more specialized chapters in the subsequent sections of this volume.

SINO–LATIN AMERICAN RELATIONS FROM A CHINESE PERSPECTIVE[2]

Sun Hongbo

Despite nuanced views regarding China's varied impacts on Latin America and the Caribbean (LAC), there appears to be a regional consensus that China's presence is now a reality and a priority for LAC. For its part, China has begun embracing the vast heterogeneity within LAC. Rather than treating LAC as a unitary actor, it views the region as a group of countries with different interests, needs, and expectations in their relations with China. Such an approach will allow China to better navigate the geopolitical and economic landscape of the region through more country-specific policies.

China and LAC face historic opportunities to grow both independently and in synergy. However, for the Sino–LAC partnership to realize its full potential, leaders from both sides need to take stock of the challenges going forward to the same extent that they value the opportunities ahead. One challenge they face is the uncertainty that looms over Sino-LAC relations amid a slow and uneven global economic recovery. As China experiences a cyclical slowdown while embarking on structural economic reforms, doubts remain over whether Sino-LAC relations can continue the impressive growth momentum of the past two decades. One key challenge lies in how to broaden the scope of economic relations beyond trade to include more investment and other long-term growth opportunities. The outlook of LAC's trade and economic relations with the United States and the EU also seems unclear in light of the lingering effects of the 2008 financial crisis and the subsequent euro-zone debt crisis. This, combined with China's deceleration, calls into question the inherent sustainability of the region's current growth model, an important determinant of future Sino-LAC relations.

As various authors in this volume point out, Sino-LAC economic ties, particularly trade and investment, require significant qualitative improvements. LAC economies on the whole seek an increase in higher-value-added exports to China. An underdeveloped institutional framework underpinning China-LAC investment activities has limited the number of Chinese companies that have successfully entered and navigated the Latin American markets. A closer look at the investment statistics reveals more concerns. The majority of the bilateral investment flows between China and LAC can be accounted for by Chinese capital flows into tax havens such as the Cayman and Virgin Islands. Furthermore, of the Chinese investments that did take place in LAC, most appeared to be brownfield or portfolio flows, as opposed to greenfield foreign direct investment (FDI). Therefore, their contribution to LAC's real economy is likely rather limited.

To fix these problems, the public and private sectors from both sides must work closely together to devise feasible solutions. On the one hand, both the Chinese and the LAC governments need to create a response mechanism through which Chinese investors can voice their concerns about investing in LAC and be offered some degree of reassurance, and vice versa. On the other hand, aside from the appropriate political and regulatory incentives, the private sector's ability to succeed also hinges on private companies' own willingness to learn, adapt, and localize.

Despite complementarities and shared agendas, China and LAC have a long way to go to achieve the full potential of their strategic partnership. As Kevin Gallagher and Rebecca Ray note, while natural resources will likely remain an important focus of cooperation, diversification into other sectors has become increasingly imperative. Such industries as manufacturing, infrastructure, and technology, especially in areas where they intersect with natural resource development, are of interest to Chinese investors and can serve as key entry points for diversification efforts in LAC. Additionally, China and LAC should hold regular dialogues to discuss sustainability-related issues, such as the potential depletion of natural resources in LAC and the resulting collapse of resource-based economies, which are of equal concern to both LAC and China.

China could also consider stepping up economic assistance to LAC as a way to solidify bilateral ties. While LAC as a region enjoys relatively high levels of income in the context of emerging market economies, there are subregions that are still in need of development aid and technology transfer. Economic assistance to these subregions could greatly complement existing Chinese diplomatic efforts and create synergies that lead to better results. LAC has long suffered ubiquitous and costly infrastructure deficits, and the region is still facing technical and financing barriers to effectively developing infrastructure on its own. Statistics show that LAC needs to invest 5.2 percent of regional GDP per year in infrastructure projects just to close the infrastructure gap with other emerging regions by 2020.[3] The scale of the Chinese economy, coupled with its capital abundance and technological superiority, makes infrastructure projects in LAC an attractive option for investors. LAC is particularly interested in seeking Chinese investment in electric grids, roads, railways, ports, and airport development, which is crucial to boosting both internal growth and trade with China.

For Sino-LAC relations to continue maturing in the longer term, mutual trust needs to be strengthened. Although Sino–LAC relations have become less politicized and ideological and more pragmatic and multidimensional over time, political cycles in LAC still play an important role in influencing the cross-regional partnership. In addition, the two decades between the mid-1990s and the mid-2010s, which saw the takeoff of Sino-LAC trade, also witnessed the emergence of a few anti-China narratives in LAC, such as "financial imperialism," "primarization" or "commodification," and "deindustrialization." Deriving from a lack of mutual understanding, these defensive discourses mainly rest on three concerns some LAC scholars have about increased Chinese involvement in the region, namely: (1) the perceived asymmetries of trade and investment ties with China, where China benefited at LAC's expense; (2) the China-induced commodity dependency, which causes LAC economies to lose competitiveness; and (3) the exploitative nature of Chinese activities as conceptualized from the perspective of the colonial and neocolonial experience.

Nevertheless, while such rhetoric and adverse political cycles could slow down the progress made in recent years, they will not be able to reverse it completely, insofar as both sides stand by the fundamental complementarity of their national interests. At the very least, both the Chinese and the LAC governments need to be more vocal and eloquent in expressing bilateral support, more attentive and responsive to the other party's needs, and more pragmatic in setting up bilateral policy goals and cooperation initiatives. In doing so, they will be able to lay out an unequivocal roadmap for the further deepening and broadening of Sino-LAC ties.

CHINA GOES GEOPOLITICAL IN ITS STRATEGIC PARTNERSHIP WITH LATIN AMERICA

Xiang Lanxin

A new strategic vision has emerged in the early 2010s touching on China's relations with Latin America. The immature and "neocolonial" phase of the relationship, driven by a single-minded strategy of raw material grabbing, is over. Starting in 2014, Beijing has adopted a comprehensive Latin America strategy in coordination with its other priority areas, especially Africa, Central Asia, and Europe. In this sense, China is increasingly treating Latin America as a region with geopolitical significance in a potential global rivalry with the United States.

During President Xi Jinping's successful Latin American tour in July 2014, Beijing established and upgraded "strategic partnerships" with Argentina, Brazil, Mexico, Peru, and Venezuela. But the question of what a strategic partnership means has so far drawn very little attention in the West. A strategic partnership is Beijing's relatively recent conception of how to prioritize its myriad bilateral ties in the world. It is considered an innovation in the process of constructing a unique Chinese version of a "great power" model to deal with the outside world. The primary objective is geopolitical, to counter the global influence and power of the United States, especially in the Asia-Pacific region.

China's traditional strategic priority is to maintain a peaceful international system in order to gain precious time and space for its "peaceful rise," without being caught in a new containment environment against its economic development. Avoiding conflict with the other great powers and maintaining China's internal stability are the twin objectives of its peaceful rise. Another priority is to promote a "harmonious world." The policy elite believes that many in the West are beginning to sense, but are not yet ready to admit, that a unified political Western coalition is disappearing and its leader, the United States, is in a serious process of decline. A historic moment has arrived for changing East-West relations, and promoting harmony among major civilizations has been put, with a degree of urgency, on China's global agenda.

The psychological foundation for this new thinking is the feeling that Chinese economic strength is nothing new in global history, because China had occupied a prominent economic position on the world stage for many centuries before its traditional international relations and domestic governance tenets were challenged. China's "restoration" in Xi's language (that is, the dream of China) will inevitably begin to influence and transform the current international system. China has acquired a new "mandate of heaven" to fundamentally change a global structure based on a Western values system. Most analysts in Beijing believe that traditional Cold Warriors will never abandon the idea of the "rise of China" because they hope that the need for dealing with an alleged Chinese threat might help create another global balance-of-power system.

In practical terms, such new thinking inevitably leads to the ending of the relatively passive and nonassertive foreign policy adopted by Deng Xiaoping (*taoguang yanghui*). But what strategy will replace Deng's low-profile one? Direct rivalry with the United States, especially in its backyard, Latin America, is unwise, only adding to the American suspicion of China's long-term intention of undermining its world leadership position. Among all the options, a strategic partnership is the least risky and most feasible. In Chinese diplomatic parlance, a strategic partnership not only stresses a kind of special economic relationship but also includes the idea of exchanging, sharing, and even coordinating views and policies on bilateral relations and major international issues. Borrowing from business language, a strategic partnership refers to two companies that will help each other over something that they are individually unable to achieve.

Latin America has increasingly become a strategic priority, for two reasons. One is the endowment of rich natural resources, the other is its proximity to the United States. Latin America is part of the subregional system that China refers to as "multipolar." It is also an important player in the global quest for economic and social justice, which the Chinese have labeled the "democratization of international relations." The geopolitical implications for a deepened Sino–Latin American relationship have to do with the potential role in modifying the existing rules of the game in the current international system. Aside from its high economic value, Latin America serves as an exemplary model not only of Beijing's diplomatic strategy but also of its economic policies toward developing nations. Beijing's approach relies on institution building and stressing "win-win" economic growth and political cooperation. Policy coordination has also increased in areas such as development strategies, diplomatic actions in international organizations, the structure of the world economy, and the advocacy of key international principles, such as state sovereignty and the principle of nonintervention in domestic affairs.

Can China's influence on foreign economic interests be translated into a long-term force of geopolitical change for the region? Opinions vary, depending on where one stands. Foreign investment has always been a crucial factor in Latin America's development. Beijing's "going out" strategy was initiated in 1999 and, in contrast to most developing nations, China has attached importance to both inward and outward foreign investment. Many on the left argue that Western investment and exploitation are tools of neocolonialism and are responsible for many of Latin America's social problems. Yet a positive consensus is emerging on Chinese investment in the region—Chinese investment is generally welcomed and seen as a positive transformative force.

The erosion of U.S. engagement with Latin America in recent decades can be attributed to distractions elsewhere, particularly the Middle East after the September 11, 2001 terrorist attacks. A parallel in history, according to one recent study, is Britain's experience in the region in the nineteenth century, when British influence began to decline as a result of other foreign entanglements (such as the Boer Wars and World War I), allowing a rising nation, the United States, to take advantage of this power vacuum.[4] Chinese leaders could hardly miss the fact that history seems to be repeating itself, in view of U.S. engagement in the Middle East and other policy priorities such as Obama's "strategic pivot" to East Asia. But is China aiming to become the new hegemonic power in Latin America?

So far, China's economic engagement with the region is a far cry from that of the United States, particularly when one takes stock of trade and investment flows.[5] However, the picture is changing. During his 2014 visit to Latin America, President Xi made a proposal known as "1+3+6," a new framework of cooperation between the two sides, with "1" referring to a unified strategic cooperation plan between China and Latin

America for 2015–19; "3" referring to three engines of growth, trade, investment, and finance; and "6" referring to six priority sectors—energy resources, infrastructure, agriculture, manufactures, technical innovation, and information technology (IT).[6] Thus, since 2014, China's new geopolitical calculus seems to be threefold. First, China's ever-closer ties to Latin America will exert pressure on the United States, and Latin America may somewhat pull U.S. attention away from its stated Asian pivot. Second, Beijing believes that, with China's influence up and U.S. influence down, Latin American countries will see China as a serious counterweight to U.S. hegemony in the region. Third, Brazil has become China's anchor in the region and an ally in international forums. As a group, BRICS members—Brazil, Russia, India, China, and South Africa—wish to have a greater voice in global economic policymaking. The creation of the BRICS Development Bank and the Contingent Reserve Arrangement reflects the emerging powers' intention and determination to challenge the existing world order.

It is in this context that Beijing increasingly views Latin America as an important geopolitical asset. While Chinese investment is not helping Latin American industry as much as it could, primarily because Chinese products also compete with industrial sectors in Latin America, the threat of deindustrialization is overblown. From a long-term perspective, China has a stake in the sustainable growth of the region, precisely for its geostrategic interest in balancing U.S. influence. A politically unstable, economically volatile, and socially restless Latin America will not serve China's long-term goal of maintaining a peaceful environment for further development. Although Latin American industry is in the difficult position of competing with China's low-cost manufactured goods, as Chinese wages rise, manufacturing will inevitably upgrade to a higher value chain.

In conclusion, China's geopolitical interests in Latin America do not undermine its economic interests. As long as China does not adopt a geopolitical strategy in military terms, the foundation of its relations with Latin American countries will remain solid. Critical voices, of course, are often heard, mainly regarding the overreliance on Latin American exports of raw materials and agricultural products. While China has demonstrated a consistent strategy with Latin America, there is no coherent regional strategy in dealing with China, as the various Latin America country chapters in this volume illustrate. The highly diversified responses to China can be attributed to a north-south divide by which some countries, such as Mexico and the economies of Central America, are more integrated with the north, while the rest are not. Political ideologies are also divided, with some favoring interventionist/

socialist policies and others more market-friendly policies. In addition, economic structures vary widely, as some countries are primarily commodity exporters and some are not.

A LATIN AMERICAN PERSPECTIVE ON CHINA'S GROWING PRESENCE IN THE REGION

Jorge Guajardo

That China has become the second-largest importer of Latin American goods and Latin America has become the third-largest destination for Chinese exports suggests a straightforward narrative: a rising China offers significant opportunities to raise economic development in Latin American nations while simultaneously presenting a geopolitical counterpoint to U.S. influence, ensuring the region's political independence. Many international commentators and, most important, Latin American leaders themselves have bought into the truth of this narrative. However, as time progresses and evidence amasses, it becomes clear that this narrative does not accurately capture reality.

In this regard, three important considerations are offered in this commentary. First, China's involvement in Latin America is guided almost wholly by economic self-interest. Many of the trade and investment deals negotiated with the Chinese deliver uncertain benefits to Latin American nations while producing clear and large benefits for Chinese corporations and the Chinese state. Second, Latin American economies are not monolithic, a theme stressed by several authors in this volume. Therefore, discussing the Chinese and Latin American relationship at the regional level threatens to obscure important heterogeneity in both the opportunities and threats posed by China, as well as the policies necessary to maximize these opportunities and minimize these threats. Finally, several policy options are available that should help Latin American nations maximize benefits and minimize costs when dealing with China on the economic and political stage.

The growth in Chinese investment in and trade with Latin America over the past decade has made China a major player in the region. However, there are a number of reasons to believe that this large increase in trade and investment has not been as beneficial to Latin America as these statistics might suggest. Chinese loan commitments—which between 2005 and 2014 totaled more than $130 billion, with the greatest part of the money dedicated to infrastructure and energy projects[7]—are often made on less favorable terms than those offered by Western creditors. The Chinese Development Bank, which has financed the vast majority of the loans, offers higher interest rates and more stringent terms than its Western counterparts. Additionally, these loans often come with requirements to use Chinese labor and purchase equipment from Chinese suppliers during the construction process.[8] These requirements cause local economies to lose much of the short-term economic benefit that infrastructure development provides and, even worse, deprive generations of young people of the opportunity to start a business or learn a skill in regions that are often short on good opportunities to begin with. The use of Chinese suppliers also prevents the diffusion of technological know-how into the local market, hampering the development of higher-value industry. Finally, although Chinese loan commitments have large headline amounts, it is unclear how much of a loan actually becomes available for discretionary use. Often loans must be used for specific purposes beneficial to the Chinese (such as purchasing Chinese imports), and long time frames imply that the announced amount may end up far overstating the amount actually received by the recipient government.

Although trade between China and Latin America has increased rapidly over the past decade, the benefits from this trade have not been spread equitably. About one-half of Latin American exports to China come from just three sources, soy, iron, and copper, while Chinese exports to Latin America include a diverse set of manufactured goods.[9] Commodity exports are subject to large price swings driven by macroeconomic trends over which the exporter has little control, increasing economic volatility. This increased volatility can be especially problematic in countries without strong institutions in place to capture surplus in times of high commodity prices to protect against periods with low prices.

Exports of commodities and other products from extractive industries also do not position countries to "move up the value chain" in the same way as manufacturing, as Robert Devlin and Theodore Kahn note in chapter 7. A country may begin by manufacturing low-value, non-technology-intensive products such as garments and leverage the knowledge gained into becoming producers of high-value products such as electronics and automobiles. A similar transition is much more difficult for an economy that relies primarily on commodity production.

In theory, it may be possible to use resources gained from commodity production and invest in the human and physical capital necessary to become a competitive manufacturer. However, trade with China also impedes this goal. Most Latin American countries cannot compete with Chinese manufacturing prices. Chinese manufacturers are the beneficiaries of cheap credit, domestic energy subsidies, protected domestic markets, and cheap domestic labor. Additionally, in response to oversupply in the Chinese market, the government has encouraged dumping overseas in some industries. Thus, trade with China has both increased the importance of extractive industries and simultaneously left Latin American manufacturing firms uncompetitive.

Finally, although China exports heavily to Latin America, there is very limited manufacturing-related FDI. This is partially for the reasons mentioned above; China's advantage in manufacturing comes largely from factors tied to domestic production and cannot be duplicated abroad. China also prefers to invest in markets with cheaper labor than China's or in countries with closed, protected markets; Latin America does not fit either of these criteria. These factors suggest not only that China has low levels of manufacturing FDI in Latin America now but also that these levels are likely to remain low for the foreseeable future.

This is not to say that Latin American countries do not gain benefits from trade: trade with China has been a boon for industries and individuals involved in the commodity sector and has increased Latin American GDP. However, if one looks at the longer term, overreliance on the commodity sector leaves Latin America vulnerable to Chinese macroeconomic performance. Further, overreliance on the commodity sector also does not allow a move into higher-value, more innovative and technologically intensive industries, potentially placing a ceiling on overall development. Finally, competition from subsidized Chinese imports impedes the creation of a home manufacturing sector.

Another challenging issue is the lack of transparency in Chinese state-owned enterprises and the Chinese government. Because they are accustomed to working with governments as authoritarian and nontransparent as their own, Chinese business leaders often do not make provisions for the community buy-in and public support for projects necessary in democracies with vibrant civil societies. This can result in misunderstandings and political headaches for Latin American leaders, as well as increased opportunities for corruption. These political costs lead to real economic inefficiencies, decreasing the gains from both trade and Chinese infrastructure development.

If the current structure for Chinese investment in Latin America is not working, how should Latin American countries think about their relationship with China in the future? Before answering this question, it is important to note, as mentioned earlier, that Latin America is not a monolithic entity—the composition of individual economies and the political tenor of each country's relationship with China differ dramatically across the region. Therefore, policies for dealing with China should also exhibit a similar level of heterogeneity. A representative set of Latin American countries can be categorized in four different groups based on their economic composition and exposure to China; specific policy recommendations for each group are warranted.

Alone among Latin American nations, Mexico has a highly manufacturing-dependent export sector, with a large focus on the U.S. market. Mexico competes with China in many industries—the largest subset of both Mexican and Chinese exports consists of manufactured machine products (35 percent for Mexico and 48 percent for China). Since China's accession to the World Trade Organization (WTO) in 2001, it has increasingly competed with Mexican manufactures in the U.S. markets. After just three years of China being a member of the WTO, total U.S. imports from China had increased from $109 billion to $192 billion, while U.S. imports from Mexico had remained nearly flat (in 2014 dollars). Mexican manufacturing also faces increased competition from China domestically. The large majority of Mexican imports from China are high-value manufactured goods, such as electronics and machines used in production.

Therefore, Mexico has a lot to lose from increased Chinese influence in the region and should be actively pursuing policies aimed at overcoming these threats to its manufacturing sector. First, Mexico should use all actions at its disposal to ensure that China does not employ unfair anticompetitive practices in industries that compete with Mexican corporations. For instance, China and Mexico are both members of the WTO, so Mexico can use the WTO as a forum to protest against Chinese domestic subsidies and dumping policies that often give Chinese corporations an unfair advantage over their Mexican counterparts. Similarly, if the WTO fails, the Mexican government can also impose unilateral import taxes in response to these policies.

Second, Mexico can build on its existing strengths. The Trans-Pacific Partnership (TPP) is one important mechanism to accomplish this. The TPP provides Mexican exporters access to many large economies, the majority of which are complements, not competitors, to Mexican manufacturing. Mexico can build on its reputation as a stable, democratic government with quality, reliable manufacturing to build market share in these countries. Although the TPP would open up the U.S. and Canadian markets to other Pacific nations, the gains from excluding China from the TPP would likely be much larger than the potential costs from additional competition in the North American market, especially because American and Canadian trade barriers are already so low. Further, if Mexico takes an active role in the TPP negotiation process, it can work to see that its key interests are protected in any final agreement.

Finally, there is still some scope to expand on Mexico's relationship with China. Tourism is a major industry in Mexico, but the country still receives relatively few Chinese tourists. Increasing Mexico's visibility and reputation to Chinese tourists is one way to take advantage of the growing Chinese middle and upper classes. Mexican agriculture may also find a growing market in China's ever-increasing demand for food products. However, Mexican leaders should not let the potential short-term and medium-term gains from these sectors obscure the larger picture. Mexico must engage with China economically—China is the second-largest economy in the world—but it must also strive to maintain its economic independence whenever possible.

The economies of both Brazil and Chile are highly dependent on commodity exports to China—copper for Chile and iron and oil for Brazil. Indeed, China is both countries' largest trading partner. However, the Brazilian and Chilean economies are not completely unidimensional: Brazil also has a large domestic industrial and financial services sector, while Chile has a growing services sector. When dealing with China, Brazil and Chile should have two major goals: first, diversifying away from a completely China-centric export strategy, and second, balancing dependence on exports with sustainable growth of industrial and service sectors. China's economy is complementary to these two countries. The goal is not to shut China out entirely but instead to use China's demand for commodities to further long-term development goals.

One mechanism for accomplishing these goals is through accession into regional trade agreements with countries outside the region. For Chile as for Mexico, the TPP is a great opportunity to diversify its export base and find new customers for both Chilean commodity/agricultural exports and the Chilean service industry. Although Brazil is not a party to the TPP, it may search for similar deals with European or Asian nations. A second mechanism is to include provisions in trade deals with China for Brazilian industry and services and Chilean services entry into the Chinese market. China is also dependent on Chilean and Brazilian raw materials; these two countries should leverage these needs into deals that allow the long-term development of their industrial and service sectors. Third, like Mexico, both Brazil and Chile have large tourism industries but relatively few Chinese tourists. More can be done to encourage Chinese tourism in the coming decade, especially in light of international events such as the 2016 Summer Olympics in Brazil. Finally, both Brazil and Chile should approach Chinese infrastructure- and energy-financing deals with caution and ensure that any deals include adequate provisions to protect Brazilian firms and workers.

Central American countries have neither access to large amounts of natural resources nor large manufacturing sectors (with the exception of Costa Rica). Primary exports are largely agricultural, but some countries have entered into garment manufacturing and electronics. All Central American countries run trade deficits with China but trade much more heavily with the United States. These countries are also highly in need of infrastructure development.

There are many potential trade opportunities with China among the Central American countries, but only if done cautiously. For instance, in many of these countries, labor may be even cheaper than in China; therefore, they may be well positioned to receive Chinese FDI in clothing and other low-tech manufacturing. Second, China may be a promising market for these countries' agricultural exports. Third, if these countries are able to negotiate infrastructure development deals that include the use of local workers and firms in conjunction with Chinese technology and logistics, this arrangement could pay long-term dividends. However, the key is to not simply accept any deal that is offered but instead negotiate for a deal that is in the true long-term interests of these countries' citizens.

Countries like Argentina and Venezuela have relied on China for financing given their lack of access to international financial markets. These countries have had fewer policy options—in some cases their choices may have been Chinese financing or default. However, again, this does not necessarily mean that these countries should simply accept Chinese financing on any terms. Countries need to consider the long-term consequences of dealing with the Chinese. For example, some of these financing deals may present options worse than an international credit default. However, given these countries' precarious financial positions, it is difficult to suggest a strict policy rule; each deal must be examined based on its individual merits. Nevertheless, the general theme remains: despite any political proclamations of solidarity made by the Chinese government, the vast majority of trade deals and infrastructure investments made by the Chinese are focused on promoting China's self-interest, not that of any recipient nation.

There is no one-size-fits-all policy for dealing with China. Each country's optimal policy is influenced by its complementarity with China's economy and leverage in negotiations. However, in general, several policies exist that would make trade and investment deals with China more beneficial for most Latin American nations. Joining the TPP or similar partnerships could open up new export markets for Latin American goods and on better terms than China provides. Approaching prospective trade and investment deals with China from the standpoint that China is acting out of calculated self-interest should push nations to perform a more rational cost-benefit analysis of any terms and conditions. Additionally, countries can use China's demand for their commodities as leverage to gain access to China's market for their own internal services and heavy manufacturing industries. Ultimately, the rise of China has completely transformed the global economic landscape, and there is no reverting back to the world before China became an economic superpower. Rather, Latin American leaders must strive to recognize China for what it is—both an opportunity and a threat—and ensure that they are using all policy levers at their disposal to make their relationships work toward maximizing the benefits for their citizens.

LATIN AMERICA'S CHINA DECADE: MANAGING BENEFITS AND RISKS

Kevin P. Gallagher and Rebecca Ray

As Devlin and Kahn explain in chapter 7, economic engagement with China was increasingly important for LAC over the 2003–13 decade. During this period, LAC exports to China surged relative to exports to the rest of the world. Chinese finance for LAC governments has risen to unprecedented heights. Chinese FDI in Latin America is also on the rise, though still relatively small. In the cases of both exports and finance, Chinese economic activity tends to be concentrated in the mining, extraction, and agricultural sectors. However, for the next decade to be fruitful, LAC governments will have to manage the benefits of this relationship to mitigate the risks of commodity-led growth in general and China-LAC economic ties in particular.

The risks to LAC associated with China's rise have become manifest on at least four levels. First, the price increases and demand for commodities led to a surge in investment for Latin American commodities and lessened demand for manufacturing. Second, the surge in investment led in part to a rise in the value of many LAC currencies during the period. Third, LAC governments and firms were not using the windfall profits from the commodity boom to increase productivity. Fourth, Chinese manufacturing producers were managing capital flows, investing in productivity, and perhaps enhancing their exchange rate, thus significantly outcompeting LAC producers in LAC markets and in markets across the world.[10]

Energy, infrastructure, and other forms of commodities extraction are also often endemic to environmental degradation and social conflict in the region. Economic activity between LAC and China is more environmentally intensive than domestic economic activity in LAC and economic activity related to LAC's trade with the rest of the world. For example, greenhouse-gas-intensive activities that contribute to climate change, such as ranching, have significantly increased because of Chinese demand for sector-related products. Currently closer to home than climate change, Chinese trade and investment have been the source of significant social and environmental conflict. Chinese energy and mining companies in Peru and Ecuador have been shown to be engaged in highly polluting activity, deforestation, poor worker relations, and a lack of transparency with respect to their activities. Although Chinese firms do not always perform worse than their counterparts in the energy and mining sectors, Chinese mines and extractive plants have increasingly become the subject of intense and contested advocacy campaigns at the local level and among transnational advocacy networks.[11]

Also important is that LAC exports to China began the 2003–13 period at a higher level of labor intensity than exports in general but ended the period well below other exports. This can be explained by the shift in the LAC-China export basket toward a greater emphasis on extraction (which supports very few jobs) and away from manufacturing (which has high labor intensity). In sum, coupled with earlier evidence on the general decline in industry in Latin America, if not managed properly, Chinese economic engagement in LAC can accentuate incentives toward deindustrialization, environmental degradation, social conflict, and a lack of job growth.

Most analysts agree that commodity prices will no longer soar upward as they have over the past decade.[12] Moreover, the era of double-digit economic growth is also considered to be over. These factors have adjusted the growth forecasts for LAC over the next five years or more considerably downward, to 2 percent per year.[13] While commodity prices may have plateaued and become volatile again, China's demand will remain strong. It should be remembered that a "slowdown" to 7 percent annual growth in China is 7 percent of 13 trillion international dollars, approximately $900 billion. The glory days of 10 percent growth in China occurred when the Chinese economy was less than half its 2013 size, at approximately 6 trillion international dollars ($600 billion). Looking ahead, however, countries such as India and Indonesia will increasingly be a source of demand for LAC commodities, and China's demand for primary products is expected to continue rising.[14] LAC has a unique opportunity to capitalize on this continued demand.

To ensure the long-run sustainability of trade-led growth, Latin America will need to orient some of the newfound economic benefits from the China-LAC economic relationship toward economic diversification, transparency, and environmental protection. While China may be a driver of environmental change and a contributor to the lack of robust employment growth in LAC, China cannot be blamed for the (mis)management of resources and environmental policy in LAC. Studies have shown that commodities go through price "supercycles" or surges in demand that are coupled with rising prices[15] even as the long-run price level is in overall decline. Over centuries, each of these surges has been a function of related booms in economic activity that led to increased demand for primary commodities—the Industrial Revolution, world wars, and, more recently, the rise of China. LAC needs to capture the benefits of these booms and use them to mitigate some of the costs the booms themselves bring to the region. That would mean channeling some of the benefits into resource conservation, economic stabilization, employment-led economic diversification, and environmental protection. That said, it will also be important for China to upgrade its business strategy, environmental standards, and the transparency of its overseas operations in order to maintain both global market share and good relations with host nations.

RECALIBRATING INDO–LATIN AMERICAN POLICY

Deepak Bhojwani

The twenty-first century introduced a new paradigm into India's relations with the world. While India is no longer pictured with a begging bowl, perceptions of this "emerging" power vary: there is apprehension in the neighborhood, enthusiasm in East and North Asia, anticipation in Europe, and expectation in the Arab world and Africa. In the Western Hemisphere, India's relations with the United States burgeoned throughout the course of the twentieth century, eclipsing India's engagement with Canada, and especially with LAC countries. Much of this had to do with the United States' superpower status and protagonism. The magnetic appeal of the "American way," contrasted with stultified conditions and prospects on the subcontinent since the 1960s, led to what was considered India's "brain drain."

India redefined its political economy priorities in the 1990s. Indian expatriate and business interests rescued an economy in free fall, while the establishment took up the challenge of sustainable development. The emergence of India in the twenty-first century has much to do with its economic and technological prowess. It is seen as a huge market for almost anything it cannot produce, from aircraft to avocados. High growth rates have meant higher demand for energy, food, minerals, and raw materials. The security dimension had long defined India's strategic priorities to a large extent, but in the twenty-first century, economic exigencies and opportunities have increasingly determined the emphasis in its international relations.

Having recalibrated its foreign policy in the past decade, India enhanced economic relations with East and Southeast Asia. Strategic connections with a reemerging Russia subsist. Historical linkages with Africa led to higher engagement, bolstered by official patronage. As New India looked around, it began to discover the potential of another region it seemed to have virtually ignored. Latin America, with more than five times India's territory and an enormous resource base of hydrocarbons, minerals, and arable land, offered India a market of more than 500 million people with a per capita annual income exceeding $10,000.[16]

India's trade with LAC, according to Indian statistics, was less than $1 billion in 2000. By 2013 it had crossed $46 billion, growing at a compound annual rate of more than 30 percent.[17] That said, the composition of this trade is skewed, as several chapters in this volume emphasize. Hydrocarbon imports by India accounted for around $20 billion that year. India's recurring trade deficit since 2006 looks likely to continue, since Latin America also supplies large volumes of copper, edible oils, and other raw or semiprocessed materials. India's manufactures have captured more space every year in Latin American markets, though they may not have achieved the brand recognition of their European or even Asian competitors. Indian investment in the region has increased in recent years to more than $16 billion, according to the Confederation of Indian Industry.

Why, then, does the feeling persist that the relationship has yet to be defined? Until the present century, Latin America was beyond India's horizon in more ways than one. The virtual absence of an expatriate Indian community, minimal historical interaction compared with other regions of the world, physical distance, and linguistic barriers combined to relegate it to the lowest priority. Yet the absence of political baggage or contention obviated active political engagement. An inadequately equipped Indian foreign service struggled to set up and maintain a diplomatic structure that still does not measure up to the full potential of the relationship. For its part, Latin America was too absorbed with the United States and Europe, and more recently China, to look toward South Asia.

In this century, Indo-LAC energy complementarity has drawn the most attention. India is expected to produce only 35.5 million tons of crude oil from domestic fields in fiscal year 2014–15. To meet an estimated demand of 224 million tons, it will need to import around 188 million tons (84 percent).[18] Indian companies have secured attractive prices for crude oil from Brazil, Venezuela, Mexico, Colombia, and Ecuador, and have even negotiated term contracts. By 2013, Latin America accounted for more than 15 percent of India's crude oil imports. This percentage could rise if turbulence persists among some of India's traditional suppliers—Iran, Nigeria, and Iraq—and other potential sources such as Libya and Sudan. Massive refining capacities have been set up on India's west coast to receive greater quantities of heavy Latin American crudes, which yield better gross refining margins. In fact, excess Indian refining capacity has helped balance the trade, with Latin America importing petroleum products from India.

Constraints on India's further involvement are primarily financial. The Indian establishment does not have pockets as deep as the Chinese and is far more stringent on the bottom line. State-owned ONGC (Videsh) Ltd. had to pull out of Cuba after seven years in 2014, unable to justify the financial viability of its exploration efforts. Private sector players such as Reliance Industries Ltd. have surrendered concessions in Colombia and Peru. There are still several billion Indian dollars in the Latin American kitty and more to come, depending on the regulatory regimes.

There is also the political dimension, which helps shape the contours and the content of India's involvement in the hydrocarbons sector. Though Latin America is seen as a more secure long-term bet than several countries in Africa or Asia, certain countries that hold promise have yet to provide the necessary confidence. Ecuador, for instance, insists on service contracts that do not allow foreign companies a share in the output. Mexico has been slow to set the terms for foreign participation in upstream projects. Will exploitation of Argentina's shale gas reserves be subject to auction or political negotiation? Venezuela has opened its arms to India but has stalled payments of significant amounts to its Indian partner. If and when Cuba's offshore exploration yields important finds, there is no clarity on the eventual terms that the communist government will offer to even state-owned companies from friendly countries.

Indian companies have invested in Latin American coal and other mines. Latin American production of coal and biofuels can be important to India, provided certain infrastructure and pricing bottlenecks can be addressed. India's growing demand for uranium, for several nuclear power plants planned for the coming years, can be partially met from untapped deposits in that region. Indian companies such as Praj (ethanol) and Suzlon (wind energy) are partnering with Latin American counterparts to achieve higher synergy.

A natural complementarity is also evident in the area of food security for the world's second-largest population, an issue examined by Mariano Turzi in chapter 6. India is subject to climate events and other vagaries of nature. Its poor land-to-population ratio, inadequate yields, and lack of sufficient water are in inverse proportion to the Latin American situation. There is an active trading relationship, primarily with Argentina, which supplies important quantities of edible oils; Brazil exports sugar and molasses. Incipient possibilities for the export of fruits, cereals, and some other niche agricultural products to India offer sufficient prospects to arouse excitement. But Indian enterprise needs to be convinced of the long-term stability and guarantee of land tenure policies and related laws on industrial-scale agricultural production for export. Unfamiliarity with local conditions, laws that do not permit ownership or long-term land tenures, and the like may inhibit serious Indian agricultural investors in Latin America.

There have been some attempts at Indo-LAC approximation in the security sector as well, such as through the sale of military aircraft and other equipment. Unfortunately, however, India's strategic and defense establishment is overwhelmingly focused in the state sector, and this nascent relationship has not received the attention it deserves. Lately, India has sought to promote bilateral cooperation with several Latin American countries in space exploration, biotechnology, nuclear energy, and other areas of high technology. These sectors have yet to yield spectacular results on par with the Chinese satellite projects with Brazil, Venezuela, and Bolivia or the Russian nuclear power plants. Nevertheless, in light of India's active programs in satellite manufacturing, launching, and tracking, nuclear power generation and technology, and a vibrant biotechnology industry, the prospects are bright. After the U.S.-India civil nuclear deal of 2005, ratified by the International Atomic Energy Agency in August 2008,[19] Latin America has accepted India's legitimate nuclear power status, and cooperation in peaceful uses of nuclear technology is taking off.[20]

Overall, India enjoys a very positive image in Latin America. Its diplomatic relations with most countries of the region date back to the 1950s. Admittedly, Latin America's perspective was dominated by the region's historical and cultural links with the United States and Europe. Nevertheless, there has been an awareness of India's ancient spiritual heritage and peaceful nonintrusive disposition. India's soft power is evident in the region's schools and disciples of yoga and meditation, ancient and present-day Indian philosophers and gurus, Indian classical dance, music, and art, as well as fascination for Indian cinema. The absence of a significant Indian diaspora has reduced prospects for greater appreciation of Indian culture and civilization, but at the same time it eliminates the frictions arising from uncontrolled migration and labor and other issues such as are present in other parts of the world. On the economic front, India needs to better comprehend the market dynamic and anticipate the trend of negotiations under way between Latin American economies and the North American, European, and even the Asia-Pacific countries. It also needs to confront the protectionist prescriptions dictated by its domestic political priorities and risk-averse establishment. India needs to take the initiative to establish better connectivity, and above all, it needs to realize the importance of political approximation as the catalyst for economic partnership.

India must make up for lost time. Its foreign policy establishment has suffered from insufficient political acknowledgment of the partnership that is on offer with Latin America. While its political and economic relationship with a growing number of Latin American countries has witnessed considerable progress, it risks being left behind as the region consolidates internally and externally. In the 1990s, India consciously embarked on a "Look East" policy, which enabled a quantum leap in its relations with Southeast Asia. It now needs to look west.

INDIA'S INTERACTION WITH ARGENTINA, BRAZIL, CHILE, AND MEXICO

Rengaraj Viswanathan

India is not likely to become a major trading partner of Brazil, Argentina, Mexico, or Chile any time soon. China, in contrast, has emerged as the largest or second-largest trading partner for Brazil, Argentina, and Chile. China's trade with the four countries in 2013 reached $200 billion, which is ten times the level of India's trade with those countries. India will remain, however, one of the top destinations for crude oil exports from Mexico and Brazil, soy oil exports from Argentina, and copper exports from Chile. However, as Jacqueline Mazza describes in chapter 8, Latin Americans are wary of the Chinese model of investment, in which labor is brought from China. An apparent disregard for environmental norms and the welfare of the local communities, especially in the mining sector, is also of concern. The possibility of illegal

Chinese immigration, the rise of the Chinese mafia, and the Chinese acquisition of local businesses are also of concern to some countries. Notwithstanding the growing number of Confucius Institutes throughout the region, there is an immense gap in culture, communication, and trust, as portrayed in the popular Argentine film *Un cuento chino* (Chinese Take-away), released in 2011.

In contrast, the Indian companies have a favorable image in Latin America, thanks particularly to the pharmaceutical and IT firms. The Latin American governments and consumers are happy with the Indian pharmaceutical companies, which have helped them reduce their cost of health care with low-cost generic medicines. They are also appreciative of the fact that Indian IT companies have provided jobs to more than 25,000 Latin American youth. Key to this positive image is that Indian companies employ local staff and managers and do not bring in many Indian nationals to run their Latin American operations. For example, Aegis, the Indian company, has a BPO operation in Argentina with a staff of more than 5,000 employees—the company is run entirely by Argentine staff led by a local manager; not a single Indian national is employed locally. Culturally, there is less of a gap; in fact, there is a certain shared comfort zone between Indians and Latin Americans.

India's relations with Argentina, Brazil, Chile, and Mexico are set to grow and diversify in the future as a result of the conscious policies of their governments and the interest shown by business leaders. Trade will be the main driver of the future growth of India's relations with Argentina, Chile, and Mexico. India's strategic partnership with Brazil will be more profound and comprehensive, with a strong political element—the two countries will continue to work closely together in global affairs. Argentina, Chile, and Mexico will cooperate with India on issues of common interest in global forums. However, Argentina and Mexico will continue to challenge the Indo-Brazilian agenda to become permanent members of the UN Security Council, but this challenge should not get in the way of bilateral relations since it is a global issue involving the big powers.

Of the four countries, it is Chile that most seriously takes India as a destination for its exports. Argentina also attaches importance to India as the largest buyer of its soy oil and as an important investor in the country. Mexican companies are relatively less enthusiastic, since their focus remains more on NAFTA and other free trade agreement partner countries, but Mexico is keen on the Indian market for its crude oil exports. Brazilian companies are the least interested in India. The main reason is the lack of competitiveness of Brazilian products except for raw materials. Furthermore, Brazilians in general appear not to share the same admiration for India as Argentina, Chile, and Mexico. Brazil's government leadership seems more interested in partnering with India in global affairs than in bilateral trade cooperation.

Indian companies are attracted by Brazil's large internal market, and they consider Mexico the gateway to NAFTA and Central America. At the moment, they focus less on Argentina, which faces numerous economic challenges. Chile is considered a rather small market. The Indian government is committed to a comprehensive partnership with Brazil and to cordial relations with the other three countries.

Trade between India and the four countries, which nearly tripled between 2007 and 2013, is likely to continue growing in the coming years (at around 15–20 percent annually). Besides a steady increase in trade, one should also expect surprises. For example, a few years back no one would have imagined that India would import raw sugar from Brazil. Today the Indian company Renuka imports several hundred million dollars' worth of Brazilian raw sugar, which it refines and exports to other countries. Renuka has invested about $500 million in Brazil and is among the top ten producers of sugar and ethanol. Reliance imports Brazilian crude oil and exports diesel to Brazil itself. The Brazilian company Surya Henna imports ingredients from India and exports henna products to India, which has a long tradition of henna use. This is an astonishing development in bilateral trade. One should expect more such surprises as both Indian and Latin American companies become more innovative, globalized, and ambitious.

The election of Narendra Modi as India's prime minister in May 2014 has given a new dimension to India's foreign policy, which is becoming more robust and proactive. The visionary Modi is expected to transform India into a stronger economy, which in turn should make it more attractive for Latin Americans. Modi's government is expected to intensify engagement with Latin America as part of his strategy to raise the global profile of India and to seek the support of the region for his global agenda.

SEEKING A BETTER DEAL FOR LATIN AMERICA: NEW OPPORTUNITIES OR MORE OF THE SAME?

Anthony Boadle

How will the Sino–Latin American relationship, which has developed so rapidly and is far from a perfect marriage, develop in a slower-growth world? What role will the more recent arrival of India play in the region? Is this emerging power the "next big thing" for Latin America? The Chinese slowdown highlighted Latin America's overreliance on low-value-added exports to China and the risk of deindustrialization posed by competition from cheaper Chinese goods. It has also shown the difficulties Latin American countries face trying to compete in the Chinese market owing to the distance and the lack of a level playing field regarding state regulations.

As China shifts away from investment-focused policies and toward a more consumer-based economy at home, economists expect there will be more investment abroad, and Latin America could expect more Chinese involvement in infrastructure projects, manufacturing industries, and services. In 2014, the flow of Chinese direct investment abroad exceeded the inflow of FDI into China for the first time.[21] But Latin America will probably not be the main beneficiary of this trend. Cash-rich Chinese state-owned companies have a growing appetite for European brands and technology that are going cheap. China has gone on a shopping spree; purchases have included the Italian tire maker Pirelli, bought by China National Chemical Corporation, and Sweden's Volvo, acquired by Hangzhou-based carmaker Geely.[22]

Instead of the promised abundant investment, the bulk of Chinese financial flows to Latin America seem to have come in the form of "loans-for-oil" deals. China is a growing source of finance for Latin American governments, state-run companies, and a handful of private companies. Since 2005, China has provided the region with more than $118 billion in loans, mainly from the China Development Bank (CDB) and the China Export-Import Bank. Almost all that financing—$108 billion—has gone to four countries that are major suppliers of food, energy, and mineral resources: Venezuela, Brazil, Argentina, and Ecuador.[23] The bulk of the lending, an estimated $56 billion, has gone to Venezuela, providing a lifeline for a country on the verge of economic collapse. Except for Brazil, these countries are risky borrowers that are unable to raise finance on international capital markets. Even Brazil's state-run oil company Petrobras got a handy $3.5 billion loan from the CDB in April 2015 as it wrestled with the financial damage of a massive corruption and political kickback scandal.

In 2010, Chinese loans to Latin America exceeded the lending from the World Bank, the Inter-American Development Bank (IDB), and the U.S. Export-Import Bank combined. Chinese interest rates are higher on average than those of international financial institutions and the regional development banks,[24] but they do not come with the policy conditions that are tied to Western multilateral lenders. Moreover, China's deep pockets could become more attractive for Latin American nations when the Federal Reserve Board raises U.S. interest rates and international liquidity shrinks.

India's arrival as a business partner in Latin America has raised hopes of a diversification in the region's trade with the Asian giants, reducing dependence on China and providing a new source of investment and technology. However, to date, India has followed a similar trade pattern as China, buying the natural resources that it needs and selling LAC countries manufactured goods. As other chapters in this volume detail, Latin America has become an important source of oil for India, with the region contributing about 10 percent of its energy imports, supplied by Brazil, Venezuela, Colombia, Mexico, and Cuba.

While Indian trade has followed China's in buying sugar, copper, oil, and other raw materials, a study by the IDB in 2010 found that India could have more to offer Latin America because of the high share of services in its exports to the region, the bulk of which are IT services and other business services.[25] India is offering a better match to Latin American exports, even though its export volumes have yet to reach their full potential. India's investments in the region are also more sophisticated. Since 2000, Indian companies have invested about $12 billion in IT, pharmaceuticals, and manufacturing, as well as mining and energy. The fact that Indian companies are private increases India's potential to expand business in Latin America through joint ventures with local entrepreneurs and less state interference, even though they will lack the advantage of abundant capital that Chinese companies enjoy. Bilateral trade has yet to reach a critical mass that would serve as a basis for more cross-border investment. Very high Indian tariffs on agricultural products, above 60 percent, are a barrier to expanded trade and an issue that has set India and Brazil on opposite sides of the negotiating table at the WTO.

The search for a more balanced and productive trade relationship with China has become a major concern for Latin American nations as economies slow down and policymakers try to add more value to commercial transactions with the world's second-largest economy. One way to diversify is to invest in China. For Latin American companies, this overcomes the disadvantage of distance by placing them in the Chinese market. An additional incentive is China's recent move to expand its domestic economy by stimulating household consumption, which will open up new opportunities for foreign companies in sectors such as food and beverages, consumer electronics, and other household goods.

China is rebalancing its economy away from a growth model driven by investment and exports and toward a model based more on consumption of a rapidly growing urban population with disposable income. Though the level of Latin American investment has been meager, a handful of firms from the region, mainly from Brazil and Mexico, have been able to establish a significant presence in the Chinese market. But cases of Latin American firms investing directly in manufacturing and services in China are still the exception rather than the rule. Recent research has shown that large Latin American multinational companies, the "multilatinas," have not yet ventured as far as China. A 2012 survey of seventy-six major overseas investments by Brazilian multinationals found that forty-six were destined for the Americas, while none went to China.[26] Brazilian Central Bank data showed that Brazilian investment in China accounted for less than 0.1 percent of the country's total outward FDI.

By early 2015, only eight Brazilian companies were producing from factories located in China, according to a report by Brazil's export promotion agency APEX.[27] The report said the low level of investment in China was because of difficulties that Brazilian companies faced in establishing themselves in the Chinese market both because of local bureaucracy and because of the lack of clear strategies in marketing their brands. The report added that many large Brazilian companies had not woken up to the fact that the Chinese market had become essential for growth. Even Brazil's most successful plane maker, Embraer, has had trouble expanding in China's regional jet market. Embraer was not able to obtain a license to build its larger E190 passenger jets at its Harbin plant and has had to focus on making executive jets because the Chinese government viewed the E190 as competition for a similar regional jet developed by Embraer's partner, the state-owned Commercial Aircraft Corporation of China (Comac), the ARJ21, China's first indigenously designed airliner.

No one would question that China has become a vital and enduring fixture for Latin America's economies and its foreign policy. Experts in the Americas would also agree today that China has no specific strategy to counter the United States' influence in Latin America and grab the region's natural resources. To the extent that China does have specific goals in the region, they are economic. China's demand for Latin America's rich array of raw materials will continue to be a major engine of growth for the region. China will probably not meet the region's expectations in terms of investment flows and a more balanced trade relationship, forcing Brazil and others to look elsewhere for new markets for manufactured goods and greater flows of investment and technology. In its seminal 2012 study on the future of Asian–Latin American ties, the IDB forecast that the commodities-for-manufactured-goods trade will continue to be the basis of the relationship for decades to come.[28] India is expected to become an increasingly important source of technology as its commercial presence grows, but China's economic policies will have a growing impact on Latin America.

It is also clear that China's investment in the region has so far been a much better deal for China than for Latin America. As global liquidity dries up and financial costs rise, Latin America could well become more dependent on Chinese lending. Ecuador's populist president Rafael Correa, whose country is one of the principal recipients of Chinese loans, said that negotiating terms with China was worse than dealing with the International Monetary Fund. Governments will have to push for better terms than the predatory conditions and long-term costs that some countries have had to accept from China.

As China moves to satisfy a rising urban middle class with consumer goods, new diets, and lifestyles, markets will open for Latin American businesses that are ready to seize the opportunity. With rising wages and increased purchasing power, Chinese consumers will want more of the protein, dairy products, fruits and vegetables, and wines and liquors that Latin America can supply and add value to in packaged foods instead of unprocessed raw materials.

NOTES

1. The commentaries presented in this chapter are significantly condensed versions of the original essays submitted for this volume.

2. The author would like to note that the original Chinese-language essay offers a broader set of considerations.

3. Alicia Bárcena, "2012 LAC Economic Outlook," *Journal of Latin American Studies* 6 (2012), pp. 4–7.

4. Council on Hemispheric Affairs, *The Dragon in Uncle Sam's Backyard* (Washington, DC: Council on Hemispheric Affairs, June 6, 2014) (http://www.coha.org/the-dragon-in-uncle-sams-backyard-china-in-latin -america/).

5. Ibid.

6. See the website http://news.xinhuanet.com/world/2014-07/25/c_1267 99227.htm.

7. Kevin P. Gallagher and Margaret Myers, "China–Latin America Finance Database" (Washington, DC: Inter-American Dialogue, 2016) (http://www .thedialogue.org/map_list/).

8. Kevin P. Gallagher, Katherine Koleski, and Amos Irwin, "The New Banks in Town: Chinese Finance in Latin America" (Washington, DC: Inter-American Dialogue, 2012) (http://www.thedialogue.org/wp-content /uploads/2012/02/NewBanks_FULLTEXT.pdf).

9. Rebecca Ray and Kevin P. Gallagher, "2013 China–Latin America Economic Bulletin" (Boston University, Global Economic Governance Initiative, 2014) (https://ase.tufts.edu/gdae/Pubs/rp/wg/WG_ChinaLA_Bulletin _2013.pdf).

10. Kevin P. Gallagher and Roberto Porzecanski, *The Dragon in the Room: China and the Future of Latin American Industrialization* (Stanford University Press, 2010).

11. Amos Irwin and Kevin P. Gallagher, "Chinese Mining in Latin America: A Comparative Perspective," *Journal of Environment and Development* 22, no. 2 (2013), pp. 207–34.

12. International Monetary Fund (IMF), *Regional Economic Outlook: Western Hemisphere* (Washington, DC: IMF, 2014) (http://www.imf.org /external/pubs/ft/reo/2014/whd/eng/wreo0414.htm); United Nations Conference on Trade and Development (UNCTAD), *Trade and Development Report, 2014* (Geneva: UNCTAD, 2014) (http://unctad.org/en/Publications Library/tdr2014_en.pdf).

13. United Nations Conference on Trade and Development (UNCTAD), *Trade and Development Report, 2014.*

14. Asian Development Bank (ADB), Inter-American Development Bank (IDB), and Asian Development Bank Institute (ADBI), *Shaping the Future of the Asia and the Pacific–Latin America and the Caribbean Relationship* (Washington: ADB, IDB, and ADBI, 2012).

15. See, for example, Bilge Erten and José Antonio Ocampo, "Supercycles and Commodity Prices since the Mid-nineteenth Century," DESA Working Paper 110 (United Nations Department of Economic and Social Affairs [DESA], 2012).

16. All currency figures are in U.S. dollars unless otherwise noted.

17. Government of India, Directorate General of Foreign Trade, Department of Commerce (www.dgft.gov.in).

18. "Africa, Latin America New Sources of Crude for India," *Financial Express,* July 27, 2014 (www.financialexpress.com).

19. "U.S.–India: Civil Nuclear Cooperation" U.S. Department of State (http://2001-2009.state.gov/p/sca/c17361.htm) (last visited April 20, 2016).

20. "India Inks Nuclear Pact with Argentina," *The Hindu*, October 15, 2009 (www.thehindu.com).

21. United Nations Economic Commission for Latin America and the Caribbean (ECLAC/CEPAL), *Primer Foro de la Comunidad de Estados Latinoamericanos y Caribeños (CELAC): Explorando espacios de cooperación en comercio e inversión* (Santiago, Chile: CEPAL, 2015) (http://repositorio .cepal.org/bitstream/handle/11362/37577/S1421104_es.pdf?sequence=1).

22. "Gone Shopping: More European Businesses Are Coming under Chinese Ownership," *The Economist,* March 28, 2015.

23. Kevin P. Gallagher and Margaret Myers, "China–Latin America Finance Database" (Washington, DC: Inter-American Dialogue, 2014) (www .thedialogue.org).

24. Amos Irwin and Kevin Gallagher, "Chinese Finance to Latin America Tops $100 Billion since 2005" (Washington, DC: Inter-American Dialogue, April 2014).

25. Mauricio Mesquita Moreira, coordinator, *India: Latin America's Next Big Thing?* (Washington, DC: IDB, 2010) (http://publications.iadb.org/handle/11319/413?locale-attribute=en).

26. Antoni Estevadeordal, Mauricio Mesquita Moreira, and Theodore Kahn, *LAC Investment in China: A New Chapter in Latin America and the Caribbean-China Relations* (Washington, DC: IDB, 2014) (http://publications.iadb.org/handle/11319/6599?locale-attribute=en).

27. Conselho Empresarial Brasil-China (CEBC) and ApexBrasil, *Oportunidades de Comércio e Investimento na China para Setores Selecionados* (Rio de Janeiro and Brasília: CEBC and ApexBrasil, 2015).

28. ADB, IDB, and ADBI, *Shaping the Future.*

Part II

CRITICAL POLICY ISSUES FOR
LATIN AMERICA, CHINA, AND INDIA

CHAPTER 5

Latin America's Changing Energy Landscape

ASSESSING THE IMPLICATIONS OF
NEW ASIAN PLAYERS

Francisco E. González

This chapter analyzes the growing energy exchange between the Asian giants China and India and Latin American countries, with particular emphasis on the more prominent case of China's oil interests in the region. Oil exchange between China and the main Latin American producers grew significantly in the 2000s.[1] Though oil accounted for only about 1 percent of total Latin American exports to China in 2003, by 2012 it had reached 15 percent. Of particular note, close to 70 percent of Chinese merger and acquisitions (M&A) activity in Latin America between 2008 and 2012 was concentrated in oil and gas investments.[2] Rather than focusing on the more common theme of China's "going out" strategy,[3] this chapter offers an assessment of the strategies and policies adopted by the main oil and gas producers in Latin America as they sought to maximize the benefits and minimize the costs of China's rapidly growing presence in the region.

This chapter also highlights the still unquantifiable but potentially strong global impact that the current shale revolution in the United States, and undoubtedly in many other countries in the near future, will have on both hydrocarbon-producing and hydrocarbon-consuming countries and on economic sectors within and across countries. The potential for disruptive change is already evident, with some projections estimating that the United States will become a significant exporter of natural gas and crude oil in the near future.[4] As U.S. shale oil and natural gas displace exports from oil-exporting countries (such as Nigeria, Venezuela, Mexico, and Colombia), growing markets in emerging Asia will play a key role in absorbing spare capacity.

The diverse political scenarios in the main Latin American hydrocarbon-producing countries, which range from a nationalistic and statist approach to an open, business-friendly one, have led to a variety of outcomes. For example, Venezuela has relied on high-stakes interventionist tactics, whereas some countries have invested in cutting-edge technologies, such as those employed in the oil sands in Canada, deep and ultra-deep off-shore drilling in Brazil and Mexico, and potential commercial level shale production in Argentina, Brazil, Mexico, and Paraguay. In this context, the scorecard for the main Chinese national oil companies (NOCs)—and the Chinese state development banks financing their investments—is likely to show mixed results into the foreseeable future. Each country presents its own unique challenges and opportunities. Hence, experience on the ground and continual adaptation to a great variety of contexts will be critical for Chinese companies operating in Latin America. Similarly, growing Chinese exchange and engagement present their own challenges and opportunities to Latin American countries. Some, such as the petro-states Venezuela and Ecuador, have become perilously dependent on Chinese financing, and have mortgaged their country's next decades of revenue streams through big loans-for-oil (in the form of ten- to thirty-year contracts), which China's development banks and main state oil companies provided.[5] In others, where the presence of Chinese oil companies such as China National Petroleum Corporation (CNPC), Sinopec, and China National Offshore Oil Corporation (CNOOC) is important—Brazil, Argentina, and potentially Mexico since its oil sector opening in 2014—are more diversified and, while eager to obtain investment from China—or anywhere else, for that matter—are not dependent on that country. They face other types of problems that have been associated with China's presence, namely, "deindustrialization" and conflicts over diverse but sensitive issues such as labor relations, indigenous communities and their rights, and environmental predation and degradation.[6]

THE GLOBAL CONTEXT

As figure 5-1 illustrates, international political and economic events can have a major impact on oil prices. The first step in analyzing the growing fossil fuel exchange between China and Latin America is to assess how governments have responded to recent changes in the global arena,

FIGURE 5-1
Crude Oil Prices and Key Geopolitical and Economic Events

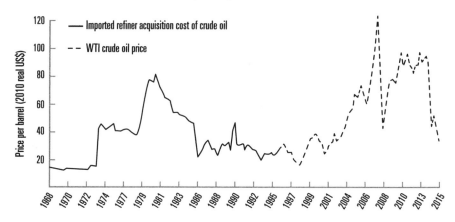

1970: U.S. spare capacity exhausted
1973: Arab Oil Embargo
1978: Iranian Revolution
1980: Iran-Iraq War
1986: Saudis abandon swing producer role
1991: Iraq invades Kuwait
1997: Asian financial crisis
1998: OPEC cuts production targets 1.7 mmbpd
2001: 9-11 attacks
2005: Low spare capacity
2008: Global financial collapse
2009: OPEC cuts production targets 4.2 mmbpd
2010: Shale gas producers start growing shale oil production
2013–14: Boom in U.S. shale oil production
2014: Growth in spare capacity and plunge of oil prices
2014–16: Saudi Arabia repeatedly refuses to cut production to keep market share and displace higher-cost producers such as shale oil companies

Source: U.S. Energy Information Administration, Thomson Reuters. Data downloaded from "Crude oil prices and key geopolitical events," www.eia.gov. Supplemented dates since 2009 by author.

with a particular view to the main disruptive changes that have shaped the opportunities and constraints that hydrocarbon producers and consumers face. Since the mid-2000s, the world of fossil fuels, especially oil and natural gas, has been through a series of major demand and supply shocks, which have produced a roller-coaster trajectory in terms of international prices, geopolitical calculations, and exploration efforts.

How have these shocks affected the main fossil fuel producers in Latin America? What impact have they had on these countries' relationship with China? What have been the consequences of this changing and growing relationship with respect to the decision-making capacity of the major oil producers in the region? Subsequent sections of this chapter address these questions, but first we turn to an overview of the global context in which these shocks unfolded, followed by an analysis of India's incipient energy relationship with the region.

Major Shocks in the Early Twenty-First Century

Three major shocks—which to different degrees continue to reverberate—have rocked global energy markets since the early 2000s. First, hydrocarbon markets experienced a positive demand shock as a result of accelerated growth in consumption and imports, driven primarily by demand from the United States and China, the world's two largest consumers. Higher demand led to a new floor in the international price of oil of $70–$80 per barrel, rather than the previous low price of $30–$40 per barrel. This trend was later reversed by the continued rapid pace of the shale revolution, which has a crowding-out effect on conventional production of oil and gas.

Second, a series of negative supply shocks has affected energy markets, mostly as a consequence of conflict affecting the big oil producers. Some examples include the U.S. invasion and occupation of Iraq in 2003; civil war and regime change in Libya in 2011; war in eastern Ukraine in 2014; and intense civil conflict, organized crime, and grand government and private business corruption in countries as different as Nigeria and Mexico. Marginal changes to the average daily world supply of oil barrels have produced big if short-term price swings, suggesting both a tight market and expectations of worsening conditions should other significant oil producers suffer destabilizing internal conflict or war.

And third, the shale revolution—since the mid-2000s in natural gas, and since 2012–13 in so-called tight oil—has produced a very powerful positive supply shock to global fossil fuel markets. The new shale technologies are widely considered a game changer. Expectations are that, as shale technologies and know-how spread beyond North America (mostly the United States), this diffusion will continue to strengthen the positive supply shock.

India's Presence, Much Smaller but Growing

Trade between India and Latin America has increased significantly in recent years, from $2.6 billion in 2001 to $44.7 billion in 2015, with oil accounting for around two-thirds of that trade (in chapter 3, Jorge Heine and Hari Seshasayee discuss the growing energy ties between India and Latin America).[7] The Reliance conglomerate was the pioneer importer of Latin American crude after building a big refinery in 2000 that could process many crude varieties. Another private firm, Essar, followed suit, and later on three state-owned Indian energy companies joined the growing trend.[8] In 2013, India's crude oil imports from the region totaled $22 billion, with $14 billion coming from Venezuela, $3 billion from Mexico, $2.8 billion from Colombia, and $1.58 billion from Brazil.[9] Between 2006 and 2010, India participated in eighteen oil extraction and development projects in Latin America, a majority of them (twelve) in Colombia and Brazil.[10] In 2014–15, oil imports from Latin America amounted to close to 20 percent of total Indian oil imports.[11] In sum, inasmuch as India continues to grow and develop, oil imports from the region are expected to continue rising, particularly if Latin American exports to the United States continue to be displaced by U.S. domestic shale oil production.[12] This trend is expected to continue as both China's and India's economic growth raises demand for more energy sources from Latin America and other regions. To put things in a broader perspective, in the 1980s and 1990s, more than 80 percent of oil from Latin American countries shipped to Asia went to Japan. In a dramatic shift, in the course of the 2000s and early 2010s, China and India became the largest destination of such oil exports. By 2013, India accounted for 50 percent and China for 45 percent of total Latin American oil exports to Asia.[13]

An interesting instance of China-India cooperation in oil exploration and production in Latin America occurred in 2006, when each partner bought 50 percent of a Colombian oil company, renaming it Mansarovar Energy Colombia Ltd. Whereas China-India cooperation in the oil sector in Latin America should not be seen as business as usual, conflict over competition for resources between the two giants cannot be assumed to be inevitable either. What seems to be increasingly probable is that the 2010s will be dominated by Latin American oil and maybe natural gas exports to both China and India, and that this is just an instance among others in one slowly emerging triangle in trading relations involving China, Latin America, and India.

MAIN TRENDS IN OIL EXCHANGE BETWEEN CHINA AND LATIN AMERICA

Since 1993, the year in which China became a net importer of oil (until then it had been a small exporter), Chinese state companies reached out across the world in search of opportunities to buy or become involved in the exploration, production, refining, and sale of this resource. In Latin America, the China National Petroleum Corporation (CNPC) carried out its first international operation, which was a service project in Peru to raise output in aging onshore fields in Talara.[14] The same company won a bid to exploit the Intercampo and East Caracoles oil fields in Venezuela in 1997.[15]

In 2001, Chinese president Jiang Zemin visited Argentina, Brazil, and Venezuela, promising more engagement and economic exchange with the region, at a time when these countries were on their knees owing to the financial crisis that had erupted in Brazil (1998–99) and the one that was about to hit Argentina (toward the end of 2001). In 2003, CNPC was given drilling rights in Ecuador, the same year that Sinochem bought off ConocoPhilipps's stake (14 percent) in a consortium that included the then Spanish-owned YPF-Repsol and a Taiwanese company, Chinese Petroleum Corporation (CPC).[16] Notable during this early phase of Chinese entry into Latin American energy markets was that Chinese companies participated in South America through a variety of contract types and operations: service contracts, bidding to explore and produce, with ownership of the resource, and entering into partnerships with consortia that included private companies from around the world (including Taipei) in prospecting, drilling, extracting, and producing.

Although planned in advance, a surprising turning point was the official visit that Chinese president Hu Jintao made to Argentina, Brazil, Chile, and Cuba in November 2004, when he famously promised $100 billion in Chinese investment in Latin America during the next decade.[17] (The Chinese government later clarified it was referring to bilateral trade rather than investment, which, as it turns out, went from $29 billion in 2003 to $270 billion in 2012, nearly a tenfold increase.[18]) This phase saw a more confident and bullish attitude by big Chinese banks and energy companies to establish oil projects in Latin America. Hefty investments were offered to Brazil and Argentina, the bulk of them in energy, infrastructure, and transport, in exchange for their recognition of the People's Republic of China (PRC) as a "market economy," which lowered barriers to the entry of myriad manufacturing products from China into these countries. Chinese manufactures ended up flooding these markets and destroying many domestic manufacturers, leading to claims of "deindustrialization." Asset acquisitions by Chinese energy companies accelerated in the region: CNPC bought out the subsidiary of Pluspetrol in Peru, Pluspetrol Norte, in 2004, and in 2005 Andes Petroleum; a consortium led by CNPC and Sinopec bought out the operations of the

Canadian firm Encana in Ecuador.[19] In the natural gas sector, China started importing liquefied natural gas (LNG) from Trinidad and Tobago in 2007.[20]

In the face of the global financial recession of 2008, and as many Western companies had to sell assets to pay off debt or cut losses, Chinese energy companies went on an acquisition spree of oil projects in Latin America. Chinese energy purchases in the region peaked in 2010, when investments totaled more than $18 billion (table 5-1). Chinese NOCs entered into all types of contracts, from service providers to partnerships, to public-private ventures, to ownership through M&As and through bidding for blocks to explore, drill, and produce oil and gas. More broadly, China's state-owned development banks, led by the China Development Bank (CDB), splashed close to $100 billion in Latin America between 2005 and 2013. Around half of that amount went to Venezuela, where financial oil infrastructure commitments continue to absorb the lion's share of Chinese financing in the region almost two years after the price of crude collapsed from $117 in June 2014 to under $30 in January 2016.

Since 2012, a significant economic slowdown in China—from 9–10 percent to 7 percent, maybe less (even a potential hard landing cannot be dismissed)—and in other emerging markets (such as Brazil, Russia, and India, the last of which became the highest-growing economy in the world in 2015–16) put a lid on China's bullishness and the ambitious pace it had sustained during the years of economic stimulus. President Xi Jinping's main early imprint after he took over in March 2013 was to impose a government spending austerity program—to include flowers, meals, watches, cars, and other luxury consumer goods and assets—and an anticorruption campaign. The latter has touched the uppermost echelons of power, including in the sphere of energy, where President Xi's campaign started a "purge of China's oil mandarins."[21] The top disgraced individuals have been two chairmen of CNPC (one current and the other from the 1990s). Thanks to its publicly traded PetroChina, CNPC was in 2013 the fourth largest corporation in the world by market capitalization (and in the energy sector number two after ExxonMobil).[22] This purge is intended not only to spotlight the immorality of self-enrichment through party–state–private business connections and operations but also as a political move to help cement the top authority of President Xi in his first years in power.[23]

These domestic political changes in China have not necessarily affected the main operations of Latin American hydrocarbon producers, but there is no question that China's two largest development banks and five main energy companies with stakes overseas will become pickier in

TABLE 5-1
China's 2010 Energy Acquisitions in Latin America[a]

Country	Local partner	Chinese NOC	Content
Argentina	Bridas	CNOOC	CNOOC acquires 50% of Bridas Energy Holdings Ltd. for $3.1 billion.
	Occidental	Sinopec	Sinopec agrees to acquire Occidental's Argentina unit for $2.45 billion.
Brazil	Petrobras	Sinopec	Concession of BM-PAMA-3 and BM-PAMA-8 to Sinopec.
	Statoil	Sinochem	China buys 40% of Statoil's share in Peregrino.
	Repsol	Sinopec	Sinopec buys 40% of Repsol's Brazil stake for $7.1 billion.
Colombia	Hupecol	Sinopec	Sinopec buys the U.S. energy firm Hupecol's assets in Colombia.
Costa Rica	Costa Rica National Oil Company	CNPC	CNPC and Costa Rica's national oil company sign a deal for a refinery upgrade that could cost up to $1 billion.
Cuba[b]	Cuvenpetrol	CNPC	CNPC won a bid to double the capacity of the Cienfuegos refinery.
Peru	Perupetro	Sinochem	Sinochem wins exploration rights for 5 oil and gas blocks in Peru.
Venezuela	PdVSA	CNPC	CNPC and PDVSA form a joint venture to develop the Junin-4 field, with CNPC being the 40% shareholder.
		Sinopec	Sinopec and PDVSA sign an agreement for the quantification and certification study of Junin 8. Sinopec also agrees to participate in building the Cabruta refinery to process Junin crude. It will be a 60:40 joint venture, with Sinopec holding 40%.
		CNOOC	CNOOC signs an agreement to join the Mariscal Sucre natural gas project.

Source: Translated from Sun Hongbo (in Chinese), "Oil and Gas Cooperation between China and Latin America: Strategy Penetration and Business Development," *International Cooperation Magazine/Journal,* January 2011.

a. The total purchases exceeded $18 billion.

b. Data for Cuba compiled by Yanan Zhao, September 6, 2014. CNOOC, China National Offshore Oil Corporation; CNPC, China National Petroleum Corporation; PDVSA, Petróleos de Venezuela, S.A.

choosing future investments in the region and elsewhere. In some places they might sell assets and look for more cutting-edge investments in unconventional oil and gas production, such as super-heavy oil and oil sands (in Canada and Venezuela), very deep offshore drilling and production (in Brazil and Mexico), and shale gas and oil extraction (in Argentina and potentially Mexico, parts of Brazil close to Paraguay, and Paraguay). At the same time, the Chinese government reiterated its intent to increase its purchase of LNG from Trinidad and Tobago during President Xi Jinping's 2013 visit.[24] The main point remains that Xi's government aim since coming to power in 2013 has been to change or accommodate the type of GDP growth driven by investment, particularly overseas (which dominated in China since its opening to the world between the 1980s and the 2000s), into one driven by domestic consumption. For hydrocarbon-related activity between China and Latin America, this change translates into different opportunities and constraints for Chinese players, reflecting the very diverse political scenarios and policy stances in the main oil- and gas-producing countries in Latin America, to which this chapter now turns.

LATIN AMERICAN REACTIONS TO CHINA'S EVOLVING ENERGY ENGAGEMENT

The three global supply and demand shocks identified earlier in this chapter have modified the financial opportunities and constraints of current and future investments. In Latin America, these global shocks led to a relative split in approach to the ownership, growth, and usage of oil and gas into two broad models: a new statist impetus (deep in Venezuela, Bolivia, and Ecuador, less so in Argentina and Brazil) and a drive toward liberalization of the energy sector (Peru, Colombia, and most recently Mexico).

Between the 1980s and the early 2000s, many countries in Latin America underwent deep, recurrent financial and economic crises and adopted internationally sponsored stabilization, adjustment, and structural reforms with the conditionality imposed by the International Monetary Fund (IMF). Of the structural reforms, the flagship policy that gained the most attention and visibility from foreign financial, industrial, and extractive firms was privatization. This flagship policy was meant to show a commitment to moving away from state ownership and industrial policy approaches that were no longer considered adequate by domestic and international bureaucrats. The end result was a very significant ownership transfer of resources to foreign investors, mainly from the United States and Europe but also from certain Asian countries such as Japan, South Korea, and, most recently, China.

Despite its traditional placement on the pedestal of nationalism, the energy sector of many countries was opened up to foreign participation in the course of the 1990s (Brazil, Ecuador, Venezuela), and in some cases most assets were sold off (Argentina, Bolivia, Peru). Colombia opened up in the early 2000s. The move from state-owned or majority-state participation in energy companies, which had been the norm in most countries since the 1930s, to private or public-private ventures and M&As, along with the embrace of global financial markets, was contentious in all countries, though to different degrees. Unlike many oil majors, such as the United States, the United Kingdom, the Netherlands, France, Italy, and particularly Spain, which entered the Latin American markets very aggressively in the 1990s and then lived to regret it, the Chinese government acted cautiously, with a few, early exploratory deals in the oil sector of just two countries, Peru and Venezuela, up until 2000.

The broad neoliberal approach applied across Latin America during the debt crisis years led to growing disenchantment and eventually to well-organized popular and radicalizing opposition to it. The alternative, promoted in several countries by new left-wing governments, in particular oil and natural gas producers (Venezuela, Argentina, Bolivia, Brazil, Ecuador), was an antiprivatization statist approach. These governments targeted big generators of U.S. dollars, namely, energy companies that had been privatized but were seen as part of the national patrimony rather than as capital gains and dividend-producing firms, and which were mainly profiting foreign private investors.

Many foreign companies, private as well as state-owned, left or were forced out of huge projects and investments: Exxon in Venezuela, Petrobras in Bolivia, most Western companies, which sold out of Ecuador, and the formerly Spanish-owned YPF-Repsol in Argentina. In turn, the big returns that most majors expected from the early market-led exploitation of Brazil's remarkable pre-salt-layer hydrocarbon abundance, discovered in 2007, evaporated after the government of outgoing President Luíz Inácio Lula da Silva changed the framework of concessions in 2010 to one based on shared production contracts, with Petrobras as the sole operator of all projects and a 30 percent minimum stake in all projects. Many energy analysts have questioned this hurdle, and it is widely believed that the government will be forced to change it in order to attract more foreign investment and, even more important, to unburden the overloaded mandate given to Petrobras to remain a technological and operations leader in ultra-deep-water drilling.[25]

The Statist Approach

Like Western energy companies (both private as well as public or national), Chinese firms also suffered losses and lower future profits after changes to terms of contract and in some cases compensated expropriations in Venezuela and Ecuador. By far the country in which China is most invested is Venezuela, which, according to some sources, owes China around $50–$60 billion pursuant to loans-for-oil arrangements. From the potential capital loss perspective, Venezuela is in a category of its own for the government of President Xi Jinping. An anti-Chávez coalition in power might reject what the previous one did. This could mean nonrecognition of past debts contracted by what a growing proportion of Venezuelans view as a tyrannical, out-of-control regime (under President Hugo Chávez himself, and as of this writing in a defensive, weakened position under President Nicolás Maduro). It is not surprising at all, therefore, to see the Chinese government keeping its finger on the pulse of developments in Caracas, and pledging more loans to raise the likelihood of repayment, because the stakes in Venezuela are high for total global Chinese foreign direct investment (FDI) and loans since its "going out" strategy started in 1999.

The CDB—the largest state-owned development bank, used by the Chinese regime to grow future returns on assets, security, and political control—has the greatest financial exposure outside China in Venezuela as a result of loans executed during the rule of President Chávez (see Gallagher and Ray's essay in chapter 4).[26] At more than $50 billion, the prospect of no repayment by Venezuela makes the Chinese government shudder, particularly after the financial losses suffered by Chinese NOCs in Libya (approximately $22 billion) following the fall and death of Colonel Muammar Qaddafi, or the situation in Sudan since it partitioned into two states.[27]

In Ecuador, Chinese oil companies and China's development bank, the CDB, also took over most of the country's oil sales once they started peddling loans-for-oil there in 2009.[28] As more oil production profits accrued to Chinese creditors rather than to Ecuador's public purse, President Rafael Correa's administration has had to keep borrowing more money from Chinese sources, and redoubling this country's dependence on Chinese finance not only to sustain Ecuador's oil industry but also to undertake projects such as big hydroelectricity dams and transport infrastructure.[29] This is an important development, for oil receipts have typically contributed 30–40 percent of Ecuador's annual budget, and the loss to the public purse is severe.

Venezuela and Ecuador, arguably the only two petro-states in Latin America, have ended up in a tight and perilous embrace with China's oil companies and development banks. Present cash flow in exchange for future Chinese control of many oil and more broadly infrastructure projects in these countries suggests an unhealthy level of dependence if not a full-blown sense of creeping neocolonialism in these countries. Paradoxically, governments that sought to distance themselves from the tyranny of short-termism of international financial markets led by the United States have ended up in a potentially longer-term dependence on Chinese inflows, which at first glance looked like loans without strings attached. The consequences of such arrangements include limiting these governments' room for future allocation of resources to promote their own goals of growth and development as a result of the long-term commitments they have established with Chinese oil companies and development banks.

A very different scenario unfolded in Bolivia and Argentina. In Bolivia, Chinese firms were not present, and hence they were not affected by nationalization. In Argentina, they had limited exposure. In particular, the nationalization of YPF-Repsol by President Cristina Fernández de Kirchner in 2012 seems to have been a one-off move specifically targeting the largest player in the country, the Spain-based Repsol (Repsol acquired majority ownership of YPF after President Carlos Menem privatized the energy sector in the early 1990s). In fact, China was bullish in Argentina, with Sinopec acquiring California-based Occidental's assets in Argentina for $2.45 billion in 2010 and, in the same year, CNOOC acquiring 50 percent of Bridas Energy for $3 billion.[30] The latter firm is Argentina's second-largest hydrocarbon producer, owned by the Argentine billionaire Bulgheroni family. This was considered to be CNOOC's proper coming into Latin America as co-owner of a major upstream oil-and-gas company.[31] However, a game changer for CNOOC was its $15 billion acquisition of the Canadian energy firm Nexen in February 2013 (the largest Chinese overseas acquisition in oil to date), which shifted its production to North America, including the Canadian oil sands and offshore Gulf of Mexico projects. As a consequence, CNOOC has put its Argentine operations on the back burner, and an eventual exit would likely be welcome.[32] Still, China's reiterated economic interest in Argentina was on full display during President Xi Jinping's official visit in July 2014, when he pledged $7 billion in loans for two hydroelectric dams and a railway to improve the movement of agricultural products, as well as an $11 billion swap line between the central banks of the two countries that would allow Argentina to pay for Chinese imports.[33] In addition, interest in Argentina's Vaca Muerta formation's world-class unconventional (shale) natural gas and oil reserves led Sinopec to sign exploration and production agreements with YPF in early 2015.[34] Even though commercial-scale production remains a future project, China has made sure it got a foot in arguably the most exciting big shale play outside the United States.

In the case of Brazil, a statist approach was manifest in the change of terms in the development of its pre-salt-layer reserves, which was implemented in 2010. The end result has been to make Brazil less attractive to foreign investment, ultimately hurting the future profits of Chinese companies that took over assets or entered into partnerships in the pre-salt-layer oil extraction projects since the 2010 reform. However, these less than ideal circumstances did not deter two Chinese companies, CNOOC and CNPC, from forming a consortium (10 percent equity each) with Royal Dutch Shell (20 percent), Total of France (20 percent), and Petrobras (40 percent) to make the only bid to exploit Libra, the world's largest offshore oil field. Analysts believed the small stakes invested by the Chinese companies reflected the post-2012 cooling off of the Chinese economy, aggressive cost cutting, and a more cautious approach to commitments abroad. But their presence is also a sign that Chinese companies want their experts to participate in the development of frontier projects, where technology, know-how, and untried conditions generate innovation that will result in comparative advantages—such as, in the case of Brazil's pre-salt-layer oil fields, in ultra-deep-water offshore drilling and production.[35] Similar to the case of Argentina, President Xi's 2014 visit reaffirmed China's interest in increasing economic ties with Brazil as Xi pledged more than $8 billion toward mining investments and purchases from Brazil's commercial aviation industry.[36] Moreover, Premier Li Keqiang reaffirmed China's commitment to keep growing its trading and broader cooperation relationship with Brazil by visiting the country in a May 2015 tour of South America, which incidentally excluded the countries where China is already most heavily invested (Venezuela, Ecuador, Argentina) and instead went on to Chile, Colombia, and Peru, countries that have adopted a more business-friendly approach, as analyzed below.

The More Business-Friendly Approach

A number of countries in Latin America—mainly Peru, Colombia, Mexico, and Chile (the latter a big energy importer but China's top copper supplier)—retained an overall pro-business, pro-foreign investment, pro-Washington stance. These countries, which in the future will be able to deal with China not only on a bilateral or a multilateral basis but also through regional trading blocs such as the Pacific Alliance and the

Trans-Pacific Partnership (TPP), have welcomed Chinese investment, which has continued to grow, despite China's economic slowdown.

Of this group of countries, Mexico presents a tantalizing case because it recently (2013–14) underwent a historic energy reform that opened up the sector to foreign participation. It is too early to tell how it will be implemented and whether the new investment opportunities will meet the high expectations formed by international players. The menu-like framework for foreign investor contracts varies according to the type of project. In low-complexity or cheap projects, conditions will not be attractive for investors focused on rate of return to capital, but in high-complexity, expensive ones, licenses will convey ownership to the investor of the extracted oil or gas (but only once it arrives on the surface). The new framework is designed to attract big operations and high-profit firms as well as the myriad oil and gas services companies, an area in which the United States dominates internationally. China will likely be interested in investing in Mexico's energy sector, given its abundance of offshore crude and some of the largest shale gas reserves in the world. In fact, with CNOOC's acquisition of Canada's Nexen Inc. for $15 billion in 2013, China already has offshore Gulf of Mexico operations and therefore is already present in the region, where large proven but yet inaccessible oil reserves lie on the Mexican side of the U.S.-Mexico maritime border.[37]

Peru is the first Latin American country where a Chinese NOC set up operations. Although mining is of greater mutual interest, China's presence in Peru's energy sector grew through CNPC's takeover of all Petrobras stakes in two oil and gas blocks and 46 percent in a third block toward the end of 2013.[38] The Peruvian government has kept an open stance with respect to foreign investment but not without controversy. Foreign companies faced conflict and tension over their investments in many local communities in areas rich in hydrocarbons or mineral deposits. In this respect, the Peruvian government must manage a delicate equilibrium between the extractive industries that have allowed Peru to grow at an average of 7–8 percent annually since the early 2000s and the rights, interests, and quality of life of the local indigenous communities, who are usually very poor and live in environmentally sensitive areas, sometimes being forced by big mining or energy companies to relocate. Although the government of President Ollanta Humala (2011–16) has managed to keep a lid on the potential spillover and escalation of extractive resources conflicts, occasional flare-ups do lead to a significant number of deaths; hence it cannot be ruled out that a change of policy would eventually result from such conflicts. The profits in Peru are high, but so are the stakes, particularly in the face of an expected

economic slowdown to less than 5 percent annual growth as a consequence of the end of the supercycle boom in commodity prices, which
produced the best terms of trade in a generation for Latin American
commodity exporters such as Argentina, Brazil, Chile, Colombia, and
Peru between 2004 and 2011.

The other hydrocarbon-rich country in the business-friendly category is Colombia. U.S.-Colombian military collaboration through Plan
Colombia served not only to severely weaken long-standing guerrilla
groups but also to strengthen the Colombian state's presence in more
parts of its territory, which ultimately helped Presidents Alvaro Uribe
(2002–10) and Juan Manuel Santos (2010–18) to promote a pro-market,
pro-foreign investment economic policy. Starting in the early 2000s, the
energy sector was opened up. The state company Ecopetrol was floated
and made to compete at a par with other oil market participants and a
new business-friendly legal and regulatory framework attracted growing numbers of small, medium-sized, and large energy companies to
prospect for oil and gas.

Attracted by low royalties and a growing buzz about Colombia as an
investment destination, in 2006 Sinopec entered into a 50-50 partnership with the International Petroleum Company of India (ONGC-VL) to
purchase (for close to $1 billion) half the stake in Omimex de Colombia,
owned by Omimex Resources of Texas. In 2010, Sinopec grew its portfolio in the country by buying the American energy firm Hupecol's assets in Colombia. Toward the end of 2012, CNPC and Ecopetrol signed
a three-year agreement for exploration, storage, and transportation of
conventional and heavy oil in Colombia.[39] Despite China's reduction
in outward investment during President Xi's early years (as part of his
strategy to support domestic consumption–based activity), Colombia remains one of the most promising and potentially lucrative countries to
grow the production and ownership of hydrocarbons. The main risk
factor for investors is the Colombian government's limited capacity to
mitigate lingering insecurity and violence by left- and right-wing organized crime syndicates and to reach a deal with the guerrillas that remain in rich hydrocarbon areas. Likewise, the rise in oil production
thanks to a flood of foreign investment since the mid-2000s has not been
accompanied by the discovery of new reserves. This hard constraint, unless
reversed, could see Colombia play a smaller role in oil markets. Nonetheless, the abundance of other raw materials and natural resources, as
well as Colombia's geostrategic location, which, as with Mexico and
some Central American countries, gives it ports in both the Pacific and
Atlantic Oceans, means that Chinese diplomatic and trading interests
will remain alive and in search of opportunities.

DUTCH DISEASE AND THE RESOURCE CURSE

China's continued presence in Latin America could force the main pro-ducers of oil and natural gas to face a two-axis trade-off. On the one hand, governments will have to remain mindful of the pros and cons of relative economic independence (an economy driven primarily by domes-tic consumption) versus dependence (an economy that relies heavily on commodity exports and is hence highly dependent on international com-modity prices). On the other hand, policymakers will need to be mindful of the tug-of-war between industrialization (more value-added manu-facturing and high-quality services) versus deindustrialization (growing the relative production of primary sectors—extractive or lightly processed industries, such as energy, mining, and basic foodstuffs—at the expense of manufacturing activity).

After the 1982 debt crisis and the subsequent "lost decade" of socio-economic development, many countries were forced to abandon protec-tionism and open up their economies. By the early 2000s, only the largest Latin American countries had retained a significant industrial base, par-ticularly Brazil but also Mexico—whose heavy manufacturing took off aggressively following the implementation of NAFTA—and manufac-turing pockets in parts of Argentina, Chile, and Colombia. All these countries have been flooded with imports of cheap Chinese manufac-tures, particularly since China's accession to the World Trade Organ-ization in 2001, and analysts have been quick to point out the challenges of deindustrialization.[40] Some of the largest manufacturing sectors in Brazil and Mexico (the automotive industry and aeronautics) have been relatively immune to Chinese competition owing to specific traits in their financing, supply chains, human capital, and geographic locations. In fact, their global viability has likely strengthened, particularly as Chinese wages, transportation costs, and fears of intellectual property theft in-creased in the course of the 2000s.

Other Latin American countries, mainly hydrocarbon exporters such as Venezuela and Ecuador, succumbed to a higher reliance on energy exports and on Chinese loans and future financial commitments for in-frastructure projects as China's appetite for raw materials grew expo-nentially beginning in the early 2000s. These are the countries where the so-called resource curse has gained in breadth and scope, making them the most vulnerable to greater dependence and deindustrialization.

In sum, the growth of Chinese demand for and investments in hydro-carbons in Latin America will continue to threaten competitive manu-facturing and lead to a host of other problems associated with external dependence and deindustrialization, such as currency overvaluation, high liquidity, and corruption. These problems will likely manifest particularly in countries with a hydrocarbon-based economic structure, including Venezuela, Ecuador, and Bolivia. In addition, countries that were excluded from international capital markets, such as Ecuador and Argentina (a potentially significant hydrocarbon producer and exporter), found it almost inevitable to turn to China for short-term financing. The political move to the right in Argentina after Mauricio Macri's victory in the November 2015 presidential elections led to a settlement with the so-called bond holdouts between February and April 2016. As a consequence, Argentina was able to reenter international capital markets and start issuing bonds, which have been in high demand since April 2016.[41] This move allowed for the diversification of financing sources, and should help to ameliorate the dependence Argentina started creating for itself through Chinese loans, swap lines, and intended future investments.

THE SHALE REVOLUTION AND IMPLICATIONS FOR THE GLOBAL HYDROCARBON SUPPLY

The fast growth of shale natural gas production (since the mid-2000s) and shale crude oil production (since 2012–13) has led to a revolution in the sense that it has disrupted and will probably change the terms of future engagement of producers and consumers, with medium- and long-term global impacts. There is no doubt that advanced and emerging economies with large future projected energy needs (such as China, Russia, some western European countries, and eastern European ones such as Poland) and those in Latin America with large shale oil and gas reserves (for example, Argentina, Brazil, Mexico, and Paraguay) will invest in developing this industry in the coming decades. Their potential for success remains uncertain, in light of the many specific conditions that allowed the United States to become the pioneer and leader of the commercial exploitation of unconventional shale resources.[42]

Oil specialists estimate that Canada's oil production will double in a few years' time to more than 6 million barrels per day (bpd; 75 percent of this increment will be from oil sands), while the United States' production of light, sweet crude from the Bakken and Eagle Ford formations will continue to grow, and the total U.S. production of liquid hydrocarbons outpaced Saudi Arabia's in 2014 and 2015. By the same token, the shale resource potential in Argentina (in the Vaca Muerta) is so great (like the Bakken and Eagle Ford, the formations have a high content of crude oil aside from natural gas) that a shale revolution is also likely to take place there if not immediately.[43]

The problem for traditional crude oil exporters in Latin America whose largest market is the United States—that is, Venezuela and Mexico—is that their production is being displaced by Canadian crude and U.S. shale oil or is being bought at a hefty discount by the large Gulf of Mexico refiners. As a consequence, Mexico has cleverly started exporting crude through its Pacific port of Salina Cruz, Oaxaca, to California and East Asia. If Mexico's energy reforms translate into big FDI inflows and a significant growth in production, Japan, South Korea, China, and India could become big markets for Mexican oil. Venezuela, which has the world's largest proven reserves of both conventional and unconventional resources, is limited by the fact that it has direct access only to the Caribbean Sea. However, the expanded Panama Canal, expected to be completed in 2016–17, will allow the passage of larger vessels that can transport between 400,000 and 680,000 barrels of oil to the Pacific Ocean, and could help Venezuela's competitiveness by reducing transportation times. The expanded Panama Canal also has the potential to revolutionize the LNG trade because it is estimated that up to 80 percent of global shipping of this product will be able to pass through the isthmus, whereas currently only very small LNG-carrying vessels can do so.[44] The bottom line is to expect China to remain engaged in Venezuela because of the highly invested position of the CDB and several Chinese NOCs.

It is important to remember that, as the shale revolution gathered steam in the United States, other big hydrocarbon producers took note and started experimenting to emulate the phenomenon. Russia and China were among the first countries to start their own pilot projects. The PRC's Ministry of Land and Resources has set as a priority the exploration and production of shale gas, and the government has established shale gas special operation zones, which are targeting 45 million hectares in provinces such as Sichuan, Chongqing, Guizhou, Yunnan, Hunan, and Hubei.[45] Linked to China's shale program is the issue of combating air pollution through the gradual substitution of coal with natural gas to generate electricity and continue powering China's industrial growth (currently, more than two-thirds of primary energy production in China relies on coal, and the Chinese regime wants to increase the proportion of natural gas used from around 6 percent in 2014 to 10 percent in 2020).[46] A shale revolution in China could change the price differentials that make coal significantly cheaper than natural gas, but powerful vested interests among the Chinese state-owned enterprises and domestic coal producers must be overcome for the shale industry to take off.[47]

In sum, the shale revolution has been a game changer in global energy markets. The main trend for the China–Latin American energy exchange will be to expand the production and trade of both conventional and unconventional hydrocarbons. Reflecting the different degrees of reliance on oil exports among Latin American countries, win-win, win-lose, and lose-lose relationships can be expected. In some cases, investments will yield significant new oil finds and their production. Perhaps more important, they could lead to new knowledge by Chinese, Indian, and other countries' energy companies that participate in cutting-edge projects in areas such as ultra-heavy oil, oil sands, deep and ultra-deep offshore production, and shale production, all of them abundant in the Western Hemisphere.

CONCLUSION

The Asia–Latin America oil and natural gas relationship, despite its short life span, has already gone through several peaks, troughs, and episodes of policy rethinking on all sides. The main changes in Latin American oil exports have been a dramatic shift from Japan and later South Korea as the principal destinations in the 1980s and 1990s to China and India in the 2000s.[48] The top driver of the overall relationship will remain the cold fact that China and, increasingly, India have to keep energy security at the top of their policy agendas because of the expected growth of their urban-industrial sectors and their unique status as the only two nation-states in the world with more than 1 billion inhabitants. These two Asian giants will remain in a class of their own.

China, moreover, faces a geographic-demographic imbalance: 70 percent of demand comes from the coastal east, yet the country's main energy sources are in the arid and underpopulated west.[49] Furthermore, because 80 percent of Chinese oil imports come from Africa and the Middle East, where political risk is high, the government will continue to diversify its sources of access to hydrocarbons, and Latin America is an obvious alternative.[50]

The catch is that Latin America is a politically plural region with markedly different governmental perspectives. The governments of some hydrocarbon-rich countries have a statist, nationalist agenda; others, in contrast, have bet on a more private-sector-driven allocation of resources. The current state-market mix in every country is not set in stone, so a continuous tug-of-war over the terms of contracts for foreign participation in the energy sector will remain a fact of life in the region. Well-organized and vocal civil societies will also continue to put pressure on their national and subnational governments, as well as on foreign and domestic firms, in areas such as labor contracts (favoring locals over foreigners), labor conditions (pursuing safe and well-remunerated jobs), indigenous communities (arguing over contact with outsiders versus isolation, and the use of these communities' territories and natural resources), and environmental standards.

For these reasons, it is difficult to make generalizations about the growing China–Latin America hydrocarbons exchange. While splash-making headlines like the $18 billion invested by Chinese companies in the region in 2010 are less likely in the near future, the pursuit of profits will continue to motivate the main NOCs. That said, the reining in of spending, the crackdown on corruption, and the imposition of a degree of frugality by President Xi in his initial years in power suggest a moderation of Chinese financing abroad. The more limited availability of Chinese credit will force banks and energy producers to engage in craftier competition for scarce resources. Therefore, it is reasonable to assume that Chinese groups will be tougher in their prioritization as they determine which energy projects to stay engaged in, which should be sold as portfolios and geoeconomic priorities change (a case in point is CNOOC as it focuses more on North America following its purchase of Canada's Nexen), and which new projects are worth pursuing.

The most rational way for the Chinese government to allocate short- and medium-term investments in Latin America would be (1) to continue investing where it already has a lot at stake and where it would be badly hurt by a crisis, such as in Venezuela; (2) to continue investing in countries where conditions are still risky in terms of the policy environment but, because of their exclusion from international capital markets (as was the case for Argentina and Ecuador, both of which have returned to capital markets, but it cannot be ruled out that these or other Latin American countries might find themselves in this situation if they are unable or unwilling to service their foreign debts in the near future) China's huge cash reserves give it a comparative advantage to more or less set terms; and (3) to continue investing where projects offer exposure to the physical and technological frontiers that spur innovation, as in unconventional oil production (such as production of the super-heavy crude and extraction from oil sands in Canada and Venezuela), in ultra-deep-water offshore drilling and production (in Brazil and Mexico), and in shale gas and oil extraction (in the United States and promising producers such as Argentina, Mexico, parts of south-central Brazil, and Paraguay).

For the largest hydrocarbon producers in Latin America, structural conditions suggest that the less diversified a given country's export basket is—and, in particular, the more concentrated it is on the production and sale of oil or natural gas (Venezuela, Ecuador, Bolivia, Trinidad and Tobago)—the higher is the risk of "Dutch disease" and other problems associated with the resource curse. Shale gas and oil production will continue to grow, possibly further lowering prices. For Latin American hydrocarbon producers, the growth in shale production in North America means more spare oil and potentially natural gas capacity (in the future) to sell elsewhere. East Asian countries such as Japan, South Korea, and China, as well as other large energy consumers with high growth rates, such as India, could become natural markets for Latin American exporters. From this perspective, talk of the twenty-first century as the "Asian century" could be a straightforward business proposition for Latin American hydrocarbon producers, sooner rather than later.

NOTES

This essay would not have been possible without the kind and excellent research assistance of Yanan Zhao. It benefited enormously from conversations with Professor Matt Ferchen of Tsinghua University in Beijing in November 2013 and July 2014, and with Hari Seshasayee of the Confederation of Indian Industry (CII) in Delhi in January 2016.

1. "Oil exchange" in this chapter refers not necessarily to the number of barrels or the volume of oil that physically moves from Latin America to China on a daily basis but rather to the oil extracted in Latin America from which Chinese firms and state development banks accrue money to their accounts. The mismatch in bilateral numbers is a variation on the problem of what counts as oil exchange. See, for example, a prescient perspective by Matt Ferchen, "China and Venezuela: Equity Oil and Political Risk," *China Brief* 13 (February 3, 2013), pp. 9–13. The author sees the mentioned bilateral relationship as "high stakes" (and growing) in light of the amount of loans-for-oil that China has extended to Venezuela (in late 2014 the value of the loans was estimated at between $45 and $55 billion). High political risk in Venezuela stems from the growing intensity of the country's internal split since the death of Hugo Chávez in early 2013. Failure to honor the contracts established between the *caudillo* and China could produce a huge loss for the Chinese Development Bank, the main lender to Venezuela, and the Chinese NOCs with super-heavy crude operations in the Orinoco.

2. Rebecca Ray and Kevin P. Gallagher, "2013 China–Latin America Economic Bulletin" (Boston University, Global Economic Governance Initiative, 2013) (http://ase.tufts.edu/gdae/Pubs/rp/wg/WG_ChinaLA_Bulletin_2013.pdf), figure 3, p. 9, and figure 8, p. 17.

3. See, for example, Deborah Brautigam, *The Dragon's Gift: The Real Story of China in Africa* (Oxford University Press, 2009); and Kevin Gallagher

and Roberto Porzecanski, *The Dragon in the Room: China and the Future of Latin American Industrialization* (Stanford University Press, 2010).

4. U.S. Energy Information Administration, "International Energy Outlook 2014," September 9, 2014 (http://www.eia.gov/forecasts/ieo/); Roger Diwan, "The Shale Revolution," lecture, Johns Hopkins School of Advanced International Studies, Washington, D.C., February 4, 2014; Trevor Houser and Shashank Mohan, *Fueling Up: The Economic Implications of America's Oil and Gas Boom* (Washington, DC: Peterson Institute for International Economics, 2014).

5. Barbara Hogenboom, "Latin America and China's Transnationalizing Oil Industry: A Political Economy Assessment of New Relations," *Perspectives on Global Development & Technology*, June 13, 2014.

6. Robert Souter, "China Has 'Big Role' in Latin America's Environmental Problems: Report," *China Dialogue*, April 16, 2015 (https://www.chinadialogue.net/article/show/single/en/7851-China-has-big-role-in-Latin-America-s-environmental-problems-report); Rebecca Ray and others, "China in Latin America: Lessons for South-South Cooperation and Sustainable Development" (Boston University, Global Economic Governance Initiative, 2015) (http://www.bu.edu/pardeeschool/files/2014/12/Working-Group-Final-Report.pdf).

7. Ministry of Commerce and Industry, Government of India, Export Import Data Bank (http://commerce.nic.in/eidb/default.asp); and Ambassador R. Viswanathan, "India and Latin America: A New Perception and a New Partnership" (Madrid: Real Instituto Elcano, July 22, 2014) (http://www.realinstitutoelcano.org/wps/portal/web/rielcano_en/contenido?WCM_GLOBAL_CONTEXT=/elcano/elcano_in/zonas_in/ari37-2014-viswanathan-india-latin-america-new-perception-new-partnership).

8. Ambassador R. Viswanathan, "Latin American Contribution to India's Energy Security," *Business with Latin America,* blog post, December 2, 2015 (http://businesswithlatinamerica.blogspot.in/2015/12/latin-american-contribution-to-indias.html).

9. Ministry of Commerce and Industry, Government of India, Export Import Data Bank (http://commerce.nic.in/eidb/default.asp).

10. Sun Hongbo, "India's Path of 'Discovering' Oil in Latin America," *Inter-American Dialogue* (in Chinese), blog post, April 11, 2014 (https://meizhouduihua.com/2014/04/11/%E6%8B%89%E7%BE%8E%E5%AF%BB%E6%B2%B9%E7%9A%84%E5%8D%B0%E5%BA%A6%E6%A8%A1%E5%BC%8F/).

11. Viswanathan, "Latin American Contribution to India's Energy Security."

12. Viswanathan, "India and Latin America."

13. See Ramón Espinasa, Estefanía Marchán, and Carlos G. Sucre, *The New Silk Road: Emerging Patterns in Asia-Latin American Trade for Energy and Minerals*, IADB Technical Note 804 (Washington, DC: Inter-

American Development Bank, June 2015), p. 5 (https://publications.iadb.org /handle/11319/6965).

14. James R. Norman, *The Oil Card: Global Economic Warfare in the 21st Century* (Walterville, OR: Trine Day, 2008), p. 165; China National Petroleum Corporation (CNPC), "CNPC in Peru" (http://www.cnpc.com .cn/en/Peru/country_index.shtml); and CNPC, "CNPC in Latin America" (http://www.cnpc.com.cn/en/America/CNPC_Latin_America.shtml).

15. CNPC, "CNPC in Venezuela" (http://www.cnpc.com.cn/en/Venezuela /country_index.shtml); and CNPC, "CNPC in Latin America" (http://www .cnpc.com.cn/en/America/CNPC_Latin_America.shtml).

16. François Lafargue, "China's Presence in Latin America: Strategies, Aims and Limits," *China Perspectives* [Online], November–December 2006 (http://chinaperspectives.revues.org/3053#tocto2n1).

17. Ministry of Foreign Affairs of the People's Republic of China, "President Hu Jintao to Visit Brazil, Argentina, Chile and Cuba and Attend APEC Economic Leaders' Meeting," press release, November 2, 2004 (http://www .fmprc.gov.cn/mfa_eng/topics_665678/huvisit_665888/t168684.shtml).

18. R. Evan Ellis, "The Rise of China in the Americas," *Security and Defense Studies Review* 6 (2014), pp. 90–105, at p. 90.

19. Lafargue, "China's Presence in Latin America."

20. Sean Douglas, "Kevin: More TT gas for China," *Trinidad and Tobago Newsday*, May 30, 2013 (http://newsday.co.tt/politics/0,178434.html).

21. David Lague, Charlie Zhu, and Benjamin Kang Lim, "Inside Xi Jinping's Purge of China's Oil Mandarins," Reuters Special Report, July 24, 2014 (http://www.reuters.com/article/2014/07/24/china-purge-cnpc-idUSL 4N0PS1ZE20140724).

22. *Financial Times*, "Global 500" (http://www.ft.com/cms/s/0/988051be -fdee-11e3-bd0e-00144feab7de.html#axzz47uMRnOrz).

23. Kerry Brown, "Why Zhou Yongkang Had to Go," *The Diplomat*, August 4, 2014 (http://thediplomat.com/2014/08/why-zhou-yongkang-had -to-go/). It is widely understood that the purge involves clashes at the very top of the Chinese leadership and a coming change during the transition from the Seventeenth (2007–12) to the Eighteenth Politburo Standing Committee (2012–present), the highest decision-making organ in the PRC. The main objective of the campaign has been to stamp, firmly and unquestionably, the authority of President Xi Jinping during his first years in office. Such assertiveness was the result of outgoing top figures' conflict with the "princeling" Bo Xilai, considered a threat because of his popularity resulting from the crony, populist system he created when he was mayor of Chongqing. Bo Xilai was arrested and ended up in prison, as have many of his supporters and fixers at the top of the party. The highest "oil mandarin" to fall to date in the course of President Xi's anticorruption campaign has been Zhou Yongkang, ex-chairman of CNPC but not just an oil man. He also held the sensitive post of chief of internal security of China, and there-

fore was one of the most powerful individuals in the country until his arrest in July 2014. Zhou was close to and supported the populist "return to the Maoist" left leadership style of Bo Xilai.

24. Douglas, "Kevin: More TT Gas for China."

25. Brian Winter, "Rousseff: 'Can't explain' Why Brazil Economy So Slow," Reuters, June 4, 2014 (http://www.reuters.com/article/2014/06/04 /us-brazil-rousseff-idUSKBN0EF04020140604); "Brazil's Disappointing Economy: Stuck in the Mud," *The Economist*, June 8, 2013 (http://www .economist.com/news/americas/21579048-feeble-growth-has-forced -change-course-governments-room-manoeuvre-more).

26. Ferchen, "China and Venezuela," p. 12.

27. Cui Shoujun, "China's Global Energy Dilemmas," seminar, Renmin University of China, Beijing, November 25, 2013.

28. Joshua Schneyer and Nicolas Medina Mora Perez, "How China Took Control of an OPEC Country's Oil," Reuters, November 26, 2013 (http://www.reuters.com/article/us-china-ecuador-oil-special-report-idUSB RE9AP0HX20131126).

29. Clifford Krauss and Keith Bradsher, "China's Global Ambitions, Cash and Strings Attached," *New York Times*, July 24, 2015 (http://www .nytimes.com/2015/07/26/business/international/chinas-global-ambitions -with-loans-and-strings-attached.html?_r=0).

30. "Sinopec Agrees to Acquire Occidental's Argentina Unit for $2.45 Billion," Bloomberg, December 10, 2010 (http://www.bloomberg.com/news /2010-12-10/sinopec-agrees-to-purchase-occidental-s-argentina-unit-for-2 -45-billion.html).

31. Yvonne Lee and Nisha Gopalan, "CNOOC Acquires Argentina Oil Assets," *Wall Street Journal*, March 14, 2010 (http://online.wsj.com/articles /SB10001424052748704416904575121130528712408).

32. Aibing Guo and Zijing Wu, "CNOOC Said to Consider Sale of $3.1 Billion Stake in Bridas," Bloomberg, April 6, 2014.

33. Brianna Lee, "Chinese President Xi Jinping Brings Billions on Visit to Latin America," *International Business Times*, July 22, 2014 (http:// www.ibtimes.com/chinese-president-xi-jinping-brings-billions-visit-latin -america-1635626).

34. Taos Turner, "Argentina's YPF, China's Sinopec to Join in Oil-and-Gas Projects," *Wall Street Journal*, January 28, 2015 (http://www.wsj.com /articles/argentinas-ypf-chinas-sinopec-to-join-in-oil-and-gas-projects -1422446008).

35. Zhang Fan, "Brazil Welcomes China's Oil Investments," *China Daily USA*, November 6, 2013 (http://usa.chinadaily.com.cn/world/2013 -11/06/content_17083995.htm).

36. Margaret Myers and Lisa Viscidi, eds., *Navigating Risks in Brazil's Energy Sector: The Chinese Approach* (Washington, DC: Inter-American Dialogue, October 2014) (http://thedialogue.org/uploads/IAD9713_China

BrazilEnergy_FINAL.pdf); Lee, "Chinese President Xi Jinping Brings Billions on Visit to Latin America."

37. Roberta Rampton and Scott Haggett, "CNOOC-Nexen Deal Wins U.S. Approval, Its Last Hurdle," Reuters, February 12, 2013 (http://www.reuters.com/article/2013/02/12/us-nexen-cnooc-idUSBRE91B0SU20130212).

38. "PetroChina Buying Peru Oil and Gas Assets for $2.6bn," Agence France-Presse, November 13, 2013.

39. Ecopetrol, "Ecopetrol y China National Petroleum Corporation suscriben acuerdo de cooperación," October 18, 2012 (http://www.ecopetrol.com.co/contenido.aspx?catID=148&conID=54775&pagID=134847).

40. Mauricio Mesquita Moreira, "Fear of China: Is There a Future for Manufacturing in Latin America?" INTAL-ITD Occasional Paper 36 (Washington, DC: Inter-American Development Bank, April 2006) (http://idbdocs.iadb.org/wsdocs/getdocument.aspx?docnum=33036625).

41. Alexandra Stevenson, "How Argentina Settled a Billion-Dollar Dispute," *New York Times*, April 25, 2016, pp. B1 and B3.

42. Diwan, "The Shale Revolution."

43. Ibid. Despite CNOOC's interest in selling its stake in Bridas, which hopes to grow its operations in Vaca Muerta as a result of CNOOC's global interest repositioning to North America after its acquisition of Nexen, few doubt that Chinese (as well as other countries') energy companies will remain interested and will try to have a presence in the Vaca Muerta.

44. Energy Information Administration, "Panama Canal Expansion Will Allow Transit of Larger Ships with Greater Volumes," September 17, 2014 (https://www.eia.gov/todayinenergy/detail.cfm?id=18011).

45. "China Considers Shale Gas Zone in Sichuan," *Energy China Forum*, Interfaxenergy.com 2014-11-07 (http://www.shalegaschinasummit.com/en/News_Show.asp?pid=7650); Zhang Dawei, "Where Are China's Special Shale Zones?" (in Chinese), Xinhuanet.com, September 27, 2014 (http://news.xinhuanet.com/energy/2014-09/27/c_127041477.htm).

46. Cui Shoujun, "China's Global Energy Dilemmas," seminar, Renmin University of China, Beijing, November 25, 2013.

47. Matt Ferchen and Francisco E. González, "Sino-Latin American Energy Ties: Current Challenges and Cooperation Opportunities," lecture, Hopkins China Forum and Young China Watchers Lecture Series, Shanghai, The Wooden Box, November 28, 2013.

48. Espinasa, Marchán, and Sucre, *The New Silk Road*, p. 5.

49. Shoujun, "China's Global Energy Dilemmas."

50. Ibid.

CHAPTER 6

Latin America on the Front Line of Food Security?

Mariano Turzi

The concept of food security is polysemous and multidimensional.[1] A recent study estimates that there are approximately 200 definitions and 450 indicators of food security in the literature.[2] The current operative definition has its origins in the Twenty-Second Conference (held in 1983) of the UN Food and Agriculture Organization (FAO), which stated that the "ultimate objective of food security should be *to ensure that all people at all times have both physical and economic access to the basic food they need.*" A decade later, the 1994 Human Development Report of the UN Development Program (UNDP) promoted a broader concept of human security, including food security as one of its components. With Indian economist Amartya Sen's ideas on human development underlying the conceptual framework, the report established that food security means that "*all people at all times have both physical and economic access to basic food.*"

At a global macrolevel, food security is understood as the overall world food supplies and the availability of sufficient food supply adequately distributed to satisfy human needs. At a domestic microlevel, food security is equated with household food security. In this chapter, food security is treated not as a humanitarian issue but rather as a foreign policy tool and a possible area of power projection by state actors. The analysis seeks to uncover how food supplies in general, and agricultural products in particular, are becoming new vectors of international relations linking Latin America with Asia. The chapter assesses the three conceptual pillars of food security from the perspective of the security of states, focusing on the absolute or relative gains in the relations of China and India with the Latin American countries.[3] Those three pillars are (1) *ensuring availability* by means of expanding, both quantitatively and qualitatively, the production of adequate food supplies; (2) *securing access* by maximizing physical and/or economic stability in the flow of supplies; and (3) *guaranteeing stability* by insulating the flow from price or political volatilities.

Guaranteeing food security is becoming an increasingly challenging task for policymakers in China and India. Several trends in global demand have come together to intensify competition for agricultural resources and food products. World demand for agricultural commodities is driven by four factors (the "four f's"): food, feed, fuel, and finance. The first factor, food, results from a demographic dynamic: the global population grows by around 80 million people per year. The first billion was reached in 1804. Owing mainly to technological advances in the fields of medicine and agriculture, from that point until 2014 the world population grew more than 600 percent, to more than 7 billion. In 2009 the renowned agronomist Norman Borlaug estimated that over the next fifty years, the world would have to produce more food than it had in the past 10,000 years.[4] The compounded result: more people in the world, living longer, means a structural upward shift in food demand. Moreover, the world population is changing not just quantitatively but also qualitatively. India and China have the largest rural populations, 857 million and 635 million, respectively. However, they are also expected to experience the largest declines in rural residents, with a 300 million reduction in China and a 52 million reduction in India anticipated by 2050. In 2010, for the first time, more than half of the world's population was urban. By 2014 the total urban population had grown to 54 percent, and this share is expected to increase to 66 percent by 2050. The UN's Population Division 2014 projections indicate that India is expected to add more than 11 million urban dwellers every year and China more than 8 million.[5]

The second driver of agricultural demand, feed, is mostly attributable to the rise of the emerging world, with a regional focus on Asia and particularly on China and India. Global poverty rates started to fall by the end of the twentieth century largely because emerging countries' growth accelerated from average annual rates of 4 percent in 1960–2000 to 6 percent in 2000–10. Around two-thirds of poverty reduction within a country comes from growth, and greater equality contributes the other third.[6] According to a World Bank estimate, between 2005 and 2012, India lifted 137 million people out of poverty.[7] For China, the World Bank calculates that, from the time market reforms were initiated in 1978 until 2004, the figure rose to more than 600 million, and in more recent years (between 2005 and 2011), nearly 220 million others have been lifted out of poverty.[8] When living standards rise, so does the demand for meat and dairy products. As people from China and India abandon poverty and move into the burgeoning global middle class—in Asia alone, the figures for 2014 were estimated at 500 million, and are projected to surpass 3 billion by 2030—they diversify their diets to include more vegetable oils, meat, and dairy products. Not only are there more people to feed, but more people are eating pork, chicken, and beef.

Against this backdrop, soybeans become the most essential input in the global food system. The bean contains 83 percent flour and 17 percent oil. When oil is extracted, the remaining residue is known as soybean cake, meal, or pellets; it is a vegetable protein concentrate (42–44 percent). Meal has found its strongest application as fodder for the industrial raising of farm animals, or "factory farming." Soybeans can also be processed for human consumption in a variety of forms: as soy meal, soy flour, soy milk, soy sauce, tofu, textured vegetable protein (found in a variety of vegetarian foods and intended to substitute for meat), lecithin, and oil. Soybean oil is the world's most widely used edible oil and has several industrial applications. Soybeans are thus a highly efficient crop: about 40 percent of the calories in soybeans are derived from protein, compared to 25 percent for most other crops. This means that the return per dollar spent is relatively high compared to that for other oilseeds.

In the lower-income segments, soy is an essential component of any dietary energy supply intended to inexpensively cover daily calorie requirements. For the better off, the crop is a cornerstone fodder component. As livestock can be fed more efficiently with soybean-based feed, the massive spread of the crop has made chicken, beef, and pork cheaper and more readily available worldwide. According to estimates from the U.S. Department of Agriculture, China and India are the world's top importers of soybean oil and are projected to remain so in the coming years.[9] China tops current importing charts and projected scenarios as soybean importer; its soybean imports were projected to reach 72 million tons in 2014–15, meaning that China alone was expected to absorb 64 percent of total global soybean exports by that year.[10]

The third factor pushing up demand for grain production is fuel. The first explanation is that the price of oil has a direct impact on prices of agricultural inputs such as fertilizers. When the price of fossil fuel rises, then it becomes a rational economic alternative to divert food crops into the production of biofuels. The debate about peak oil and the subsequent expectations of oil price hikes, plus the risk of supply shortages, have triggered a growing demand for energy from the biofuels industry. Supported by policy mandates, countries are seeking to diversify their energy sources by incorporating renewables. The FAO estimated in 2013 that biofuel prices would continue to rise—16–32 percent higher in real terms compared to the previous decade—over the next ten years, with expected high crude oil prices and continuing biofuel policies around the world that promote demand.

The financial component of agricultural demand is more indirect and more controversial, but nevertheless equally important in light of the speculation in food commodity markets, particularly by institutional investors such as hedge funds, pension funds, and investment banks. Since the year 2000 there has been a fiftyfold increase in dollars invested in commodity index funds. After the 2008 financial crisis, global investors seeking safe hedges for their portfolios in the face of depreciation of the U.S. dollar turned commodities into an asset class. In 2003 the commodities futures market totaled $13 billion.[11] In the first two months of 2008, $55 billion flowed into commodity markets, and by July of that year, $318 billion were inside the market. By 2012, assets under management rose to a record $412 billion. The financialization of commodity markets is self-perpetuating: as new investment products—food derivatives and indexed commodities—create speculative opportunities in grains, edible oils, and livestock, prices for food commodities increase. More money flows into the sector, and a new round of price increases follows. Although food inflation and food volatility have increased alongside commodity speculation, there is no conclusive evidence of the impact of finance as a driver of price developments.

THE DEMAND SIDE

The international-level variables (the four f's) are structural constraints within which both India and China find themselves bound. The strategic relevance of agricultural products has been undervalued relative to that of other natural resources such as gold, silver, or oil. Since the mid-twentieth century, oil has been regarded as the most critical commodity. But agricultural commodities are much more vital goods: one can substitute driving for public transportation, but there is no substitute for eating and drinking. If energy scarcity can disrupt the normal functioning of a society, the absence of food can cause its sudden breakdown.

Both India and China are driven to Latin America's agricultural products and land by a mixture of economic and security motives. The pursuit of scarce resources is a growing vector of foreign policy for the Asian giants.[12] In such an increasingly competitive and energetic economic and ecologic international scene, private business is seeking to maximize opportunities for profit and state actors are striving to gain an upper hand in providing for their populations. But although structural constraints and motives are alike, strategies have differed. The reason behind these differences is in the domestic political economy structures of both countries, which give rise to different international political economy configurations.

If the global structure conditions explain the *why*, the domestic political economy structures in both China and India can account for the *how*. The preferences and relative power of actors within these societies—economic and political, national and subnational, public and private—within certain institutional and policymaking frameworks is giving way to differential patterns in the food security quest in Latin America. How are both China and India responding to the challenge of food provision? By which means and strategies are they ensuring availability, securing access, and guaranteeing stability of food supplies? The following discussion delves into the individual characteristics of the two Asian giants.

China

After the 2008 financial crisis, Beijing decided to steer the economy away from export-led growth and into domestic consumption. This pattern of development was deemed too dependent on overseas sources of finance and international markets. As relative food scarcities continue to deepen and move the world into a new age of geopolitical and geoeconomic competition, securing agricultural resources in Latin America is fast becoming a priority of Chinese foreign policy and a key element in guaranteeing food security. For Beijing, the strategic aim of securing supplies is directly linked with guaranteeing social stability and regime preservation.

More important for the Chinese Communist Party (CCP), as demand outstrips supply—and it is currently physically impossible to move the frontier of production because of lack of land[13] and water scarcity—is to use importing as a way to keep up with domestic demand increases. The CCP leadership knows protests for specific grievances can snowball into massive civil unrest. The so-called food riots showcase the close relationship between food insecurity and conflict. This can manifest as famine, a humanitarian disaster, but also as externally generated food volatility or price shocks that trigger political instability. Empirical evidence supports the hypothesis that international food price shocks can reverberate in local markets, causing spontaneous, mostly urban (food consumers) political unrest.[14] But the countryside also worries the Chinese leadership. Rural living standards have stagnated compared with urban standards, and few in the countryside see their future there. The most recent official figures show a threefold gap between urban and rural incomes, fueling discontent and helping to make China one of the most unequal societies in the world.[15] In consequence, the Xi government has made it a priority to maintain social stability through economic restructuring, unveiling in 2013 a blueprint for reform with agricultural policy as a centerpiece.

Unlike its Indian counterparts, the PRC leadership deems access to food a source of security and power. In light of rising protectionism and price volatility, the Chinese government has concluded that food supplied through free trade is insufficient to provide for the population. The Chinese government's decisions about international agriculture in Latin America aim to protect production from the volatilities of foreign trade, potential market disruptions, or breakdown through war, sanctions, or foreign government policies. The price premium usually offered is intended to guarantee access against uncertainty rather than to secure an asset. Compelled by China's "going out" strategy, Chinese agricultural companies have ambitions to expand far beyond China. And Chinese government officials are eager for local companies to break into the ranks of the global corporate agribusiness elite. However, because these organizations are part of the state, they have different resources, aims, and strategies from those of private investors. Consequently, state investment is led by political motives and seeks not only economic profit but also political security.

China has concluded that the best way to serve its food security interests is through building its own, state-owned international food supply chain. State-owned companies are guided by both economic demands and political imperatives. As economic actors, Chinese companies enjoy advantages their competitors cannot offer: an effective mix of deep financial pockets and broad political shoulders. Thus, Chinese state investors have moved gradually toward owning ever-larger stakes of agriculture companies, leading to total consolidation of the value chain. This was evidenced in early 2014, when the China National Cereals, Oils, and Foodstuffs Corporation (COFCO) moved to control two overseas grain operations in the space of a week. In late March of that year, COFCO bought 51 percent of the Dutch company Nidera, the largest-ever international acquisition in the history of the Chinese agricultural industry.[16] Soon after, COFCO acquired a 51 percent stake in Noble Agri Limited from Noble Group in an all-cash transaction. Noble Agri, the agriculture platform of the Noble Group, engages primarily in the agricultural trading and processing business; it originates agricultural commodities from low-cost producing regions, such as South America, to supply regions with high demand, such as Asia. Taken together, both investments enable COFCO to extend its product offering and value chain overseas, thereby gaining access to core world grain market value chains. They provide direct access to grain and oilseeds in South America, consolidate a global supply chain system, and guarantee origination capabilities that complement the Chinese giant's domestic logistics, processing, and distribution network. With the operational streamlining and consolidation that will come from these deals, China will have a powerful global agricultural trader with the capacity to procure directly from around the world. Thus, it will be able to leverage its dominant position to ensure food security in China while at the same time using the advantages of its massive scale to compete more effectively against the historically dominant "big four" or "ABCD" grain firms: ADM, Bunge Ltd., Cargill Inc., and Louis Dreyfus.

By late 2014, China was at a critical turning point that signaled the launch of an overt attempt to establish a closed-circuit global agricultural value chain. From an economic point of view, COFCO, a corporate actor, attempted to remove itself from the global grain trading networks, sidelining the big international Western conglomerates. From a political standpoint, the Chinese government secures a food supply by exerting control from soil to store. COFCO's strong operational and strategic linkages with the state are also evident, as it is the key actor and policy tool of the CCP for ensuring food security. From an international political economy standpoint, the agricultural relationship between China and Latin America is also delineating the contours of an emerging model of international state capitalism the PRC seems to be embracing.[17]

India

Like China, India is also driven into Latin America by food security concerns. The *OECD-FAO Agricultural Outlook 2014* (with market projections to 2023) portrays a relatively optimistic scenario for India, assuming with considerable certainty that the country will be able to reduce food insecurity in the next decade.[18] However, the way in which India has approached the agricultural sector has been fundamentally different from China's approach. Indian actors are mostly private entrepreneurs rather than state-owned enterprises (SOEs). Indeed, most Indian agricultural trade and investment with Latin America is done by private Indian agribusiness companies. The Adani Group is the main importer of edible oil—sunflower and soybean oils—which is India's third largest import from Latin America, amounting to $1 billion in 2013. India's largest sugar refiner, Shree Renuka Sugars, was Brazil's main sugar producer, where it has more than 60 percent of its total international capacity. Olam International Ltd. has more than 35,000 hectares of peanuts, soybean, corn, alubias, and rice. It has also established two peanut-processing plants. Argentina is the second-largest exporter of peanuts after China, accounting for 25 percent of the world trade. In 2014, Breedens Investments, a unit of Singapore's state-owned sovereign wealth fund Temasek Holdings, gained control of Olam and its operations in the eleven Latin American countries where it has a direct presence.[19]

As a result, the Indo–Latin American agricultural relationship exhibits a distinctive pattern. The foreign policy and security interests of Delhi have been aligned with private, profit-seeking Indian firms rather than being centrally directed, as is the case with Beijing. To the extent of its direct involvement, the central government fosters and supports the creation of complementarities and collaborative synergies between Indian and Latin American businesses in accordance with India's food security priorities. The Indian Ministry of External Affairs has explicitly recognized it as a powerful factor that is driving the country's deepening engagement with the Latin American region.[20]

The Latin American agribusiness sector is not the result of natural endowments and comparative advantage. It is the product of a technological revolution that radically transformed the means of agricultural production. This technology stems from the simultaneous, mutually reinforcing adoption of three components: genetically modified seeds, agrochemicals, and no-till or direct seeding. These technological advances are making Latin American agriculture globally competitive. Production is carried out commercially, scientifically, and professionally. Because of the characteristics of the product itself as much as for the productive linkages it generates, it is difficult to properly refer to such technology-intensive products simply as raw materials. China and India both have taken note of this. But Indian companies have taken the lead in seeking more than just the natural advantages Latin America offers in terms of fertile land and water abundance. They are seeking also the technological know-how that some of these countries have developed in such areas as food storage (Brazil) and biotechnology (Argentina).

Because Indian firms do not seek to create wholly integrated value chains with a commanding presence of SOEs, the opportunities for synergistic integration at different stages is broader, as is the case for equipment and machinery parts. China's business model "crowds out" participation from Latin American companies and entrepreneurs, but India's business model allows for the participation of private actors (firms) in synergistic or convergent sectors at different stages in the value chain. The assertive proposals of Chinese companies to establish long-term lease agreements for large areas of agricultural land in South America have triggered public reaction and governmental restrictions on foreign ownership of agricultural land in Brazil, Argentina, and Uruguay. Indian officials have been exploiting these differences with their Chinese counterparts to make the case that Indian investments have a greater potential to reduce Latin American production costs and to increase the chances of Latin American products becoming globally competitive.[21] Aside from this posture playing well in the context of apprehension about the Chinese presence in Latin American agriculture, there is a material basis for the claim. The role of the Indian government is much less top down, and not as centrally controlled. For example, the state of Gujarat has become the most important actor in Indo–Latin American business, accounting for more than 60 percent of India's trade with Latin America. India's prime minister, Narendra Modi, was previously the chief minister of Gujarat state. It remains to be seen whether this trend toward an "entrepreneurial state" will become national in scope.[22]

THE SUPPLY SIDE

The nature and composition of Asia's agricultural demand and the developing world's supply have a structural relationship, for they are being driven by the demographics and economics behind the rising demand of the growing Asian middle classes. There are many factors empowering Latin American producers, stemming from changing ecological conditions that are affecting economic destinies. First, climate change is generating increased temperature volatility and alterations in precipitation patterns. The global mean sea level rise has gone from a rate of 1.5 mm/year in the 1901–90 period to 3.2 mm/year in the 1993–2010 period, according to the 2013 Fifth Assessment Report of the Inter-Governmental

Panel on Climate Change (IPCC).[23] The IPCC also states it is "virtually certain" that global mean sea level rise will continue, and that about 70 percent of coastlines worldwide are projected to experience sea level change, which means a reduction in arable land and, in consequence, of food availability. Climate change is also identified by the IPCC as increasingly contributing to extreme events such as heat waves, droughts, flash floods, and sea storms. Economic losses and damages from disasters have been rising over the past three decades, from an annual average of $50 billion in the 1980s to just under $200 billion each year in the past decade, totaling $3.8 trillion in the period from 1980 to 2012.[24] Weather-related economic impacts are especially high in fast-growing, middle-income countries such as China and India as a result of shrinking and increasingly exposed assets. Over the six years from 2001 to 2006, the average impact of disasters in middle-income countries equaled 1 percent of GDP, ten times higher than the average for high-income countries over the same period.[25]

Finally, natural limitations and policy deficiencies such as water mismanagement and land degradation have resulted in increased water pollution and desertification, while relentless urbanization is reducing previously arable land. Arable land data (hectares per person) alone are impressive: Argentina (0.96) is twelve times the proportion in China (0.08) and seven times that in India (0.13). Brazil (0.37) is more than four times that of China, Paraguay (0.66) more than eight times that of China, and Uruguay (0.52) quadruples India.[26] Renewable internal freshwater resources per capita show comparably staggering differences: the regional average for developing Latin American and Caribbean countries is five times bigger than for developing East Asian and Pacific countries. By this metric, Colombia has more than forty times the resources of India and Peru twenty-six times those of China. Even Chile and Bolivia are forty-three and twenty-four times more freshwater abundant than India.

The question for Latin America then becomes how to translate natural resources into national wealth. Economically, this means a cautionary tale of past experiences of development. Growth based on "star" products (oil, copper, soybeans, iron ore, bananas) has in the past led countries in the region into commodity bubbles that went bust when international conditions turned adverse. Countries got locked into excessive commodity dependence, exposure to international price volatility, lack of diversification, and, ultimately, an unbalanced pattern of development. More often than not, populist leaders capitalized on this, creating a cycle of political polarization, nationalist rhetoric, protectionist policies, institutional instability, and even regime breakdown. Will this

China- and India-led agricultural boom be just another new version of the old third world model of integration into the international economy as commodity exporters?

Global investment and trade are increasingly formed by production networks of firms investing in productive assets worldwide and trading inputs and outputs in cross-border value chains.[27] These can have different degrees of diversification and complexity (intrafirm and interfirm, regional and global). The UN Conference on Trade and Development (UNCTAD) estimates that global value chains shaped by multinational corporations or transnational corporations account for some 80 percent of international trade.[28] Estimates of developing country share in global value-added trade increased from 20 percent in 1990 to 40 percent in 2013. Economies with the fastest-growing participation in global value chains have GDP per capita growth rates around two percentage points above the average.[29] Although there are several distinct development paths to boost competitiveness in order to succeed in this new global value chain economic structure,[30] the public and private actors involved in the Latin American agricultural and food value chains being structured with the emerging Asia-Pacific countries still lack understanding of their governance and lack effective national or regional policy interventions.

Strategically, the emerging agricultural international political economy could recreate old (inter)dependencies. Will Chinese and Indian foreign relations with Latin American agricultural exporters resemble the ones the United Kingdom had during the nineteenth century? In the oil geopolitics of the twentieth century, such countries as Saudi Arabia, Kuwait, Oman, Qatar, the United Arab Emirates, Bahrain, Iran, and Iraq became strategically relevant for U.S. foreign policy. Will the rising powers of the twenty-first century define core strategic interests in South American food production? If the coming age is more about soil than oil, then the South American green giants might become for Asia the geopolitical equivalent of the Gulf countries for the United States.

CONCLUSION

Food production in the contemporary world is no longer a domestic economic issue. It is an international, political dynamic involving complex interdependencies at multiple levels and numerous overlapping actors manipulating a shifting combination of resources. The global reach of China and India in agriculture is fundamentally restructuring patterns of production, trade, and consumption. The changing circulation of food is reshaping economic, political, social, and international relations between Asia and Latin America, creating and restructuring international political economy networks, international trade patterns, multinational corporate structures, and investment flows. This is also transforming domestic political economy coalitions and public policies both in the Atlantic and in the Pacific countries.

The business models of both China and India are heavily dependent on their domestic political economy structures. While China has exhibited a definite preference for SOEs, Indian agricultural links with Latin America are clearly more private sector driven. While the Chinese business model seeks autonomy and vertical integration, the Indian model seeks also complementarily productive chains within the agricultural sector at different stages of the production process. Politically, China directs the search for profit of its state-owned companies with a firm, centralized grip directed by national (food) security concerns. The regime type in India allows for lesser degrees of political control over markets and corporate actors. As both countries compete for agricultural resources in Latin America, they showcase two models of emerging international capitalism.

Engagement by China and India in the global agricultural business value chains carries the risk of locking developing countries into the role of low-cost agricultural producers. There is growing international economic pressure from the global restructuring of agricultural trade patterns. The demand behind this massive realignment is not exclusively Chinese or Indian but, because of the magnitude of both powers, the direction China and India take in international agricultural provision and food security will determine the global pace and direction. Because of this, the main challenge for Latin American leaders is to create governance structures that translate the newfound wealth into sustainable development, social well-being, and international relevance. The comparative advantages of both parties involved create structural complementarities undergirding the relationship. However, this does not prevent the creation of foreign economic enclaves as producing countries rise.[31] Another challenge for the Latin American countries will be the territorial reshaping according to foreign—corporate or state—needs. The agricultural sector is the bargaining chip these countries have vis-à-vis hungry Asian giants such as China and India. In an increasingly competitive world, private and public actors, both Western and non-Western, are offering generous conditions that include construction or renovation of infrastructure, logistics, and networks (such as railways and waterways) for transportation and shipping.

In geopolitical terms, agricultural producers have an opportunity to capitalize on these needs and constraints to serve their own development needs. The notion that Latin America is a *place* rather than an *actor* leaves the region in a passive state. It assumes Latin American countries can only respond to these dynamics instead of actively shaping them or even anticipating them. Therein lies the risk of acritically acquiescing to the "win-win" relations much touted by the Foreign Ministries of China and India. If Latin American agricultural products support Asia's rising wealth and power, can they not as well support Latin America's? Dismissing this question as chauvinistic rhetoric risks failing to acknowledge nationalistic populist politics that could derail the relationship.

The entrance of Chinese and Indian agricultural companies into Latin America is also an indicator of a larger trend: the increasing restructuring of international capitalism around non-Western actors who have a different balance between the public and the private sector. The traditional distinction between the invisible hand of the market and the visible fist of the state is being re-created constantly, redefining the boundaries of economics and politics at local and global levels. This is a growing trend, posing new and complex questions for Latin American foreign policies and also for U.S.–Latin American relations. Indeed, there are many geoeconomic complementarities that the United States should explore to find new areas for cooperation with Latin America. As Chinese and Indian agricultural ties with Latin America fast become a new dimension of international relations, they are also opening up a new geography of power. The United States and the Southern Cone of Latin America combined account for more than 50 percent of global soybean and soybean-derived world exports. Turning producers of the same resource into a coherent organized bloc might not be desirable or even possible. However, moving toward coordination in international grain trade might increase the bargaining power of Latin American countries vis-à-vis Asian countries, especially in the context of the ongoing Trans-Pacific Partnership (TPP) negotiations and the U.S. foreign policy pivot to Asia. Just as agricultural trade has become a new vector of integration between Latin American and Asia-Pacific countries, it could also be an avenue for renewed hemispheric relations.

NOTES

1. For a detailed discussion on the conceptual evolution, see Eduardo Bianchi, "Food Security, the Right to Food and the Human Development

Report 1994," GREEN Working Paper 48 (University of Warwick, May 2014).

2. Anamaria Toma-Bianov and Oana Saramet, "The Concepts of Food Security and the Right to Safe Food from the International and European Perspective," *Bulletin of the Transilvania University of Brasov* 5 (54), no. 1 (2012), pp. 153–58.

3. Robert Powell, "Absolute and Relative Gains in International Relations Theory," *American Political Science Review* 85, no. 4 (December 1991), pp. 1303–20.

4. Norman Borlaug, "Population Growth Requires Second Green Revolution," Nobel Laureates Plus interview, *New Perspectives Quarterly* (April 7, 2009) (http://www.digitalnpq.org/articles/nobel/353/04-07-2009/norman _borlaug).

5. United Nations, *World Urbanization Prospects: The 2014 Revision, Highlights,* ST/ESA/SER.A/352 (UN Department of Economic and Social Affairs, Population Division, 2014).

6. A 1 percent increase in incomes in the most unequal countries produces a 0.6 percent reduction in poverty; in the most equal countries, it yields a 4.3 percent reduction.

7. World Bank, *India Development Update*, Report AUS5757 (Washington, DC: World Bank, Economic Policy and Poverty Team, South Asia Region, October 2013), p. ii (www-wds.worldbank.org/external/default/WDS ContentServer/WDSP/IB/2013/10/16/000356161_20131016171237/Rendered /PDF/AUS57570WP0P140Box0379846B00PUBLIC0.pdf).

8. The more recent figures correspond to poverty at the $2 per day (PPP) level. World Bank, "Results Profile: China Poverty Reduction" (Washington, DC: World Bank, March 19, 2010) (www.worldbank.org/en/news/feature /2010/03/19/results-profile-china-poverty-reduction); and World DataBank, *Poverty and Inequality Database* (Washington, DC: World Bank, 2005–2011) (http://databank.worldbank.org).

9. U.S. Department of Agriculture, *World Agricultural Supply and Demand Estimates (WASDE)* 534 (October 10, 2014) (www.usda.gov/oce /commodity/wasde/).

10. Ibid.

11. All currency figures are in U.S. dollars unless otherwise noted.

12. Daniel Yergin, *The Quest: Energy, Security, and the Remaking of the Modern World* (New York: Penguin Books, 2012); Michael Klare, *The Race for What's Left: The Global Scramble for the World's Last Resources* (New York: Picador, 2012); and Dambisa Moyo, *Winner Take All: China's Race for Resources and What It Means for the World* (New York: Basic Books, 2012).

13. This is the result not only of desertification and urbanization but also of speculation. In 2013, agricultural rental prices topped $1,200 per acre in some parts of China. By contrast, the average acre of farmland in the United States rented for $136 in 2013.

14. Joshua D. Angrist and Adriana D. Kulger, "Rural Windfall or a New Resource Curse? Coca, Income, and Civil Conflict in Colombia," *Review of Economics and Statistics* 90, no. 2 (2008), pp. 191–245; Henk-Jan Brinkman and Cullen S. Hendrix, "Food Insecurity and Violent Conflict: Causes, Consequences, and Addressing Challenges," Occasional Paper 24 (Rome: World Food Programme, 2011); Markus Brückner and Antonio Ciccone, "International Commodity Prices, Growth and the Outbreak of Civil War in Sub-Saharan Africa," *Economic Journal* 120 (2010), pp. 519–34; Rabah Arezki and Markus Brückner, "Food Prices, Conflict, and Democratic Change," Research Paper 2011-4 (University of Adelaide, School of Economics, 2011); Oeindrila Dube and Juan F. Vargas, "Commodity Price Shocks and Civil Conflict: Evidence from Colombia," *Review of Economic Studies* 80, no. 4 (2013), pp. 1384–1421; Julia Berazneva and David R. Lee, "Explaining the African Food Riots of 2007–2008: An Empirical Analysis," *Food Policy* 39 (2013), pp. 28–39; and Christopher B. Barret, ed., *Food Security and Sociopolitical Stability* (Oxford University Press, 2014).

15. China National Bureau of Statistics, *China Statistical Yearbook 2013* (Beijing: China Statistics Press, 2013) (www.stats.gov.cn/tjsj/ndsj/2013 /indexeh.htm).

16. The name Nidera stems from the names of the countries in which the company focused its activities: the Netherlands, India, Deutschland (Germany), England, Russia, and Argentina.

17. For a discussion of how the rise of multinational corporations from emerging markets has been a major development during the last decade that is not exclusively or even primarily Chinese, see Andreas Nölke, ed., *Multinational Corporations from Emerging Markets: State Capitalism 3.0* (New York: Palgrave Macmillan, 2014).

18. OECD/Food and Agriculture Organization of the United Nations, *OECD-FAO Agricultural Outlook 2014* (Paris: OECD Publishing, 2014) (http://dx.doi.org/10.1787/agr_outlook-2014-en).

19. Olam has a significant upstream presence across South America for peanuts (Argentina), dairy (in Uruguay through majority shareholding in New Zealand Farming Systems), soy, corn, cocoa (Ecuador), cotton (Brazil), and coffee (Peru, Colombia, and Brazil). In Central America, the company is among the top exporters in tea (Costa Rica and Panama) and one of the leading players in the coffee market (Honduras).

20. Government of India, Ministry of External Affairs, "India and Latin America: It's Time to Tango" (New Delhi, July 12, 2014) (www.mea.gov.in /in-focus-article.htm?23616/India+and+Latin+America+Its+time+to+tango).

21. Ambassador R. Viswanathan, "India and Latin America: A New Perception and a New Partnership," Real Instituto Elcano Paper ARI 37/2014 (Madrid: Real Instituto Elcano, July 22, 2014) (www.realinstitutoelcano.org /wps/portal/web/rielcano_en/contenido?WCM_GLOBAL_CONTEXT= /elcano/elcano_in/zonas_in/ari37-2014-viswanathan-india-latin-america -new-perception-new-partnership#.VEMOPWebCSo).

22. Mariana Mazzucato, *The Entrepreneurial State: Debunking Public vs. Private Sector Myth* (London: Anthem Press, 2014).

23. Inter-Governmental Panel on Climate Change, *Climate Change 2013: The Physical Science Basis* (Cambridge University Press, 2013).

24. World Bank, "Building Resilience: Integrating Climate and Disaster Risk into Development; Lessons from World Bank Group Experience" (Washington, DC: World Bank, November 18, 2013).

25. Ibid.

26. The latest available arable land data are for 2012 and include land defined by the FAO as land under temporary crops (double-cropped areas are counted once), temporary meadows for mowing or for pasture, land under market or kitchen gardens, and land temporarily fallow. Land abandoned as a result of shifting cultivation is excluded. World Bank, "Arable Land (hectares per person)" (http://data.worldbank.org/indicator/AG.LND .ARBL.HA.PC).

27. Gary Gereffi, "A Global Value Chain Perspective on Industrial Policy and Development in Emerging Markets," *Duke Journal of Comparative & International Law* 24 (2014), pp. 433–58.

28. United Nations Conference on Trade and Development (UNCTAD), *Global Value Chains and Development: Investment and Value Added Trade in the Global Economy: A Preliminary Analysis*, UNCTAD document UNCTAD/DIAE/2013/1 (February 27, 2013).

29. Ibid.

30. The ones identified by UNCTAD are "engaging," "preparing," "upgrading," "competing," "converting," and "leapfrogging."

31. See H. W. Singer, "The Distribution of Gains between Investing and Borrowing Countries," *American Economic Review* 40 (1950), pp. 473–85; Paul A. Baran, *The Political Economy of Growth* (New York: Monthly Review Press, 1957); and Kevin P. Gallagher and Lyuba Zarsky, *The Enclave Economy. Foreign Investment and Sustainable Development in Mexico's Silicon Valley* (MIT Press, 2007).

CHAPTER 7

Latin American Trade with India and China

THE REGION NEEDS A "BUSINESS PLAN"

Robert Devlin and Theodore Kahn

Postwar world trade has expanded twice as fast as world gross domestic product (GDP), providing a major stimulus to growth of the world economy.[1] Dynamic articulation with international trade has, moreover, been an important policy tool for encouraging investment, economic upgrading, and growth in all the developing countries that have succeeded in achieving economic catch-up with rich countries.

Over the past two decades, Latin America has seriously embraced international trade. Trade as a share of regional GDP increased steadily from 33 percent in 1993 to 51 percent in 2012, as governments throughout the region liberalized trade regimes after decades of inward-looking development policies. Tariffs were brought down from a regional average of more than 40 percent in the mid-1980s to around 10 percent a decade later,[2] and the region now boasts a large network of bilateral and plurilateral free trade agreements spanning the globe. Meanwhile, in many countries public trade promotion agencies were reformed and professionalized, with several of these institutions now considered world class. Between 2003 and 2008, in particular, Latin America enjoyed an unprecedented trade boom, with the value of exports growing by an average annual rate of 21 percent. This strong performance of the external sector contributed significantly to a marked uptick in growth in nearly every country in the region, signs of economic catch-up, and significant reductions in poverty and, to a lesser extent, inequality.[3] Moreover, the consolidation of good macroeconomic management insulated the region from the most devastating effects of the U.S.-EU financial crises and the outbreak of the global recession in 2008.

Below the surface, however, the picture is less rosy. Latin America continues to lag behind developing regions such as East Asia and Eastern Europe both in productivity growth and in many indicators of international economic integration, including the share of global exports and intraregional trade.[4] In addition, while economic growth in Latin America between 2003 and 2008 was the highest it had been in forty years, in relative terms it was less spectacular: to wit, it fell short of the rate achieved by other developing regions of the world, including sub-Saharan Africa.[5] More worryingly still, much of the growth was underpinned by the commodity bonanza of the 2000s. This favorable commodity cycle, moreover, appears to be over.[6] Beginning in 2011, growth has decelerated considerably, and prospects for the mid-2010s are not encouraging; growth was 1.3 percent in 2014, −0.3 percent in 2015, and projected to be negative again in 2016.[7] The mediocre performance is influenced by a variety of factors, but perennial issues such as generalized low productivity growth, low value-added in manufactured exports, and many countries' static export concentration in natural resources are especially salient.

This chapter argues that, for trade to be a driver of productivity and sustained high rates of growth, Latin America needs an effective "business plan" to guide the direction of trade policy. The moniker "business plan" is shorthand for the use of industrial policies to give trade policy a sharper and much more determined focus on the end objective of productive transformation and on identification of the best opportunities for achieving that through trade. While the use of industrial policies is a source of continued debate in economics, this chapter does not refer to the old 1960s approach of the state as demiurge. Rather, it refers to the "new industrial policies" of the twenty-first century, put into effect by various economies, that express modern market-friendly modalities for generating a medium- to long-term national vision and forward-looking proactive strategies for scaling up the global hierarchy of production and international trade.[8] When used effectively in this framework of market enabler, state interventions can be a catalyst for generating productive transformation with faster and more sustained economic growth. Indeed, all countries that have been successful in economic catch-up have had national strategic visions implemented with industrial policies of one vintage or another where trade policy played a central role.[9]

As discussed later in this chapter, integration with the global economy provides opportunities for diversification, transformation, and productivity gains beyond what is possible in most domestic contexts. World trade growth has recently suffered a sharp slowdown, and some speculate about structural, as opposed to purely cyclical, characteristics behind the phenomenon.[10] Even if growth of world trade were not to sustain the historical rates of the past decades, the promotion of trade and export upgrading to exploit the opportunities that do exist must be part of any development strategy. This is especially true for small and medium-sized economies and in the context of today's "hyperglobalized" economic activity.[11] The incipient development of new industrial policies can be observed in Latin America, where international competitiveness and export diversification have a prominent place in countries' strategic objectives.[12] However, the vision for trade policy needs a sharper strategic focus and an intensified discipline to enable countries to go beyond their static comparative advantage. Indeed, countries' goals for diversification and upgrading of exports unfortunately have been overpowered by the sirens of the commodity boom and reliance on easy preferential market access for low-valued-added exports.

For Latin America, future strategic thinking about trade will inevitably bring China and India into consideration. These nations are respectively the world's second- and third-largest economies, with populations approaching 1.4 and 1.3 billion. China's economy has experienced three decades of double-digit growth, while India grew at an annual average of slightly less than 7 percent over the two previous decades. Both economies have recently experienced slowdowns but still have relatively robust growth rates. Preliminary data suggest that in 2013, China edged out the United States as the largest merchandise trader, with 22 percent of total world merchandise trade, while a less trade-oriented India was at 4 percent. In commercial services trade, the United States is the largest, with 12 percent of the world's total value; China and India measure at 6 percent and 3 percent, respectively. Using World Bank classifications for per capita income, China is in the upper tier of middle-income countries, while India has lower-middle-income status.[13]

China's rapid rise to global economic power status and the expectation that India could do the same have made the countries a focal point for export and foreign direct investment (FDI) attraction strategies in the developing and developed worlds alike. China in particular has also garnered attention as a source of import competition for domestic firms in many countries. Latin America has been no exception. The global rise of China has left a large footprint in the region since trade took off in the early 2000s. India's footprint is still light, but some analysts are nonetheless asking whether the country will be Latin America's "next big thing."[14]

However, policymakers in Latin America must ask how much strategic weight should be given to these two markets in light of other global and regional opportunities. Have some countries depended too much on China for growth? What are the alternatives to current patterns of trade? Does India's rise mean Latin America has overlooked an untapped opportunity hidden in the shadow of China's much publicized success?[15] Should it become a new focal point of attention for trade? Answering these questions will require transcending the region's propensity for short-term thinking about China and India and starting to think about the region's trade strategy more broadly.[16]

This chapter argues that Latin America's trade-related industrial policy should be more strategically focused on exploiting those markets that already offer the best opportunities to diversify into more knowledge-intensive and technologically advanced exports, rooted in domestic value-added. However, to make this future a reality, Latin America must reassess current trade patterns being driven by China, and reinforced by India, with a view to exploring the feasibility of generating new patterns with these two markets and better leveraging real, existing opportunities at the region's doorstep. Indeed, the chapter posits that the most feasible place to achieve trade diversification and upgrading is close to home—within the region itself and North America—and not so much across the Pacific, where many eyes are cast.

This chapter first provides an overview of the role of trade in growth and economic catch-up. It then outlines the global profile of trade for China, India, and Latin America. The next section examines the nature of the bilateral trade between Latin America and the two Asian giants, followed by a comparison of exports of manufactures by Latin America, China, and India to the United States and the European Union. The chapter then examines strategies to upgrade exports to China and India and concludes that such opportunities will probably be limited by a number of factors. The chapter also explores markets closer to home for their potential as platforms for diversification and upgrading. The final section offers some conclusions and argues that Latin America's efforts to diversify and upgrade exports indeed should focus closer to home. It is important to note that, in light of the strong heterogeneity in the trade patterns of Latin America, the analysis focuses on the two subregions of Mexico–Central America–Dominican Republic (DR) and South America. The analysis also recognizes the strong relation between trade and FDI; however, in a short essay, the discussion is limited to trade, with a minimal comment on FDI.[17]

THE ROLE OF TRADE IN GROWTH, TRANSFORMATION, AND CATCH-UP

In promoting competitiveness and high rates of economic growth the issue of productivity is of central importance and an area where Latin America has seriously lagged.[18] Another central issue is diversification of production and exports along with movement into more complex production activities.[19] Latin America has lagged here too.[20] As mentioned earlier, trade can be a tool to move forward on these objectives.

Trade affects these objectives through a number of channels. At the firm level, opening to trade (in a way that does not expose firms to predatory pressures) increases competition in the domestic market and provides incentives to raise productivity by lowering costs ("doing more with the same resources"), investing in product and process innovation, and importing embodied technological upgrades. At the sector level, laggard firms will be pushed out of the market and resources reallocated to healthier firms, which will raise overall productivity, even if productivity at the firm level is constant. Of course, positive outcomes are not automatic and will depend on the broader constellation of public policies that condition the effect of trade on markets and incentives.[21]

Promoting exports to foreign markets has advantages too. Among them is the ability, especially for small and medium-sized domestic markets, to achieve economies of scale that lower unit costs of production. Moreover, for countries exporting goods that are not highly specialized, diminishing returns on investment can be postponed, as Jaume Ventura argues happened for the investment-intensive, export-led growth in East Asia.[22] Consumers' preference for variety also creates diversification opportunities through intra-industry trade, as opposed to the classic textbook interindustry trade.[23] Efforts to export additionally can stimulate flows of cross-border knowledge and incorporation of technology, as well as "learning by doing," with positive dynamic spillover effects, diversification of production structures, and construction of new comparative advantages. Here also the outcome is not automatic. There is a need for public policy interventions that encourage entrepreneurial experimentation, learning, capability development, and innovation in new activities that discover latent comparative advantages.[24] Moreover, migrating to new, higher-knowledge-based activities may be easier or harder, depending on whether current comparative advantage is in the center or the periphery of the world's product space and on the ability of a country to "learn" and expand its knowledge domain.[25]

Another trade channel involves the emergence of global value chains.[26] This refers to the fragmentation of the full productive process of conceiving, making, and delivering a final product to the consumer.

Traditionally, production processes took place within an integrated firm or industry in the domestic market. As a result, developing countries wishing to industrialize and diversify their economic base faced the challenge of creating entire industries. By contrast, today developing countries can specialize in one stage of production processes that are often divided up among different firms across national borders. Participating in a chain is often termed "vertical specialization."[27] The emergence of global value chains has changed the nature of trade: countries trade intermediate goods within narrow product categories, as goods cross borders several times in the process of being produced. Global value chains thus represent an opportunity for developing regions such as Latin America to leverage trade to diversify their productive structure, move into higher-value-added activities, participate in market segments with dynamic demand, and raise productivity. Firms need not remain stuck at one node in the chain. Upgrading can entail developing better-performing products, adopting more efficient processes, "moving up the value chain" by engaging in higher-value-added activities within a value chain, or applying new technology or knowledge to move into entirely new sectors.[28]

However, these gains are by no means guaranteed. First, value chains are usually organized and driven by large multinationals, which demand a high level of standards and capabilities from their suppliers. Second, to move up a chain may require successful displacement of entrenched incumbents. Third, global value chains remain highly regionalized, with the major value chains geographically clustered in East Asia, the EU, and North America, so that distance and transport infrastructure are strategic factors.[29] Finally, there is evidence that the trend toward fragmentation of production may be reversing, at least in certain industries, as a result of upgraded productive capacities in some countries (such as China), with a consequent reduced degree of vertical specialization or multinational corporations (MNCs) "reshoring" segments of their chains.

While Latin America is linked to North American value chains through the North American Free Trade Agreement (NAFTA, Mexico) and the Central American Free Trade Agreement (CAFTA, Central America and the DR), its participation is mostly at the margin of the chain in low-value-added "maquila" activities.[30] Aside from the maquiladora industry's limited links to the domestic economy and low growth effects, dependence on inputs creates balance-of-payments pressures. While the valued-added of the exports of South America, which does not participate intensively in global value chains, is relatively high, exports are dominated by commodities and commodity-based manufactures with limited connections to domestic markets and placement at the more upstream parts of supply chains.[31] This makes these countries' growth very vulnerable to the vagaries of international commodity cycles. Successfully entering and moving up value chains requires deployment of effective industrial policies that encourage capability building, experimentation, learning by doing, innovation, technological upgrading, and increased productivity. FDI attraction and cooperation is often a platform for supply chain participation and hence can be an important dimension of industrial policies and trade development.[32] Reviewing the role of trade in growth, transformation, and economic catch-up provides the context for this chapter's examination of the trade dynamics between Latin America and India and China.

GLOBAL TRADE PROFILES OF INDIA, CHINA, AND LATIN AMERICA

Between 2003 and 2013 the value of the goods trade grew much faster in China and India than in South America and Mexico–Central America–DR—it expanded roughly six times for the two Asian countries and three and two times, respectively, for the latter two subregions of Latin America. Between India and China, China is by far the more intensive trader, valued at $2,700 per capita, compared to India's $711.[33] Indeed, China has become the first or second trading partner for nearly eighty countries in the world.[34]

China

China's exports to the world are dominated by manufactured goods and its imports are dominated by commodities and manufactured goods (figure 7-1). As an importer, China's high level of domestic investment has made it one of the world's top importers of many commodities but especially metals; on the eve of the global recession, China accounted for roughly 30 percent of net world metal imports, 65 percent in the case of iron ore.[35] Meanwhile, roughly 50 percent of its manufactured exports passed through specially dedicated processing zones, explaining the strong participation of manufactured imports. Estimating the domestic value-added of exports is difficult, but recent estimates put the value-added of processed exports at about 49 percent in 2006 (up from 25–30 percent in the late 1990s), while domestic value-added in total exports has been estimated to be more than 70 percent.[36] Given China's strategic ambitions and fast technological development, one should suspect that the value-added figure is higher today and significantly growing.[37]

FIGURE 7-1
China's Exports and Imports, 2002–13

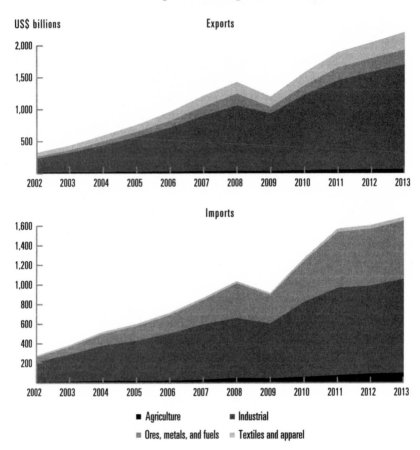

US$ billions   Exports

Source: UN Comtrade.

Table 7-1 shows China's top ten merchandise exports and imports worldwide. The data reflect a highly diversified export structure, with the top ten categories accounting for only 23 percent of total exports. Moreover, exports are dominated by manufactured goods that are medium and high tech. The top ten imports are almost evenly split in value between raw materials and manufactured goods, the latter being mostly intermediate inputs. As for China's top five markets, the United States, Japan, Korea, and the EU stand out on both the export and import sides, while Hong Kong is a base for reexports and Australia is a major supplier of raw materials, especially iron ore (table 7-2).

In contrast to manufacturing, China's service sector is inefficient and operates with low productivity. While registering surpluses in merchan-

TABLE 7-1

China's Top Export and Import Products, 2013

	Amount (US$ thousands)	Product description	Share (percent)
EXPORTS	110,802,220	Portable digital automatic data processing machines, weighing not more than 10 kg, consisting of at least a central processing unit, a keyboard, and a display	5.0
	95,640,415	Transmission apparatus for radio telephony	4.3
	87,563,878	Digital electronic integrated circuits	4.0
	47,116,398	Parts of electrical apparatus for radio telephony	2.1
	36,048,022	Other devices, appliances, instruments, liquid crystal devices	1.6
	30,252,689	Other apparatus, for carrier current line systems or for digital line systems	1.4
	28,598,928	Parts and accessories for automatic data processing machines	1.3
	28,034,769	Articles of jewelry of other precious metals	1.3
	27,387,019	Input or output units of automatic data processing machines	1.2
	19,488,963	Other petroleum oils	0.9
IMPORTS	219,660,366	Petroleum oils and oils obtained from bituminous minerals, crude	12.3
	206,510,523	Digital electronic circuits	11.5
	102,080,390	Nonagglomerated iron ores	5.7
	39,681,134	Other devices, appliances, and instruments	2.2
	38,009,394	Soya beans, whether or not broken	2.1
	36,289,072	Motor vehicles with a cylinder capacity exceeding 1,500 cc but not exceeding 3,000 cc	2.0
	28,264,372	Other oils	1.6
	23,059,443	Cathodes and sections of cathodes	1.3
	19,966,553	Airplanes and other aircraft, of an unladen weight exceeding 15,000 kg	1.1
	19,775,885	Bituminous coal	1.1

Source: UN Comtrade.

dise trade, the country consistently runs a significant deficit in trade in services, estimated at about $90 billion in 2012. Notwithstanding significant liberalization following World Trade Organization (WTO) accession, China is still a difficult market to penetrate, as many upstream industries and service sectors are strategically controlled by state-owned enterprises (SOEs) or are difficult to enter because of tariffs and the

TABLE 7-2
China's Top Trading Partners, 2013

	Exports/Imports	Total (US$ thousands)	Share (percent)
EXPORTS	Hong Kong	$384,876,899	17.4
	United States	369,006,713	16.7
	European Union	339,273,554	15.3
	Japan	149,912,337	6.8
	Korea	91,174,355	4.1
IMPORTS	European Union	$219,726,030	11.3
	Korea	182,881,542	9.4
	Japan	162,219,410	8.3
	United States	146,979,147	7.5
	Australia	91,558,190	4.7

Source: UN Comtrade.

regulatory environment, including "buy national" policies.[38] Millennia-old cultural barriers are sometimes also an issue for Western exporters. Overall, in 2008 the OECD's Product Market Regulation Index put China at 3.17, compared to 1.11 for the United States.[39]

China has more than twenty regional trade agreements (RTAs), mostly clustered in Asia. In Latin America, Chile, Costa Rica, and Peru have signed free trade agreements (FTAs) with China. They are comprehensive in goods trade, covering more or less 7,000 products with maximum liberalization horizons of ten, fifteen, and sixteen years, respectively.[40] Being an export juggernaut, China traditionally has run large trade surpluses. However, recent strategic goals include a "rebalancing" of the economy's growth away from investment and exports to more domestic consumption, opening up the service sector, and strategic technological development that aims to accelerate upgrading of production and exports. Environmental protection now also gains a high profile.[41]

India

India's merchandise exports are much less intensive in manufactured products than China's and much more intensive in natural resources (figure 7-2). Its top ten exports also account for a much larger share of total exports (41 percent) than China's top ten exports. India's top ten

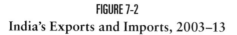

FIGURE 7-2
India's Exports and Imports, 2003–13

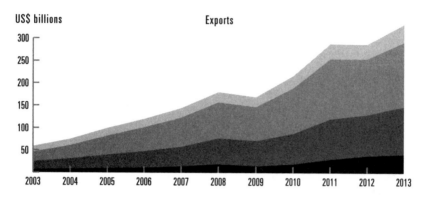

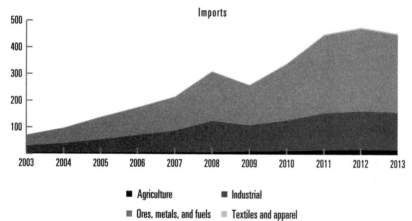

■ Agriculture   ■ Industrial
■ Ores, metals, and fuels   ▪ Textiles and apparel

Source: UN Comtrade.

imports account for more than half of total imports and are dominated by natural resources, especially petroleum-related products (table 7-3). India's main markets for merchandise exports are the United States and the United Arab Emirates (UAE), while China and the Middle Eastern states of Saudi Arabia and the UAE, largely because of the petroleum trade, stand out as the most important sources of imports (table 7-4). Preliminary figures indicate that, in 2013, India's services trade was in surplus by $65 billion, owing almost entirely to software exports.[42] However, the surplus was not sufficiently large to compensate for the large deficit in goods trade.

Among India's recent stated objectives for its industrial policy is the promotion of employment-intensive manufacturing and exports, including

TABLE 7-3
India's Top Export and Import Products, 2013

	Amount (US$ thousands)	Product description	Share (percent)
EXPORTS	46,973,477	Other petroleum oils	14.2
	27,084,559	Diamonds, other	8.2
	19,765,201	Light oils and preparations	6.0
	9,572,682	Articles of jewelry of precious metals	2.9
	8,375,464	Other medicaments	2.5
	7,754,818	Semi-milled or wholly milled rice, whether or not polished or glazed	2.3
	4,513,411	Cotton, not carded or combed	1.4
	4,410,700	Bovine meat, boneless	1.3
	3,540,087	Motor vehicles with cylinder capacity between 1,000 cc and 1,500 cc	1.1
	2,860,253	Oilcake and other solid residues, from the extraction of soybean oil	0.9
IMPORTS	148,046,659	Petroleum oils and oils obtained from bituminous minerals, crude	31.8
	34,388,815	Other unwrought forms, base metals	7.4
	15,386,950	Diamonds, unworked or simply sawn, cleaved or bruted	3.3
	14,571,854	Other coal	3.1
	8,311,492	Natural gas	1.8
	7,443,378	Copper ores and concentrates	1.6
	7,136,329	Other diamonds	1.5
	5,962,984	Transmission apparatus incorporating reception apparatus	1.3
	4,884,715	Crude oil	1.0
	4,177,563	Unwrought silver	0.9

Source: UN Comtrade.

the development of backward linkages to export sectors to reduce imports. Technological upgrading of exports is also highlighted, with an interesting focus on entirely new emerging industries in the global economy.[43] India's more extensive tariff-reducing regional trade agreements are concentrated in Asia.[44] In Latin America, India has regional trade agreements only with Chile and the Mercosur regional pact countries (Argentina, Brazil, Paraguay, Uruguay, and Venezuela). The agreements are for goods only and are of relatively limited scope, in contrast to the

TABLE 7-4
India's Top Trading Partners, 2013

Exports/Imports		Total (US$ thousands)	Share (percent)
EXPORTS	United States	41,956,732	12.5
	United Arab Emirates	33,980,431	10.1
	China	16,416,825	4.9
	Singapore	14,189,022	4.2
	Hong Kong	13,666,555	4.1
IMPORTS	China	51,635,444	11.1
	Saudi Arabia	36,596,585	7.9
	United Arab Emirates	32,964,585	7.1
	Switzerland	24,659,313	5.3
	United States	22,600,341	4.8

Source: UN Comtrade.

aforementioned Chinese agreements. In the case of Chile, the agreement covers slightly fewer than 300 products; for Mercosur, the count is 450 products.

Finally, India is also a difficult market to penetrate. Average tariffs are relatively high, and additional duties often apply. The country also has an extensive list of import licensing.[45] A millennia-old culture and twenty-two official languages pose a challenge for traders and investors. The OECD's Product Market Regulation Index put India at 3.40—even higher than China. But India has the advantage that, notwithstanding the importance of state enterprises, most business is oriented to the private sector, while English is an official language and of common use in commerce. It remains to be seen what reforms the new pro-business prime minister, Narendra Modi, will undertake.

South America

The value of the subregion's merchandise exports expanded threefold between 2003 and 2013, while imports rose nearly fivefold (figure 7-3). Exports are very much dominated by natural resources, with a high profile for petroleum oils, while imports are dominated by manufactured goods. The top ten exports—all natural resource–based—accounted for

FIGURE 7-3

South America's Exports and Imports, 2003–13

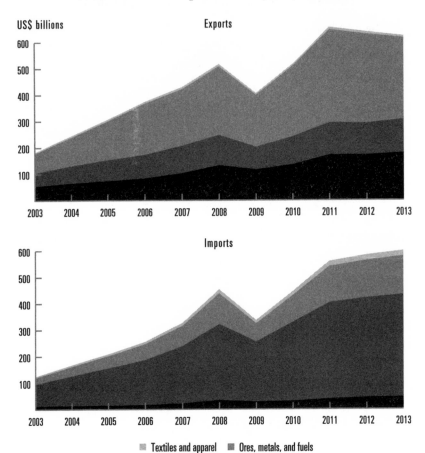

Source: UN Comtrade.

almost 50 percent of total merchandise exports, reflecting an important concentration. The top ten imports—representing only 22 percent of the total—are dominated by energy-related trade and automobiles (table 7-5). Excluding intra-South America trade, the major export markets are the United States, China, the EU, and India, in that order, while the top three import markets are also the top three export markets (table 7-6). South America's services exports amounted to nearly

TABLE 7-5

South America's Top Export and Import Products, 2013

	Amount (US$ thousands)	Product description	Share (percent)
EXPORTS	115,932,997	Petroleum oils and oils obtained from bituminous minerals, crude	18.6
	31,561,298	Soya beans, whether or not broken	5.1
	28,573,980	Iron ore, non-agglomerated	4.6
	27,644,767	Copper ores and concentrates	4.4
	21,626,894	Other petroleum oils	3.5
	21,596,863	Refined copper cathodes	3.5
	18,983,413	Oilcake and other solid residues from the extraction of soya bean oil	3.0
	15,117,109	Gold, other unwrought forms	2.4
	12,364,492	Maize, other	2.0
	9,546,149	Cane sugar	1.5
IMPORTS	36,966,555	Other petroleum oils	6.2
	27,759,280	Petroleum oils and oils obtained from bituminous minerals, crude	4.6
	16,342,067	Motor vehicles with cylinder capacity between 1,500 cc and 3,000 cc	2.7
	13,086,818	Light oils and preparations	2.2
	7,491,696	Other medicaments	1.2
	7,425,873	Natural gas	1.2
	6,059,105	Transmission apparatus incorporating reception apparatus	1.0
	5,765,724	Other natural gas	1.0
	5,496,216	Parts of electrical apparatus	0.9
	5,422,049	Digital electric integrated circuits	0.9

Source: UN Comtrade.

$88 billion in 2013, while imports were $162 billion. The main drivers of this trade deficit in services were large imports of travel, transport, and business services.

Most of the economies in the subregion are quite open to trade, although Mercosur is a very imperfect common market that also has had protectionist instincts. Peru, Chile, and Colombia have an extensive array of regional trade agreements, including agreements with the large markets of the United States, the EU, and China (except Colombia).[46] Chile and Peru are partners in the negotiations to create the Trans-Pacific

TABLE 7-6
South America's Top Trading Partners, 2013

Exports/Imports	Total (US$ thousands)	Share (percent)
EXPORTS		
United States	122,540,806	20.4
China	109,868,350	18.3
European Union	96,386,218	16.0
Brazil	32,094,711	5.3
India	28,584,370	4.7
IMPORTS		
United States	111,531,404	21.3
European Union	105,023,077	20.1
China	84,343,364	16.1
Brazil	41,312,542	7.9
Argentina	29,490,481	5.6

Source: UN Comtrade.

Partnership (TPP), a mega-international trade agreement.[47] Chile, Colombia, and Peru are also members of the Pacific Alliance aiming at very deep integration of their economies and development cooperation.[48] Mercosur has been attempting to negotiate a regional agreement with the EU for many years, with little success so far. For a more detailed analysis of the main regional trade schemes, see chapter 2.

Mexico–Central America–Dominican Republic

The subregion's exports expanded twofold between 2003 and 2013, while imports increased by a comparable amount. This subregion's exports and imports are dominated by trade in manufactures, and even more so if largely Mexican petroleum trade is excluded. The aforementioned maquila processing underpins much of the trade in manufactures. Excluding petroleum and gold, the top exports and imports are all manufactured goods (figure 7-4 and table 7-7). The subregion's exports are very North America-centric, followed at great distance by the EU. Along with China, these two regions are also the major sources of imports (table 7-8). In terms of services, the subregion saw a slight trade surplus of around $360,000 in 2013, although the composition of exports and imports differs. Tourism clearly drives exports, accounting for nearly 60 percent of the total for 2013, while the largest services imports are in the transportation sector.

FIGURE 7-4

Mexico–Central America–Dominican Republic Subregion Exports and Imports, 2003–13

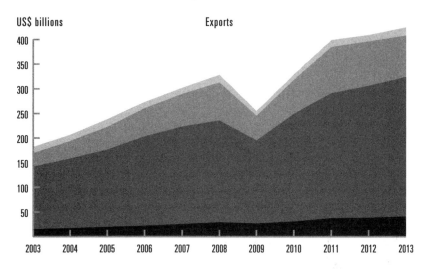

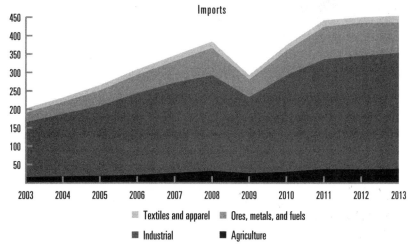

▨ Textiles and apparel   ▨ Ores, metals, and fuels
■ Industrial   ■ Agriculture

Source: UN Comtrade.

The Mexico–Central America–DR subregion is very open to trade. Central America has an incomplete common market arrangement. The subregion also has an extensive array of FTAs, including very comprehensive ones with the United States, Canada, and the EU.[49] Mexico also is part of the aforementioned TPP and the Pacific Alliance.

TABLE 7-7
Mexico, Central America, and Dominican Republic's
Top Export and Import Products, 2013

	Amount (US$ thousands)	Production description	Share (percent)
EXPORTS	43,081,113	Petroleum oils and oils obtained from bituminous minerals, crude	10.3
	22,767,345	Motor vehicles with a cylinder between 1,500 cc and 3,000 cc	5.4
	15,957,209	Reception apparatus for color television	3.8
	11,513,437	Motor vehicles for transport of goods, g.v.w. not exceeding 5 tonnes	2.7
	7,250,052	Other electrical apparatus, for telephone line systems or digital line systems	1.7
	6,966,015	Ignition wiring sets and other wiring sets of a kind used in vehicles, aircraft, or ships	1.7
	6,701,348	Other automatic data processing machine systems	1.6
	5,651,746	Gold, other unwrought forms	1.3
	5,485,781	Parts of electrical apparatus for telephony	1.3
	5,404,634	Other parts and accessories of motor vehicles	1.3
IMPORTS	22,744,058	Light oils and preparations	4.9
	14,997,477	Digital integrated circuits	3.2
	14,629,427	Other petroleum oils	3.2
	9,303,356	Other parts of electrical machinery	2.0
	8,560,925	Transmission apparatus incorporating reception apparatus	1.8
	5,983,153	Motor vehicles with a cylinder between 1,500 cc and 3,000 cc	1.3
	5,602,549	Parts and accessories of automatic data processing machines	1.2
	4,550,633	Other medicaments	1.0
	4,417,691	Other parts and accessories of motor vehicles	1.0
	4,293,494	Parts of electrical apparatus for line telephony	0.9

Source: UN Comtrade.

INDIA/CHINA–LATIN AMERICA BILATERAL TRADE PATTERNS

China and India may be the world economy's two emerging giants, but bilateral trade relations with Latin America have followed different paths. In the better-known case of China, trade took off in 2002 and continues to be one of the region's most dynamic trade relationships,

TABLE 7-8
Mexico, Central America, and Dominican Republic's
Top Trading Partners, 2013

Exports/Imports		Total (US$ thousands)	Share (percent)
EXPORTS	United States	314,697,397	67.2
	European Union	33,042,677	7.1
	Canada	28,847,357	6.2
	China	15,840,110	3.4
	Brazil	6,320,028	1.4
IMPORTS	United States	218,926,528	52.4
	China	45,250,741	10.8
	European Union	45,213,768	10.8
	Japan	20,825,872	5.0
	Korea	14,488,097	3.5

Source: UN Comtrade.

driven by China's demand for natural resources and the region's readiness to absorb low-cost final goods and inputs from Chinese manufacturers. India, by contrast, remains a sleeping giant from the perspective of the region's trade, although trade flows to date suggest a similar commodities-for-manufactures pattern is at play.

Latin America–China Trade

The dynamism of the Latin America–China trade since 2002 has been much discussed, and for good reason. Trade increased at an annual average rate of 27 percent between 2003 and 2013, reaching $289 billion that year. However, the Sino–Latin American story is really a tale of two subregions. For natural resources–rich South America, Chinese demand for metals, fuel, and basic agricultural commodities has driven an export boom. Countries such as Chile, Peru, and Venezuela—with strong commodity-exporting sectors and relatively small domestic manufacturing bases—have, in fact, accumulated trade surpluses with China since 2000. In Argentina and Brazil, the two South American countries with the most significant manufacturing base, the commodity-boom dividend has been tempered by stiff competition for domestic firms, as consumers and firms in these markets have readily adopted Chinese products.

FIGURE 7-5
South American and Central American–Mexican–DR
Trade with China and India

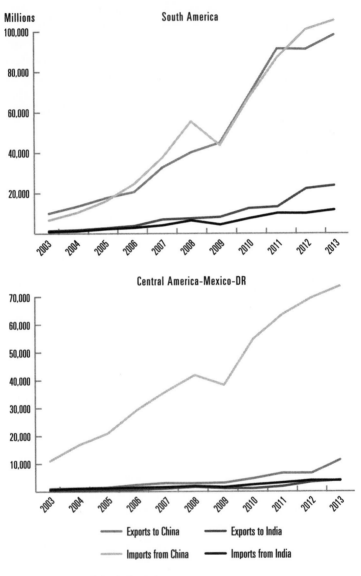

Source: IMF Direction of Trade Statistics.

Further north, the impact of China has been less salutary. The Mexico–Central America–DR subregion witnessed a major influx of Chinese manufacturing goods and industrial inputs, which have displaced domestic producers in these manufacturing-intensive economies. With little to gain from Chinese demand for commodities, the subregion built up large trade deficits with China. As figure 7-5 shows, trade with China consists almost entirely of imports. In fact, Mexico alone absorbed a full 37 percent of all Chinese imports to Latin America, making it a major contributor to Latin America's much-discussed trade deficit with China, which has accumulated to over $27 billion since 2000. Most of the trade is interindustry.

Even within these subregions, the emergence of China has not affected all countries equally. While China's share of Latin American countries' exports and imports has risen across the board since 2003, the cases of Brazil, Chile, Peru, and Uruguay stand out. China now accounts for between 17 and 25 percent of these countries' exports, and for 15–20 percent of imports. By contrast, for other South American countries, such as Bolivia, Ecuador, and Paraguay, China is the destination of less than 3 percent of total exports (although China is a considerable source of imports for these countries). By the same token, a few countries in the region dominate total trade with China. Brazil and Chile together account for 60 percent of the region's exports to China, while Mexico, as mentioned, has absorbed 37 percent of Chinese imports and Brazil another 23 percent.

Latin America–India Trade

Trade with India, by contrast, has yet to reach a critical mass. Though growth has been fast—17 percent per year on average since 2003—total trade reached only $43 billion in 2013, about 15 percent of the region's trade with China. As of 2013, no country in the region can count India as a major trading partner, except Venezuela and perhaps Colombia. A series of agreements to sell oil beginning in 2008 has made India an important market for Venezuela's main export product. India accounted for 16 percent of Venezuelan exports in 2013, while absorbing 5 percent of Colombian exports, mostly coal. Likewise, the region's trade with India is dominated by a few countries. These patterns largely reflect complementarity of resource endowments, although they are particularly sensitive to large irregular commodities sales. As alluded to above, Venezuela made up nearly half of the region's exports to India in 2013 (compared with 0.2 percent in 2002). Mexico and Colombia account for

FIGURE 7-6

A. LAC Exports to China and India, 2003–13

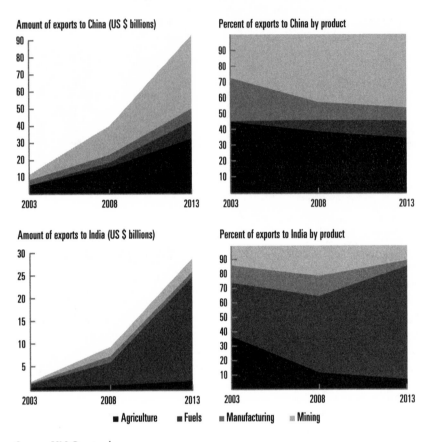

Source: UN Comtrade.

an additional 17 and 10 percent each, driven by petroleum and coal, respectively. Imports from India, not surprisingly, are concentrated in the region's largest markets, Brazil and Mexico, which absorbed 45 and 20 percent, respectively, of the 2013 total. Brazil's share is still disproportionate to its size relative to the region and may partly reflect deeper diplomatic engagement and cooperation in the context of the BRICS and IBSA initiatives.[50]

The combination of significant commodities exports from Latin America to India and relatively little penetration (to date) of Latin American markets by Indian exporters translates into a trade surplus with India for the region. Exports to India since 2000 exceeded imports

FIGURE 7-6
B. LAC Intraregional Exports and Exports to the United States

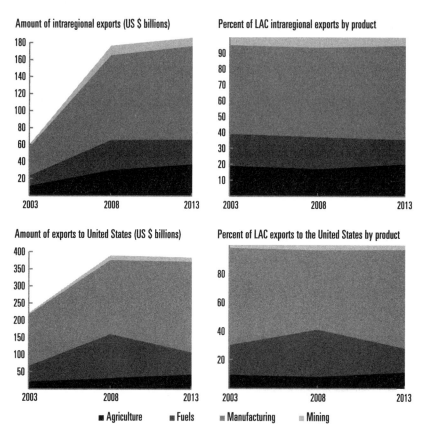

Amount of intraregional exports (US $ billions)

Percent of LAC intraregional exports by product

Amount of exports to United States (US $ billions)

Percent of LAC exports to the United States by product

■ Agriculture   ■ Fuels   ■ Manufacturing   ▦ Mining

Source: UN Comtrade.

by $42 billion, an outcome that largely resulted from a strong jump in commodity exports from a handful of South American countries since 2009. Meanwhile, the Mexico–Central America–DR subregion has had consistent trade deficits with India.

Bilateral Trade Patterns

Sino–Latin American trade has epitomized the "typical" pattern of Latin American trade with Asia. A full 70 percent of Latin American exports to China consist of minerals, fuels, and agricultural commodities. As figure 7-6 shows, this trend has only accelerated over the course of the Sino–Latin American trade boom, with the share of minerals and fuels gaining ground since 2003 at the expense of manufactures. Another (related) feature of the region's export performance in China is its high concentration in a handful of commodities. Taken as a whole, the region's top five export products—a familiar list consisting of soya beans, petroleum, iron ore, copper ore, and copper cathodes—made up a combined 75 percent of total exports to China in 2013. Central America and Mexico's exports to China are somewhat distinct. They are less concentrated—the top five products accounted for 53 percent of the 2013 total, and automobile are the second-largest export product, accounting for 15 percent of the total. Of the top ten export products from the subregion, four are manufactured goods. Mexico, which accounts for 91 percent of the subregion's total, is driving this result, although Costa Rica exports a significant quantity of digital electronic equipment, a result of its vibrant information technology (IT) sector.

The region's trade relationship with India displays this general pattern of trade, although its exports to India are dominated by fuels, which made up 78 percent of the total in 2013, as opposed to trade with China where there are a number of export commodities. This is true of both subregions within Latin America, although South America accounted for a full 86 percent of the region's exports to India in 2013. On the import side, India, like China, is mainly a source of manufactured products. However, India's manufacturing sector is small—despite its potential to mobilize a large low-cost labor force—and the region has not experienced a major influx of Indian manufactures. Overall, imports from India reached only $15 billion in 2013, 63 percent of which were manufactured products. While one sees in India the broad outline of a commodities-for-manufactures pattern, overall trade is still highly responsive to one-off natural resource deals. Hence, to some degree, the contours of Indo–Latin American trade have yet to be fully defined.

The discussion so far has been limited to merchandise trade, but services represent an increasingly important component of global trade. Services are now the most dynamic sector of the global economy and also provide crucial inputs for most goods. Trade in services, however, has traditionally been overlooked by economists, partly owing to the difficulty of measuring the flow of services across borders and partly to the belief of many that manufacturing is the major driver of technology, learning, and innovation that provides platforms for high-valued services.[51] While data limitations continue to complicate analysis of trade in services, a brief glance at the numbers that are available confirms that trade in services has taken on growing importance for the economies of Latin America, China, and India. India, in particular, has developed a world-class service sector in areas such as IT outsourcing and business process outsourcing (BPO). This success is evident in its services exports, which grew from $38 billion in 2004 to $151 billion in 2013. Computer and information services and other business services have accounted for around two-thirds of India's service exports over the past decade.

As previously mentioned, China's service sector is relatively inefficient and the country is a large net importer of services. In addition, China's demand for services is expected to grow at a faster rate than the overall economy in the medium term, leading some analysts to see a market opportunity for Latin American services exports. While the data do not allow for a direct analysis of the bilateral services trade, this potential is addressed later on in the chapter.

For several years now, Latin American countries have worried about the impact of slower growth in China on their economies. While we cannot predict the future, China has continued to be a dynamic export market for the region despite slower growth since 2011. The rate of growth of exports to China since the first quarter of 2010 (92 percent) has outpaced that of exports to the rest of the world, which only grew 30 percent. As table 7-9 shows, the period between the first quarter of 2010 and the first quarter of 2014 saw particularly dynamic export growth from the Mexico–Central America–DR subregion to China, which increased more than threefold. In India, the region also saw its exports grow much faster than overall exports, at 93 percent since the first quarter of 2010. Again, the subregional patterns tell completely different stories—South American exports took off during this period, more than doubling, while the Mexico–Central America–DR subregion surprisingly saw only 24 percent export growth to India, below the subregion's overall trade performance.

INDIA, CHINA, AND LAC MANUFACTURING EXPORTS TO THE UNITED STATES

One major implication of the rise of China as a global economic power has been increasing competition in third markets. This indirect effect has been especially relevant for countries such as Mexico that export similar products as China and depend heavily on the U.S. market, where China has made major inroads. As figure 7-7 confirms, China has indeed been a formidable competitor in the United States and Europe, the region's traditional export markets. China accounted for a full 25 percent of U.S. manufacturing imports in 2013, up from less than

TABLE 7-9

Growth of Exports, Q1 2010–Q1 2014

(US$)

Exporter

	Central America and Mexico			South America		
	Q1 2010	Q1 2014	Percent change	Q1 2010	Q1 2014	Percent change
China	829,850,634	2,672,944,159	222.1[a]	11,841,537,787	21,688,584,290	82.3
India	496,360,734	615,405,672	24.0	3,071,474,919	6,262,066,003	103.9
Rest of world	73,693,642,899	104,039,934,086	41.2	94,284,883,959	113,928,086,094	20.8

Source: UN Comtrade.

a. Excluding Costa Rica, only 118.5 percent.

FIGURE 7-7
China, India, and LAC Share of U.S. Manufactures Imports, 1998–2013

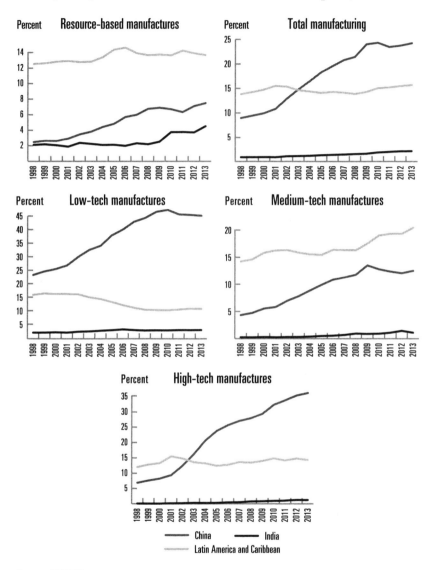

Source: USITC.

10 percent in 1998.[52] Latin America, meanwhile, has seen its share hover around 15 percent during that period, with Mexico alone contributing around 10 percent. It is highly probable that competition from Chinese products in the U.S. market is partly responsible for the region's disappointing performance; indeed, recent analysis has shown the

region's export products to be under "direct threat" from growing Chinese imports.[53]

At the same time, there is some evidence that the nature of China's competitive challenge is evolving. Its share of low-technology manufactures in the U.S. market has fallen off in recent years, albeit from a remarkable peak of 47 percent in 2010. Meanwhile its share of high-technology manufactures continues to rise apace, consistent with a story of China moving up to higher-value-added activities in value chains and potentially squeezing opportunities for more advanced Latin American manufacturers.[54]

India, by contrast, has yet to emerge as a relevant competitor in the United States. It has seen some gain in resource-based manufactures since 2008 but still lags well behind Latin American producers in this area.

CHINA AND INDIA: CAN LATIN AMERICA UPGRADE THE BILATERAL TRADE RELATIONSHIP?

Export diversification and upgrading can be tools to promote the sustained growth and economic transformation that Latin America lacks, especially in a global trade environment characterized by cross-border production in manufacturing. However, the region's trade with China is heavily weighted toward classic interindustry trade, which has reinforced static comparative advantages, especially in natural resource–based export activities. The share of natural resource products in the region's exports to China and India has only increased since the global recession of 2008–09. To the extent that diversifying and upgrading the region's export basket are desirable objectives for the region's industrial policy—and this chapter posits that they are—policymakers in the region need to ask themselves two sets of questions.

First, does the potential exist for Latin America to develop more diverse economic relationships with China and India? If so, how can countries take steps in that direction? Are the most important policy measures in the realm of promotion of productivity growth generally, or should efforts in this area be more targeted, based on informed judgments of potential success for competing with these two giants and penetrating new markets there? What is the role for trade promotion and direct trade negotiations (either bilateral or part of a regional grouping) in creating new opportunities in China and India? Second, and perhaps more important, policymakers need to ask how China and India fit in the broader context of global trade priorities. Even if satisfactory answers are available for the above questions, strategically it may still be the case that the best opportunities to generate trade patterns that allow for diversification, upgrading, and dynamic productivity gains lie in other markets.

Answering the first question requires us to peer into the future and speculate on how Latin American trade with China and India may evolve. While doing so may be risky, insofar as Latin America–Asia trade was barely on the agenda a mere decade ago, and post–global recession trends are still to be defined, the following points are important considerations. First, the general commodity-for-manufactures pattern in the bilateral relations will be hard to reverse because of disproportionate resource endowments, with China and India very abundant in labor and scarce in natural resources, whereas most of Latin America is just the opposite. In addition, growth of demand from China and India for the products that have driven the trade relationship to date, while possibly less robust, should nevertheless remain relatively strong well into the future if those countries' consumption patterns follow the trajectories of more developed countries.[55] Moreover, China's prowess in manufacturing, the peeling off of low-wage segments of manufacturing by Asian neighbors as China upgrades, and India's strategy to prioritize growth of low-wage, employment-creating manufacturing for export, coupled with entrance into new short-technological-cycle industries, all create more resistance to using these markets for upgrading the region's exports. Thus, much of the existing pattern of trade may prove to be sticky. The silver lining is that there still seems to be time to exploit the income from Asian-driven demand for natural resources to finance economic strategies at home for upgrading.[56]

The potential channels for diversifying the region's trade with China and India face a host of obstacles. First, although pursuing more free trade areas with China, coupled with rising wages in that country, could possibly open up opportunities for Latin American firms to enter East Asian manufacturing value chains, this will be very difficult to achieve in practice. Incumbency, established trade patterns, geography, and the fact that China's size and diverse endowments may allow it to hold on to many old positions in value chains while simultaneously moving up them,[57] all militate against the region's participation in Asian value chains. Moreover, the region's poor infrastructure exacerbates the problem of distance, creating another major obstacle to the region's entry into Asian production networks.[58] While a small number of LAC firms have used direct investment in China as an entrée into Asian value chains, the universe of firms in the region with the resources and capabilities to pursue such a strategy remains small.[59]

Second, while shifts in China's growth model will raise import elasticities and generate more demand for imports in new areas, the region's ability to take advantage of these opportunities is far from certain. China's anticipated transition to more consumption-driven growth has led observers to suggest that new demand for Latin American exports could arise in two particular areas. The first is in consumer goods, where a combination of rising wages and a growing urban middle class should lead to increased demand for products such as processed foods, wine, snacks, and higher-priced meat products. This group of products does represent an area where Latin America could enjoy a comparative advantage based on its advanced agribusiness firms, and indeed, there have been some success stories. However, tariffs are high in China (and India), as can been seen in tables 7-10 and 7-11. The region's exports of more processed, higher-value-added agricultural goods also face a host of other obstacles, including tariff escalation, in which more processed products are subject to a higher tariff rate, nontariff barriers arising from cumbersome approval processes for food imports, and the challenge of lengthy shipping times for products where in-time delivery is a priority. In addition, Latin American firms aiming to meet growing demand from the Chinese middle-class consumer will have to contend with a highly competitive field of multinationals that enjoy the advantage of a direct presence in China.

The prospect for addressing the aforementioned tariff and nontariff barriers through further trade agreements between Latin America and the Asian partners, moreover, appears limited. China, as discussed, has FTAs with Chile, Costa Rica, and Peru—all small, open economies that absorb a negligible share of China's total exports to the region and whose exports to China are of little consequence for competition in the domestic market. The politics of these agreements were particularly auspicious, with China willing to accept restrictions on imports of "sensitive" products that its negotiators would be unwilling to grant to larger countries such as Argentina, Brazil, or Mexico.[60] Moreover, negotiations could be onerous (for example, it took Australia a decade to negotiate its recent FTA). In the case of India, the outlook is even dimmer, unless the Modi government can overcome important political obstacles to much-needed economic reforms. Existing agreements with Chile and Mercosur are quite limited in their coverage of goods and the extent of liberalization, as seen by the still high average tariffs facing

TABLE 7-10

Tariffs Imposed by China on Selected Countries, 2011

Percent

Country	Agriculture	Materials Industrial	Ores and metals
Brazil	14.0	5.2	0.6
Chile	3.6	0.4	0.0
Mexico	5.1	4.5	0.9

Source: TRAINS.

TABLE 7-11

Tariffs Imposed by India on Selected Countries, 2011

Percent

Country	Agriculture	Materials Industrial	Ores and metals
Brazil	26.7	4.6	1.2
Chile	24.6	2.5	3.2
Mexico	18.8	3.4	0.7

Source: TRAINS.

exporters from Brazil and Chile (see table 7-11). In any event, while neither market can be ignored, unless there is a strong reversal of current policy, a major turnaround in prospects on this front will be especially challenging.

Another area where the Chinese market should see considerable demand growth is in services. As mentioned earlier, China faces a "deficit" in the service sector, as its domestic services are relatively inefficient, while demand for services is expected to experience fast growth of around 7 or 8 percent over the next two decades.[61] Indeed, both China and India (despite the latter's strengths, especially in IT and BPO services) have seen services imports grow dramatically over the past decade, from $21 billion to $128 billion in the case of India and from $47 to $330 billion for China.

Before concluding that China and India represent fertile markets for Latin American services exports, we need to look more closely at where demand is strongest and whether firms from the region have the capability to meet that demand. Services encompass a wide variety of economic activities, and Latin America has had some recent success in exporting services.[62] However, these experiences may not necessarily translate to the Chinese market.

For China, the largest component of services imports has been in travel. Here, there is conceivably an opportunity for the region to attract more tourism as Chinese travelers could become increasingly interested in the region. A number of years ago, the Inter-American Development Bank (IDB) identified tourism as a potential new export market for the region.[63] In 2013, China had 97 million outward trips, of which half were for tourism.[64] Moreover, official China in 2014 estimated that 500 million Chinese tourists would travel abroad over the next five years.[65] However, success in attracting Chinese tourists requires structural adaptation to the special cultural demands of the Chinese market (such as dining, language, and easy access to high-end or exotic shopping), facilitation or waiver of visas, a more dedicated air transport infrastructure, effective promotion that highlights attractions that can compete for attention with the traditional first overseas vacation choices of Europe and the United States, and in some cases better security.

Some Latin American countries, such as Chile, have creative retail service sectors that cater to low-income budgets and hence could possibly find niche service export opportunities to retailers in China and India; however, the challenges may be daunting.[66] And as Chinese and Indian firms penetrate Latin American markets through trade and investment in intermediate and consumer goods, there may be opportunities to export business, technical, and professional (BTP) services to them by exploiting regional knowledge, time zones, and language. Spanish and Portuguese language services for Chinese and Indian multinational firms also could become a growing opportunity, as could design services given an emerging middle class in China and India that will be ever more attuned to the cultural motifs of globalization. Moreover, their firms with trade and investment in the Americas will need to appeal to the tastes of local consumers (as well as the Hispanic diaspora in North America). Even in IT, there may be niche opportunities to sell services to Chinese and Indian firms with interests in the Latin America market. But as recent studies point out, the region's potential in service exports will be in the low-end activities until the region's relatively limited supply of knowledge-based skill sets (in engineering, science, and technology) is successfully addressed.[67] Another area where Latin American firms may have a chance to gain market share in China is in financial services, where the region has a number of top firms, especially from Brazil, with experience in China. While financial services imports have been limited, the anticipated opening of China's cross-border capital accounts could create a dynamic scenario in the future.

LOOKING CLOSER TO HOME

The next strategic question is how China and India fit into the big picture. This chapter has pointed out some opportunities to obtain more development "bang" out of the existing bilateral trade relations. But it also points out that it will be difficult to markedly change the pattern given the nature of these economies, the respective strong complementarity of their comparative advantages, and other obstacles. This scenario suggests that the region's "business plan" should perhaps look closer to home for export markets in which trade can more easily be a handmaiden for capability building, diversification, and upgrading. Moreover, success on this front would strengthen capabilities to penetrate markets worldwide, including China and India.

In fact, the region's trade with the rest of the world already elicits markedly different and more favorable patterns than its trade with China and India. Latin America also has in place a broad and deep network of formal integration agreements with North America, Europe, and within the region itself. By developing a trade strategy that privileges these markets, the region can build on existing strengths.

The Regional Market

Closest to home is the Latin American regional market. As pointed out and well documented by the UN Economic Commission for Latin America and the Caribbean (ECLAC), regional trade is laden with characteristics that suggest it can be a driver of dynamic structural change:

- The Latin American market absorbs by far the largest number of the region's export products, indicating it is a vehicle for diversification.

- For many countries in the region, it is the major market for the export of medium- and high-tech manufactured products.

- Intraregional trade is intensive in intra-industry trade, which is conducive to gaining economies of scale, technological spillovers, and the development of incipient regional value chains, such as in textiles and apparel, medicine, chemicals, and auto parts.

- The regional market has the largest number of participating export firms, many of which are small and medium-sized enterprises.

- The regional market has given birth to "multilatinas," large Latin American firms with important cross-border direct investments in the region and increasingly in the world.[68]

The numbers bear this out. Trade within Latin America is heavily weighted toward manufactured products, which made up 59 percent of intraregional exports in Latin America in 2013, up from 55 percent in 2003. The dynamics of the subregions are also interesting. While exports within and between the two subregions—South America and Mexico–Central America–DR—all have manufactures as their largest share, Central America's and Mexico's exports to South America stand out, with 84 percent in manufactures. At the other end of the spectrum is trade within South America, which is more diversified among manufacturing (55 percent), agriculture (21 percent), and fuels (17 percent).[69]

Notwithstanding these positive characteristics, intraregional trade's share of Latin America's total trade has remained at around 20 percent since the early 1990s, considerably lower than for other principal economic regions of the world. Meanwhile, countries such as Argentina, Brazil, Paraguay, and Uruguay have seen intraregional shares of total exports decline since 2000, despite their participation in Mercosur. Even a proliferation of intra–Latin America FTAs over the past decade and a half has failed to catalyze intraregional trade. These agreements increased exports by only 18 percent, compared with 47 percent for the region's total FTAs.[70] Moreover, most of the manufactured goods trade is in final goods (90 percent), as opposed to the high representation of intermediate goods found in intra–East Asia trade (34 percent), which is laden with value chains.[71]

The limited intraregional trade and low profile of intermediate goods do not seem to be related to tariffs as such because all countries have gone through stages of unilateral and multilateral liberalization, while most regional agreements and bilateral free trade areas have further sharply reduced these barriers.[72] Indeed, many of the agreements have modern trade disciplines.[73] Some of the problems pointed out by ECLAC are exceptions in liberalization schedules, the lack of connectivity or convergence among the web of agreements in the region, technical barriers, a shortage of trade facilitation measures, and pockets of protection on third-party imported inputs. Another important area not yet mentioned is the rule of regional law: a number of the agreements (such as Mercosur) are subject to unpredictable policy behavior of the partners without clearly defined recourse, which discourages investments in segmented regional value chains. The lack of stable political leadership of regional initiatives is another shortcoming. Finally, targeted incentives to coax large multilatinas to lead regional supply chains is another ingredient in need of reinforcement.[74] ECLAC, interestingly, points out that if Brazil and Mexico could overcome their traditional rivalry and negotiate a comprehensive trade agreement, that could serve as a regional manufacturing hub which would draw in links with the other Latin American countries and be a catalyst for the development of regional value chains.[75]

As Roett details in chapter 2, there has been much talk in Latin America about regional integration since the days of independence, but advances over history have fallen far short of stated ambitions. Deepening regional integration is a goal well worth pursuing. As pointed out in a recent study, regional integration and cooperation is the only way Latin America will ever have a significant voice and economic and political weight in the a globalized world.[76]

North America

As figure 7-6 illustrates, the region's exports to the United States are dominated by manufactured products, which make up over two-thirds of total exports in 2013 and have consistently gained share since 2008.[77] Of course, most of these exports arise from value chains based in the NAFTA and CAFTA spaces. While the exports from these member countries to the United States are dominated by manufactures (79 percent of the total for 2013), for South America the figure is 20 percent. However, the South American figure, which reflects large petroleum exports from Venezuela, actually understates the importance of the United States as a market for manufactured goods from many South American countries. For Brazil, a full 62 percent of its $24.5 billion worth of exports to the United States were manufactured goods, while Argentina's U.S. exports consisted of 42 percent in manufactured goods. Hence, the United States continues to be an important market for South American manufactured products.[78]

Another feature of the region's trade with the United States that distinguishes it from trade with China or India is a relatively high share of intra-industry trade (IIT), often taken as a proxy for cross-border production chains. This is especially true in the case of the Mexico–Central America–DR subregion, whose IIT index with the United States was 0.42 in 2013 (see table 7-12), again reflecting that subregion's integration in North American value chains. Even for South America, however,

TABLE 7-12
Intra-Industry Trade Index, by Partner Country, 2013

Partner	Central America and Mexico	South America
China	0.11	0.03
India	0.08	0.04
European Union	0.32	0.20
South America	0.39	0.52
Central America and Mexico	0.71	0.39
United States	0.42	0.23

Source: UN Comtrade.

Note: Industries defined at three-digit SITC 2 categories; values weighted by trade flows.

an IIT index of 0.23 for trade with the United States is considerably higher than the IIT index for trade with China (0.03) or India (0.04). Trade of this type with the EU is also significant. These patterns also hold for some of South America's major commodity exporters, even when primary products are excluded (see table 7-13).

This trade platform is an underexploited opportunity. For one, trade flows with the United States have grown relatively slowly since 2008 compared with Latin America–Asia trade. The reasons for this are not hard to divine. China and India have continued to experience relatively fast growth in the half decade since the global recession, while North America (and Latin America itself) turned in middling growth performances over this period. However, with the U.S. market finally picking up steam since 2012 and outperforming that of many other industrialized countries, and with the Canadian market, which is not examined here, poised for fiscal stimulus, the region would be remiss to overlook this large source of demand close to home.

While trade with North America has generated important employment opportunities in the Mexico–Central America–DR subregion, domestic value-added tends to be low, while participation in value chains tends to be at the low-end segments of components production and assembly. This positioning minimizes growth effects in the economy, while remaining there makes the region vulnerable to low-wage competition from Asia and Africa. Moreover, upgrading is the only way for the region to avoid competing through compressed real wage levels. Restric-

TABLE 7-13

Intra-Industry Trade Index by Partner Country, Selected Countries, Excluding Primary Goods, 2013

Partner	Argentina	Brazil	Colombia
China	0.03	0.05	0.01
India	0.03	0.09	0.01
European Union	0.15	0.26	0.07
South America	0.60	0.48	0.42
Central America and Mexico	0.22	0.29	0.33
United States	0.18	0.33	0.12

Source: UN Comtrade.

Note: Industries defined at three-digit SITC 2 categories; values weighted by trade flows.

tions on adding value and moving up value chains are related to many factors: shortages of required skills, modern infrastructure and logistics networks, finance, entrepreneurial ambition, innovation effort, and flaws in existing industrial policies are just some of them.[79] The strategies of producers and distributors in the United States that lead value chains also are not entirely malleable and hence are a conditioning factor as well. However, U.S. trends in "reshoring" as a result of China's appreciating exchange rate and increasing wages may displace established suppliers and offer opportunities to attract value chain segments home to the region.

South America's exports of manufactured goods are only 21 percent of total exports.[80] This subregion is not well articulated with any global value chain (although Brazil has significant intra-industry trade with the United States).[81] The commodity boom, with the consequent exchange rate appreciation, has moreover accelerated the decline in manufacturing. This is damaging since, despite popular messaging about the alternative of services, manufacturing is still the major world platform of innovation, including in services. The prescription outlined earlier for building value-added around commodity exports to China and India is equally valid for North America. However, there could be greater prospects for expanding exports of non-resource-based manufactured exports because this market, while not bereft of important areas of protection, is generally more open and a global value chain hub. Moreover, automation is reducing dependence on low-wage labor, and proximity matters. If Mercosur could achieve comprehensive FTAs with the United

States and Mexico, that would be a way to energize investment in non-resource-based manufacturing and services and would open up more doors for participation in global value chains.[82]

Although exchange rate corrections were under way in 2014, there are many challenges to diversifying exports to North America, including the relatively specific technological domain of many dominant resource-based industries (which makes migration to new activities harder), infrastructure and logistics capabilities, weak innovation systems and innovation effort (except for Brazil), skill shortages in some of the countries, the up-to-now market-seeking bias of non-natural-resource-based FDI, and so on.

Finally, the TPP and the U.S.-EU Transatlantic Trade and Investment Partnership (TTIP) are huge mega-trade initiatives, the impact on the region of which is potentially large but still uncertain. The recently signed, but not ratified, TPP would undoubtedly affect the region's ability to upgrade and participate in value chains.[83] For the countries participating in the TPP—Chile, Mexico, and Peru—the agreement may open doors to Asian value chains and encourage FDI.[84] At the same time, the agreement risks further dividing the region between those countries that are integrated with global value chains and those that are not (primarily the Mercosur countries). We believe that our prescription to better integrate LAC itself is also the best way to mitigate this risk. The TTIP negotiations, meanwhile, face considerable political headwinds. If the agreements do come to fruition, preference erosion in the North American market is one potential outcome that the region would face. This complexity underscores the need to evaluate this major strategic issue at the detailed level of products and investments and to prepare a course of action.[85]

CONCLUSIONS: WHERE DO WE GO FROM HERE?

This chapter has argued that Latin America's trade-related industrial policies need more focused, disciplined, and effective strategies that can better underpin export diversification and upgrading. Without such strategies, international economic integration will not reach its potential as a driver of sustained growth for the region. The experience of the past decade underscores this point. Much of the region enjoyed a trade boom from 2003 to 2008 based on a commodities supercycle, favorable external financial conditions, and preferential access to some important markets. However, with prices for the region's main export commodities in decline since 2011, external pressures for adjustments in emerging markets after the end of quantitative easing in the United States, and continued trade preferences erosion, the region finds itself mired in a period of slow growth. Trade can be an important ingredient in the recipe for reviving investment and growth. However, trade's effects are undermined if the region continues to rely excessively on the easy rents from the commodity trade and on positioning in low-value-added segments of manufacturing/services value chains in preferential agreements with North America.

To break the existing pattern of trade that reinforces static comparative advantage, the region must move forward on two major (and interrelated) policy fronts. At the domestic level, countries need to deploy industrial policies to promote entrepreneurial experimentation, learning, and technological absorption that generates new knowledge capabilities that are invested in upgraded productive capacities and productivity growth. In the realm of trade-related industrial policy, Latin America should prioritize regional integration (including with North America), as this strategy holds the greatest potential for leveraging trade for export diversification and upgrading.[86]

Intraregional trade is characterized by greater product diversity, more manufacturing exports, and a higher share of intra-industry trade compared to trade with extraregional partners. At the same time, the performance of intraregional trade over the past two decades has been disappointing. Latin America has witnessed countless regional projects that failed to deliver real progress on integration, and the region should avoid reviving pipe dreams of a continent-wide FTA. Rather, the current scenario presents opportunities to take piecemeal steps toward a more integrated region. First, success in signing (mostly bilateral) intraregional FTAs over the past two decades has led to an unintended consequence in the form of overlapping and divergent regulatory regimes for different trading partners within the region—the so-called spaghetti bowl effect.[87] The existence of multiple trade rules, especially in the all-important area of rules of origin, tends to raise costs, divert trade flows, and critically impede the development of intraregional trade and regional value chains. Negotiations to achieve convergence in the rules embodied in current FTAs would go a long way toward creating a regulatory framework more conducive to intraregional trade and regional value chains without embarking on new agreements. And as mentioned earlier in this chapter, rules in regional agreements, reformed or otherwise, need to be enforced with transparency and consistency if cross-border trade and investment are to be encouraged.

Efforts at convergence are already under way in the aforementioned Pacific Alliance bloc, where member countries are working to harmonize the rules of origin and other disciplines contained in the existing bilateral agreements between members. The considerable progress of the Pacific Alliance, moreover, may encourage Mercosur, the other major subregional grouping in Latin America. In particular, Mercosur, which began in 1991 with intentions of evolving into an ambitious common market, has been plagued by protectionism and poor governance. The two blocs have at times been portrayed as occupying opposite ends of the spectrum on economic policy. However, there is great potential for the creation of a manufacturing hub and new value chains from closer ties if Mercosur's dysfunctional behavior does not spill over to the Pacific Alliance. Recent diplomatic and political stirrings suggest the time may be ripe for a rapprochement. In late 2014, Mercosur and Pacific Alliance foreign ministers met for the first time and agreed to explore opportunities for cooperation to expand trade. Positive trade outcomes will depend to a large extent on leadership from Brazil, although the recent transition in Argentina, to a pro-trade government under Mauricio Macri, would also help.

In terms of integration agreements between Latin America and the United States, a barrier to a preferential trade agreement between Mercosur and the United States is the latter's protection of agricultural goods in which this subregion has a strong comparative advantage. If the two parties can reengage on this issue, the attention of the Mercosur countries could return to the U.S. market more broadly.

Regardless of what happens on the trade policy front, poor physical infrastructure continues to be a major barrier to trade for Latin American economies, the relief of which must be a major strategic objective. A series of detailed analyses by the IDB have shown that transportation costs represent a more significant trade cost than tariffs for nearly every country in the region.[88] As a result, the gains from trade brought about by reducing transport costs exceed those from tariff reductions in much of the region. In addition, transport costs naturally have an unequal impact on the region. The evidence suggests that far-flung, less connected locales in countries throughout Latin America have export opportunities that are not being exploited because of lack of access to transport infrastructure. While this issue is not exclusive to intraregional trade, it is likely that regional trade would receive the greatest boost from better connectivity, owing to the challenging geography in much of Latin America.

The two Asian giants, China and India, remain hugely important economies, and trade with these countries will continue to be relevant for the region—above all, as markets for natural resource exports. At the same time, policymakers in Latin America should be realistic about the prospects for these economic relationships to change fundamentally from the patterns established over the past decade. The margin for policies to affect the overall contours of Latin America's trade with Asia is limited. The commodities-for-manufactures pattern will probably define the relationship for decades to come. This does not mean that the region should not try to produce and export higher-value-added goods to China and India. It undoubtedly should. It simply means that achieving this goal should not distract from the policies needed to exploit more promising opportunities for upgrading exports in the region and North America.

NOTES

1. World Trade Organization (WTO), *World Trade Report 2008: Trade in a Globalizing World* (Geneva: WTO, 2008).

2. Mauricio Mesquita Moreira, Christian Volpe, and Juan S. Blyde, *Unclogging the Arteries: The Impact of Transportation Costs on Latin American and Caribbean Trade* (Washington, DC: Inter-American Development Bank and David Rockefeller Center for Latin American Studies, 2008).

3. Chile reversed a long trend of a widening GDP gap with rich countries in the late 1980s.

4. Antoni Estevadeordal, Paolo Giordano, and Barbara Ramos, "Trade and Economic Integration," in *Routledge Handbook of Latin America in the World,* edited by Jorge I. Domínguez and Ana Covarrubias (New York: Routledge, 2015), pp. 249–64.

5. Robert Devlin and Graciela Moguillansky, "What's New in the New Industrial Policy in Latin America?," in *The Industrial Policy Revolution I: The Role of Government beyond Ideology,* edited by Joseph E. Stiglitz and Justin Lin Yifu (New York: Palgrave Macmillan, 2013).

6. Inter-American Development Bank (IDB), "All That Glitters Is Not Gold" (Washington, DC: IDB, 2008); and Bilge Erten and José Antonio Ocampo, "Super-Cycles of Commodity Prices since the Mid-Nineteenth Century," DESA Working Paper 110 (New York: United Nations, Department of Economic and Social Affairs, February 2012).

7. UN Economic Commission for Latin America and the Caribbean (ECLAC), "Preliminary Overview of the Latin American and Caribbean Economies" (Santiago, Chile: ECLAC, December 2015); and IMF, "World Economic Outlook Update" (Washington, DC: IMF, January 2016).

8. There is no official definition of industrial policies. But the authors would characterize them as public policies framed in a medium- to long-term national vision that guides strategic and proactive public policy interventions

in markets with a variety of instruments. The new industrial policies emphasize the goal of promoting individual and collective learning that generate knowledge capabilities for investment in new industrial and technological capacities of a higher order than those prevailing in the economy, which in turn will accelerate structural change and growth beyond what static comparative advantage may provide. This approach encourages public-private dialogue and problem solving to foster entrepreneurial experimentation, the identification of new opportunities, and binding constraints, as well as market-friendly policies to address them. Promoting learning and new knowledge capabilities is central, as is the objective of good governance, to ward off rent seeking, including rigorous evaluation of impacts of policy interventions, honest and accountable political leadership, and technically competent public officials. For the "new industrial policies" see, among others, Dani Rodrik, "Industrial Policy for the Twenty-first Century," in *One Economics, Many Recipes: Globalization, Institutions and Economic Growth* (Princeton University Press, 2007); Ricardo Hausmann and Dani Rodrik, "Economic Development as Self-Discovery," *Journal of Development Economics* 72, no. 2 (2003), pp. 603–33; Mario Cimoil, Giovanni Dosi, and Joseph E. Stiglitz, *Industrial Policy and Development* (Oxford University Press, 2009); Justin Lin and Celestin Monga, "Growth Identification and Facilitation: The Role of the State in the Dynamics of Industrial Change," World Bank Research Working Paper 5313 (Washington, DC: World Bank, May 2010); Keun Lee, "Capability Failure and Industrial Policy to Move beyond the Middle Income Trap: From Trade-Based to Technological-Based Specialization," in *The Industrial Policy Revolution I,* edited by Stiglitz and Lin, pp. 244–272; Irmgard Nübler, "A Theory of Capabilities for Productive Transformation," in *Transforming Economies,* edited by José Salazar-Xirinachs, Irmgard Nübler, and Richard Kozul-Wright (Geneva: International Labor Organization, 2014); and Joseph E. Stiglitz and Bruce Greenwald, eds., *Creating a Learning Society* (Colombia University Press, 2014).

9. Ja-Joon Chang, "Kicking Away the Ladder: The 'Real' History of Free Trade," FPIF Special Report, Foreign Policy in Focus, December 2003.

10. Cristina Constantinescu, Aaditya Mattoo, and Michele Ruta, "The Global Trade Slowdown: Cyclical or Structural?," IMF Working Paper WP/15/6 (Washington, D.C.: IMF, January 2015); Larry Summers, "Why Stagnation Might Prove to Be the New Normal," *Financial Times,* December 15, 2013.

11. ECLAC, *Structural Change and Productivity Growth 20 Years Later: Old Problems, New Opportunities* (Santiago, Chile: ECLAC, 2008); and Arvind Subramanian and Martin Kessler, "The Hyperglobalization of Trade and Its Future," Working Paper 13-6 (Washington, DC: Peterson Institute for International Economics, 2013).

12. Devlin and Moguillansky, "What's New in the New Industrial Policy in Latin America?"

13. Lower-middle income is $1,046–$4,125 and upper-middle income is $4,126–$12,745. Country and Lending Groups Data, World Bank (http://data.worldbank.org/about/country-and-lending-groups [accessed April 21, 2016]).

14. Mauricio Mesquita Moreira, coordinator, *India: Latin America's Next Big Thing?* (Washington, DC: IDB, 2010).

15. Jorge Heine, *La Nueva India* (Santiago, Chile: Aguilar Chilena Ediciones S.A., 2012).

16. Chile has been the economic leader in Latin America, but it, too, is a short-term thinker. See Sergio Bitar, "Acuerdos para una estrategia de largo plazo," *El Mercurio* (Santiago, Chile), October 23, 2014.

17. For additional discussion of FDI between LAC and China and India, see ECLAC, *India and Latin America and the Caribbean: Opportunities and Challenges in Trade and Investment Relations* (Santiago, Chile: ECLAC, 2011); ECLAC, "Chinese Direct Foreign Investment in Latin America and the Caribbean" (Santiago, Chile: ECLAC, 2013); and the Heritage Foundation's China Global Investment Tracker (Washington, DC: Heritage Foundation) (www.heritage.org). Official statistics put total inflows from China at just over $6 billion from 2003 to 2012, while the region received a total inflow of FDI from all sources of $175 billion in 2012 alone. The large majority of Chinese investment appears to be directed to the agriculture, mining, and energy sectors in LAC—these sectors accounted for 84 percent of Chinese investments in the region since 2005. The total stock of India's FDI in the region stood at only $1.2 billion in 2012.

18. ECLAC, *Structural Change and Productivity Growth 20 Years Later*; IDB, *The Age of Productivity* (Washington, DC: IDB, 2010); José Gabriel Palma, "Why Has Productivity Growth Stagnated in Most Latin American Countries since the Neo-Liberal Reforms?," in *The Oxford Handbook of Latin American Economics*, edited by José Antonio Ocampo and Jaime Ros (Oxford University Press, 2011).

19. Jean Imbs and Romain Wacziarg, "Stages of Diversification," *American Economic Review* 93, no. 1 (2003), pp. 63–86; Bailey Klinger and Daniel Lederman, "Discovery and Development," World Bank Policy Research Working Paper 3450 (Washington, DC: World Bank, November 2004); Celine Carrère, Vanessa Strauss-Kahn, and Oliver Cadot, "Export Diversification: What's behind the Hump?," mimeo, Institut CREA d'economie appliquée, Université de Lausanne, 2007; Ricardo Hausmann and Bailey Klinger, "The Structure of the Product Space and the Evolution of Comparative Advantage," CID Working Paper 36 (Harvard University, Center for International Development, April 2007).

20. ECLAC, *Structural Change and Productivity Growth 20 Years Later*; and ECLAC, *Structural Change for Equality* (Santiago, Chile: ECLAC, 2012).

21. For the theoretical basis of industry-level productivity gains resulting from reallocation from less to more productive firms, see Marc J. Melitz,

"The Impact of Trade on Intra-Industry Reallocations and Aggregate Industry Productivity," *Econometrica* 71, no. 6 (2003), pp. 1695–725. A real life example of this is China—see Ashvin Ahuja, "De-monopolization Towards Long-Term Prosperity in China," IMF Working Paper WP/12/75 (Washington, DC: IMF, March 2012). For policy issues, see IDB, *The Age of Productivity.*

22. Jaume Ventura, "Growth and Interdependence," *Quarterly Journal of Economics* 112, no. 1 (1997), pp. 57–84.

23. WTO, *World Trade Report 2008.*

24. Hausmann and Rodrik, "Economic Development as Self-Discovery"; Lin and Monga, "Growth Identification and Facilitation"; and Lee, "Capability Failure and Industrial Policy to Move beyond the Middle Income Trap."

25. The first argument is that certain activities have highly specific technological and knowledge domains that are not easily adaptable to other activities of a higher order (the periphery of product space), while other activities have more adaptable domains that cluster in, or closer to, the center of the product space and better facilitate migration to a new, higher order of productive activities (see Hausmann and Klinger, "The Structure of the Product Space and the Evolution of Comparative Advantage"). However, Nübler ("A Theory of Capabilities for Productive Transformation") emphasizes that migration is by no means automatic; raising productive capacities requires prior expansion of a country's capabilities to learn and expand its knowledge domain.

26. ECLAC, "Preliminary Overview of the Latin American and Caribbean Economies"; Juan Blyde, ed., *Synchronized Factories: Latin American and the Caribbean in the Era of Global Value Chains* (New York: Springer Open, 2014).

27. Vertical specialization is high for low-income countries that assemble imported materials. As countries develop linkages and produce inputs themselves, vertical specialization declines. However, as income rises, further vertical specialization intensifies again, but at the top end of the value chain. Conceptually, the evolution is U-shaped. William Milberg, Xiao Jiang, and Gary Gereffi, "Industrial Policy in the Era of Vertically Specialized Industrialization," in *Industrial Policy for Economic Development: Lessons from Country Experiences,* edited by Irmgard Nübler, José Manuel Salazar-Xirinachs, and Richard Kozul-Wright (Geneva: ILO-UNCTAD, 2013).

28. Karina Fernández-Stark, Penny Bamber, and Gary Gereffi, "Global Value Chains in Latin America: A Development Perspective for Upgrading," in *Global Value Chains and World Trade,* edited by Rene Hernández, Jorge Mario Martínez-Piva, and Nanno Mulder (Santiago, Chile: ECLAC, 2014).

29. Antoni Estevadeordal, Juan Blyde, and Kati Suominen, "Are Global Value Chains Really Global? Policies to Accelerate Countries' Access to In-

ternational Production Networks," E15 Initiative, ICTSD–IADB think piece prepared for the E15 Expert Group on Global Value Chains: Development Challenges and Policy Options, Geneva, Switzerland, 2012.

30. *Maquila* refers to manufacturing operations, often operating in designated zones, which enjoy duty-free imports of capital goods and imports, under the condition that their products be exported. Strictly speaking, maquilas can operate at any stage of the value chain, but the most common activities are low value-added processing and assembly, and the term "maquila" has thus become synonymous with this type of productive activity. Even in Mexico, the most sophisticated manufacturing economy in the subregion, the value-added of total exports is only 60 percent, and that is twelve percentage points below the pre-NAFTA 1990 level. Hugo Beteta, "Inserción comercial y políticas de desarrollo productivo en México" (Mexico City: Taller de la Comisión de Competitividad, Secretaría de Economía y Secretaría de Hacienda de México, February 17, 2014).

31. Ibid.; Blyde, ed., *Synchronized Factories.*

32. Theodore Moran, "Industrial Policy as a Tool of Development Strategy: Using FDI to Upgrade and Diversify the Production and Export Base of Host Economies in the Developing World" (Washington, DC: Center for Global Development, 2014).

33. All currency figures are in U.S. dollars unless otherwise noted.

34. IMF, "People's Republic of China: Spillover Report for the 2011 Article IV Consultation and Selected Issues," IMF Country Report No. 11/193, Washington, DC, July 2011.

35. Shaun Roache, "China's Impact on World Commodity Markets," IMF Working Paper WP/12/115 (Washington, DC: IMF, May 2012).

36. Yuqing Xing, "Measuring Value Added in People's Republic of China's Exports: A Direct Approach," ADBI Working Paper 493 (Tokyo: Asian Development Bank Institute, August 2014).

37. Ernest Preeg, *The Emerging Chinese Advanced Technology Superstate* (Washington, DC: Manufacturer's Alliance and Hudson Institute, 2005).

38. United States Trade Representative (USTR), "National Trade Estimate on Foreign Trade" (Washington, DC, 2012).

39. Organization for Economic Cooperation and Development (OECD), Product Market Regulation Statistics for 2013, OECD.Stat, (http://stats .oecd.org/Index.aspx?DataSetCode=PMR [accessed April 21, 2016]).

40. Organization of American States (OAS), "Foreign Trade Information System (SICE)," (http://www.sice.oas.org/agreements_e.asp); WTO, "Participation in Regional Trade Agreements" (http://www.wto.org/english /tratop_e/region_e/rta_participation_map_e.htm [accessed April 21, 2016]).

41. CBI China Direct, "China's 12th Five Year Plan (2011–2015): The Full English Version," May 11, 2011 (http://cbi.typepad.com/china_direct /2011/05/chinas-twelfth-five-new-plan-the-full-english-version.html [accessed April 21, 2016]).

42. Data are for fiscal year April–March.

43. Government of India, Ministry of Commerce and Industry, *Annual Report 2012–13* (New Delhi, 2014); Victor Mallet, James Crabtree, and Amy Kazmin, "India Gears Up for an Industrial Revolution," *Financial Times*, January 12, 2015. The focus on entirely new industries seems to follow the Korean strategy of focusing on "short cycle time" technologies, which are less controlled by incumbents. See Keun Lee, *Schumpeterian Analysis of Economic Catch-up: Knowledge, Path-creation, and the Middle-income Trap* (Cambridge University Press, 2013).

44. WTO, *Trade Policy Review India* (Geneva: WTO, 2011).

45. USTR, "National Trade Estimate on Foreign Trade" (Washington, DC, 2014); Mesquita Moreira, *India: Latin America's Next Big Thing?*; WTO, *Trade Policy Review India*.

46. OAS-SICE, "Trade Agreements in Force," Foreign Trade Information System (SICE), OAS, (http://www.sice.oas.org/agreements_e.asp [accessed April 21, 2016]). The United States and the EU agreements are very comprehensive WTO-plus agreements that go beyond trade in goods.

47. USTR, "The Trans-Pacific Partnership" (Washington, DC, April 2016) (http://www.ustr.gov/tpp [accessed April 21, 2016]). Members are Australia, Brunei, Canada, Chile, Japan, Malaysia, Mexico, New Zealand, Peru, Singapore, the United States, and Vietnam.

48. For more details, see Barbara Kotschwar, "The Pacific Alliance and Mercosur: Narrowing the Gap?," (Washington, DC: Peterson Institute for International Economics, November 24, 2014), (http://blogs.piie.com/real time/?p=4630 [accessed April 21, 2016]).

49. WTO, "Chronological List of Dispute Cases," Dispute Settlement, WTO (http://www.wto.org/english/tratop_e/dispu_e/dispu_status_e.htm); OAS-SICE, "Trade Agreements in Force," Foreign Trade Information System (SICE), OAS, (http://www.sice.oas.org/agreements_e.asp [accessed April 21, 2016]).

50. India and Brazil both participate in the BRICS and IBSA regional blocs, which have established various initiatives aimed at facilitating trade, investment, and political cooperation among member countries. The BRICS forum unites Brazil, Russia, India, China, and South Africa, while IBSA consists of India, Brazil, and South Africa. For an analysis of IBSA, see Sean Woolfrey, "The IBSA Dialogue Forum Ten Years On: Examining IBSA Cooperation on Trade," Tralac Trade Brief S13TB05/2013 (Stellenbosch: Tralac Law Center, August 2013. (http://www.tralac.org/files/2013/08/S13TB052013 -Woolfrey-IBSA-Dialogue-Forum-ten-years-on-20130827-fin.pdf).

51. Mario Cimoli, "The Need for Structural Change and Its Main Implications for a New Industrial Policy in Mexico" (Mexico City: Taller de la Comisión de Competitividad, Secretaría de Economía y Secretaría de Hacienda de México, February 17, 2014).

52. United States International Trade Commission (USITC), Trade and Tariff Dataweb (https://dataweb.usitc.gov/). It should be recalled that Chi-

nese exports are laden with inputs imported from many countries; i.e., in value-added terms Chinese exports are considerably less than their dollar value.

53. USITC, Trade and Tariff Dataweb (https://dataweb.usitc.gov/); Kevin P. Gallagher and Roberto Porzecanski, *The Dragon in the Room: China and the Future of Latin American Industrialization* (Stanford University Press, 2010).

54. USITC, Trade and Tariff Dataweb (https://dataweb.usitc.gov/). In the European market, China has also made impressive inroads, increasing its share of low-tech manufactured imports from 9 percent to 19 percent and its share of high-tech manufactures from 4 percent to 16 percent between 2000 and 2013. The main difference is that Latin American manufacturers never established a significant beachhead in the European market. With the exception of South American primary products, the region has failed to capture a relevant share of the European import market. Meanwhile, India has not been a relevant competitor in Europe.

55. IDB, *Shaping the Future of the Asia-Latin America and the Caribbean Relationship*, IDB Publication (Books) 74638 (Washington, DC: IDB, January 2012). The authors plot GDP per capita against consumption of copper and soy per capita for a set of developed and developing countries and show that China and India are both several decades away from the inflection point where demand decreases with income.

56. In some studies, natural resource specialization has been characterized as a type of "curse" for development. It is true that natural resource dependence encounters risks that can stall development (see Jeffrey Frankel, "The Natural Resource Curse: A Survey," NBER Working Paper 15836 [Cambridge, MA: National Bureau of Economic Research, March 2010]). However, to characterize natural resources as a curse is an exaggeration. Development outcomes of countries reliant on natural resources depend on how natural resources are produced and how the revenue they generate is used to promote new capabilities that are channeled into industrial upgrading (see Jean Philippe Stijns, "Natural Resource Abundance and Economic Growth Revisited," *Resource Policy* 30 [2005]: 107–30; David de Ferranti and others, *From Natural Resources to the Knowledge Economy* [Washington, DC: World Bank, 2002]). However, diversification and upgrading often require especially strong industrial policy incentives in order to counterbalance the sirens of easy rents in primary commodities.

57. Philip Schellenkens, "A Changing China: Implications for Developing Countries," *Economic Premise* 118 (May 2013).

58. For an analysis of Latin America's infrastructure deficits and its effect on trade performance, see Mesquita Moreira, Volpe, and Blyde, *Unclogging the Arteries;* and Mauricio Mesquita Moreira, *Too Far to Export* (Washington, DC: IDB, 2013).

59. ECLAC, *Panorama de la inserción Internacional de América Latina y el Caribe* (Santiago, Chile: ECLAC, 2012); ECLAC, *Panorama de la*

inserción Internacional de América Latina y el Caribe (Santiago, Chile: ECLAC, 2014).

60. Carol Wise, "China's Free Trade Agreements in South America," Economics Brief, Inter-American Dialogue, Washington, DC, November 2012.

61. World Bank, Office of the Regional Chief Economist, *Latin America's Deceleration and the Exchange Rate Buffer* (Washington, DC: World Bank, October 2013).

62. Andrés López, Andrés Niembro, and Daniela Ramos, "Latin America's Competitive Position in Knowledge-Intensive Services Trade," *CEPAL Review* 113 (August 2014), pp. 21–39.

63. Robert Devlin, Antoni Estevadeordal, and Andrés Rodriguez Clare, eds., *The Emergence of China: Opportunities and Challenges for Latin America and the Caribbean* (Harvard University Press, 2007).

64. "Good, in Parts," *The Economist*, October 4, 2014.

65. Jamil Anderlini, "China Foresees Outbound Investment of $1.25tn in a Decade," *Financial Times*, November 9, 2014.

66. Large multinational retailers have found the Chinese market very difficult. India's retail markets enjoy much protection.

67. Mesquita Moreira, *India: Latin America's Next Big Thing?*; and López, Niembro, and Ramos, "Latin America's Competitive Position."

68. ECLAC, "Panorama de la inserción" (2014).

69. Ibid.

70. Estevadeordal, Giordano, and Ramos, "Trade and Economic Integration."

71. ECLAC, "Panorama de la inserción" (2014).

72. IDB, *Beyond Borders: The New Regionalism in Latin America* (Washington, DC: IDB, 2002).

73. Table III.5 in ECLAC, "Panorama de la inserción" (2014), has a good summary.

74. Devlin and Moguillansky, "What's New in the New Industrial Policy in Latin America?"

75. ECLAC, "Panorama de la inserción" (2014).

76. Enrique V. Iglesias, "Las ideas y la praxis en la experiencia de un servidor público internacional," in *América Latina en una era de globalización*, edited by Robert Devlin, Oscar Echevarría, and José Luis Machinea (Amazon Publishers, 2014).

77. This trend partly reflects lower commodity prices since the global recession of 2008–09.

78. UN Comtrade, International Trade Statistics Database (http://comtrade.un.org/).

79. These shortcomings are examined in Robert Devlin and Graciela Moguillansky, *Breeding Latin American Tigers: Operational Principles for Rehabilitating Industrial Policies* (Washington, DC: ECLAC and World

Bank, 2011); and Devlin and Moguillansky, "What's New in the New Industrial Policy in Latin America?"

80. This figure does not include natural resource–based manufactures.

81. Its IIT index for non-primary commodity exports was 0.33 in 2013.

82. From the standpoint of negotiations, agriculture is a sticking point for the United States, while Mercosur has been sensitive to opening up industry to free trade.

83. U.S. ratification of the TPP remains a question mark due to domestic political environment uncertainty surrounding the November 2016 elections.

84. According to Petri and Plummer, the main Latin American beneficiary of the TPP would be Peru, due to the easing of restrictions on adding value to commodities. Those most hurt will be Central America and the Dominican Republic, due to U.S. preference erosion. In addition, TPP's "accumulation of origin" will allow inputs from other TPP members to comply with the rules of origin standard. Mexico, for example, could import high-quality inputs from Asia for its exports to NAFTA; see Peter A. Petri and Michael G. Plummer, "The Economic Effects of the Trans-Pacific Partnership: New Estimates," Working Paper 16-2 (Peterson Institute for International Economics, Washington, DC, January 2016).

85. Osvaldo Rosales and Sebastián Herreros, "Mega-regional Trade Negotiations: What Is at Stake for Latin America?," Trade Policy Working Paper (Washington DC: Inter-American Dialogue, January 2014).

86. The EU, with a significant IIT index, may also be attractive, but not until it shows signs of serious economic recovery.

87. IDB, *Beyond Borders*.

88. See Mesquita Moreira, Volpe, and Blyde, *Unclogging the Arteries;* and Mesquita Moreira, *Too Far to Export.*

CHAPTER 8

Migration in a Mobile Age

PERSPECTIVES FROM CHINA, INDIA, AND THE AMERICAS

Jacqueline Mazza

Migration has shaped and characterized Latin American and Caribbean (LAC) development from its very beginning. Historical immigration from Europe, slave populations from Africa, indentured servants from China, India, and Asia, and indentured indigenous peoples helped build the region. Today, LAC's development is characterized by two-way migration—high rates of out-migration, largely to the north, and new inflows of immigrants, principally from within the region and other developing countries, China among them. In today's more mobile and global economy, China, India, and LAC have each become among the top migrant-sending nations/regions of the world. This chapter traces the changing profile of migration in LAC countries, analyzing particularly new inflows from China and the much more limited inflows from India, trends that provoke both tensions and new promise between China, India, and the region.

The first section briefly reviews the historical role of Chinese and Indian migration in the region's economy. The second section takes us up to the current day, examining global and regional migration patterns of the three emigrating "giants"—China, India, and LAC. The third section analyzes new and traditional forms of Chinese migration to the region, as Indian migration appears to be occurring at much more reduced levels. The chapter concludes with policy reflections regarding both the current tensions over rising Chinese migration in the region and positive changes that could come from more explicitly considering and linking migration to the region's development.

HISTORICAL PERSPECTIVES

Foreign workers, slaves, and indentured servants played a critical role in LAC countries' early growth, as did the region's indigenous populations. Foreign workers built the region's railroads, harvested sugar, and established farms and factories; they came first principally from Europe but later from Japan and China. Indian indentured servants arrived in the Caribbean region principally to work on plantations.

Historical Chinese migration to the region, which was often labeled as "coolie" labor, can be traced to an intense period lasting from 1868 to 1939. These workers, who operated in near slave conditions, were imported to build the railroads and work on plantations from Mexico to Panama to Argentina. As slaves were gradually freed in the region, these chiefly male laborers moved into indentured, low-wage labor in the region's fields and plantations, later migrating to the cities for work in the service sector, creating grocery stores (now *chitzas* in Peru), restaurants, and shops. Discrimination and legal restrictions on the Chinese in particular characterized this early history in Latin America. Overcoming years of restrictions, Chinese communities transformed into now long-established communities of Chinese-Latinos who may still retain market ties with China but have long lost their cultural ties to their land of origin.

Historical Indian migration, which has been less comprehensively studied, occurred on a smaller scale and was concentrated in the British and Dutch colonies in the Caribbean. Indian migration specialist Daniel Naujoks notes that Britain began exporting Indian labor in the form of indentured servants to its colonies.[1] France and the Netherlands began doing so in 1834, and by 1878, Indian laborers were working on plantations in Suriname, Guyana, and Trinidad and Tobago. Indentured servants typically accepted contracts of five years; and after their term of labor ended, many accepted payment in the form of land or money in lieu of payment to return home. These workers came mainly from the present-day Indian states of Bihar and Uttar Pradesh.[2] Over time, Indian laborers migrated a bit more widely in the region; many were later hired into businesses established by Indian businessmen and professionals, but, according to Deepak Bhojwani, the reaction to such Latino-Indian businesses back in mainstream India was "tepid."[3] Distinct from Chinese migration to the region, and perhaps as a result of its concentration in the Caribbean, the Indian diaspora (descendants) rose to political power in the countries of Trinidad and Tobago, Guyana, and Suriname.[4]

The year 1970 marks the point when LAC's development pattern "flipped." By then the region was no longer a net importer of labor from abroad. European emigration had slowed markedly (after 1950), while migration to the United States skyrocketed, particularly from Mexico and Central America after 1980, and migration *between* countries in the region began to grow.[5] For slowing Chinese migration, it was not only that the economic "pull" of the region slowed in the twentieth century but also that political restrictions following the Cultural Revolution took over. Chinese migration to the region all but halted, with the exception of a brief spurt of Chinese fleeing China's civil war in the late 1940s. China highly restricted both internal (rural-to-urban) and outward migration for political-social control and to manage foreign exchange. Migration overseas prior to 1980 had a negative political connotation—one termed "betraying" or "fleeing" *(pantao)*. Officially permitted flows were thus effectively halted after the Cultural Revolution; hence the substantial numbers of Chinese who migrated to the region in the 1950s and 1960s came from Taiwan.

Political controls also held back Indian emigration, particularly for low-skilled workers from 1930 to 1966. In 1966, however, passports were liberalized, and with passports no longer discretionary, the first wave of new Indian immigration went to the United Kingdom. Noticeable in this period in the 1970s was a "secondary migration" of descendants of Indian indentured servants, born in the Caribbean, who emigrated to the United States and Canada, mostly for economic reasons, and after 1975 to the Netherlands, following Suriname's independence.[6]

The Chinese and Indian workers who were compelled or coerced to move to the Americas in the nineteenth century predominantly remained in the region, forming diaspora communities that now have their own Latino-Caribbean characteristics; they are found in Chinatowns from Lima to Buenos Aires to Santo Domingo and in Indian shops and restaurants throughout the Caribbean. The historical contribution of Chinese migrants to Latin America and of Indian migrants to the Caribbean has been documented in several studies.[7]

Today's labor migration trends in LAC look nothing like these nineteenth-century labor flows. Outflows to the "north"—principally the United States and Canada, but also to Europe—account for more than two-thirds of migrant flows. Inflows are now characterized by three source groups: LAC intraregional migrants, Asian migrants (now more frequently from mainland China), and transit migrants from all regions who are making their way to the United States. As this immigration trend accelerated since 2005, national statistics have yet to catch up with these shifts. Census figures from 2000 still recorded Japan as the largest source of Asian immigrants to the region (26 percent in 2000).[8]

CHINA, INDIA, AND LAC MIGRATION: A GLOBAL PERSPECTIVE

Today China, India, and LAC have among the world's most mobile populations—China, India, and Mexico more so for sheer numbers, and LAC as a percentage of its population. The three migration giants, however, vary greatly in the principal destination countries and in the market connections each maintains with its migrants. Worldwide, Chinese and Indian mobility after the 1990s through its sheer size pushed India to becoming the world's second-largest migrant-sending nation (14.1 million in 2013) and China to becoming the fourth largest (sending 9.3 million Chinese abroad in 2013).[9] Mexico, with its relatively smaller population, has occupied a top spot for decades (table 8-1). Large-scale out-migration from LAC countries, principally to the United States, has a long historical trajectory but accelerated particularly in the 1980s as a result of civil conflicts in Central America. Only in 2013 did the estimated number of Chinese living abroad exceed the total number of LAC migrants abroad (7.9 million).

Table 8-1 presents the three large emigrating nations in 2010 and the LAC region along with their immigration figures. Although all three nations send and receive migrants, only Mexico is both a top world sender and receiver. These migrating giants have different primary destinations—two-thirds of LAC migrants go to the United States and Canada, half of Chinese migrants go to Asia (Hong Kong, Singapore, and Thailand, though many also go to the United States and Canada), and nearly 70 percent of all Indian migrants go to South Asia and the Middle East (top destinations are the UAE, the United States, Saudi Arabia, and Bangladesh).[10] The large workforces overseas of China, India, and Mexico return the largest dollar amounts of remittances worldwide: India is at the top ($71 million in 2013), followed by China ($60 million), then Mexico (in fourth place worldwide) at much reduced, and currently declining, levels ($22 million). However, as these are large economies, in none of the three countries do remittances constitute a large percentage of GNP as found in smaller, high-emigration countries such as Haiti.[11]

Again, owing to sheer volume, foreign-born persons in China and India do not constitute as high a percentage of the local population as in LAC countries. Regionwide, 1.1 percent of the residents of LAC are

TABLE 8-1

China, India, Mexico, and LAC Migration: Global Comparisons, 2010

Country/ region	Emigration			Immigration	
	Stock (in millions)	% of population	World rank	Stock (in thousands)	% of population
China	8.3	0.6	4	685.8	0.1
India	11.4	0.9	2	5,436.0	0.4
Mexico	11.9	10.7	1	725.7	0.7
Latin America and the Caribbean	30.2	5.2	...	6,600.0	1.1

Source: World Bank, *Migration and Remittances Fact Book* (Washington, DC, 2011).

foreign-born (including other Latin Americans), but this figure is much larger in the countries of Argentina, Brazil, and Costa Rica. India quite possibly is more similar to LAC in the larger foreign-born population as unauthorized migration from Bangladesh is thought to be particularly undercounted.[12]

Migration to LAC: Trend Lines from China and India

How significant is Chinese and Indian migration to LAC? While LAC is clearly not a top destination for migrants from either country, new migration flows, particularly from China, are poorly captured in regional data; south-south flows around the world are thought to be exponentially undercounted.[13] UN data for the Chinese, Indian, and foreign-born populations in Latin America and the Caribbean are presented in table 8-2.

Few believe that these totals represent accurate estimates of the precise numbers of immigrants. Rather, because of significant data deficiencies, table 8-2 is best interpreted as a rough approximation of trend lines, as it does not include the local diaspora (children born of Chinese and Indian parents) or any number of other forms of migration. The trends from 1990 to 2013 garnered from the UN data do coincide with some qualitative observations in the region,[14] but in the broadest sense: Chinese migration is shown to increase 58 percent just from 2000 to 2013; Indian migration increased as well (66 percent), but at dramatically lower aggregate levels than the Chinese, with Chinese migration being seven times the level of Indian migration. In this data set, Chinese migration is shown to be principally to South America (66 percent) and

TABLE 8-2

Chinese and Indian-Born Residents of LAC, 2000–13

Country of origin

Region	2000		2010		2013	
	China	India	China	India	China	India
Caribbean	5,490	3,080	6,222	3,844	6,365	3,946
Central America	16,038	2,965	24,864	4,730	27,041	5,382
South America	41,263	2,337	64,239	2,831	67,850	2,969
Latin America and the Caribbean (total)ᵃ	66,449	8,875	99,257	13,825	105,059	14,801

Source: United Nations, UNDESA (2014).

a. Regional totals differ slightly from the sum of UNDESA subregional totals because the following were excluded in the latter: *Caribbean*—Angola, Aruba, British Virgin Islands, Caribbean Netherlands, Cayman Islands, Curaçao, Guadeloupe, Martinique, Montserrat, Puerto Rico, Saint Maarten, Turks and Caicos Islands, and U.S. Virgin Islands; *South America*—Falkland Islands, French Guiana.

Indian migration principally to Central America and the Caribbean (63 percent).

If we focus just on the relatively larger Chinese migration, the numbers of foreign-born Chinese (technically "stock") still appear small in percentage terms in LAC in comparison to other groups of foreign-born migrants. In most LAC countries, the largest groups of foreign-born persons are from other LAC countries, such as Bolivians and Paraguayans in Argentina. In this, LAC's "south-south" trends reflect a similar regional concentration, with the greatest numbers of migrants moving between neighboring countries, much as China and India do with their Asian and Middle Eastern neighbors.

Specifically with regard to post-2000 Indian migration to the region, a review of a number of international and national data sets detected clear increases, but from a relatively reduced base. This finding appears consistent with historical patterns and with the more limited level of Indian investments (relative to China) to date over the same period. In 2002, the Indian High Level Committee on the Indian Diaspora estimated that just over 1 million persons of Indian descent (both born in India and born in the Caribbean) resided in only three countries in the Caribbean (Guyana, Suriname, and Trinidad and Tobago), representing only 6 percent of the total Indian diaspora worldwide.[15] The UN system registered Indian foreign-born migrants to Mexico (775 in 2010), El Salvador (10 in 2007), and Brazil (821 in 2010) as permanent residents. Interestingly, more than half of the Indian foreign-born persons in Mexico and Brazil had higher education.[16] The Continuous Reporting System on International Migration in the Americas (SICREMI) of the Organization of American States (OAS), which measures legal permanent residents each year,[17] noted only sixty-three Indian legal permanent residents in Belize in 2012 and none in more than twelve other reporting countries.[18] While the following analysis pertains particularly to new Chinese migration, the final section of this chapter discusses whether changes in Indian migration may come in the future as Indian investment diversifies in the region.

An additional look at the profile of Chinese and Indian migrants can be garnered from the census data of select countries, which provide details of gender, age, and education of foreign-born residents. Census data from Brazil in 2010, for example, permit comparisons of the education and gender of Chinese and Indian foreign-born migrants compared to other migrants. One sees a clear trend toward working-age, highly educated male immigrants from India to Brazil (64 percent were male and 70 percent of these men had finished the second year of tertiary education or above). Chinese workers, who migrated to Brazil in much larger numbers, were only 54 percent male (the average of all foreign-born migrants) and had relatively less education (only 24 percent had tertiary-level education, but the majority had at least upper secondary level).[19]

Overall, the figures cited in UN statistics appear particularly low if used as an estimate of the total number of Chinese- and Indian-born persons living in the region (such as a total of 105,059 Chinese-born persons living throughout LAC). Census data often greatly underestimate foreign-born populations, as they tend to cluster in certain cities and regions. Other estimates of the total Chinese stock vary widely and, when the diaspora is included, can stretch to 1.8 million.[20] Even the official Chinese estimate of migrants sent just in 2012 for work in Latin America (presented in the next section) is 87,436, a one-year inflow that constitutes 87 percent of the UN estimate for the total number in residence.

In those countries where Chinese migration is reportedly particularly high, such as Guyana, Suriname, and Venezuela, the data are simply unreliable or unavailable. One press report from Suriname alone stated that an estimated 40,000 Chinese workers had come to work on Chinese investment projects.[21] Chinese workers coming specifically for investment projects, perhaps the type of migration most visible within the region, constitute the newest type of flow in the region and are not likely to show up yet in these international statistics. Due to the greater relative volume attributed to both recent Chinese investment and migration to the region, the next section focuses specifically on new and traditional forms of recent Chinese migration to LAC.

EMERGING TYPES OF MIGRATION FROM CHINA TO LAC

Migration from China and India were both highly restricted for significant portions of the mid-twentieth century, opening up officially in 1966 in India and in the mid-1970s in China. When restrictions on Indian migration were lifted, the United Kingdom was the destination of an overwhelming majority (with migration levels tripling); migration to the Gulf countries also skyrocketed after 2000.[22] Increased Chinese migration to LAC seems to have come even later, picking up in parallel with a growing Chinese investment presence in the region.

The Chinese opening to emigration in the 1970s is described by the scholar Biao Xiang as a new "mobility regime."[23] In this new mobility regime, passports were liberalized, and labor export was permitted in various forms. Sending teams of workers abroad (labor export or *laowu shuchu*) started with overseas aid programs and accelerated with foreign investments by state-owned companies. The term "Chinese overseas" has substituted for the earlier negative term "fleeing," and overseas migrants are now seen as more integral to China's expansion and a key source of income and new market connections. By the mid-1990s, East and Southeast Asia had become the top receiving destination of these official Chinese workforces, displacing the Middle East.[24] By the turn of the twenty-first century, a series of academic studies had traced increased Chinese workforces to Africa accompanying investment projects.

The impact of this new Chinese mobility regime, as noted, reached Latin America much later, coinciding with the growth of Chinese investment in the region. R. Evan Ellis characterizes the expansion of the Chinese "footprint" in LAC as occurring in three stages: limited before 2002, increasing with simple trade expansion through 2007, and increasing further after 2007 with the dual expansion of investment and trade, coordinated with the Chinese government's "going out" five-year plan.[25]

For LAC countries, increases in Chinese migration are particularly noticeable after 2005 and can be classified into three types: type 1 consists of workforces related to Chinese investments or donations, type 2 corresponds to independent or diaspora-linked migration, and type 3 refers to transit migration to the United States or within the region. The majority of new Chinese migrant workers (internal and external, all types) are classified as low- and medium-skilled and the majority are male.[26] Unfortunately, human trafficking persists. Although this chapter focuses on voluntary economic migration, the issue of forced migration is discussed briefly at the end of this section, particularly because of perceived links between trafficking and criminal enterprises, which feed negative perceptions of migrants.

Type 1: Investment- or Donation-Related Workforces

The newest type of Chinese labor migration—associated with China's economic and trade expansion after 1990—is that of Chinese laborers brought in as part of a Chinese construction or infrastructure investment. Such projects typically reflect a direct investment by Chinese state-owned companies, donations made by the Chinese government, or investments made with Chinese bank (sometimes state-owned) financing. In a comprehensive survey of China in Latin America, R. Evan Ellis notes that "virtually all" Chinese investments[27] in the region have led to contracts for Chinese companies to carry out the projects.[28] When construction is involved in these investments or in donations to the region, Chinese workforces are often employed. Chinese state-based companies and Chinese financing, it should be emphasized, often come in when there is no other willing investor, saving failing firms and industries in the host country while serving key raw material needs and ensuring a package of strategic investments for China.

Investment-Related Workforces
The vast majority of Chinese workers formally accompanying Chinese investments in Latin America and the Caribbean work in two broad sectors, tourism and infrastructure for primary production. There appear to be limited manufacturing-related workforces, principally found in larger countries such as Brazil.

This first type of investment-related migration is most visible in several large projects in the region. For sheer size, perhaps the best known is the Baha Mar Casino and Hotel complex investment on the island of Nassau (the Bahamas). Chinese banners can be seen at the site surrounding a fenced compound where Chinese construction workers are building the hotel's skyscrapers. The contract with China State Construction and Engineering Cooperation Company (CSCEC), China's largest contractor and executor of the project, provided up to 7,000 workers in stages.[29] Proportionately larger numbers of Chinese laborers have been reported in projects in Central America, the Caribbean, Venezuela, Guyana, and Surinam. Public disclosures of workforce size in the ALBA countries (in particular Venezuela, Cuba, and Nicaragua) are rarely found. Publicly available estimates include an estimated 200 for a highway construction project and the Trelawney Stadium in Kingston, Jamaica; 750 Chinese and 2,000 Hondurans for the Patuca III hydroelectric facility in Honduras;[30] and in Rio, 600 authorized Chinese workers in the context of 4,000 workers requested for the German ThyssenKrupp coke plant.[31]

Investment-related laborers are typically provided visas by LAC national immigration authorities. Work visas are relatively routinely provided around the globe for the investors themselves and those in key management positions; a more recent trend for LAC is the provision of visas for low-skilled or moderately skilled workers, as all countries in the region have large unskilled labor forces. In LAC, official public announcements of the numbers of Chinese workers accompanying Chinese investments are relatively rare; most estimates for this chapter were assembled from press accounts and discussions with migration officials, who indicated that press accounts often underestimate the number of visas provided.[32] Particularly unknown are the numbers of Chinese workers in the ALBA countries of Venezuela and Cuba. More commonly, a press report announces the new investment, and possibly the presence of Chinese workers, but often without indicating what the agreement, numbers, or terms are for laborers. For example, press reports noted the appearance of Chinese workers in Britto, Nicaragua, after President Ortega's announcement of a construction deal with the Chinese company HK Nicaragua Canal Development Investment Ltd.[33]

This type 1 migration appears to be more prevalent in the smaller nations of the Caribbean and Central America and the ALBA treaty nations, which may be more likely to accept Chinese labor as part of the investment deal (Venezuela, Nicaragua, Bolivia). Reports of large-construction workforces are more limited in countries such as Brazil, Chile, and Argentina. In Brazil, for example, investments with China are more typically made jointly; although Chinese technical workers are noted to accompany infrastructure or manufacturing investment, the numbers appear to be somewhat limited, possibly as a result of Brazilian labor laws or Brazilian bargaining power.

Official Chinese Estimates of Workforce Migration

Data for 2012 published by the Chinese Academy of Social Sciences (CASS) and the Center for China and Globalization provide the only regionwide official estimate of Chinese workers sent to Latin America for "labor or workforce related issues"—87,436 in 2012.[34] This figure represents a 3.6 percent increase compared to 2011 but does not include the Caribbean, which the report notes also saw increased Chinese migration. These data, only recently published, represent the largest comprehensive figures for type 1 migration (labor or investment related) to the region, exceeding numbers compiled from press accounts, perhaps because they may include Venezuela and other ALBA nations. Such figures put LAC closer to estimates for the number of Chinese workers in Africa. Emmanuel Ma Mung puts the stocks of investment-related workers going to Africa at 80,000 (roughly 1985–2009), 90 percent of whom work for state-owned companies.[35]

Donation Labor Forces

Over the past decade, the Chinese government has donated buildings to LAC countries as a form of foreign assistance, including largely soccer stadiums and government buildings, and have used Chinese workforces to accomplish the construction. To date, these donation buildings have been built exclusively in Central American and Caribbean countries, principally as a result of switching diplomatic recognition from Taiwan to the People's Republic of China (PRC). Examples include soccer stadiums in Costa Rica, Grenada, Antigua, Jamaica, and St. Kitts and public buildings in Trinidad and Tobago (the National Academy of Performing Arts, the prime minister's residence) and Suriname (the Foreign Ministry). The typically all-Chinese construction workforce often numbers 500–700 workers, who are granted short-term work visas.[36] The visas permitted for these workers are only for the purpose of constructing the donated building. However, in a notable scandal, Costa Rican officials discovered that workers on the donated "Bird's Nest" soccer stadium in San José were being transported in the evenings to work on the construction of Chinese-financed condominium buildings, in violation of both their visas and local employment regulations. Construction materials, which had entered tax-free as donated materials, were also being moved. The government suspended 100 visas in May 2010; however, there remains much disagreement on both sides over what transpired.[37]

Keeping track of Chinese workers granted temporary visas after project completion has not been simple for regional immigration officials, who indicate they are under pressure to extend visas for workers on other Chinese projects. Long after the July 2007 completion of the Trelawny soccer stadium in Kingston (which involved mostly Chinese but also some Jamaican construction workers), more than 200 Chinese laborers were still living in the housing compound. Press reports indicated that the workers were staying to work on a new Montego Bay convention center.[38] Africa clearly has seen the "leakage" of investment-related migration, which blends into the local service sector; this trend, however, has been less well documented in LAC countries. Such construction work groups typically are housed in fenced compounds, though allowed to leave the premises. While these investment- and donation-related workers come for specific projects or work, LAC has also seen increases in a second, more historic type of migration—Chinese coming independently to create businesses or to work in Chinese businesses.

Type 2: Independent or Diaspora-Fed Migration

Throughout the twentieth century, LAC countries saw independent migration, mostly of Chinese hoping to work in or set up Chinese businesses and to a much more limited extent of Indians searching for the same among Indian businesses. This type 2 independent migration is focused principally in the service sector: in shopkeeping, restaurant work, or fisheries. From China, type 2 migration came largely from Taiwan after the Cultural Revolution, but beginning in the 1970s, with the liberalization of exit rules, it came increasingly from the coastal areas of China. This form of migration followed a more concentrated regional pattern of migrants journeying from one Chinese region to connect with a specific Chinese diaspora in Latin America and the Caribbean. Key examples of such concentric movement include migration from Shanghai (1970–90), then Fujian (after 2000), to Greater Buenos Aires; from Guangdong to São Paolo and Rio, Brazil; from southern China (Guangdong and Fujian) to Santiago and northern Chile; and from Fujian to Venezuela.[39]

After the 1990s, however, these traditional Chinese regional links appear to have given way to a greater diversity of Chinese regions sending migrants, with newer Chinese populations who spoke different languages or dialects blending in, and sometimes creating tensions, with extant Chinese populations residing in Latin America and the Caribbean. While this trend of regional diversity from China is not as highly documented as it is in Africa, Europe, and the United States, the case of Lima, Peru, has recently been documented: the post-1980 immigration was of Mandarin-speaking Fijians, while the historical population, which arrived between 1900 and 1930, was Cantonese.[40]

A key example of type 2 migration in terms of visibility can be found in greater Buenos Aires, in the neighborhood of Belgrano. Most of the Chinese migration to Argentina occurred within the last forty years, with the biggest wave migrating in 1970–90.[41] Chinese merchants took over grocery chains from inefficient Spanish producers in Greater Buenos Aires and now own an estimated 30 percent of the chains, leading to tensions and sporadic local strikes. The Chinese consulate estimated that around 60,000 Chinese live in Argentina, with more than 30,000 "regularized" in 2009 when the Argentine government undertook a large-scale effort to provide documents to foreign migrants working in the country.[42]

A sharp spike in independent Chinese migration occurred after 2007 when Ecuador, Colombia (for one year), and Venezuela lifted their visa requirements for immigrants from most countries, including Chinese nationals. By one estimate, Ecuador's removal of visa restrictions in 2007 led to a 500 percent increase in Chinese migration in one year.[43] Migration officials in the neighboring Southern Cone and Andean countries (Chile, Peru) say they also have seen an increase in Chinese migration across borders, which they attribute to the eased travel to Ecuador and Venezuela.[44] Independent migrants, particularly cross-border in the region, are difficult to capture in national migration statistics.

Independent and diaspora-related migration is a mix of both documented and undocumented migration, or it may involve a change from one migration status to the other. A Chilean Foreign Ministry official noted that Chile has seen the increased entry of low-skilled Chinese on family visas or investor visas (*compra de negocios*), whom they later find migrating to work in the mines in the north.[45]

Type 3: Transit Migration

Perhaps the most difficult migration to identify and quantify is that involving people in transit through the Americas, most destined for the United States and Canada, but some also going to the higher-income Latin American countries such as Brazil and Argentina. Transit migration has been noted in LAC countries not only of Chinese but also of African and other nationalities. Mexican officials, for example, have observed an uptick at their southern border crossings of many foreign nationals making their way to the U.S. border. Official inflows of Chinese into Mexico went from 600 in 2007 to 2,000 in 2009, rendering China the second-largest source of inflows into Mexico after the United States.[46] Immigration officials across the region have noted as well intra-regional migration of Chinese from Guyana and Suriname to Brazil and Argentina, and from Ecuador to Peru and Chile.

Accounting for exiting workers or exiting investors who might pass through LAC countries en route to the United States has been difficult, but such transit is clearly of concern to U.S. and regional officials. U.S. cables disclosed in Wikileaks worried openly that Chinese workers brought to the Bahamas to work on the Baha Mar resort would find their way to the United States, owing to the proximity and eased immigration controls between the two countries.[47] Guatemala noted a particular incident after approving investor visas for a conference in Guatemala City in 2010. Once they saw the group of "investors" and observed their age, unskilled status, and lack of investment knowledge, the officials assessed that this group instead would be searching for ways to cross the border into Mexico and the United States, and their visas were revoked.[48]

Trafficking and Criminal Migration

Finally, Chinese workers still are brought to LAC shores against their will. The U.S. State Department estimates external Chinese migration at 600,000 annually, "many of whom are recruited by false promises of employment and later coerced into prostitution or forced labor worldwide."[49] Costa Rica foiled an attempt by the Chinese mafia in April 2009 to traffic 300 underage children. The mafia had paid Chinese immigrants in Costa Rica to pose as the parents of these children and forced the children to remain silent by threatening to harm their families back in China. The Costa Rican embassy in China noticed forged documents used in the visa application. The 2009 operation was similar to one foiled in 2007, when the Chinese mafia tried to bribe then Costa Rican migration director Mario Zamora for 500 child visas.[50]

Chinese criminal gangs have become notably associated with both human trafficking and other criminal activity (drugs, weapons). The association of Chinese migration with the Chinese mafia—the Dragón Rojo, as it is called in Peru and elsewhere—renders policies to expand and better protect authorized migration more politically challenging. The truckers' strike in greater Buenos Aires in 2007, a move aimed at Chinese merchants, was precipitated by the perceived links between Chinese merchants and criminal organizations.[51] Colombia reinstated its visa restrictions in 2007 after the surge in migration became associated with increased criminal activity. Ecuador kept its lack of visa requirements in place, which, according to Logan, meant "Ecuador's role as the staging area for [this] human smuggling network has all but replaced Colombia, which used to be considered South America's springboard for Chinese illegal immigrants who sought entry into the United States."[52]

The three types of migration for work described in this chapter form the principal trend lines in the region, colored by serious concerns regarding forced or coerced migration. A few caveats regarding other types of migration that have not yet appeared on any scale in LAC should also be noted. Temporary Chinese migration for trading as seen in Africa, which consists of Chinese workers coming for two or three years to sell goods and then return to China, has not yet been noted significantly in Latin America.[53] Migration for the purposes of work should be seen as distinct from the temporary inflows of Chinese trainers and service personnel that accompany Chinese investments or military activities.[54] And finally, although China and India rank as the first- and second-largest senders of students to foreign universities, there do not appear to be significant numbers of students from either nation going to LAC countries. In the case of both China and India, the United States and the United Kingdom are top destinations; Spain largely receives those Chinese seeking a Spanish-language education.

GROWING TENSIONS AND FUTURE PROSPECTS

Growing investment, trade, and commercial relations with China and India have captured the first set of headlines from LAC. But it is new influxes of semi-skilled and unskilled labor (largely Chinese to date) into a region suffering, as China and India are, from poor-quality job generation that could provoke greater tensions and undermine economic advances for all. These labor tensions are already present in the region, but they are not inevitable. Tensions can be seen from the secrecy surrounding the number of Chinese workers present, their living in compounds, and limited policy attention to innovation in migration.

The Caribbean, Central America, and Andean region in particular have seen Chinese workers appearing suddenly in large numbers without disclosures to the public or clarity about employment possibilities for local workers. Most dramatically, tensions have led to kidnapping and violence against Chinese workers (in Caqueta, Colombia, and Tarapoa, Ecuador); the robbery and murder of Chinese shop owners in Surinam;[55] and the sending in of the Honduran armed forces to the Patuka hydroelectric site to protect Sinohydro workers in 2010.[56]

The current pattern of silence on both sides and housing labor forces in compounds both isolates Chinese communities in ways that are contrary to the history of LAC societies and neglects opportunities to bolster support for Chinese investments through more openings for employment of local lower-skilled labor, as well as joint training and skill development. Deborah Brautigam indicates that a number of African countries, such as Angola, have moved to public announcements of the number of Chinese migrants and related jobs in response to concerns about the creation of local jobs.[57]

The employment tensions can be seen today in Jamaica, a country that considers itself multiracial and has historically hosted arriving Chinese and Indian populations, who have integrated well. The unemployment rate is among the highest in the entire region, and tensions arose over Chinese construction crews—housed in local compounds—who were perceived to be displacing Jamaican construction crews in the building of the soccer stadium and airport road. In the Bahamas, the local Construction Industry Association, experienced in tourism construction, indicates it was not even consulted about undertaking any work related to the Baha Mar Casino and Hotel complex, the biggest project in the country.[58]

In the future, LAC officials will need to look more strategically at Chinese and Indian investments for better integration with the local labor market and better gains for local workers. There are many feasible alternatives to the "bring your own workers" approach to infrastructure investment. Singapore, for example, required that it manage the project, and learned the training methods of its foreign investors, greatly strengthening the human capital improvements brought by foreign investment.[59] Particularly as both Chinese and Indian investments are diversifying away from primary products, there will be more opportunities in the near future for sharing local employment gains with local labor forces. A prime example is Chinese auto assembly and manufacturing in the Southern Cone—investments such as Lenovo in electronics (Brazil, Mexico, and Argentina) and Chery and JAC in the automotive sector (Brazil).[60] While Indian investment has largely concentrated on energy and primary products to date, the next wave of investment, expected in mining in Peru, Colombia, and Brazil, could also bring greater local employment possibilities.[61]

The LAC countries in their turn could learn from China and India different approaches to linking their own large network of émigrés, principally in North America, to national and local market development. The Chinese, whether at the state, local government, or company level, have seen migration as a way to advance local market relations, with Chinese migrants selling Chinese products and goods linked to their home regional markets. Chris Alden has noted that in Africa, local Chinese governments encourage emigration not only for remittances but also to open up trade and market relations for local industries and crops.[62] In a more targeted way, India has created links between its high-tech migrants in the United States and the United Kingdom and firms in India. Ethnic Chinese communities have made remarkable contributions to Southeast Asian economies,[63] but this phenomenon has been less considered in LAC, and remains outside current thinking of the region's economic leaders either for incoming migrants or their own migrants abroad. The region has not yet embraced a concept of migration as being linked to their home country's external trade and investment.

Rather than looking at individual Chinese or Indian investment deals as single events that one seeks to either "contain" or "keep quiet" about employment losses, LAC countries might think more strategically about how to better link and profit from the growing interrelationships of trade, investment, and migration with China and India. The challenge in the next decade is to make south-south migration more human capital and market enhancing and thus less politically charged. Migration in a more mobile and global world economy is, or could be, a more integrated feature and player in the future economic advances of Latin America, China, and India.

NOTES

The author would like to especially thank Caitlyn McCrone and Ge "Pepe" Zhang for their research assistance on this chapter.

1. The British Parliament ended indentured servitude only in 1916.

2. Daniel Naujoks, "Emigration, Immigration, and Diaspora Relations in India" (Washington, DC: Migration Policy Institute, October 15, 2009) (www.migrationpolicy.org).

3. Deepak Bhojwani, "India's Prospects in Latin America and the Caribbean," *Indian Foreign Affairs Journal* 7, no. 4 (2012), pp. 433–45.

4. Ibid.

5. Jacqueline Mazza and Eleanor Sohnen, "Crossing Borders for Work: New Trends and Policies in Labor Migration in Latin America and the Caribbean" (Washington, DC: Inter-American Development Bank, 2011).

6. Naujoks, "Emigration, Immigration, and Diaspora Relations in India."

7. Haiyan Zhang, "The Role of Migration in Shaping China's Economic Relations with Its Main Partners," Migration Policy Center (MPC) Research Report, MPC and European University Institute Robert Schuman Center for Advanced Studies; Biao Xiang, "A New Mobility Regime in the Making: What Does a Mobile China Mean to the World?," paper presented at the "Development Assistance and Emerging Countries" workshop, Seminaire Regulier, 2006; Ronald Skeldon, "China: From Exceptional Case to Global Participant" (Washington, DC: Migration Policy Institute, 2004)

(http://www.migrationpolicy.org/article/china-exceptional-case-global
-participant); Jane J. Cho, *Asians in Latin America: A Partially Annotated
Bibliography of Select Countries and People* (Stanford University Center
for Latin American Studies, 2000); Binod Khadria, "The Future of International Migration to OECD Countries, Regional Note, South Asia," Organi-
zation for Economic Cooperation and Development (OECD), 2008; Mary
Chamberlain, *Caribbean Migration: Globalized Identities* (Abingdon, UK:
Taylor & Francis, 2002); Steven Vertovec, "Indian Indentured Migration to
the Caribbean," in *The Cambridge Survey of World Migration,* edited by
Robin Cohen (Cambridge University Press, 1995), pp. 57–62; Hugh Tinker,
A New System of Slavery: The Export of Indian Labour Overseas (Oxford
University Press, 1974).

8. Census data notoriously undercounts immigration populations and
showed a 2000 census total of only 28,716 Chinese in all of Latin America.
Guyana alone is believed to have more than this figure. Latin American and
Caribbean Demographic Center (CELADE), "Investigación de la Migración
Internacional en Latinoamérica," United Nations Economic Commission
for Latin American and the Caribbean, Santiago, Chile (http://celade.cepal
.org/bdcelade/imila/).

9. United Nations Department of Economic and Social Affairs (UN
DESA), International Migration, Population Division, 2014, (http://www
.un.org/en/development/desa/population/migration/data/estimates2/index
.shtml).

10. Author calculations for 2013 from UNDESA, 2014.

11. World Bank, "Migration and Remittance Flows: Recent Trends and
Outlook: 2013–2016," Migration and Development Brief 21 (Washington,
DC: World Bank, October 2, 2013), p. 5.

12. Naujoks, "Emigration, Immigration, and Diaspora Relations."

13. Jacqueline Mazza, "Chinese Migration to Latin America and the Caribbean," Inter-American Dialogue Report, Washington, DC, 2016.

14. Author interviews, 2010–12.

15. Indian High Level Committee on the Indian Diaspora, 2002.

16. United Nations Statistics Division, 2014 (http://unstats.un.org/unsd
/default.htm).

17. Legal permanent residency often implies an application of current
residents to change migration status to permanent or are supported by
employers.

18. Organization of American States (OAS), *International Migration in
the Americas, SICREMI 2012* (Washington, DC: OAS, 2012) (https://www
.oecd.org/els/mig/G48952_WB_SICREMI_2012_ENGLISH_REPORT
_LR.pdf).

19. The 2010 census records only 881 Indians and 19,396 Chinese,
likely highly undercounted in both cases. UNDESA, author calculations of
"foreign-born population 15 years of age or over by country/area of birth,
educational attainment and sex."

20. Mazza, "Chinese Migration to Latin America and the Caribbean."

21. Simon Tomero, quoted in R. Evan Ellis, "The Expanding Chinese Footprint in Latin America: New Challenges for China, and Dilemmas for the US," *Asie.Visions* (Institut Français des Relations Internationales) 49 (February 2012).

22. Semi-skilled and unskilled Indian workers to Gulf countries tripled from 160,000 in 1999 to 770,000 in 2007 (Naujocks, "Emigration, Immigration, and Diaspora Relations in India").

23. Xiang, "A New Mobility Regime."

24. Ibid.

25. Ellis, "The Expanding Chinese Footprint in Latin America."

26. State Council of China, "China National Plan of Action on Combating Trafficking in Women and Children (2008–2012)," December 13, 2007 (http://www.hsph.harvard.edu/population/trafficking/china.traf.08.pdf).

27. Excluding investments by Chinese banks.

28. Ellis, "The Expanding Chinese Footprint in Latin America."

29. Minister of Social Services for the Bahamas, Ms. Loretta Butler-Turner, estimated the number closer to 8,000 Chinese who would be in and out of the Bahamas for the construction of the project (author interview, June 2012). See also Juan McCartney, "Baha Mar, Bahamas Resort Complex: Backed by Chinese Government," *Huffington Post,* February 21, 2011.

30. Ellis, "The Expanding Chinese Footprint in Latin America."

31. "Rio Industries Agree to Hire Chinese Workers," *People's Daily Online,* December 21, 2006.

32. Author interviews with immigration officials, 2010–12.

33. Patricia Rey Mallén, "Chinese Workers Arrive in Nicaragua to Do Viability Studies for Controversial Canal," *International Business Times,* December 13, 2013 (http://www.ibtimes.com/chinese-workers-arrive-nicara gua-do-viability-studies-controversial-canal-1507360).

34. Hulyao Wang, *Annual Report on Chinese International Migration* (Beijing: Center for China and Globalization and the Social Sciences Academic Press, January 2014) (translation). They report 2012 data from the Chinese National Bureau of Statistics, p. 17. Also reviewed for this chapter were data from the Bureau of Exit and Entry Administration of the Ministry of Public Security, the Chinese Ministry of Commerce, and the Chinese International Contractors' Association.

35. Emmanuel Ma Mung, "Chinese Migration and China's Foreign Policy in Africa," *Journal of Chinese Overseas* 4, no. 1 (2008), pp. 91–109.

36. An estimated 700 Chinese workers for the Costa Rican stadium were cited in *Mata,* July 1, 2010. Estimates for 500 workers include Grenada and the two public buildings in Trinidad and Tobago (cited in Ellis, "The Expanding Chinese Footprint in Latin America").

37. Alonso Mata Blanco and Johan Umaña, "Gobierno pasado aprobó visas a 100 chinos para construir condóminos," *La Nación,* June 10, 2010

(http://wfnode01.nacion.com/2010-06-03/ElPais/NotasSecundarias/N03 -FALTA.aspx).

38. Adrian Frater, "Trelawny Stadium Intact," *Jamaica Gleaner,* July 9, 2007 (http://jamaica-gleaner.com/gleaner/20070709/sports/sports10.html).

39. Author interviews, 2010–12; Ellis, "The Expanding Chinese Footprint in Latin America."

40. Ge Zhang, "Being 'Chinese' in Peru: The Chinese Success in Lima in Perspective," unpublished undergraduate thesis, Pomona College, California, 2013.

41. R. Evan Ellis, *China in Latin America: The Whats and Wherefores* (Boulder, CO: Lynne Rienner Publishers, 2009).

42. Oficina del Consejero Económico-Comercial de la Embajada de la República Popular China en la República Argentina, "Intercambios de visitas," May 9, 2005 (http://ar2.mofcom.gov.cn/article/bilateralvisits/200505 /20050500086780.shtml).

43. Samuel Logan, "Ecuador: Back Door to America," The International Relations and Security Network, January 29, 2009 (http://www.isn.ethz.ch /Digital-Library/Articles/Detail/?lng=en&id=95896).

44. Author interviews, 2010–12.

45. Author interview, November 2010.

46. Organization for Economic Cooperation and Development (OECD), *International Migration Outlook 2013,* (Paris: OECD, 2013).

47. Jeffrey Todd, "It Takes a Village to Build Baha Mar," *Nassau Guardian,* February 14, 2012.

48. Author interview, Guatemalan migration official, 2010.

49. State Council of China, "China National Plan."

50. Daniel Zueras, "Rights–Costa Rica: Persons for Sale," *Inside Costa Rica,* May 12, 2009 (http://insidecostarica.com/special_reports/2009/2009 -05/costa%20_rica_persons.htm).

51. "Tras una mediación del Gobierno, los camioneros levantan el boicot a los autoservicios chinos," *Clarín,* June 26, 2006 (http://edant.clarin .com/diario/2006/06/26/um/m-01222980.htm).

52. Logan, "Ecuador."

53. Frank N. Pieke and Tabitha Speelman, "Chinese Investment Strategies and Migration: Does Diaspora Matter?" Report for the Migration Policy Center and the European University Institute, Leiden University, the Netherlands, 2013) (http://media.leidenuniv.nl/legacy/pieke—mpc-report -final-draft-130117.pdf).

54. Ellis, "The Expanding Chinese Footprint in Latin America."

55. Simon Romero, "With Aid and Migrants, China Expands Its Presence in a South American Nation," *New York Times,* April 10, 2011.

56. Ellis, "The Expanding Chinese Footprint in Latin America."

57. Author interview with Deborah Brautigam, November 2013; and Giles Mohan and May Tan-Mullins, "Chinese Migrants in Africa as New

Agents of Development? An Analytical Framework," *European Journal of Development Research* 21, no. 4 (2009), pp. 588–605.

58. Author interview, 2012.

59. Monika Aring, "Best Practices in Labor and Economic Development: Malaysia, Singapore, and Ireland." Inter-American Development Bank, 2015 (unpublished).

60. Gayle Allard and Jacqueline Mazza, "China's Expansion into Latin America: Trends in Investment and Labor Migration," Latin American Policy Lessons: Perspectives for Europe Series, Bologna Institute for Policy Research (BIPR), Johns Hopkins University-SAIS Europe, 3 April 2014, (http://www.bipr.eu/eventprofile.cfm/idevent=711B769E-BD29-A8D4-06412F341D8CEB48/Gayle-Allard-and-Jacqueline-Mazza-Chinas-Expansion-in-Latin-America-Trends-in-Investment-and-Labor-Migration &zdyx=1).

61. Bhojwani, "India's Prospects in Latin America and the Caribbean."

62. Chris Alden, *China in Africa* (London: Zed Books, 2007).

63. Guotu Zhang, and Wangbo Wang, "Migration and Trade: The Role of Overseas Chinese in Economic Relations between China and Southeast Asia," *International Journal of China Studies* 1, no. 1 (2010), p. 174; and literature cited in Zhang, "Being 'Chinese' in Peru."

CHAPTER 9

The Security Dimension of Chinese and Indian Engagement in the Americas

R. Evan Ellis

In October 2013, a flotilla including two Chinese guided missile frigates crossed the Pacific, where for the first time they conducted a series of bilateral exercises with their counterparts in Chile[1] and Brazil,[2] as well as making a port call in Argentina. In August 2014, the Indian Ministry of Defense announced that it had decided to permit the sale of the hypersonic anti-ship missile, BrahMos, to interested clients in Latin America.[3] The missile is considered by defense analysts to be a weapon so difficult to defend against that its introduction into the region could fundamentally change the strategic calculus for naval forces operating there. In June 2014, Mexican authorities arrested "El Chapo" Guzmán, the leader of the Sinaloa Cartel. Despite his subsequent escape and recapture, media coverage of the arrest and ensuing "roll-up" operations highlighted the cartel's extensive operations in Asia, including not only cocaine sales but also the purchase of precursor chemicals from companies in China and India for the production of methamphetamines. Each of these developments highlights how the People's Republic of China (PRC) and, to a lesser extent, India, are increasingly altering the security environment of Latin America and the Caribbean (LAC).

Although much has been written on the growing economic ties between Asia and the LAC countries, the security dimension of that relationship has received much less attention.[4] Moreover, although there is growing literature on China's engagement with the region, there are almost no scholarly articles on India's activities there.[5] The present chapter takes a step toward filling that gap by examining Chinese and Indian military activities in LAC and the impact of such activities, as well as other forms of engagement, on the regional security environment.

In general terms, the strategic objectives of the PRC and India in LAC are similar: to secure reliable access to the primary products, markets, and technologies that each nation needs for its development and to obtain the agricultural products that each needs to help feed its enormous population. In pursuing such objectives, however, the PRC has arguably demonstrated more, and more effective, coordination between the activities of its government, commercial entities, and financial institutions than has India. Moreover, the greater scale and more rapid pace of PRC industrialization and urbanization have driven the Chinese to pursue such activities in LAC to a far greater extent and across a broader range of countries and sectors than has India.

Within the domain of military engagement, both the PRC and India are pursuing arms sales to the nations of the LAC region and conducting military-to-military interactions. In both areas, the activities of the PRC and its defense companies are far greater and stretch across a broader range of countries than do those of its Indian counterparts.

For both China and India, military sales to LAC countries are part of their expansion into defense markets globally and contribute to the development and sustenance of their respective defense industrial bases. Benefits from such sales include the improvement of key defense-relevant technologies through the codevelopment of products with partners in the region, and refinement of that technology through use in the field. Both the PRC and India also exchange limited numbers of personnel with LAC partner nations for training and professional military education, which helps each to develop relationships with defense institutions in those countries as part of their broader engagement with the region.[6]

MILITARY ACTIVITIES BY THE PRC AND INDIA IN LATIN AMERICA AND THE CARIBBEAN

Chinese and Indian activities of an explicitly military character in LAC are more extensive than commonly realized, although those of the PRC are far greater than India's. For both Eastern countries, such activities have expanded significantly in recent years and are helping to change the dynamics of the regional arms trade. In so doing, India and the PRC are forging greater multipolarity in the region's security partnerships.

Chinese Military Sales to the Region

By comparison with the limited progress of Indian companies in selling arms to LAC countries, the advances of Chinese military suppliers have been remarkable, including sales by the China North Industries Corporation (NORINCO), Poly Technologies, the China National Aero-Technology Import & Export Corporation (CATIC), the China National Electronics Import and Export Corporation (CEIEC), the China Aviation Industrial Corporation (AVIC), and the China Shipbuilding Industries Corporation (CSIC). Contracts with these companies in the region in recent years have expanded from the provision of nonlethal goods to making available sophisticated end items, and from sales to the politically sympathetic regimes of the Bolivarian Alliance for the Peoples of Our America (ALBA) to contracts with a broader range of regimes for major end items. Although Chinese companies have sold light arms, military clothing, and other basic goods to Latin American militaries, Venezuela provided China with the first significant opportunity to sell sophisticated military systems in the region, announcing the purchase of Chinese JYL-1 radar systems in August 2005,[7] K-8 fighter aircraft in October 2008,[8] and, in 2010, Y-8 and Y-12 military transport aircraft as well.[9] From Venezuela, Chinese companies diversified their sales to ALBA partners Bolivia and Ecuador. In October 2009, Bolivia agreed to acquire six Chinese K-8 fighters of its own, and in 2011 Bolivia contracted with the Chinese firm Harbin Aircraft Manufacturing Corporation to acquire six H-425 helicopters for $108 million.[10]

Ecuador, which had already leased Chinese MA-60 military transports, followed Venezuela's lead by purchasing Chinese radar systems from the China Electronics Technology Corporation (CETC), although Ecuador subsequently terminated the contract following a legal dispute.[11]

Concurrent with the addition of Bolivia and Ecuador to their client base, Chinese military companies expanded their existing position in Venezuela, securing commitments for nine more K-8 transport aircraft[12] and twenty-six more radar systems.[13] Expanded sales to Venezuela also included amphibious assault vehicles, SR-5 multiple launch rocket launchers, and SM-4 self-propelled grenade launchers,[14] the Harbin H-425/Z-9 helicopter, and the L-15 fighter,[15] which is considered more advanced than the previously acquired K-8s. Leveraging their growing position in and experience with the ALBA countries, in addition to selling less sophisticated goods throughout the region, Chinese military companies then began to move into more competitive markets, such as Peru and Argentina.

The initial forays of Chinese arms companies into Peru and Argentina were embarrassing failures, with the Peruvian Ministry of Defense unexpectedly cancelling a purchase of Chinese MBT-2000 tanks in April 2010[16] after having displayed the tanks in a military parade in Lima in December 2009 and after the highest levels of government had confirmed the acquisition.[17] Similarly, in November 2013, Chinese defense companies lost a bid for a Peruvian air defense system to a team led by the U.S. company Raytheon.[18] In Argentina, the government suspended its 2009 acquisition of Chinese WMZ-551 armored vehicles after the delivery of only four units, while China's attempt to sell the X-11 helicopter to Argentina stalled when France objected that the helicopter was based on designs and technology stolen from the French company Aerospatiale and threatened to scale back French cooperation with Argentina if the X-11 purchase from China went forward.[19]

Despite such initial setbacks, by 2014, Chinese arms companies had sold the Peruvian armed forces Beiben, Dong Feng, and Shaanxy military trucks and had won contracts to supply forty type 90B multiple-launch rocket vehicles,[20] the first twenty-seven of which were delivered in July 2015.[21] Chinese military shipbuilders are now beginning to register sales in the region, with a contract for a long-range patrol vessel to be sold to Trinidad and Tobago in 2014[22] and a public attempt to sell a similar type of vessel to Uruguay.[23]

The most significant Chinese advance in military sales beyond the nations of ALBA, however, came in January 2015, when the Argentine government announced plans to procure $1 billion in equipment from the Chinese, including 110 8×8 VN-1 armored personnel carriers, five P-18 "Malvinas" class patrol ships, and fourteen Chengdu Aircraft Corporation JF-17/FC-1 multirole fighters,[24] although with the election of Mauricio Macri to the Argentine presidency in November 2015, the policy direction of the country changed and the contract was never realized.

The new role of the PRC as a seller of military goods in the region has arguably expanded arms procurement options for LAC security establishments, particularly for rogue regimes such as that in Venezuela, which cannot purchase U.S. arms. In the process, such sales have generated concerns in neighboring states such as Colombia and have increased the risk of sophisticated arms falling into the hands of terrorists or criminal organizations.

Even for LAC regimes that are not limited in their access to other sources of arms, Chinese companies offer an increasingly broad selection of military products, from basic goods to increasingly sophisticated end items, generally at lower prices than their competitors and with financing available through Chinese banks. Chinese companies have also become regular participants in the region's military shows, including FIDAE (Feria Internacional del Aire y del Espacio) in Chile, LAAD (Latin

America Aero and Defence) in Brazil,[25] and SITDEF (Salón Internacional de Tecnología para la Defensa y Prevención de Desastres Naturales) in Peru.[26]

Indian Military Sales to the Region

By comparison with their Chinese counterparts, Indian defense companies' sales to the region have been modest. Cases include Hindustan Aeronautics (HAL), which has sold its Dhruv light helicopters to Ecuador, Peru, and Suriname. HAL's advance in the Latin American arms market has arguably been impeded, however, by the loss of four of the seven helicopters sold to Ecuador, including a crash in October 2009 in front of military leaders and other spectators during an air show in Quito, Ecuador,[27] a second crash in February 2014 during a routine flight from Guayaquil to Quito,[28] and the subsequent termination of its contract by the government of Ecuador.[29]

Beyond HAL's sales of the Dhruv, India's military Defense Research and Development Organization (DRDO) has collaborated with the Brazilian Ministry of Defense and the Brazilian aircraft company Embraer to develop and produce an airborne radar platform,[30] with the first three aircraft developed through this collaboration delivered to India in August 2012.[31]

More recently, and potentially more significant, in February 2014 the Indian Ministry of Defense authorized the sale of the hypersonic missile BrahMos to the region.[32] Brazil, Chile, and Venezuela have reportedly expressed interest in the missile.[33] Beyond aircraft, the vehicle manufacturer Mahindra has sold light military trucks to Argentina, Uruguay, Honduras, and Belize,[34] among others.

Military-to-Military Relationships between China, India, and LAC Countries

In addition to arms sales, both the Chinese and Indian governments have sought to build military-to-military ties in the region in such areas as visits by senior military leaders to each other's countries, training, and professional military education. In breadth and intensity, such activities on the part of the Chinese far exceed those of India, and of the two nations, only the Chinese People's Liberation Army (PLA) has regularly deployed military forces to the region to conduct both humanitarian engagements and combat exercises. Such engagement is contributing to an expanding multipolarity of security partnerships in the region through increased training, professional military education, and other military activities.

With respect to exercises, professional military education, training activities, or other exchanges, and with the exception of military attachés, India's military has almost no presence in LAC countries. Indeed, in the 2012 Indian Ministry of Defense's annual report cataloguing the nation's foreign defense engagements, the only mention of Latin America is a reference to "regular exchanges of high level visits and exchange of views" with Brazil.[35] Nonetheless, in July 2014, for the first time, an Indian frigate participated in the multinational naval exercises known as RIMPAC, or Rim of the Pacific Exercise,[36] in the company of Mexico, Chile, Colombia, and Peru.

In contrast to the modest Indian military-to-military activities in LAC, the PRC's military engagement with the region has been far more robust. From the beginning of the millennium, as the PRC has expanded its commercial presence in the region, it has also hosted an increasing number of LAC military officers and civilian defense personnel in Chinese institutions, among them the Defense Studies institute in Chanping and the PLA navy command and general staff schools near Nanjing. It has also regularly visited, and received delegations from, Latin American institutions, such as Colombia's Escuela Superior de Guerra, and conducted training for operators and maintainers of the equipment purchased from Chinese arms companies, including not only the aircraft, vehicles, and ships mentioned in the previous section but also satellites built and launched by Chinese companies.

The PLA is also operating in the region. Chinese personnel have been sent to Colombian bases such as Tolemaida for training in special skills such as jungle survival and riverine and urban combat, and to attend Brazil's jungle warfare school near Manaus. China also maintained a contingent of military police in Haiti from 2004 through 2012 as part of the UN multinational force there, MINUSTAH. In November 2010 it conducted a bilateral humanitarian exercise with the Peruvian army titled Peace Angel, and in December 2011 it deployed its recently commissioned hospital ship *Peace Ark* to the Caribbean for a four-nation goodwill-building medical mission.[37] In October 2013, while U.S. policymakers were distracted by a national budget crisis, the PRC deployed a naval flotilla to the Southern Cone, conducting separate bilateral exercises with its counterparts in Chile,[38] Argentina, and Brazil.[39]

While the PLA has yet to establish exclusive military alliances or basing agreements with countries in the hemisphere, its official white paper on Chinese defense strategy, released in June 2015, recognizes protection of global commercial interests and maintaining relationships with foreign militaries as important missions of the Chinese military.[40]

Arguably, the development of such relationships with the region's militaries undercuts the traditional role of the United States as the security partner of choice, and opens the door for the PLA to operate from the region's ports, airfields, bases, or other facilities on very short notice in the future should the PRC, and counterpart regimes in the region (such as Venezuela, Cuba, Nicaragua, Ecuador, or Bolivia), choose to do so.

BROADER IMPACTS OF CHINA'S AND INDIA'S REGIONAL ENGAGEMENT ON THE REGIONAL SECURITY ENVIRONMENT

The impacts of Chinese and Indian engagement on the security environment of LAC go far beyond arms sales and other explicitly military activities. This section discusses some of those effects, both positive and negative.

Reshaping of the Physical Infrastructure and Commercial Patterns of the Region

Expanded commerce with China and other parts of Asia continues to fuel the growth of ports, highways, railroads, and other infrastructure in LAC, with the goal of facilitating the extraction of its primary products and agricultural goods and easing access to its markets for Asian products. Such dynamics can be seen in the expansion of Pacific coast ports from Manzanillo and Lázaro Cárdenas (Mexico) to Iquique, Valparaíso, and Concepción (Chile), as well as new port projects on the Atlantic side of the continent tied to the expanding trans-Pacific trade, including the ports of Goat Island in Jamaica,[41] Mariel and Santiago in Cuba,[42] and La Rocha in Uruguay.[43]

The new trans-Pacific commerce is also driving infrastructure connecting those ports to the interior of the continent, including a Peru-to-Brazil transcontinental rail project announced during the August 2014 visit to the region by Chinese president Xi Jinping,[44] and "bioceanic corridors" connecting the interior of Brazil to Pacific coast ports such as Iquique, Ilo, Callao Paita, and Manta.[45]

Both the widening of the Panama Canal and the proposed new Nicaragua Canal[46] are similarly driven by the logic of expanding commerce with Asia, as is the series of transcontinental highway and rail corridors contemplated to be built by Chinese construction companies with Chinese loan funds, including one from Veracruz to Oaxaca, Mexico,[47] and others across Honduras,[48] Guatemala,[49] and Colombia.[50]

While such projects, if completed, may facilitate commerce and development, they will also alter patterns of human interaction and criminal activity in the region. Such infrastructure is likely to give new importance to previously isolated Pacific coast cities such as Machala, Ecuador, or Paita and Ilo, in Peru. New highway and rail corridors will make the interior of the continent more accessible for illegal loggers and drug laboratories.[51] It will also bring new immigrants to previously isolated areas, putting them into contact with indigenous peoples living there and expanding opportunities for social conflict.[52]

Chinese Companies as Local Actors with Interests in the Outcomes of Local Government Decisions

Since approximately 2009, Chinese companies have expanded from exporting products to, and importing products from, LAC countries to establishing commercial operations on Latin American soil. This new physical presence encompasses not only mining and petroleum operations but also Chinese construction projects, final assembly facilities, and retail operations, plus activities in banking, telecommunications, logistics, and other service sectors.[53]

In establishing themselves in the region, Chinese companies become social and political actors there as local employers, taxpayers, and members of the community. From market entry, Chinese companies establish relationships with national and local governments, dealing with tax and regulatory authorities, working to secure the approval of projects, and competing for public bids. In the process, they must navigate a web of interested parties, including local communities, environmentalists, and competitors. Once established, Chinese companies generate social impacts, from positive pecuniary effects on the persons and subcontractors they employ to negative effects on those not hired to the displacement of persons in projects such as construction or hydroelectric facilities; issues of security also arise quickly, particularly for construction, petroleum, and mining projects operating in remote areas.[54] Although the PRC has repeatedly proclaimed its commitment to "noninterference" in the sovereign affairs of foreign countries, it is not clear to what degree the Chinese government will use its economic leverage and other forms of soft power to advance or protect the interests of its companies and personnel in the region. In a possible foreshadowing of how it might conduct itself in LAC countries, in September 2014 the PRC deployed 800 troops to Sudan to protect its oil operations against violence in that country.[55] It is not unthinkable that the PRC would similarly deploy forces to protect its commercial interests in a Latin American country such as Venezuela if invited to do so by the host government.

The Question of Special Protection for Chinese Communities in the Region

As PRC commerce with LAC countries has expanded, Chinese communities, long established there, have increasingly drawn the attention of other communities and the national government. This phenomenon has been accentuated by the growth of these populations through immigration, fueled by both illegal immigration and by Chinese personnel who decide to remain in the country after having been brought in for work projects under liberal visa policies in countries such as Suriname and Guyana.[56]

The expansion of Chinese communities has been particularly felt in the smaller nations of the Caribbean Basin, where some non-Chinese perceive the increasing Chinese presence as a threat to their livelihood. Such tensions have given rise to ethnic violence against Chinese in Maracay and Valencia, Venezuela, in 2004; in Papitam and Maripaston, Suriname, in 2009 and 2011, respectively; and in Buenos Aires in 2013, and to massive protests against Chinese shopkeepers, which shut down the central portion of Santo Domingo, the capital of the Dominican Republic, in July 2013.[57]

Although ethnic Chinese residing abroad have long been considered part of the greater Chinese civilization, for more than a century the Chinese state has been too weak to protect them. As the PRC's power grows, and as its presence in and economic leverage over the LAC countries expand, its government is becoming increasingly active in defending the interests of "overseas Chinese" communities there.[58] In October 2011, for example, the Chinese ambassador, Yuan Nansheng, was notably vocal and critical of the Surinamese government following violence against the Chinese community in Maripaston.[59] Similarly, in August 2013, during a state visit to China by Jamaican prime minister Portia Simpson-Miller, her PRC counterpart, Li Keqiang, raised the issue of criminal violence against Chinese Jamaicans, forcing Simpson-Miller to implement a special program of protection for the community on her return.[60]

Trans-Pacific Organized Crime

The expanding flow of goods, capital, and people between the PRC and Latin America has been accompanied by growth in trans-Pacific Chinese organized crime. Activities include human trafficking (discussed in more detail by Jacqueline Mazza in chapter 8), contraband goods, sales of precursor chemicals by China and India to the region, the sale of cocaine and other drugs from the region to China,[61] the illegal purchase of minerals by Chinese companies from Latin America's informal mining sector,[62] weapons trafficking,[63] and money laundering involving Chinese companies and institutions.[64]

While there is no evidence that the PRC government is involved in such activities, cooperation between Chinese and Latin American authorities has been limited.[65] Moreover, Latin American law enforcement authorities are ill-equipped to deal with the phenomenon, having few personnel who speak mandarin Chinese, let alone dialects common among Chinese immigrants to the region, such as Cantonese and Hakka, and with limited technical contacts between Latin American law enforcement personnel and their counterparts in the PRC.

Decreased Incentives for Countries of the Region to Follow the United States and Western Institutions

The availability of the PRC as an alternative export destination and as a source of investment and finance has arguably lessened enthusiasm in the region for U.S.-led initiatives such as the Free Trade Area of the Americas and the Trans-Pacific Partnership, as well as U.S.-led multilateral institutions, such as the Organization of American States (OAS).[66] In similar fashion, the availability of financing from PRC-based institutions such as the China Development Bank (which dispensed more than $120 billion between 2005 and 2014)[67] has decreased incentives within the region to follow the precepts of Western financial institutions such as the World Bank and the International Monetary Fund (IMF).

Beyond providing material alternatives to the United States and Western institutions, the PRC has also undercut the influence of U.S. and Western positions on issues of trade, democracy, and human rights. While the PRC has been careful not to advance a specific political, economic, or social model to rival those of the United States, it has done so in an even more effective fashion by demonstrating to countries of the region that nations can achieve developmental goals without adhering to U.S. positions on such issues.

Extended Life of Populist Regimes

In its pursuit of "friendships," raw materials, and business for its banks and companies, China is indirectly extending the life of populist regimes in the region and indirectly contributing to the adverse effects that those regimes have on the security environment of the region. Such support includes more than $50 billion in Chinese bank loans to Venezuela—of which $4 billion was disbursed in the months prior to the reelection bid by the country's late president, Hugo Chávez—plus $11 billion in new commitments as Chávez's successor, Nicolás Maduro, struggled to consolidate power.[68] Indeed, Chinese banks approved an additional $5 billion for Venezuela in 2015, with disbursement occurring shortly before the nation's December 2015 congressional elections, to the benefit of the regime.[69]

China similarly has extended more than $11 billion in loans to Ecuador,[70] including a $1 billion loan in 2009 as the country struggled with solvency issues associated with its default on IMF loans the previous year,[71] and $1.4 billion during February 2013, the month of the elections that gave a new mandate to Ecuadoran president Rafael Correa.[72] It has extended approximately $500 million in construction projects for Bolivia, as well as a $7.5 billion line of credit for further work.[73]

As a by-product of helping anti-U.S. regimes such as those of Hugo Chávez, Nicolás Maduro, and Rafael Correa remain in power, Chinese resources have allowed those regimes to minimize cooperation with U.S. and international law enforcement authorities[74] as transnational criminal organizations, insurgent groups such as the FARC, Islamic fundamentalists such as Hezbollah, and others operate from their territory.[75]

Changed Strategic Calculus for the United States in the Event of a Global Conflict with the PRC

Although a military conflict between the United States and the PRC is neither desirable nor likely, it is probable that both countries have personnel charged with planning how to conduct such a conflict if the need arose. For such planners in the United States, the significant and growing PRC commercial presence in the Western Hemisphere creates substantial vulnerabilities with respect to both what the PRC could do and how the U.S. global response might be limited.

In the period preceding a conflict, China's economic and political leverage in the region could help it convince LAC nations not to support U.S. actions against the PRC in Asia. Withholding support for U.S. actions could take the form not only of refusing to join a coalition or blocking resolutions in the UN but possibly of denying the United States intelligence cooperation or the use of bases and logistics infrastructure important for U.S. power projection beyond the hemisphere. Chinese commercial facilities in the region also expand PRC options for the clandestine introduction and sustainment of operatives there. From LAC countries, such agents could act in a variety of ways to distract or paralyze the U.S. military response, including attacking the canals, ports, logistics, transportation facilities, and telecommunications infrastructure in the region supporting U.S. operations. Such activities could even be used to attack Latin American financial, manufacturing, agricultural, or other targets to create an economic crisis in the United States that would undermine the sustainability of its operations in Asia.

In the event of hostilities between the United States and the PRC or of a prolonged global crisis, China's friendships with and economic leverage over Latin American countries, such as those of ALBA, could induce them to allow the PRC to use their territory for military purposes. If permitted to do so, China could begin conducting military operations from the region relatively quickly, owing to the working relationship that it is building with the region's militaries today and the detailed technical knowledge of the region's ports, airfields, logistics, and other infrastructure possessed by Chinese companies such as Hutchison-Whampoa, COSCO, China Shipping, China Airport Holdings, and China Airlines, which operate there currently. Indeed, on repeated occasions historically, Chinese commercial companies have made their knowledge and assets available to the Chinese government when called on to do so in support of the national interest. As examples, in 1991 the Chinese shipping company COSCO supported the evacuation of Chinese personnel from Somalia,[76] and in February 2011 China Airlines and China Southern Airlines supported the evacuation of Chinese from Libya.[77]

CONCLUSIONS

Chinese engagement and to a lesser extent Indian engagement with LAC countries are profoundly transforming the regional security environment. Though the activities of each actor in the LAC region are primarily economic, the military activities in the region of both countries are nontrivial and growing, and the indirect effects of the two Eastern nations' commercial activities are reshaping the region. These effects are manifested in a host of areas: in the new economic and sociopolitical dynamics associated with the transformation of the region's infrastructure, in a new role for Chinese and Indian companies on the ground in the region, in the evolving position of Chinese communities and their relationship with the Chinese government, in the expanding threat of trans-Pacific organized crime, in the diminished ability of the United States to advance its policy agenda in the region, in the extended life of anti-U.S. regimes such as those of ALBA, and in new options for China to use its presence in the region in a future conflict involving the United States. None of these developments implies malevolent intentions by either the PRC or India toward the region or toward the United States through their presence there. Yet Chinese and Indian engagement in LAC countries has transformed the regional security environment in profound ways that should be carefully considered by scholars, politicians, and security planners in the region as well as in the United States.

NOTES

The views expressed in the article are strictly those of the author. The author would like to thank Jenny Lafaurie, Joseina McKenzie, and Brett Carpenter for their research assistance.

1. "Armadas de China y Chile Realizaron Ejercicios Navales," *Noticias FFAA Chile,* October 16, 2013 (http://noticiasffaachile.blogspot.com/2013/10/armadas-de-china-y-chile-realizaron.html).

2. China Ministry of National Defense, "PLAN Taskforce Conducts Joint Maritime Exercise with Brazilian Navy," October 28, 2013 (http://eng.mod.gov.cn/DefenseNews/2013-10/28/content_4472787.htm).

3. "BrahMos Missile Can Be Exported to SE Asian, Latin American Nations," *Times of India,* August 3, 2014 (http://m.timesofindia.com/india/BrahMos-missile-can-be-exported-to'SE-Asian-Latin-American-nations/articleshow/39561883.cms).

4. The modest literature on the strategic dimension of this relationship principally focuses on China–Latin American military ties. See, for example, R. Evan Ellis, *The Strategic Dimension of China's Engagement with Latin America* (Washington, DC: William J. Perry Paper Center for Hemispheric Defense Studies, 2014). See also Gabriel Marcella, "What Is the Chinese Military Doing in Latin America?," *America's Quarterly* (Winter 2012); and R. Evan Ellis, *China–Latin America Military Engagement* (Carlisle Barracks, PA: U.S. Army War College Strategic Studies Institute, August 2011) (http://www.strategicstudiesinstitute.army.mil/pubs/). Nonetheless, journalistic accounts periodically mention individual Chinese economic activities as potential strategic threats to the United States, including the

government of Panama's granting of Panama Canal port concessions to the Chinese company Hutchison Whampoa in 1999, rumors of the China's operation of signals intelligence facilities in Cuba, and possible Chinese financing for the proposed Nicaragua Canal.

5. One of the most important of the limited number of works on India's activities in Latin America is Mauricio Mesquita Moreira, *India: Latin America's Next Big Thing* (Washington, DC: Inter-American Development Bank, 2010).

6. The PRC explicitly addressed such military engagement in its 2008 policy white paper on the region, promising to "deepen exchanges in military training, personnel training and peacekeeping," "expand cooperation in the non-traditional security field," and "provide assistance for the development of the army in Latin American and Caribbean countries." See "Full Text: China's Policy Paper on Latin America and the Caribbean," *People's Daily Online,* November 8, 2008.

7. "Venezuela y China suscriben acuerdo para adquisición de radares," *El Universal,* April 8, 2005 (http://www.eluniversal.com/2005/08/04/pol _eva_04A588957).

8. Rebeca Fernández, "Venezuela comprará a China dieciocho aviones K8," *El Universal,* October 31, 2008 (http://www.eluniversal.com/2008/10 /31/pol_art_venezuela-comprara-a_1122802).

9. "Venezuela compra a China 12 aviones de transporte," *El Universal,* November 29, 2010 (http://www.eluniversal.com/2010/11/29/pol_art_vene zuela-compra-a-c_2119611).

10. Inigo Guevara, "Bolivian Army Receives H425 Helicopters," *IHS Jane's 360,* July 14, 2014 (http://www.janes.com/article/40813/bolivian -army-receives-h425-helicopters). See also "Las Fuerzas Armadas de Bolivia recibirán 14 helicópteros," *Infodefensa,* April 30, 2014 (http://www.info defensa.com/latam/2014/04/30/noticia-fuerzas-armadas-bolivia-recibiran -helicopteros.html).

11. "Ecuador recupera $39 millones que pagó por los radares chinos que nunca funcionaron," *El Universo* (Guayaquil, Ecuador), May 21, 2013 (http://www.eluniverso.com/noticias/2013/05/21/nota/942886/ecuador -recupera-39-millones-que-pago-radares-chinos-que-nunca).

12. "Venezuela inaugura un simulador de aviones de transporte Y-8F-200W," *Infodefensa,* May 27, 2014 (http://www.infodefensa.com/latam /2014/05/27/noticia-venezuela-inaugura-simulador-aviones-transporte -y8f200w.html).

13. "Venezuela firma la compra de más radares chinos," *Defensa,* April 24, 2014 (http://defensa.com/index.php?option=com_content&view =article&id=12115:venezuela-firma-la-compra-de-mas-radares-chinos &catid=55:latinoamerica&itemid=163).

14. "La Armada de Venezuela fortalecerá sus medios de combate y apoyo en 2014," *Infodefensa,* January 7, 2014 (http://www.infodefensa .com/latam/2014/01/07/noticia-armada-venezuela-fortalecera-medios

-combate-apoyo.html). See also "Venezuela activa un nuevo Grupo de Artillería armado con sistemas de la china Norinco," *Defensa*, September 13, 2013 (http://defensa.com/index.php?option=com_content&view =article&id=10085:venezuela-activa-un-nuevo-grupo-de-artilleria -armado-con-sistemas-de-la-china-norinco&catid=55:latinoamerica &Itemid=163).

15. "Venezuela adquiere aviones chinos de entrenamiento de combate L15," *Infodefensa*, April 4, 2014 (http://www.infodefensa.com/latam/2014 /04/04/noticia-venezuela-adquirio-aviones-entrenamiento-combate.html). See also "Venezuela habría cerrado la compra del avión de entrenamiento chino L15 'Falcón' y piensa también en Sukhoi," *Defensa*, April 9, 2014 (http://defensa.com/index.php?option=com_content&view=article&id =12011:venezuela-habria-cerrado-la-compra-del-avion-de-entrenamiento -chino-l15-falcon-y-piensa-tambien-en-sukhoi&catid=55:latinoamerica &itemid=163).

16. "Gobierno suspende indefinidamente compra del tanque chino MBT-2000," *La Republica*, April 7, 2010 (http://www.larepublica.pe/08-04 -2010/gobierno-suspenda-indefinidamente-compra-del-tanque-chino-mbt -2000).

17. Ángel Páez, "Factor precio influyó en elección del tanque chino MBT 2000," *La República*, December 12, 2009 (http://www.larepublica .pe/12-12-2009/factor-precio-influyo-en-eleccion-del-tanque-chino-mbt .2000).

18. "Se frustra la adquisición en Perú del Sistema de Defensa Aérea de factoría china valorado en 155 millones de dólares," *Defensa*, November 25, 2013 (http://www.defensa.com/index.php?option=com_content&view =article&id=8050:se-frustra-la-adquisicion-en-peru.del-sistema-de-defensa -aerea-de-factoria-china-valorado-en-155-milliones-de-dolares&catid =55:latinoamerica&intemid=163).

19. "Negocia la Argentina comprar helicópteros militares a China," *La Nación*, May 17, 2007 (http://www.lanacion.com.ar/909317-negocia-la -argentina-comprar-helicopteros-militares-a-china).

20. "Perú selecciona el sistema táctico de lanzacohetes múltiples Norinco tipo 90B," *Infodefensa*, January 10, 2014 (http://www.infode- fensa.com/latam/2014/01/10/noticia-selecciona-sistema-tactico-lanzaco- hetes-multiples-norinco.html). See also "El Ejército de Perú adquiere sistemas de artillería chinos por 38 millones de dólares," *Defensa*, December 27, 2013.

21. "Peru Gets 27 China-Made 90B Self-Propelled Rocket Launchers," *Economic Times (India)*, July 21, 2015 (http://economictimes.indiatimes .com/news/defence/peru-gets-27-china-made-90b-self-propelled-rocket -launchers/articleshow/48152490.cms).

22. "China entregará un buque patrullero a Trinidad y Tobago," *Info- defensa*, March 11, 2014 (http://www.infodefensa.com/latam/2014/03/11 /noticia-china-entregara-buque-patrullero-trinidad-tobago.html).

23. "La Armada Uruguaya recibe una propuesta china para tres OPV," *Infodefensa*, May 6, 2014 (http://www.infodefensa.com/latam/2014/05/06 /noticia-uruguay-recibe-propuesta-china-buques-patrulleros-maritima.html).

24. "China, Argentina Set for Defence Collaboration, Malvinas-Class OPV Deal," *Pakistan Defense*, February 2, 2015 (http://www.thinkdefence .co.uk/2013/07/chengdu-fc-1-xiaolong-argentinas-silver-lining/).

25. See, for example, "Arranca en Brasil LAAD Security 2014," *Defensa*, April 9, 2014 (http://defensa.com/index.php?option=com_content &view=article&id=12004:arranca-en-brasil-laad-security-2014&catid =55:latinoamerica&Itemid=163).

26. "Expositores chinos en el SITDEF 2013," *Poder Militar*, 2013 (http://podermilitar.blogspot.com/2013/05/expositores-chinos-en-el-sitdef -2013.html).

27. "Auditora dice que los Dhruv tienen 'peligrosa limitación,'" *El Universo* (Guayaquil, Ecuador), April 16, 2010 (http://www.eluniverso.com /2010/04/03/1/1355/auditora-dice-dhruv-tienen-peligrosa-limitacion.html).

28. "3 militares mueren en accidente aéreo," *El Universo* (Guayaquil, Ecuador), February 21, 2014 (http://www.eluniverso.com/noticias/2014/02 /21/nota/2213376/3-militares-mueren-accidente-aereo).

29. "Ecuador Grounds Made-in-India Dhruv Chopper, Terminates Contract," Hindustan Times, October 16, 2015 (http://www.hindustantimes.com /india/ecuador-grounds-made-in-india-dhruv-chopper-terminates-contract /story-f6vT6lwzTxliJUS4nM1SFL.html).

30. "Embraer Delivers First Airborne Radar Aircraft to India," *Aviation Today*, August 20, 2012 (http://www.aviationtoday.com/the-checklist /Embraer-Delivers-First-Airborne-Radar-Aircraft-to-India_77056.html# .U91tuWcg_IU).

31. "India's First Embarer AWAC Headed Home," *Space Daily*, August 23, 2012 (http://www.spacedaily.com/reports/Indias_first_Embarer _AWAC_headed_home_999.html).

32. "BrahMos Attracts Buyers at Latin American Defence Expo," *Economic Times (India)*, April 26, 2009.

33. Brazil and Chile's longstanding interest in the missile is mentioned in Peerzada Abrar, "BrahMos Order Book Swells to $13 Billion," *Economic Times (India)*, September 2, 2010 (http://articles.economictimes.indiatimes .com/2010-09-02/news/27601065_1_supersonic-cruise-missile-npo -mashinostroyenia-brahmos-aerospace). Venezuela's interest is documented in "BrahMos Missile Can Be Exported to SE Asian, Latin American Nations."

34. "Belice mejora los medios de su Fuerza de Defensa," *Defensa*, July 24, 2013 (http://www.defensa.com/index.php?option=com_content&view =article&id=9677:belice-mejora-los-medios-de-su-fuerza-de-defensa&catid =55:latinoamerica&Itemid=163).

35. Government of India, Ministry of Defense, "Annual Report Year 2012–2013" (New Delhi) (http://mod.nic.in/forms/List.aspx?Id=57&display ListId=57 [accessed August 3, 2014]).

36. Indian Navy, "INS Sahyadri joins 'RIMPAC' at Pearl Harbour" (http://indiannavy.nic.in/press-release/ins-sahyadri-joins-rimpac-pearl -harbour [accessed August 2, 2014]).

37. See Ellis, *China–Latin America Military Engagement.*

38. China Ministry of National Defense, "PLAN's Taskforce Conducts Maritime Joint Exercise with Chilean Navy," October 12, 2013 (http://eng .mod.gov.cn/TopNews/2013-10/12/content_4470459.htm). See also "Armadas de China y Chile realizaron ejercicios navales," *Noticias FFAA Chile,* October 16, 2013 (http://noticiasffaachile.blogspot.com/2013/10/armadas -de-china-y-chile-realizaron.html).

39. China Ministry of National Defense, "PLAN Taskforce Conducts Joint Maritime Exercise with Brazilian Navy," October 28, 2013.

40. China Ministry of National Defense, "China's Military Strategy," May 2015, 2014 (http://eng.mod.gov.cn/Database/WhitePapers/).

41. Balford Henry, "Government Dismisses Uncertainty about Goat Islands Project," *Jamaica Observer,* May 15, 2014 (http://www.jamaicaob server.com/news/Government-dismisses-uncertainty-about-Goat-Islands -project).

42. "China Grants Credit to Cuba to Build Port Terminal in Santiago," *Havana Times,* July 23, 2014 (http://www.havanatimes.org/?p=105054).

43. W. Alejandro Sanchez, "President Jose Mujica's Prized Rocha Port Project," *La Opinion,* June 12, 2014 (http://www.laopinion.com/president -jose-mujicas-prized-rocha-port-project&template=mobile_redesign).

44. "China propone trabajar con Perú y Brasil en construcción de ferrocarril transcontinental," *Gestion,* June 16, 2014 (http://gestion.pe/politica /china-propone-trabajar-peru-y-china-construccion-ferrocarril-transconti nental-2103133.

45. For a general discussion of contemplated and in-progress bioceanic corridors, see Guillermo Háskel, "Transport Savings from Bioceanic Corridors May Be Not That Significant," *Buenos Aires Herald,* November 4, 2013 (http://www.buenosairesherald.com/article/144422/%E2% 80%98transport-savings-from-bioceanic-corridors-may-be-no-that-signi ficant%E2%80%99). See also R. Evan Ellis, *China and Latin America: The Whats and Wherefores* (Boulder, CO: Lynne Rienner Publishers, 2009).

46. For a good brief overview of the project and associated issues, see Richard Feinberg, "A Transoceanic Canal for Nicaragua?," *Confidencial,* July 16, 2014 (http://www.confidencial.com.ni/articulo/18496/a-transoceanic -canal-for-nicaraguan).

47. "México quiere competir con Panamá en construir su propio canal," *El Siglo,* July 22, 2014 (http://elsiglo.com/internacional/mexico-quiere-com petir-panama-construir-propio-canal/23788884).

48. "Se acerca construcción del último tramo del 'canal seco,'" *La Tribuna,* February 14, 2014 (http://www.latribuna.hn/2014/02/14/se-acerca -construccion-del-ultimo-tramo-del-canal-seco).

49. "Con corredor seco Guatemala se alista para competir con Canal de Panamá," *Agencia EFE,* August 3, 2013 (http://www.telemetro.com/inter nacionales/corredor-Guatemala-competir-Canal-Panama_0_612238771 .html).

50. "BID financiaría canal seco en Colombia," *Portafolio,* September 14, 2014 (http://www.portafolio.co/economia/bid-financiaria-canal-seco -colombia).

51. Indeed, the bioceanic south corridor has already opened up the previously isolated Peruvian region of Madre de Dios.

52. See R. Evan Ellis, "The Impact of China on the Security Environment of Latin America and the Caribbean," in *Routledge Handbook of Latin American Security Studies,* edited by David Mares and Arie Kacowicz (New York: Routledge, 2015). See also R. Evan Ellis, "The Rise of China in the Americas," in *Reconceptualizing Security in the Western Hemisphere in the 21st Century,* edited by Hannah Kassab, Bruce Bagley, and Jonathan Rosen (New York: Lexington Books, 2015).

53. R. Evan Ellis, *China on the Ground in Latin America* (New York: Palgrave-Macmillan, 2014).

54. Ibid., pp. 167–70. While Chinese companies are not the only ones to generate such impacts, the Chinese preference for using a significant portion of their own laborers and subcontractors to execute the projects, along with the linguistic and cultural distance between those Chinese managers and workers and other actors, tends to exacerbate the perceived impact of the Chinese in the Latin American contexts in which they operate, as well as the associated levels of conflict.

55. Nicholas Bariyo, "China Deploys Troops in South Sudan to Defend Oil Fields, Workers," *Wall Street Journal,* September 9, 2014 (http://online .wsj.com/articles/china-deploys-troops-in-south-sudan-to-defend-oil-fields -workers-1410275041).

56. See, for example, R. Evan Ellis, "Suriname and the Chinese: Timber, Migration, and the Less-Told Stories of Globalization," *SAIS Review* 32, no. 2 (Summer–Fall 2012), pp. 85–97. See also "Chinese Commercial Engagement with Guyana: The Challenges of Physical Presence and Political Change," *China Brief* 13, no. 19 (September 27, 2013).

57. Omar Santana, "Protestan contra "nuevos comerciantes chinos," *Diario Libre,* July 30, 2013 (http://www.diariolibre.com).

58. For a general discussion of China's growing challenge to defend overseas Chinese communities in Latin America, see Ellis, *China on the Ground in Latin America,* pp. 179–96.

59. Ellis, *China on the Ground in Latin America.*

60. "Police to Ramp Up Security Measures for Chinese Community in Jamaica," *Go Jamaica,* August 27, 2013 (http://go-jamaica.com).

61. In one recent case, Chinese and U.S. authorities intercepted 71 kilograms of cocaine in a container moving from Peru through Mexico to Shanghai. "China, U.S. Jointly Bust Cocaine Trafficking," China.Org.Cn,

August 28, 2014 (http://www.china.org.cn/china/off_the_Wire/2014-08/28 /content_33369304.htm).

62. Hugo Ruvalcaba, "Asian Mafias in Baja California," *Insight Crime,* August 20, 2013 (http://www.insightcrime.org/news-analysis/asian-mafia -in-mexico).

63. "Colombia: Capturan al capitán del buque chino con armas para Cuba," *InfoBae,* March 3, 2015 (http://www.infobae.com/2015/03/03 /1713666-colombia-capturan-al-capitan-del-buque-chino-armas-cuba).

64. For an overview, see R. Evan Ellis, "Chinese Organized Crime in Latin America," *Prism* 4, no. 1 (December 1, 2012), pp. 67–77.

65. Based on off-the-record author interviews with Latin American police and government officials between 2010 and 2014.

66. For a more in-depth discussion of such impacts, see Ellis, "The Impact of China on the Security Environment of Latin America and the Caribbean." See also Ellis, "The Rise of China in the Americas."

67. China-Latin America Finance Database. Inter-American Dialogue (http://thedialogue.org/map-list [accessed September 14, 2014]). See also Kevin Gallagher, Amos Irwin, and Katherine Koleski, *The New Banks in Town: Chinese Finance in Latin America* (Tufts University, Global Development and Environment Institute, November 2012) (http://www.ase.tufts .edu/gdae/policy-research/NewBanks.html).

68. This includes an initial $5 billion loan given to the Maduro regime in September 2013, an additional $4 billion infusion to the Heavy Investment Fund announced during the visit of Chinese president Xi Jinping to the country in July 2014, plus approximately $2 billion in separate credits announced during the same trip. See "Xi brinda más préstamos a Venezuela, especialmente para comprar en China," *MercoPress,* July 22, 2014 (http://es .mercopress.com/2014/07/22/xi-brinda-mas-prestamos-a-venezuela-espe cialmente-para-comprar-en-china).

69. "Venezuela recibe 5.000 millones de dólares por préstamo de China," *El Universal,* April 20, 2015 (http://www.eluniversal.com/eco nomia/150420/venezuela-recibe-5000-millones-de-dolares-por-prestamo -de-china).

70. Nathan Gill, "Ecuador Says China Signed $2 Billion Oil Deal to Access Crude," Bloomberg.com, July 3, 2014 (http://www.bloomberg.com/news/2014 -07-03/ecuador-says-china-signed-2-billion-oil-deal-to-access-crude.html).

71. For a more detailed discussion of Chinese financial support for Ecuador, see R. Evan Ellis, "El compromiso de China con los países del ALBA: ¿Una relación de conveniencia mutual?," in *¿La hegemonía norteamericana en declive? El desafío del ALBA y la nueva integración latinoamericana del siglo XXI,* edited by Bruce M. Bagley and Magdalena Defort (Cali, Colombia: Universidad ICESI, 2014), pp. 529–56.

72. "Ecuador Receives $1.4 Billion Disbursement from China Loan," *America's Forum,* February 26, 2013 (http://www.americas-forum.com /ecuador-receives-1-4-billion-disbursement-from-china-loan/).

73. Wálter Vásquez, "Cada préstamo tendrá dos tipos de tasas de interés," *La Razón*, October 25, 2015 (http://www.la-razon.com/suplementos /financiero/prestamo-tipos-tasas-interes-financiero_0_2367963320.html).

74. See Humberto Marquez, "Drugs—Venezuela: More Seizures, But Decertification by US," Inter Press Service, September 11, 2009 (http:// www.ipsnews.net/2009/09/drugs-venezuela-more-seizures-but-decertifica tion-by-us/).

75. For a good brief summary, see Paul D. Shinkman, "Iranian-Sponsored Narco-Terrorism in Venezuela: How Will Maduro Respond?," *U.S. News and World Report*, April 24, 2013 (http://www.usnews.com/news /articles/2013/04/24/iranian-sponsored-narco-terrorism-in-venezuela-how -will-maduro-respond).

76. Christopher D. Young and Ross Rustici, *China's Out of Area Naval Operations: Case Studies, Trajectories, Obstacles, and Potential Solutions,* China Strategic Perspectives 3 (Washington, DC: National Defense University Press, December 2010).

77. "China Continues to Bring Citizens Evacuated from Libya Back Home," Xinhua News Agency, March 5, 2011 (http://news.xinhuanet.com /english2010/china/2011-03/05/c_13762503_2.htm).

Part III

CASE STUDIES: THE INTERACTION OF CHINA AND INDIA WITH KEY ACTORS IN LATIN AMERICA

CHAPTER 10

Chile

A BRIDGE TO ASIA?

Alicia Frohmann and Manfred Wilhelmy

The dynamic nucleus of global wealth has been shifting toward emerging economies, which have become the principal drivers of growth. In Asia, emerging economies were responsible for 41 percent of global growth between 2005 and 2012, while Latin America produced only 9 percent of global growth during the same period.[1] In the next decade, this shift will continue to increase: while Asia (excluding Japan) will be responsible for 57.8 percent of global growth between 2014 and 2024, Latin American participation will amount to only 6.3 percent.[2]

Chile is a small market economy. As such, the intensification of economic ties between Chile and Asia is feasible only in association with its Latin American neighbors. Within this framework, the idea of Chile serving as a bridge or gateway between South America and Asia Pacific has been a central theme in the discourse of many Chilean political and business actors.

THE BRIDGE COUNTRY CONCEPT

What is a bridge country? It is a nation or territory that serves as a link, either real or figurative, for a group of other countries or territories in a variety of exchanges.[3] In this case, the central idea is that Chile could facilitate access for its South American neighbors—especially those on the Atlantic coast—to the countries of Asia Pacific, and serve as a business intermediary. As bridges are bidirectional, Chile would also facilitate access for Asian Pacific countries to South American economies.

The purpose of the bridge is developed subjectively: it is proposed by a country's certain political and economic actors to potential regional and neighboring partners. This idea is grounded in geographic and economic characteristics according to which Chile is in a favorable position to serve as a bridge country. Among these are its extensive coastline and many ports, and its network of trade agreements with the principal economies of Asia Pacific.

Of course, this idea is in contrast to certain insular traits that have historically characterized traditional Chilean attitudes toward diverse external actors, such as the country's long period of geographic isolation and its relative economic decline within the region since the end of the nineteenth century. Another attribute that departs from the bridge concept is the notion of Chilean exceptionalism, linked to a history of conflicts with neighboring countries and the Chilean elite's portrayal of the country as more stable and democratic than the rest of Latin America.[4] This issue is addressed later in this chapter.

The objective of this chapter is twofold: (1) to analyze the bridge country concept, its characteristics, and its conditions; and (2) to contrast public and private discourses that place this role within the reality of Chile's development, its relations with the Asia-Pacific region, and its position within the current regional dynamic. An analysis of the ties between Chile and its South American and Asian partners in economic, commercial, financial, physical connectivity, transportation, and logistical terms allows an assessment of the feasibility and soundness of Chile serving as a bridge country.

THE CHILEAN PROPOSAL

Within the realm of government and trade policy, the proposal of Chile serving as a bridge country was first developed in the late 1990s and the beginning of the 2000s. The idea stemmed from the consolidation of economic ties with the Asia-Pacific region, the strengthening of its participation within the Asia-Pacific Economic Cooperation (APEC) member economies, an increase in bilateral trade, and negotiations of free trade agreements. The bridge country proposal became state policy during the Eduardo Frei Ruiz-Tagle (1994–2000) and Ricardo Lagos (2000–06) administrations and was reiterated by the Michelle Bachelet (2006–10) and Sebastián Piñera (2010–14) administrations. The second Bachelet administration (2014–18) has carried on the bridge country proposal.

During his inaugural address before the Twelfth General Meeting of the Pacific Economic Cooperation Council (PECC) in Santiago (1997), President Frei stated:

> We are building a network of regional relationships and free trade instruments with the goal of positioning Chile as a provider of services and a port of entry into South American markets and a port of exit toward markets across the Pacific. Roads connecting Chilean ports with centers of production and neighboring countries are important commercial corridors serving regional integration and trans-Pacific interaction.[5]

In the 2000s, President Ricardo Lagos continued to develop this concept. In light of the 2004 APEC Summit, held in Chile, Lagos stated the following:

> Chile would like to be the link between Asia and Latin America. . . . What will give us the edge will not be just our FTAs with Asian countries but our connectivity to Asia. . . . We believe we can be a launching pad for Asia as it develops ties with Latin America, and East Asia can be a launching pad as we move farther from China to India.[6]

Prominent businessman Andrónico Luksic, who presided over the 2004 APEC CEO summit, spoke along similar lines: "Chile can serve as a two-way platform for goods to and from Asia, not just to Chile . . . but also to much larger economies, like Argentina and Brazil."[7] Also, former ambassador to Japan and Argentina Eduardo Rodríguez Guarachi suggested that "Chile's role is to integrate the rest of the countries in order to benefit from free trade agreements. In order to do so, it must maintain its role as a bridge, a link between local economies and the economies of Europe and Asia."[8]

During the end of the first Bachelet administration in 2010, the General Directorate of International Economic Relations (DIRECON)[9] of the Ministry of Foreign Relations issued a review of contemporary Chilean trade policy and reiterated the proposal to convert Chile into a platform country. The review highlighted the following conditions necessary for achieving this: strong institutions, political stability, respect for and compliance with laws, the quality of services and logistical support systems for production and distribution, a well-trained workforce, modern and efficient telecommunications systems and infrastructure, a favorable security situation, and an adequate quality of life for international executives.[10]

Additional necessary conditions are purportedly a consolidated financial and foreign investment system, a high number of residents who speak a foreign language (in particular English, the lingua franca for business and technology), and transparency and low levels of corruption within public and private institutions. Favorable international rankings of Chile in areas such as economic freedom, economic competitiveness, ease of doing business, and perceptions of corruption support this point of view.[11] Some Asian observers have added their voices to this discussion. For example, Pithaya Pookaman, former Thai ambassador to Chile, maintained that Chile was "a logical location as a business hub and a staging post for Latin America for enterprising Thai businessmen. Although all roads do not necessarily lead through Chile . . . the importance of Chile as a springboard for Thailand should not be underrated."[12] It should be noted that all these qualifications highlight Chile as an individual actor.

More recently, initiatives within the Pacific Alliance framework—founded in 2011 and comprising Chile, Colombia, Mexico, and Peru—have demonstrated a more associative Chilean approach to relations with Asia without abandoning the basic bridge concept. Building ties with Asian Pacific countries is an explicit objective of this new regional bloc. However, in spite of its potential for joint initiatives regarding trade and investment in Asia, beyond some trade promotion initiatives and exploratory political communications, the Alliance has not consolidated a strategy for developing a joint relationship between its members and Asian Pacific countries. This new bloc has raised suspicions among Atlantic South American countries of Mercosur. During the Lula da Silva and Rousseff administrations, Brazil has reacted negatively to the Alliance, considering it a neoliberal political-economic bloc that would exclude Brazil and compete, in practice, with more ample Latin American integration frameworks. In the face of such criticism, the second Bachelet administration, beginning in March 2014, proposed refocusing the Alliance by means of joint rapprochement policies with Brazil and Mercosur. This proposal was aimed at developing a flexible integration framework that would work at dual speeds and seek a convergence of the diversity between the Pacific Alliance and Atlantic countries. A first initiative in this direction was the November 2014 "Dialogue about Regional Integration: The Pacific Alliance and Mercosur" in Santiago, organized by Chile, with the participation of the foreign relations, trade and finance ministers of both country groups, as well as the heads of regional organizations, such as the Organization of American States (OAS), the UN Economic Commission for Latin America and the Caribbean (CEPAL), the Development Bank of Latin America (CAF), and the Latin American Integration Association (ALADI).

Mercosur, entangled in its own economic and political problems, has not demonstrated continued interest in this Chilean proposal. In fact, in July 2014 it expanded its outreach in a different direction by signing an agreement to establish a Complementary Economic Zone with the Bolivarian Alliance for the Peoples of Our America (ALBA), Petrocaribe, and the Caribbean Community and Common Market (CARICOM) countries.[13] However, post–2016 political changes in South America could bring about a shift in the region's geopolitical orientation and facilitate joint Mercosur-Pacific Alliance initiatives.

The proposal to convert Chile into a bridge between Asian Pacific countries and South America is based on the premise that Chile has significant advantages over its neighbors in the aforementioned areas, as well as more robust political and economic relations with Asian countries. This view is not widely shared by those in neighboring countries conducting or wanting to conduct business with Asia Pacific.

On the other hand, it also seems unlikely that Asian Pacific countries are seeking a specific partner to serve as a bridge to Latin America. In July 2014 the leaders of three leading Asian Pacific countries, Vladimir Putin of the Russian Federation, Xi Jinping of China, and Shinzo Abe of Japan, visited Latin America. They demonstrated a great interest in the region as a supplier of natural resources, a market for industrial goods, and a destination for direct investment. All three secured long-term agreements regarding energy and natural resources, awarded or committed to loans, and signed various cooperation agreements.[14] Russia and China proposed providing Cuba with financial relief. Putin and Xi participated in the BRICS summit held in Brazil. Only Abe traveled to Chile, after visiting Mexico, Colombia, and Trinidad and Tobago. In early 2015, President Xi Jinping announced that Chinese companies would invest $250 billion in Latin America over the next ten years. Chinese investors are also becoming interested in agriculture, the food sector, manufacturing, and infrastructure. Premier Li Keqiang visited Brazil, Colombia, Peru, and Chile in May 2015, focusing mainly on big infrastructure projects.[15]

Even though some of the arguments in favor of the bridge country concept seem convincing, the Chilean political discourse contains an element of wishful thinking regarding the possibility of serving as a potential Asia–South America intermediary. This is related more than anything to the aspirational or programmatic nature of the proposal. It is not realistic—except in isolated cases—to consider that Chile is on its way to becoming a regional service provider connected to Asia in conjunction with its neighbors.

The bridge country discourse is based on a new version of the aforementioned notion of Chilean exceptionalism vis-à-vis its neighbors. This new exceptionalism is based on globalization and association rather than on insularity, as well as on Chile's aspiration to hold a position of relative privilege within the framework of integration policies.

Whereas in some areas Chile demonstrates strength for future cooperation with Asia Pacific, it has not consolidated progress in other areas that would allow it to act as an efficient intermediary. In terms of links with neighboring countries, the Chilean proposal is more unilateral than associative; it does not arise from consensus, effective dialogue or integration with neighboring countries, or participation in regional value chains. As such, its potential is significantly limited.[16] Differences between Chile and some of its neighbors over border issues contribute to making implementation of the bridge country concept impracticable.

Chile is far from being a South American version of Singapore, which serves as a commercial, financial, logistical, and educational hub for much of Southeast Asia, or a Panama, whose ports and logistics systems serve as points of entry and exit for maritime routes between Latin America and Asia Pacific. Rather, Chilean businesses are important customers of the Panama Canal. Neither are there parallels between Chile and Hong Kong, East Asia's metropolitan business center, which, despite China's international opening, continues to serve as an important broker for the People's Republic of China. Hong Kong has indeed been complemented rather than supplanted by Shanghai and continues to compete with Singapore.

CHILE'S ECONOMIC RELATIONS WITH ITS MAIN PARTNERS IN ASIA PACIFIC

In the decade between 2003 and 2013, trade between Chile and its main partners in Asia grew spectacularly (table 10-1). This owed in large part to the shift in global industrial manufacturing (and the demand for natural resources) from the United States and the European Union to Asia, as well as to the increase in the price of commodities exported by Chile to those markets, spurred by China's dynamic growth. Chile has become dependent on its commerce and trade surplus with China, Japan, and South Korea, which jointly accounted for 42 percent of Chilean exports and 30 percent of imports in 2015.[17]

However, Chile was not the only country in the region whose trade with Asia, especially China, increased notably in the years between 2003 and 2013. Other South American exporters of natural resources demonstrated very similar tendencies (table 10-2).

Conversely, Latin America is still of little relevance to Asia as a trade partner, although it is of increasing interest to investors. Trade with

TABLE 10-1

Chilean Trade with China, Japan, South Korea, and World, 2003, 2008, 2010, 2013, and 2015
(US$ millions)

	China	Japan	South Korea	World
2003				
Exports	1,900	2,400	1,100	21,700
Imports	1,600	700	500	19,300
2008				
Exports	8,500	6,300	3,300	64,500
Imports	8,300	3,200	3,300	62,800
2010				
Exports	17,300	7,700	4,200	71,100
Imports	10,000	3,400	3,500	59,200
2013				
Exports	19,200	7,700	4,300	77,400
Imports	15,700	2,500	2,800	79,600
2015				
Exports	16,800	5,500	4,100	63,400
Imports	14,800	2,100	2,000	63,000

Source: COMTRADE.

TABLE 10-2

Exports to China from Argentina, Brazil and Peru, 2003 and 2013
(US$ millions)

Year	Argentina	Brazil	Peru
2003	2,500	4,500	700
2013	5,500	46,000	7,300

Source: COMTRADE.

Latin American countries—with Brazil and Chile as principal partners—represented only 6.3 percent of China's total trade in 2013.[18] There is still less trade between Latin America and India, the value of which is less than half that of India's trade with Africa. Trade with members of the Association of Southeast Asian Nations (ASEAN), Hong Kong, and South Korea is even more reduced. Nevertheless, South America is already a consolidated provider of natural resources for the leading Asian economies and an interesting market for Asian industrial products. Countries exporting raw materials to Asia, such as Chile, experienced a true boom in exports to that market, and natural resources regained predominance in their exports at levels similar to those of the 1960s and 1970s. This reflected both the impact of elevated commodity prices and the limited effect of Latin American efforts to diversify exports, often aggravated by increased local currency values, the so-called Dutch disease. The natural resources boom waned after 2012 as a direct consequence of the deceleration of Chinese economic growth, prompting a fall in commodity prices and a drop in the value of Latin American exports and GDP growth.

TRADE AGREEMENTS BETWEEN CHILE AND ASIA PACIFIC: THE REGIONAL CONTEXT

An important part of the Chilean bridge country discourse has been to emphasize the country's vast network of free trade agreements (FTAs), which allows for the creation of a true free trade zone with its partners (table 10-3). Chile could become a hub for a series of value chains that transform intermediate goods or imported consumer goods to final value-added goods for export to other markets. Another related aspiration is to become a platform for services and investment for Asian Pacific businesses in Latin America. There has not been a significant response from that region, as Asian businesses interested in manufacturing in the region operate directly in the principal markets—Brazil and Argentina, because of their size, and Mexico, because of its role as an exporter to the United States. In general, South American businesses export final and intermediate goods (especially natural resources) directly to Asian markets.

For some time, Chile's trade relations with leading Asian markets were developed in the context of a special economic institutional framework. This began with Chile's participation in APEC (starting in 1994) and continued in the mid-2000s with the bilateral FTAs with its principal partners in the region. Active participation within APEC, a showcase for Chile in the Asia-Pacific region, prevailed as an official policy between 1994 and 2004. Despite being relatively unknown by many APEC member countries, this participation allowed Chile to position itself as a player that, despite its small economy, presented solid and creative proposals to promote APEC's economic integration and cooperation agenda. Within this context, the proposal to create a Free Trade Area of Asia Pacific, initially developed by the APEC Business Advisory

TABLE 10-3

Preferential Trade Agreements, in Effect May 2016, between Chile and Asia Pacific

Country	Year implemented
South Korea	2004
Trans-Pacific Partnership Agreement (P4) (Brunei, New Zealand, Singapore)	2006
China	2006
India	2007
Japan	2007
Australia	2009
Malaysia	2012
Vietnam	2014
Hong Kong	2014
Thailand	2015

Source: DIRECON.

Council (ABAC), was enthusiastically supported by the government of Chile.

One of the first initiatives to liberalize trade on both sides of the Pacific was the Trans-Pacific Strategic Economic Partnership Agreement (P4), with Chile, Brunei, New Zealand, and Singapore as signatories. The P4 contained an accession clause for other countries and was conceived as an initial step for promoting regional integration. At first the principal regional actors did not consider the P4 to be relevant because of the small size of the member economies. However, five years later the P4 became the foundation of the 2009 U.S. proposal to develop the Trans-Pacific Partnership (TPP) as a mechanism for Asian–Pacific regional integration.

Participation in APEC gave Chile the opportunity to negotiate trade agreements with the leading Asian economies. However, after hosting the APEC summit in 2004, Chile's commitment to multilateralism gradually declined, as bilateral agreements with South Korea, China, and Japan became the main priority in regional economic diplomacy. Subsequently Chile signed FTAs with several other Asian Pacific economies.

This development was not unique to Chile, however. Peru soon implemented a similar strategy, joining APEC in 1998 and signing trade agreements with China, South Korea, and Japan between 2010 and 2012. Notwithstanding the attractiveness of these agreements, it is difficult to evaluate their real impact, as the dynamism of links with Asian economies derived mostly from market incentives rather than from preferential agreements. For example, Argentina and Brazil have not followed suit in terms of bilateral agreements, but their trade results have also been excellent, especially with China.

Beginning in 2010, negotiations on the Trans-Pacific Agreement, promoted by the United States in its new version as the TPP[19], came to dominate Chile's trade agenda. TPP negotiations concluded in October 2015 and the agreement was signed in February 2016, with no fixed date for coming into effect. The country is the only TPP member that already has trade agreements with all other partners. As such, rather than serve as a bridge between partners, Chile is relatively blocked: it had little to gain in negotiations and its own market preferences were eroded. However, contrary to expectations, Chile did not make additional significant concessions to its commitments within the framework of the 2004 FTA with the United States.

The main appeal of the TPP for Chile will be regional cumulative rules of origin to facilitate the development of value chains with its neighbors and Asian partners, as has been promoted for years. Currently, only three Latin American countries participate in the TPP: Chile, Peru, and Mexico. Chile's Atlantic neighbors have tended to view the TPP as a threat rather than an opportunity, as this agreement would renew the prominence of U.S. trade policy in the region.

As mentioned earlier, a new regional integration initiative, the Pacific Alliance,[20] was created in April 2011 with the participation of Chile, Colombia, Mexico, and Peru.[21] Since its inception, the Pacific Alliance has served two functions: to promote the liberalization of trade and finance and to serve as an integrated business platform toward Asia and the world. A common approach to and strategy for enhancing business with Asia is an interesting element of the Alliance. Presently, trade with Pacific Alliance countries makes up less than 4 percent of Asia's total trade and is already covered to a large extent by bilateral trade agreements. A first concrete institutional arrangement is the bilateral framework agreement between the Pacific Alliance and ASEAN, addressing issues such as economic cooperation, education, and academic and business exchanges, due to be signed in New York in September 2016.

The beginning of the second Bachelet administration in 2014 signaled the resurgence of the bridge country concept, with a new twist. The concept has been retooled to promote rapprochement among Atlantic and Pacific South American countries by means of dialogue between the Pacific Alliance and Mercosur regarding a convergence of customs procedures, infrastructure development, and the facilitation of tourism and cultural integration.[22] This dialogue began in Chile in November

2014 during a summit of foreign ministers and vice ministers of trade from both blocs, with the presence of the heads of inter-American organizations such as ECLAC, the OAS, and CAF.[23]

Interest in this initiative has grown considerably. By May 2016, 42 countries were participating as observers of the Pacific Alliance process, among them Paraguay and Uruguay which are members of Mercosur. The Macri administration in Argentina joined as observer at the Alliance's July 2016 summit.

CONDITIONS AND FACTORS LIMITING CHILE'S BRIDGE COUNTRY ASPIRATIONS

Despite the significant internationalization of Chile's economy, the conditions necessary for serving as a relevant actor in connecting South America and Asia Pacific are limited. The following section describes these conditions in terms of connectivity (transport, logistics, and information technology), the ease of doing business (capital markets, financial centers, marketplace, multilatinas), and the availability of qualified human resources.

Connectivity: Transportation, Logistics, and Information Technology

Maritime Transport

The vast majority of products traveling between South America and Asia Pacific are shipped by sea. Shipments by air are limited to certain high-value goods and some perishable products.

Maritime traffic and ports are a focus from which to evaluate whether Chile is, or can be, a bridge to or platform for trade with Asia, which is the main destination for cargo exiting Chilean ports. In 2013, China, Japan, and South Korea were among the top six export destinations in terms of total tonnage, especially in bulk. Almost one-third of total tonnage exported was to China alone. More than 90 percent of this cargo consisted of exports from the different regions of Chile. Goods in transit represented no more than 9 percent of exported tonnage and exited mainly through Arica, the principal port of exit for Bolivian products.[24]

Chile's location in the far Southeast Pacific results in its ports being among the last points of entry for imports or among the first ports of exit for exports traveling along the West Coast of South America (WCSA) shipping route. Many shipping services dock at ports in the country's northern (Arica, Iquique, Antofagasta), central (San Antonio and Valparaíso), or southern regions. Chilean ports have limited capacity; the number of containers entering or exiting San Antonio and Valparaíso combined is only slightly higher than the volume (in TEUs, or twenty-foot-equivalent units) of those entering or exiting the port of Callao in Peru. The most frequent Pacific crossings are between Manzanillo, Mexico, and East Asian ports.

The main destinations for imports along the WCSA shipping route are Chile (an average of 50 percent of TEUs transported between 2008 and 2011), Peru (20 percent), Colombia (17 percent), and Ecuador (13 percent). In terms of TEUs exported, 72 percent exited from Chile, 20 percent from Peru, 6 percent from Ecuador, and only 2 percent from Colombia.

With few exceptions (such as the aforementioned case of Bolivian goods), cargo entering or exiting Chilean ports originates in Chile or is destined for Chile. A small number of Argentine goods (such as wine exported from Mendoza) exit from Chilean ports. In general, the use of trucks to ship cargo across the Andes is not profitable owing to high operational costs and bureaucratic requirements regarding international overland travel.[25]

Ground Transportation

South American infrastructure for ground transportation remains insufficient. Several countries are participating in an initiative to develop bioceanic corridors in South America with the support of international financing institutions. The Initiative for the Integration of the Regional Infrastructure of South America represents a modest step forward. Reaching an efficient operational level would require not only accelerating the construction of international roads but also streamlining border controls (migration, customs, sanitation) that raise costs and delay the flow of cargo.

The Aconcagua Bi-Oceanic Corridor is a joint Chilean-Argentine public-private infrastructure megaproject. It aims to connect the town of Lujan de Cuyo in the Argentine province of Mendoza with the town of Los Andes in the Valparaíso region of Chile by means of a 52-kilometer-long, low-altitude (between 1,500 and 2,400 meters above sea level) trans-Andean rail tunnel. This low-altitude tunnel is meant to replace the Cristo Redentor tunnel, which, at 3,200 meters above sea level, is frequently closed because of winter snow. The new tunnel would be located at the same latitude as the current one, which carries more than two-thirds of the 7.5 million tons of cargo traveling between the two countries, some of which originates in or is destined for other countries, such as Brazil.

An additional protocol to the Agreement for Physical Integration and Economic Complementation between Chile and Argentina, signed in October 2009, created a binational entity to bid on the project and regulate its construction and operation. The private sector has organized itself by means of Corporación América, comprising businesses from both countries and the multinational Mitsubishi Corporation. Proponents of the corridor argue that the new road would meet current demand and projected demand until the mid-twenty-first century and would provide better security, reliability, continuity of service, and energy efficiency. The project would cost approximately $3.5 billion.[26] According to Corporación América, it would be Argentina's most convenient option for shipments to the Pacific coast of the Americas, Oceania, and the Far East, and would provide a new route to East Asia and Oceania for Brazil. For Chile, the corridor would serve as a link to parts of South America and an advantageous route for shipping and receiving cargo to and from Africa, Europe, and Indian Ocean countries. There is an estimated 15 percent freight savings in relation to current costs for shipping from the inland provinces of Argentina to Manzanillo, Mexico.[27] The project has advanced slowly, a result of inconsistent governmental support and uncertainty as to development and operational costs. Additionally, there is not a detailed plan for operating the binational regulatory and administrative entity.

Two important trans-Andean road projects are the Agua Negra and the Las Leñas tunnels. The first would link the Chilean area of Coquimbo, about 280 miles north of Santiago, and the Argentine province of San Juan. The estimated cost is around $2.5 billion, of which Chile would contribute about 28 percent. The second is to be located about 60 miles south of Santiago, connecting the Argentine province of Mendoza with roads leading to ports in central Chile. Initial cost estimates are in the magnitude of $1.3 billion. While both governments support these projects, so far there are no binding agreements to initiate construction.

Furthermore, the surplus of available cargo space for shipments from the Atlantic coast of South America to Asia Pacific (East Coast of South America, or ECSA, shipping route, using the Panama Canal or crossing the Atlantic and Indian Oceans), because of a higher number of imports than exports, significantly lowers freight charges to Asia Pacific. Under these conditions, and with a few exceptions, the use of Chilean ports utilizing intermodal transportation would be uneconomical for shipments from Atlantic Southern Cone countries. This situation leaves Chile far from being an effective bridge or gateway and is one of the challenges affecting the consolidation of the Aconcagua Bi-Oceanic Corridor project.

Air Transport

The Latin American market for air transport is dynamic and demonstrates significant growth potential. Between 2012 and 2015, the number of passengers traveling by air increased from 124.4 million to 187.5 million (50 percent). Of these, 90 percent traveled within Latin America and 10 percent traveled to destinations outside Latin America. In Chile, air transport grew rapidly from 10.9 million to 14.3 million passengers between 2011 and 2015. In 2013, 177,528 tons of cargo were exported by air, representing a 6.7 percent increase from 2012. Despite a certain imbalance in costs owing to a higher volume of exports, it is estimated that the Chilean market for air transport is one of the most dynamic in the region.[28]

Chile's aspiration to serve as bridge or gateway to Asia by air is limited by geography. The distances between cities in Asia and Lima by air, for example, are shorter than those between Santiago and Asian cities. The location of Chile's capital is favorable only in relation to certain points on the opposite side of the Pacific, such as Sydney and Auckland. As such, international connections through Santiago are scarce; it is not a true hub for air transport. The Chilean airline LAN (now part of the Chilean-Brazilian LATAM holding company), which has subsidiaries in Argentina, Peru, Ecuador, and Colombia, extensively uses Jorge Chávez Airport in Lima as a connecting point for international flights, including some to or from Santiago.

To date, no Chilean or Asian airlines offer flights between Chile and Asia, although Air China has reported that it is considering operating a route to Lima or Santiago. Los Angeles, Frankfurt, Paris, and Sydney are generally used as connecting airports for flights to and from Santiago. These trips can easily last more than thirty hours. Malaysian Airlines, on the other hand, has been flying to the Atlantic coast of South America via the Indian Ocean and South Africa, and Singapore Airlines has flights to Brazil via Barcelona. Air transport infrastructure is another limiting factor. While Santiago's airport boasts favorable operational security, its number of slots and facilities for customer service and baggage handling become insufficient whenever demand rises. A new expansion of the international terminal aims to ameliorate this situation.

Telecommunications and Information Technology

Chile's telecommunications and information technology infrastructure is modern and ever evolving. While local prices are still higher than in the majority of developed countries, they are competitive within Latin American, allowing for approximately 11.7 million Internet access connections. This number amounts to 67 percent of the 17.4 million population and is significantly greater than the South American average of 57 percent coverage.[29] Most mobile devices in the country have the ability to access the Internet, as tends to be the case globally. Internet use among businesses and institutions is practically universal, although some medium-sized and small businesses lag behind. The growing use of the Internet to pay bills, carry out bank transactions, file tax and customs declarations, and complete other administrative tasks stimulates demand for Internet access. However, more regulation of service providers is required in such a concentrated market. Lack of competition and weak regulations still allow for poor services, affecting both individuals and businesses and limiting economic competitiveness.

Ease of Doing Business

Capital Market and Financial Center
A global or regional financial center is defined as a marketplace that brings together a significant number of commercial and investment banks, as well as other financial institutions and businesses, such as stock and commodity exchanges, securities companies, fund administrators and other institutional investors, investment funds, financial consultants, risk managers, and the like. Relevant financial centers are host to a high volume of daily currency-exchange and short-term credit transactions, as well as frequent high-value transactions with global reach, such as initial public offerings (IPOs), mergers and acquisitions (M&As), and debt transactions, such as credit syndication and the emission and transaction of corporate bonuses.

Santiago de Chile is on its way to becoming a regional financial center. According to the World Economic Forum's 2014 *Global Competitiveness Report* on financial systems, Chile's WEF ranking rose to nineteenth, the highest of any Latin American economy. The report highlighted some of Chile's strengths, such as the availability of financial services and the soundness of banks, but also addressed the weakness and high service cost of the financial market, as well as the low venture capital availability. These factors are associated with the relatively reduced size of the Chilean market.[30] Economic stability, especially that of the financial system, the development of local capital markets (tied to pensions funds, among other factors), and the high quality of supervision and regulation fuel the aspirations of Chilean actors. Chilean banks gradually become internationalized as they carry out more foreign transactions, acquire subsidiaries in other countries, and open offices in new markets, such as China. Meanwhile, important foreign banks operate in the local market by means of subsidiaries, associations with Chilean banks, or local offices.

It is worth noting that Chile's aspiration to be a Latin American financial center does not include utilizing any offshore elements to attract business to Santiago. Insofar as the Chilean financial system is one of the most internationally open in Latin America, businesses and regulators have warned of the need to manage and prevent risks, such as the use of financial institutions for money laundering. As such, the Ministry of Finance has established a Financial Analysis Unit to monitor and prevent certain international financial transactions.

The Santiago Stock Exchange (Bolsa de Comercio de Santiago) participates in the Integrated Latin American Market (Mercado Integrado Latinoamericano, or MILA), along with the stock exchanges in Lima, Bogotá, and Mexico City. The combined market cap is close to $987 billion). MILA, which is a private sector contribution to the Pacific Alliance, has considerable potential but is still in the initial development phase, has a low transaction volume, and requires improvements to its regulation and operations, such as payment and custody procedures.

"Chile Day" is a public-private promotional event periodically carried out in financial centers such as London and New York with the goal of persuading the international financial community to increase trade, financing, and investment with Chilean businesses. Notwithstanding, the Global Financial Centers Index (GFCI) identifies only São Paulo, Rio de Janeiro, and Panama in the main index of global financial centers. While Santiago is indeed considered a dynamic marketplace, it is still not included on the GFCI, due to an insufficient number of assessments. The possibility of Santiago serving as a relevant bridge for financial transactions between South America and Asia Pacific is not considered in international reports.

Chilean Multilatinas

A new type of transnational corporation, known as the multilatina or translatina, has emerged in Latin America over the past two decades.[31] There is a significant presence of Chilean businesses among multilatinas, especially those in the service sector. Multilatinas have made large investments: between 1990 and 2014, Chilean investments abroad (1,200 companies in sixty countries) reached $100 billion.[32] Of these investments, 86 percent were in Latin America, mainly Brazil, Argentina, Colombia, and Peru, countries in which the presence of Chilean investment is important.

Investments made by Chilean businesses abroad have added a new dimension to Chile's international presence. Reactions from neighboring countries range from respect for Chile's economic success to a certain aversion because of the perceived use of aggressive tactics by some businesses. Associative initiatives, such as the business committees established between the Chilean private sector and counterparts in Peru, Colombia, and other countries, seek to consolidate investment gains in the region and identify new businesses opportunities.

Marketplace

Despite its limited scale, Santiago is an international marketplace in which businesses and organizations from a diverse range of regional markets operate. These businesses and organizations are frequently tied to multilatinas investing in the region. The majority of transactions carried out in this environment are conducted privately and unknown to the public. Some, however, are related to large-scale and specialized events, and the largest-scale transactions are reported in the media. The periodic hosting of important trade shows and business conventions is relevant. For example, the Santiago International Air and Space Fair (FIDAE) and Expomin trade show attract numerous international and Latin American businesses from industries such as defense, air transport, electronics, mining equipment and services, and heavy machinery, among others.

Because Chile has a highly centralized economy, few international transactions are carried out in regional cities. Nevertheless, the northern city of Iquique is playing an important part in trade with neighboring countries by means of the Iquique Free Trade Zone (Zona Franca de Iquique, or ZOFRI). Because of the exemption laws governing the Free Trade Zone, such as the elimination of import costs and processes, it is possible that certain merchandise has entered the country illegally. The operational value of ZOFRI in 2013 was $8.98 billion. The principal markets of origin were China, the United States, Japan, and Korea (some Chilean goods also passed through) and the principal destinations were Bolivia, Paraguay, and Peru.[33] In this way, special legislation has fostered ZOFRI's role as a regional center for trade with neighboring countries.

Decisionmakers, Human Resources, and Immigration

The Chilean political, business, and bureaucratic elites have traditionally used the West as their frame of reference. Following a strong orientation toward Europe during the first century of the country's existence, elites opened up to the influence of the United States. Cooperation initiatives with Asian Pacific countries, while with precedent, are generally recent and tied to the globalization process. This rapprochement has required individual actors to learn about this part of the world, as even twenty years after joining APEC, Chilean understanding of Asia is tentative and lacking depth.

Some actors, such as ambassadors with relevant experience in Asian Pacific countries, and business leaders, such as the representatives to ABAC, have worked to deepen political and economic relations with Asian counterparts. However, ties with these new partners have generally been pragmatic in nature. With few exceptions (such as business relationships with Australian and Japanese partners), important trans-Pacific associations with Chilean businesses have not been established.

There are significant cultural gaps, as demonstrated by the contrast between the ubiquity of Asian products in Chile (automobiles, electronic devices, home appliances, clothing, toys) and the general attitude of the people, for whom Asia remains a distant and unknown point of reference. These cultural gaps, as well as the high cost of doing business with Asia owing to geographic distance, continue to limit the development of trans-Pacific relations.

Culturally, Asia is not yet considered a relevant location. Potential ambassadors prefer posts in European or Latin American countries rather than in Asian capitals, which hinders the establishment of more significant political ties. There has been a generational shift, as some young people of Asian descent and Chilean graduates of Asian Pacific universities have contributed to the development of new relations with Japan, South Korea, and China. These young people, however, do not yet constitute a critical mass.

One requirement for serving as an efficient bridge between regions is the availability of qualified human resources. Some business organizations (such as the American Chamber of Commerce in Chile) note that there is a scarcity of professionals skilled and trained in sectors that are in high demand internationally. The mining boom, as well as the recent boom in commodities exports, has increased demand for qualified engineering and business management personnel. The installation of important astronomical observatories belonging to international scientific consortia has generated additional demand for technical personnel. Some multinational businesses and institutions from developed countries have established research and development centers in Chile, while others have opened back offices, such as call centers. Some IT companies, such as those based in India, work extensively with foreign professionals.

In general, the lack of English-proficient professionals remains an obstacle for the internationalization of the country. According to the 2014 English Proficiency Index (EPI), Chile is classified as a country with very low English proficiency, ranking forty-first out of sixty-three countries examined. While Chile has made progress, according to the EPI, it remains behind Argentina, Brazil, and Peru, among other countries in the region. This shortage also reflects a weakness in the competency among Chileans in their mother tongue. The low availability of bilingual professionals and technical personnel affects the hiring potential of international businesses and institutions.

The market has welcomed the recent arrival of professional immigrants or temporary residents from countries such as Spain, Argentina, Peru, and Colombia, while some businesses rely on professionals from their country of origin and expatriate executives. Chileans are finally beginning to recognize that a national policy of opening up to foreign migrants or temporary residents can significantly contribute to the country's competitiveness by strengthening and diversifying the pool of qualified human resources. A recent study concluded that the influx of foreigners has been increasing significantly but that the country does not have an adequate institutional framework:

> Entering the national territory is highly regulated. . . . Visitors from 108 countries require visas, all due to reciprocity. The migration reform bill submitted in 2012 is bogged down in Congress, in spite of the fact that Chile has been the largest receptor of immigrants in South America over the past two years.[34]

According to census data, the percentage of foreigners living in Chile increased from 0.76 percent to 2.3 percent between 1976 and 2014. In recent years the number of temporary residence visas issued has increased dramatically, from 41,377 in 2005 to 137,372 in 2014. Some Asians have immigrated to the country in recent years, but local Chinese, South Korean, Japanese, Indian, and other Asian communities remain small.[35]

CONCLUSION: CHILE–ASIA PACIFIC RELATIONS IN THE NEW REGIONAL CONTEXT

The proposal to convert Chile into a bridge country is entrenched in the discourse of political and business elites. However, as mentioned above, this proposal has its limitations and weaknesses.

A Misguided Self-Perception

A basic weakness of the proposal is its long-standing unilateral character. There seems to be a self-perception of Chile as a leader in Asia Pacific–South America relations among local actors, as well as a presumption that

Chile has certain advantages with respect to neighboring countries. This stems from the perception of the country's special assets and opportunities for developing economic relations with that dynamic region.

Inasmuch these opportunities do not become evident to other actors, it will be difficult for the proposal to come into force. The prevailing assumption among the largest South American actors (such as Brazil) is that Chilean mediation (or any external mediation) is superfluous; these countries have their own policies and instruments for executing them, and, in some cases, possess clear advantages over Chile in terms of participation in international networks, such as the BRICS bloc.

Other actors (such as Peru) believe that, while Chile did indeed anticipate developing trans-Pacific relations, it is possible to compete with Chile in this vast economic and political space. They have reached preferential trade agreements over the past decade, similar to those arranged by Chile, and offered to provide their own infrastructure for intra and interregional connectivity. While the Chilean discourse is not refuted in these countries, it is generally ignored. One exception is Chile's commitment to support Colombia's bid to join APEC, which has bestowed an associative character to rapprochement with Asia Pacific, and influenced the Pacific Alliance at a subregional level.

Problems of Scale

Chile suffers from a problem of scale with regard to its ties with Asia. The asymmetry between Asian Pacific and South American economies, with the exception of Brazil, is a key challenge to upgrading levels of cooperation between the two. As a result of this imbalance, South American countries are not a priority to the large Asian economies, aside from certain high-demand products. Hence South America has little leverage in negotiating with Asia.[36] Within this context, the associative efforts of subregional groups such as Mercosur and the Pacific Alliance are fundamental for achieving a deeper trade relationship with increased value-added. Relations between the two regions must transcend the current situation in which bilateral trade grows dynamically, but South America remains stuck in its role as an exporter of natural resources and importer of manufactured goods.

Opportunities Arising from "De Facto" Integration

While the formalization of South American integration, as well as of agreements between governments, has suffered from frequent difficulties and setbacks, a "de facto" integration has developed. This is demonstrated by the dynamic flow of investment and goods and services, the migration of workers between countries in the region, the international mobility of professionals, increased air transport connectivity, Internet communications, and cultural and academic exchanges, among other aspects. Consequently, taking into account these indicators, Latin America appears more integrated than ever before, although political obstacles and weak institutional arrangements remain.

De facto integration is creating a more fluid, flexible, and dynamic interdependence that will improve Chile's regional and global position. Chile and its neighbors should adopt a model similar to that of ASEAN, which has allowed member countries to consolidate Asian integration and whose systems are flexible and functional with respect to international trade and business.[37] De facto integration can be seen in the investments made by Chilean multilatinas in Argentina, Brazil, Colombia, and Peru—all with a strong Chilean trade and business presence—which give regional scale to their operations. This occurs similarly in the case of multinational businesses, some of them of Latin American origin, that have established operations in Chile.

Associative Initiatives between the Atlantic and Pacific

Chile is well positioned within this new context of regional integration, in large part because of the dynamism and openness of its economy. However, on its own, it faces limitations in expanding its trade relationship with Asia Pacific beyond exporting natural resources. The goal of becoming a bridge country unilaterally remains elusive, but Chile is making strides in terms of plurilateral initiatives. Its participation in the Pacific Alliance is an important step toward building a bloc of Latin American countries that can be a more relevant partner for Asia Pacific as a supplier, market, and destination for investment.

In addition to this participation, the promotion of joint subregional initiatives is a good opportunity for Chile, as it is a member of both the Pacific Alliance and an associate member of Mercosur. Chile can play a relevant role as a broker of joint initiatives between the two blocs to strengthen ties with Asia Pacific. Cooperation between Pacific and Atlantic partners would offer Chile the best opportunities in the medium and long term. The policies of President Michelle Bachelet's second administration point in that direction and could be successful, owing to the region's urgent need to consolidate its economic ties with more dynamic markets in order to confront the deceleration of the global economy and international trade.

NOTES

1. Inter-American Development Bank/Economic Commission for Latin America and the Caribbean/Organization for Economic Cooperation and Development, *Perspectivas de América Latina 2014: Logística y competitividad para el desarrollo*, LC/G.2575 (Paris, 2013).

2. Alvaro Ortiz and others, *EAGLEs Economic Outlook: Annual Report 2015* (Bilbao: BBVA, April 13, 2015).

3. The idea of Chile as a bridge country has arisen in several different contexts. For example, the belief that it could develop Antarctic activities and serve as a key actor in the Antarctic System because of its geographic proximity to the continent. See Javier Urbina Paredes, "El Tratado del Antártico, posición de Chile como país puente," UNISCI Discussion Paper 21 (Swiss Federal Institute of Technology Zurich, UNISCI [Research Unit on International Security and Cooperation], 2009).

4. See Joaquín Fermandois, *Mundo y fin de mundo—Chile en la política mundial, 1900–2004* (Santiago, Chile: Ediciones UC, 2005), pp. 203–07 and 215–23 ("El problema del 'excepcionalismo'" and "Visiones sobre la política mundial" sections).

5. H. E. Eduardo Frei Ruiz-Tagle, President of the Republic of Chile, speech, reprinted in *América Latina y Asia-Pacífico: Oportunidades ante la crisis*, edited by Pilar Alamos, Luz O'Shea, and Manfred Wilhelmy (Santiago, Chile: Fundación Chilena del Pacífico–Instituto de Estudios Internacionales de la Universidad de Chile, 1998), p. 39.

6. "Chilean Model," *Asia Inc.* (November 2004), p. 25.

7. "Man of Summits," *Asia Inc.* (November 2004), p. 30.

8. Eduardo Rodríguez Guarachi, "Chile, País Puente," Fundación Chilena del Pacífico (Santiago, Chile: RIL Editores, 2006), p. 97.

9. The Dirección General de Relaciones Económicas Internacionales del Ministerio de Relaciones Exteriores (DIRECON) is in charge of international economic negotiations.

10. DIRECON, "Chile: 20 Años de Negociaciones Comerciales" (Santiago, Chile, 2009), p. 23.

11. Chile is ranked seventh in economic freedom (Heritage Foundation 2016), thirty-third in economic competitiveness (World Economic Forum 2015–2016), twenty-third in perceptions of corruption (Transparency International 2015), and forty-eighth in ease of doing business (World Bank 2015).

12. Pithaya Pookaman, "Chile: An Economic Hub for Latin America" (Santiago, Chile: Universidad Santo Tomás, 2005), p. 6.

13. Communications and declarations made at the Summit of Mercosur Heads of State, Caracas, July 29, 2014.

14. Between 2005 and 2013, the China Development Bank granted $98 billion in loans to countries facing difficulties in accessing international credit. More than 90 percent of these loans were awarded to Venezuela,

Argentina, Brazil, and Ecuador in exchange for long-term contracts for the extraction of oil and other commodities.

15. See "The Chinese Chequebook," *The Economist*, May 23, 2015.

16. Osvaldo Rosales, director of the International Trade and Integration Division, ECLAC, interview by Alicia Frohmann, July 15, 2014.

17. DIRECON, "Comercio Exterior de Chile 2015."

18. China National Bureau of Statistics, *China Statistical Yearbook 2014* (Beijing: China Statistics Press, 2014).

19. The twelve TPP member economies are Australia, Brunei, Canada, Chile, the United States, Malaysia, Mexico, Japan, New Zealand, Peru, Singapore, and Vietnam.

20. The Pacific Alliance was a successor to the Pacific Arc, which included all Pacific Rim Latin American countries and was unable to come to fruition because of the excessive heterogeneity of its members.

21. See Sebastián Herreros, "The Pacific Alliance: A Bridge between Latin America and Asia Pacific?," in *Trade Regionalism in the Asia-Pacific: Developments and Future Challenges*, edited by Sanchita Basu Das and Masahiro Kawai (Singapore: ISEAS-Yusof Ishak Institute, 2016).

22. A CEPAL study, *La Alianza del Pacífico y el MERCOSUR: Hacia la convergencia en la diversidad* (November 2014), presents the feasibility and potential benefits of convergence between the two blocs.

23. See *La Tercera*, November 24, 2015.

24. Armada de Chile, Dirección del Territorio Marítimo (DIRECTEMAR), *Boletín Estadístico Marítimo* (2014).

25. The authors would like to acknowledge Catalina Viancos of Ultramar network for providing statistics for this section.

26. All currency figures are in U.S. dollars unless otherwise noted.

27. See the website http://www.corporacionamerica.com/corredor-bioceanico-aconcagua.

28. Figures based on World Bank data, information received from the Asociación Latinoamericana de Transporte Aéreo (ALTA), and "Estimación de demanda por transporte aéreo nacional e internacional en Chile," consultora Qualimet, Santiago, Chile, November 2013.

29. See the website http://www.internetworldstats.com/.

30. See Klaus Schwab, ed., *Global Competitiveness Report 2015–2016* (Geneva: World Economic Forum, 2015) (www.weforum.org).

31. See José Pablo Arellano, *Inserción internacional 2.0: Las multilatinas chilenas* (CIEPLAN/UTALCA, 2015).

32. DIRECON, "Presencia de Inversiones Directas de Capitales Chilenos en el Mundo, 1990–diciembre 2014" (www.direcon.gob.cl).

33. Zona Franca de Iquique ZOFRI, S.A., Anuario Estadístico 2013.

34. Alvaro Bellolio and Hernán Felipe Errázuriz, *Migraciones en Chile: Oportunidad ignorada* (Santiago, Chile: Ediciones LYD, 2014), p. 13.

35. See the websites www.ef-chile.cl/epi and www.extranjeria.gob.cl.

36. Barbara Stallings, "Expandiendo los vínculos económicos de América Latina con Asia," in *Desafíos post crisis de América Latina: Vínculos con Asia y rol de los recursos naturales,* edited by Alejandro Foxley (Santiago, Chile: CIEPLAN, 2012).

37. Alicia Frohmann, "Regionalismo en Asia: Oportunidades para Chile," Universidad de Chile, *Revista de Estudios Internacionales* 167 (December 2010).

CHAPTER 11

Mexico's Relationship with China and India

RECENT DEVELOPMENTS

Enrique Dussel Peters

The Latin America and Caribbean (LAC) region's relationship with China and the broader Asian region could be understood in several stages over the last centuries, starting as early as the sixteenth century with maritime trade and most recently at the end of the twentieth century and the beginning of the twenty-first century, when we have witnessed a qualitative change and significant growth in the economic relationship between the regions. Mexico, an active member of the Trans-Pacific Partnership (TPP), the Asia-Pacific Economic Cooperation forum (APEC), and the Pacific Alliance, among other regional economic schemes related to Asia, has a critical role to play in the future of LAC's relationship with China and India.

This chapter examines Mexico's current relationship with China and India, both in terms of available analysis on the subject and in terms of recent developments in the bilateral relationships. The first section offers an overview of the main issues highlighted in contemporary analyses. The second section offers a brief summary of the issues driving Mexico's relations with the two Asian giants, including recent institutional, commercial, and financial trends in the 2000–13 period. The third and final section presents a set of policy issues that are most pressing from a Mexican perspective.

RECENT ANALYSES OF MEXICO'S RELATIONS WITH THE ASIAN GIANTS

At least three types of analyses can be highlighted regarding Mexico's relationship with China and India during the 2000–13 period. First are the LAC regional perspectives. The Economic Commission for Latin America and the Caribbean (ECLAC), along with the Inter-American Development Bank (IDB) and the Organization for Economic Cooperation and Development (OECD), led the way with a group of publications in the first part of the twenty-first century. In general, the studies conducted by these institutions highlighted the increasing relevance of both regions in terms of trade, investment, and finance—the "seismic changes" experienced in recent years were the result not only of market forces but also of the active policies of the respective governments.[1]

Indeed, LAC's relationship with Asia and the Pacific—and particularly with China and India—proved to be one of the most dynamic and relevant in terms of trade, with an average annual growth rate of 20.5 percent. Trade between the two regions accounted for more than 20 percent of LAC's total trade since 2011. The costs of trade, including tariffs, transportation, and overall transaction costs, were highlighted as important agenda items between the two regions.[2] The new Asia-focused trade diversification trends also posed massive opportunities and challenges for LAC in this new "south-south" relationship, specifically in terms of trade and investment cooperation, infrastructure, competitiveness and innovation, climate change, and policy dialogue on cooperation, among other areas.[3]

A number of studies have deepened the analysis of the Sino-LAC relationship, covering a broad range of economics topics, strategic and political relationships, and key issues such as energy and manufacturing.[4] Particularly relevant for the case of China—as also for India, and for Asia in general—is that LAC's trade deficit with the region is significant in terms of its content: LAC's exports to Asia and China include mostly raw materials, with little value-added or technological content, while LAC's imports from the region are manufactured goods with increasing value-added content and products of medium- and high-level technological content. These topics have been discussed in detail for most of LAC in its relationship with Asia, and particularly with China.[5] These findings have been updated periodically by institutions such as ECLAC, the IDB, and the Red Académica de América Latina y el Caribe sobre China (RED ALC-CHINA), among others.

There has also been increased analysis of the Mexico-China relationship—and to a lesser extent of the Mexico-India relationship—from a general or macroeconomic perspective, discussing trade and business experiences, and whether China's involvement in the region poses an opportunity or a threat, but also in terms of cooperation, cultural and educational exchanges, and history. Up until the present, the Mexican government has continued, with few exceptions, a consistent liberalization strategy that started at the end of the 1980s, and only very recently has it begun to seriously consider Asia an important strategic partner in the context of globalization and beyond the North American Free Trade Agreement (NAFTA), particularly in terms of the diversification of its economic ties.[6]

Earlier analysis on Mexico tended not to explicitly include Asia, as it remained difficult for policymakers to incorporate the region into their strategic thinking.[7] While Mexico has maintained important political relations with China and India in several multilateral groups, such as the G-20 and the UN system, and has long been a participant in Asian forums, among them APEC, the Association of Southeast Asian Nations (ASEAN), the Forum for East Asia–Latin America Cooperation (FEALAC), and the Pacific Economic Cooperation Council (PECC), it is only since 2013 that the government's strategic plan, the Plan Nacional de Desarrollo, or PND (2013–2018), has presented a set of "lines of action" with specific goals and strategic objectives for interactions with Asia (though there is not a single direct reference to India in the PND).[8] The TPP and the Pacific Alliance have also played a role in bringing Asia into focus in terms of Mexico's policy reform path.[9]

Analysis regarding Mexico-China relations indicates that public, private, and academic institutions are weak in terms of their capacity to devise proposals and provide funding for particular projects of relevance to bilateral ties.[10] Since 2004, China and Mexico have set up a number of bilateral institutions, including the Mexico-China Binational Commission and the High-Level Group, which have focused on most of the relevant bilateral issues. However, there is still a long way to go in addressing these issues, which range from statistics to education, tourism, immigration, trade, and investment. New qualitative improvements in the bilateral relationship since 2013, the result of several presidential meetings between Enrique Peña Nieto and Xi Jinping, have raised expectations that important results in the Mexico-China agenda are imminent.

China has consolidated its position as Mexico's second-largest trading partner, but it also accounts for a significant trade deficit and an increasing "primarization" of Mexico's trade with the Asian giant—increasing exports in raw materials (oil and copper)—while more than 60 percent of Mexico's imports from China have a medium- and high-level technological content. Until 2013, Foreign direct investment (FDI) from China accounted for less than $260 million (less than 0.1 percent) of Mexico's total FDI (in firms such as Hutchinson Ports, Sinatex, Golden Dragon, and Huawei), manifesting an important gap with overall economic and trade intensification.[11] Several Mexican "multilatinas" have also been actively investing in China, reaching around $320 million in investments by 2011. They include Bimbo, Nemak, Katcon, Gruma, Softek, Cemex, Interceramics, and Grupo Kuo, among others.[12]

The administrations of Enrique Peña Nieto and Xi Jinping have placed emphasis on Chinese investment in Mexico.[13] The Mexican Finance Ministry has overseen these investment initiatives as part of the stated goal to become "integral strategic partners." Thus, one of the most important challenges in the Mexico-China relationship is the implementation of concrete projects in the prioritized agenda regarding Chinese investment. Formal agreements in the areas of tourism, education, culture, and scientific cooperation, among others, have been reached, in addition to the Agreement for the Promotion and Reciprocal Protection of Investments (APPRI) in 2008. Finally, on the cultural front, China has made important inroads in Mexico through five Confucius Institutes, among the highest number of centers in any country worldwide.

On Mexico's relations with India, research has been much more scarce.[14] Mexico's diplomatic relationship with India started in 1950, much earlier than with China (1972). Beginning in 2007, the Mexico-India relationship was elevated to a "privileged association," and several bilateral institutions have been established—in particular, the Mexico-India Binational Commission. As well, cooperation agreements in education, culture, and science and technology have been updated since the 1970s, though they have remained relatively low profile.[15] In terms of trade and investment, both countries signed an APPRI in 2007. Rather surprisingly, India has so far developed a more significant relationship in investment than in trade: though India is not among Mexico's top ten trading partners, investment since the 1990s has been noteworthy, particularly in steel, other manufacturing, and software (see Jorge Heine and Hari Seshasayee's discussion of Indian investments in chapter 3).[16] Both countries have also increased efforts in the cultural, agricultural, and educational fields (in 2010, the Professorship Octavio Paz on Indian Studies was established in Mexico).

The number of microlevel studies on China's FDI in Mexico is also increasing.[17] These case studies generally highlight that Chinese FDI in Mexico is still very low as a result of a lack of coordinated promotion from the Mexican side and the complexity of Mexico norms and rules of origin. Certain benefits to investing in Mexico are clear, such as its membership in NAFTA and other free trade agreements (FTAs), which allows access to some forty-four partner countries. Chinese firms have been slow to learn and adapt to the Mexican system, for example in relation to public contract bidding.[18] As a result, both countries must invest significant time to prepare in detail. Mexico in particular must adjust to the specific requirements of Chinese firms, which are substantially different from those of other foreign firms that have already established investment relationships with Mexico and have a rather in-depth knowledge of supplier systems and particular products and processes, relationships with other firms and the public sector, logistics, and access to specialized labor and training.

OVERVIEW OF INSTITUTIONAL RESOURCES AND TRADE AND INVESTMENT TRENDS

Mexico's Foreign Ministry has the highest-ranked unit specializing in Asia, the General Directorate for Asia-Pacific, which is part of the portfolio of the deputy secretary of foreign relations and covers both China and India.[19] Other government institutions in Mexico, such as the Economics Ministry, do not have specific dependencies dedicated to Asia.[20] Under the Peña Nieto administration, however, the Finance Ministry has increased its focus on Mexico's relationship with China. Mexico's public sector has also substantially pushed for an active strategy in the TPP, categorizing it as "the most important and ambitious trade negotiation worldwide."[21] The Pacific Alliance is a more recent Latin American initiative, led by four countries (Chile, Colombia, Mexico, and Peru), to allow for the free exchange of goods, services, capital, and people. The four countries account for 34 percent of Latin America's GDP and 50 percent of trade in the region.[22]

A number of business organizations in Mexico work on Asia, but they tend to focus on specific countries and not to look more broadly at the region. The following organizations are the most significant in Mexico today: the Mexican Business Council for Foreign Trade, Investment, and Technology (COMCE), which organizes events and presents analysis on both China and India; a small but growing group of business organizations specializing in China issues, such as the Mexican Chamber of Commerce in China and the Mexico-China Chamber of Commerce and Technology; and the Confederation of Chinese Associations in Mexico. In the case of India, the India-Mexico Business Chamber (IMBC) was created in 2006.

Academic institutions specializing in China and India are rather new in Mexico, with the important exception of El Colegio de México. The Center for Asian and African Studies at El Colegio has the oldest tradition in Mexico and Latin America of studying Asia.[23] The National

Case Studies

TABLE 11-1
Mexico: Main Trade Structures, 1993–2013

Exports

	Year	Total	United States	European Union	Asia	China	India	O
$US (MILLION)	1993	51,886	42,912	2,704	1,348	45	10	4
	1996	96,000	80,570	3,570	2,601	38	21	9
	2000	166,121	147,400	5,743	2,158	204	60	10
	2005	214,233	183,563	9,144	4,779	1,136	561	16
	2010	298,473	238,684	14,432	10,703	4,183	1,015	34
	2013	380,027	299,439	19,710	18,499	6,470	3,795	42
GROWTH RATE	1993–2000	18.1	19.3	11.4	7.0	24.2	29.8	11
	2000–2013	6.6	5.6	10.0	18.0	30.5	37.6	11
SHARE OVER TOTAL (PERCENTAGE)	1993	100.00	82.70	5.21	2.60	0.09	0.02	9
	1996	100.00	83.93	3.72	2.71	0.04	0.02	9
	2000	100.00	88.73	3.46	1.30	0.12	0.04	6
	2005	100.00	85.68	4.27	2.23	0.53	0.26	
	2010	100.00	79.97	4.84	3.59	1.40	0.34	11
	2013	100.00	78.79	5.19	4.87	1.70	1.00	11
TRADE BALANCE	1993	−13,481	−2,383	−5,204	−6,025	−342	−79	
	1996	6,531	13,034	−4,303	−6,397	−721	−103	4
	2000	−8,337	19,866	−9,586	−18,113	−2,676	−229	
	2005	−7,587	65,016	−16,838	−48,875	−16,561	−398	−6
	2010	−3,009	93,677	−18,065	−85,215	−41,425	−782	6
	2013	−1,184	112,178	−23,062	−100,937	−54,851	927	10

Source: Author's own elaboration based on Banco de México data ("Balanza comercial de mercancí México") for 1993–2013 (www.banxico.org.mx, 2014).

Autonomous University of Mexico also offers various academic options for studying Asia, both through the School of Philosophy and through the School of Economics, in addition to foreign languages. The Center for Chinese-Mexican Studies (CECHIMEX), part of the School of Economics, has offered in-depth studies in the last decade on trade and investment, and has conducted detailed research on value-added chains, urbanization, agriculture, the environment, and the increasing exchange with Chinese counterparts.[24] In several cases, academic institutions co-

Imports

Total	United States	European Union	Asia	China	India	Other
65,367	45,295	7,908	7,373	386	89	4,791
89,469	67,536	7,873	8,998	760	125	5,061
174,458	127,534	15,328	20,271	2,880	288	11,324
221,820	118,547	25,981	53,654	17,696	959	23,637
301,482	145,007	32,497	95,918	45,608	1,797	28,060
381,210	187,262	42,772	119,436	61,321	2,868	31,740
15.1	15.9	9.9	15.5	33.2	18.4	13.1
6.2	3.0	8.2	14.6	26.5	19.3	8.3
100.00	69.29	12.10	11.28	0.59	0.14	7.33
100.00	75.49	8.80	10.06	0.85	0.14	5.66
100.00	73.10	8.79	11.62	1.65	0.17	6.49
100.00	53.44	11.71	24.19	7.98	0.43	10.66
100.00	48.10	10.78	31.82	15.13	0.60	9.31
100.00	49.12	11.22	31.33	16.09	0.75	8.33
100.00	75.23	9.05	7.44	0.37	0.08	8.28
100.00	79.86	6.17	6.25	0.43	0.08	7.72
100.00	80.73	6.19	6.59	0.91	0.10	6.50
100.00	69.28	8.06	13.40	4.32	0.35	9.26
100.00	63.95	7.82	17.77	8.30	0.47	10.45
100.00	63.94	8.21	18.12	8.91	0.88	9.74

SHARE OVER TOTAL TRADE

operate with business organizations to formulate policy-oriented agendas.[25] A number of institutions offer courses on Asia (Universidad de Guadalajara, Instituto Tecnológico de Monterrey, Universidad de Colima), but with little specialization in China and India.[26] In general, it is clear that Mexican institutions, whether in the public, private, or academic sector, are ill prepared for the qualitatively new relationship with China and India and for generating conditions of extensive and in-depth knowledge of both countries.

TABLE 11-2

**Mexico: Trade with Asian Countries by Medium
and High-Technology Levels[a]
(share over respective total)**

	1995	2000	2005	2010	2013
Mexico, Total					
Exports	54.34	62.01	56.89	59.19	59.28
Imports	45.91	53.84	51.44	50.84	50.75
United States					
Exports	58.56	65.03	59.68	62.01	63.60
Imports	45.07	53.67	43.29	38.54	38.40
China					
Exports	3.62	89.20	34.39	27.92	40.39
Imports	38.39	51.15	70.36	77.46	74.67
India					
Exports	12.66	6.17	2.76	20.92	9.52
Imports	8.81	14.69	27.22	29.11	37.14

Source: Author's own elaboration based on World Trade Atlas data (available through IHS Maritime & Trade, www.ihs.com, 2014).

[a] Refers to chapters 84–90 of the Harmonized Tariff System.

In terms of Mexico's current trade and investment trends with respect to China and India, table 11-1 highlights that the share of exports to the United States, but particularly of imports from that country, have fallen substantially—the share of imports fell from 75 percent to less than 50 percent, and the share of total trade fell from 81 percent in 1999 to below 63 percent since 2010. In contrast, the share of total trade between Mexico and Asia almost tripled during the 2000–13 period, and increased almost tenfold for both China and India. Table 11-1 also shows that Mexico has a large trade deficit with China (a 10:1 import-export relationship in 2013). In 2013, India was Mexico's ninth-largest trading partner, ranking above such historical trading partners as the United Kingdom, France, and Colombia. In addition, since 2011, Mexico has had a small but increasing trade surplus with India.

As table 11-2 illustrates, while Mexico has substantially improved the technological level of its exports since the 1980s, particularly with its main trading partner, the United States, this structural change is not witnessed in Mexico's trade with Asia, and especially not with China. In 2013, for example, 40 percent of Mexico's exports to China

TABLE 11-3
Mexico's Trade with China and India (at the chapter level of the Harmonized Tariff System, 1995–2013)
(main ten chapters of the HTS, according to 2013)

		1995	2000	2005	2010	2013
	Imports from China	521	2,880	17,696	45,608	61,321
85	Electrical machinery	140	904	7,110	21,755	26,687
84	Auto parts	38	415	4,567	10,658	14,422
90	Optical instruments	20	114	414	2,066	3,032
87	Automobiles	2	39	336	824	1,591
98	Special classification	9	123	424	925	1,497
39	Plastics	26	101	511	1,023	1,435
95	Toys, games	68	204	625	1,353	1,390
73	Articles of iron and steel	10	54	316	707	1,147
72	Iron and steel	8	69	194	125	257
27	Oil	40	92	129	134	129
	Exports to China	37	204	1,136	4,198	6,465
87	Automobiles	0	5	52	641	1,615
27	Oil	0	0	0	724	717
85	Electrical machinery	0	19	39	301	670
84	Auto parts	1	157	296	198	252
39	Plastics	0	3	35	103	160
90	Optical instruments	0	1	5	32	74
73	Articles of iron and steel	21	0	15	7	18
72	Iron and steel	0	4	102	15	8
95	Toys, games	0	0	1	0	2
98	Special classification	0	0	0	1	2
	Imports from India	121	288	959	1,797	2,868
87	Automobiles	8	19	133	168	521
85	Electrical machinery	1	13	65	222	279
84	Auto parts	1	7	48	118	227
27	Oil	0	0	26	156	181
73	Articles of iron and steel	2	6	17	84	117
98	Special classification	0	4	22	61	92
39	Plastics	1	3	14	39	64
90	Optical instruments	1	4	15	15	37
72	Iron and steel	18	20	23	24	35
95	Toys, games	0	1	3	3	2

(continued)

TABLE 11-3
(continued)

		1995	2000	2005	2010	2013
	Exports to India	25	60	561	1,009	3,525
27	Oil	0	41	487	591	3,001
85	Electrical machinery	0	0	2	107	179
84	Auto parts	3	3	12	38	122
72	Iron and steel	0	0	8	47	39
87	Automobiles	0	0	0	49	29
39	Plastics	0	0	6	25	23
90	Optical instruments	0	0	1	1	3
73	Articles of iron and steel	1	7	2	5	2
95	Toys, games	0	0	0	0	0
98	Special classification	0	0	0	0	0

Source: Author's own elaboration based on World Trade Atlas data (available through IHS Maritime & Trade, www.ihs.com, 2014).

and 75 percent of its imports consisted of medium- or high-tech items, and throughout the 2000–13 period the technological gap in trade increased steadily. To a different degree, this technological gap is also relevant for Mexico's trade with India.

As shown in table 11-3, electrical machinery, auto parts, and optical instruments accounted for 72 percent of Mexican imports from China in 2013, while the three main import categories originating from India—automobiles, electrical machinery, and auto parts—accounted for 36 percent. Though Mexico's exports to China also included automobiles, auto parts, and electrical machinery, the categories related to raw materials—oil, plastics, and minerals—accounted for more than 50 percent; in the case of India, Mexican oil exports alone accounted for 85 percent of total exports in 2013.

Despite difficulties in tracking FDI, several general trends in Mexico's FDI inflows stand out.[27] First, in the 1999–2013 period, almost 111,000 firms invested in Mexico. In the case of China and India, it was 968 and 195, or 0.9 percent and 0.2 percent, respectively. Second, Chinese and Indian FDI in Mexico accounted for 0.08 percent and 0.02 percent of Mexico's accumulated FDI for the period, and those figures have remained steady (table 11.4). And third, from a sectoral perspective, Chinese FDI in Mexico has concentrated in mining, commerce, and manufacturing (accounting for 79 percent of total Chinese FDI during the stated period), while India's FDI in Mexico has been primarily in manu-

TABLE 11-4
Mexico: FDI Flows by Country of Origin, 1999–2013
(according to 2012)

		1999	2000	2005	2010	2011	2012	2013	1999–2013
$US (MILLION)	Total FDI to Mexico	13,940	18,302	24,741	23,491	23,720	17,810	39,172	305,676
	China	5	11	15	14	22	83	19	259
	India	0	28	2	6	8	2	0	64
SHARE (PERCENTAGE OVER TOTAL)	Total FDI to Mexico	100.0	100.0	100.0	100.0	100.0	100.0	100.0	100.0
	Top 5	73.1	103.6	79.3	87.2	79.6	64.8	47.4	94.4
	United States	54.2	72.0	48.0	28.4	50.9	49.3	33.5	56.3
	Spain	7.5	11.6	6.9	8.7	15.4	-5.2	-2.1	13.7
	Holland	7.8	14.7	16.2	39.3	11.8	8.2	9.2	15.5
	Canada	5.0	3.7	2.8	7.9	5.9	9.9	3.5	5.9
	United Kingdom	-1.3	1.6	5.5	3.0	-4.4	2.5	3.2	3.0
	Asia (selected)	10.0	3.3	1.4	3.1	5.5	12.2	5.8	3.1
	Japan	8.9	2.4	0.7	2.3	3.9	10.2	4.1	1.9
	China	0.04	0.06	0.06	0.06	0.09	0.47	0.05	0.08
	India	0.00	0.15	0.01	0.03	0.03	0.01	0.00	0.02

Source: Author's own elaboration based on data from the Dirección General de Inversión Extranjera, Secretaría de Economía, 2014 (www.gob.mx/se/).

facturing and mass media storage, accounting for 91 percent of total FDI for the same period.

CONCLUSIONS AND POLICY PROPOSALS

There is no doubt that Mexico will continue to improve its political and economic relationship with China and India in the future, particularly in terms of the increasing global presence of these countries in multilateral institutions, in LAC, and specifically in Mexico's trade and FDI. But how well prepared is Mexico for such a qualitatively different relationship?

Mexico needs to improve and invest substantially in institutions to enhance its dialogue with China and India. As analyzed, so far the public, private, and academic sectors do not account for the increasing presence of the Asian giants in Mexico—in fact, there is an increasing gap between the growing economic ties and the institutional capacity to address this new reality. The current Mexican administration has recognized the strategic importance of Asia for Mexico after several decades of focusing almost exclusively on NAFTA.

Interestingly, neither China nor India is currently participating in the TPP or the Pacific Alliance, and China so far has explicitly rejected the possibility of adhering to these groups.[28] In addition, neither the Pacific Alliance nor the TPP is particularly relevant for Mexico from a trade or FDI perspective.[29] While it is true that Mexico's trade with TPP countries accounted for 71.50 percent of Mexico's total trade in 2013, it is also true that if we exclude all the countries with which Mexico already has FTAs—Canada, Chile, Japan, Peru, and United States—the share of Mexico's total trade was 1.47 percent in 2013. The three countries of the Pacific Alliance, all of whom have FTAs with Mexico, accounted for 1.51 percent of Mexico's total trade. In addition, Mexico's trade with the TPP and the Pacific Alliance countries is much less dynamic than with other countries, particularly China and India, and the TPP's and Pacific Alliance's share of Mexico's FDI is even smaller. Hence, while there might be important arguments to participate actively in the TPP and the Pacific Alliance, it seems to be much more relevant to update, modernize, and reform already existing FTAs, which so far has not been set as a priority by the Mexican government. From a strategic perspective, and to effectively allow for a broader and deeper relationship with both China and India, Mexico must strengthen its bilateral institutions and devise more robust bilateral agendas, as regional or multilateral options will not be sufficient in either case.

In its relationship with China, Mexico needs to integrate the existing sectors that work effectively, including the public, legislative, business, and academic sectors, to develop a detailed agenda.[30] A dedicated task force or working group should prioritize items in the short, medium, and long term, from statistics to immigration and visas, tourism, infrastructure (particularly regarding ports and direct flights), financing of trade activities, and trade and investment opportunities in specific segments of value-added chains (from telecommunications and auto parts/automobiles to electronics and yarn-textile garments). Mexico and China have already established an important group of bilateral institutions such as the Binational Commission and the High-Level Group; however, the public and legislative sectors have thus far been unable to integrate additional sectors into these institutions and address new issues as they emerge.

In the Indian case, systematic knowledge building and proposals for a strengthened Indo-Mexico bilateral agenda in the short, medium, and long term have not taken place to the degree necessary, although the Mexico-India Binational Commission has done important work in this regard. Unlike China's significant trade presence—as well as the accompanying social and political expectations to solve related issues—the Mexico-India relationship has not gained prominence on the policy agenda, but it has great potential in the short and medium term. Improved research on investment flows between India and Mexico are a step in the right direction.

In sum, in the case of both China and India, Mexico needs to make important investments in existing and new institutions. Clearly, a NAFTA-only strategy is insufficient to meet Mexico's needs in a changing global environment. In approaching the growing opportunities with China and India, Mexico will have to devise specific bilateral strategies rather than rely on multilateral forums such as the TPP and the Pacific Alliance.

NOTES

1. Economic Commission for Latin America and the Caribbean (ECLAC), *India and Latin America and the Caribbean: Opportunities and Challenges in Trade and Investment Relations* (Santiago, Chile: ECLAC, 2011); Osvaldo Rosales and Mikio Kuwayama, "América Latina al encuentro de China e India: Perspectivas y desafíos en comercio e inversión," *Revista de la CEPAL* 93 (2007), pp. 85–108; Inter-American Development Bank (IDB), *Shaping the Future of the Asia–Latin American and the Caribbean*

Relationship (Washington, DC: IDB, 2012); Javier Santiso, "¿Realismo mágico? China e India en América Latina y África," *Economía Exterior* 38 (2006), pp. 59–69.

2. IAB, *Shaping the Future of the Asia–Latin American and the Caribbean Relationship;* Santiso, "¿Realismo mágico?"

3. ECLAC *India and Latin America and the Caribbean.*

4. Cynthia Arnson, Jorge Heine, and Christine Zaino, eds., *Reaching across the Pacific: Latin America and Asia in the New Century* (Washington, DC: Woodrow Wilson Center, 2014); Riordan Roett and Guadalupe Paz, eds., *China's Expansion into the Western Hemisphere: Implications for Latin America and the United States* (Brookings, 2008); Enrique Dussel Peters, "The Implications of China's Entry into the WTO for Mexico," Global Issue Paper 24 (Berlin: Heinrich Böll Stiftung, 2005), pp. 1–38.

5. Arnson, Heine, and Zaino, eds., *Reaching across the Pacific.* For a detailed analysis and discussion of LAC's relationship with China, see several studies, statistics, and books of the Red Académica de América Latina y el Caribe sobre China (RED ALC-CHINA) (http://www.redalc-china.org/).

6. Plan Nacional de Desarrollo 2013–2018 (PND) (Mexico City: Government of Mexico, 2013), p. 148; Enrique Dussel Peters, "Mexico and the Asian Challenge, 2000–2012," in *Reaching across the Pacific,* edited by Amson, Heine, and Zaino, pp. 187–252; Rafael Fernández de Castro and Laura Rubio Díaz Leal, "Falsa ilusión: China, el contrapeso de Estados Unidos en el Hemisferio Occidental," in *China y México: Implicaciones de una nueva relación,* edited by Enrique Dussel Peters and Yolanda Trápaga Delfín (Mexico City: National Autonomous University of Mexico [UNAM]/ Center for Chinese-Mexican Studies [CECHIMEX], ITESM, and *La Jornada,* 2007), pp. 105–17.

7. Marcelo M. Giugale, Olivier Lafourcade, and Vinh H. Nguyen, eds., *Mexico: A Comprehensive Development Agenda for the New Era* (Washington, DC: World Bank, 2001); José Luis León, "México y el mundo del futuro: Cinco posibles escenarios," in *La política exterior de México,* edited by El Colegio de Mexico/Instituto Matias Romero (Mexico City: El Colegio de Mexico/Instituto Matias Romero, 1997), pp. 167–85.

8. Dussel Peters, "Mexico and the Asian Challenge"; PND 2013–2018, p. 148.

9. Francisco Rosenzweig, "El Acuerdo de Asociación Transpacífica: un impulso a América del Norte," in *Reflexiones sobre la política comercial internacional de México (2006–2012),* edited by Beatriz Leycegui Gardoqui (Mexico City: ITAM and Secretaría de Economía, 2012), pp. 434–45.

10. For a full discussion, see various studies, statistics, conferences, and books published by the Centro de Estudios China-México (CECHIMEX) (http://www.economia.unam.mx/cechimex/index.php/es/); Dussel Peters, "Mexico and the Asian Challenge"; and Enrique Dussel Peters, "La inversión extranjera directa de China en América Latina: 10 estudios de caso" (Mexico City: RED ALC-CHINA, UNAM/CECHIMEX, and UDUAL, 2014).

11. All currency figures are in U.S. dollars unless otherwise noted.

12. Enrique Dussel Peters, ed., *América Latina y el Caribe-China: Economía, comercio e inversiones* (Mexico City: RED ALC-CHINA, UDUAL, UNAM/CECHIMEX, 2013).

13. Dussel Peters, "La Inversión extranjera directa"; Qiu, Xiaoqi, "China: Profundización integral de la reforma y sus relaciones con México," *Cuadernos de Trabajo del Cechimex* 3 (2014), pp. 1–8.

14. Some studies on the Mexico-India relationship include Shri Sujan R. Chinoy, "The India-China Relationship," presented at a conference at the Center for Chinese-Mexican Studies (Cechimex) at the National Autonomous University of Mexico, April 9, 2014 (http://www.economia.unam.mx /cechimex/index.php/es/pagina-inicio/2-uncategorised/156-2014-2); ECLAC, "India and Latin America and the Caribbean"; Francisco E. González, "El ciclo de dominación de un solo partido: México, India y Japón en perspectiva comparativa," *Foro Internacional* 49 (1) (2009), pp. 47–68; Julio Millán Bojalil, "México e India: Intensificar las relaciones comerciales" (Mexico City: Consultores Internacionales, 2011); Benjamín Preciado Solís, "Las Relaciones entre México y la India, 1995–2000," *Foro Internacional* 41 (4) (2001), pp. 891–900; Benjamín Preciado Solís, "Las Relaciones entre México e India, 2000–2006," *Foro Internacional* 48 (1–2) (2008), pp. 487–93.

15. Secretaría de Relaciones Exteriores (SRE), "Nuevos espacios para México en Asia-Pacífico," SRE, Mexico, 2012.

16. Since 1992, Indian ISPAN has acquired the former state-owned Lázaro Cárdenas-Las Truchas for $250 million, in addition to a concession for the terminal at the Lázaro Cárdenas port. More recently, Indian firms in informatics and software, such as TCS, Infosys, Wipro Technologies, and Patni Computers Systems, and in pharmaceuticals (including Claris Life-sciences and Dr. Reddy's Laboratories), have invested in Mexico (Indian Embassy 2014). Mexican investments in India are smaller but also present (Homex and Cinépolis).

17. Dussel Peters, "La inversión extranjera directa."

18. The issue arose in November 2014 when, first, Mexico's secretary of communication and transportation selected the Chinese firm China Railway Construction as the winner of the Mexico City–Querétaro high-speed railway construction but only a few days later canceled the bid as a result of irregularities. Public opinion and the public sectors in China, as well as the CRC, were upset, and the action affected the Mexico-China relationship.

19. The lack of institutional relevance of Asia in Mexico's public sector contrasts, for example, with the existence of an undersecretary for North America and another on Latin America and the Caribbean in the case of Mexico's Foreign Ministry.

20. However, in June 2013 the Secretariat of the Economy noted that it would create a unit on China.

21. PND 2013-2-18, p. 95.

22. Ibid.

23. For more details, see the website http://ceaa.colmex.mx/.

24. For more details, see the website http://www.economia.unam.mx /cechimex.

25. Particularly interesting, for example, is the agenda that Agendasia established for the case of China, with 100 proposals on specific topics (including trade, investments, political links, culture, and education and tourism). Agendasia, "Agenda estratégica México-China. Dirigido al C. Presidente Electo Enrique Peña Nieto" (Mexico City: Agendasia, 2012).

26. Dussel Peters, "Mexico and the Asian Challenge."

27. Enrique Dussel Peters and others, eds., *Inversión extranjera directa en México: Desempeño y potencial. Una perspectiva macro, meso, micro y territorial* (Mexico City: Siglo XXI, Secretaría de Economía, and UNAM/ CECHIMEX, 2008).

28. In November 2014, as the host of the APEC meeting, China seemed to strategically support APEC and an APEC FTA, although there is the possibility of China either negotiating directly with the United States or participating in a later stage in TPP.

29. The official argument highlights the relevance of the Pacific in general— not considering Mexico's already existing trade and FDI agreements—and the possibility of "conserving benefits obtained through NAFTA [and] NAFTA as an export platform for the Asia-Pacific." See Secretaría de Economía (SE), "Tratado de Asociación Transpacífico (TPP)," H. Senado de la República, Sesión de trabajo, 4 de noviembre de 2015 (Mexico City, 2015) p. 6.

30. Agendasia, "Agenda estratégica México-China"; Dussel Peters, "La inversión extranjera directa."

CHAPTER 12

Argentina and Brazil

TOWARD AN ATLANTIC STRATEGY?

Henrique Altemani de Oliveira

The establishment of diplomatic relations with the People's Republic of China (PRC) during the military dictatorships in Argentina (1972) and Brazil (1974) shows that the foreign policies of these two countries were not determined essentially by ideological concerns but pragmatically by their national interests, encompassing both economic and political considerations. In addition, in the late 1970s, Argentina and Brazil began to pursue a process of rapprochement with the objective of removing the strategic military constraints and obstacles to integration so as to bring about conditions more propitious for development.

In this context, Mercosur, the Common Market of the South, was created in the early 1990s, with Argentina and Brazil at its core. From that moment on, there was an expectation of South American integration, which was seen as a way of leveraging the two countries' possible insertion into the international system. Despite Argentina's efforts to implement a special alliance with the United States, Argentina and Brazil, as well as Latin America and the Caribbean (LAC), also came to see East Asia as strategic in their process of international insertion. It is thought that beyond commercial interests, political interests were also present on the Mercosur agenda, the result of member countries' efforts to craft a regional identity and retake a place of their own in the international system, relatively disconnected from inter-American arrangements.

The basis of this political agenda and of the subsequent formation of institutions such as the Union of South American Nations (UNASUR) is the consideration that the United States does not have and has never presented a genuine intention of regional integration, formal or informal, with LAC directed toward the commercial, industrial, financial, and technological sectors,[1] such as the role played by Japan in Asia or by Germany in the European Union. In this sense, Mercosur did not (and does not) represent an ideological alternative or an Atlantic option. To the contrary, it sought a regional reorganization for repositioning in the international system not only because of the end of the Cold War but also because of regional integration trends. The emergence of Asia as an actor with greater economic, commercial, financial, and technological capabilities, in addition to great political weight, also presented important opportunities for the Mercosur member countries.

Initially, the economic rise of Asia was led by Japan, with players such as South Korea and other Southeast Asian countries constituting what was called at the time the "Asian economy." The ties that Argentina and Brazil had maintained with India and China during the Cold War induced a stronger political relationship around the process of renegotiating the post–Cold War international order. More recently, assuming leading roles in the international economy, China and India have come to figure more prominently in the economic and political prospects for LAC.

China and India are both interested in the region as a source of natural and mineral resources and also as a space with significant opportunities to absorb their manufactured goods. This commercial relationship has room to expand with a new flow of investments to ensure the supply of natural resources or to establish productive units in situ with a view to the local and regional markets. Diplomatically, seeking joint action in multilateral forums is a strategy pursued by both India and China, often characterized as south-south cooperation. In this context, Brazil is considered a strategic partner, owing to its relatively active role in the international system and its emphasis on coalition building.

This chapter highlights the significance of the relationships that Argentina and Brazil have developed with the Asian giants, China and India. The analysis is based on the premise that these relationships express the interests and perspectives of each state more than they do a regional approach. The first section considers Mercosur as a nonexclusionary project geared toward regional expansion (South America). Subsequent sections focus on the political-strategic objectives of each country's bilateral and multilateral relations, with particular attention paid to the economic, commercial, and financial aspects of these relationships and their implications.

ARGENTINA AND BRAZIL: A GAMBLE ON MERCOSUR AND SOUTH AMERICA

In the late 1970s, Brazil's foreign policy, without discarding its universalist orientation, began to invest in a regional perspective and started a process of rapprochement with the rest of Latin America.[2] Emblematic stages of this process, displaying the endeavors not only of Brazil but also of Argentina in relation to the region, included the following: (1) the Amazon Cooperation Treaty of 1978;[3] (2) the resolution of the Itaipu dispute, with the signing of the Argentine-Brazilian-Paraguayan Tripartite Agreement in 1979;[4] (3) the signing of an agreement between Brazil and Argentina on the peaceful uses of nuclear energy in 1980;[5] (4) the formation of the Rio Group in 1986;[6] (5) the integration of Brazil and Argentina; and (6) the creation of the Brazilian-Argentine Agency for Accounting and Control of Nuclear Materials (ABACC) and the signing of the Quadripartite Agreement.[7] In this context, the creation of Mercosur in 1991 represented a joint effort to establish a more cooperative environment in the Southern Cone. Mercosur was a response to real problems that stemmed from the debt crisis and from the lag in acceding to liberalism, which required economic restructuring and greater possibilities of international insertion.[8]

There are many interpretations to explain the creation of Mercosur, but in practice, they converge as an Argentine-Brazilian gamble on regionalism[9] and, even more clearly, on a new direction for South America.[10] Mercosur's creation did not represent an "Atlantic" strategy. Coupled with clear economic and cultural interests, Brazil's power politics should not be dismissed. Consistent with its universalist foreign policy, Brazil understood (and understands) that "regionalism is one of the most efficient instruments for increasing a nation's room to maneuver in a unipolar world."[11] Hence, these ideas reveal that "in Brasília, regionalism is seen in instrumental terms as power calculus—a means for obtaining certain foreign policy aims."[12] Accordingly, the creation of Mercosur had a political dimension, one that was brought into sharp relief by Brazil's intention to use Mercosur/South America as leverage for its own international insertion and by member countries' equally clear goals of seeking mechanisms for economic and commercial cooperation to support the recovery of the respective weakened economies.

It should be noted that the degree of autonomy enjoyed by Brazil's diplomatic and economic agencies, in contrast to Argentina's alignment with the United States in the 1990s, weakened the process of institutionalization and consolidation of Mercosur. Nonetheless, in keeping with the view that Mercosur was for the benefit of South America, in 1993 Celso Amorim launched a proposal for a South American Free Trade

Area (SAFTA), and that same year negotiations began that were aimed at strengthening ties with the Andean Community of Nations (CAN). An emphasis on Mercosur and South America was maintained throughout the administrations of Fernando Collor, Itamar Franco, Fernando Henrique Cardoso, and Luís Inácio Lula da Silva.[13]

As the difficulties stemming from the financial crises took their toll, in the second half of the 1990s the negotiations lost intensity, yet Brazil remained active, and went on to organize the First Meeting of Presidents of South America (Brasília, 2000). At that meeting Brazil pointed to the need to expand regional physical integration, which found expression in the Initiative for the Integration of the Regional Infrastructure in South America (IIRSA).[14] This process was completed by the formation of the Community of South American Nations (CSN, 2004), which subsequently evolved into UNASUR (2008), and was supplemented, in the strategic security dimension, by the South American Defense Council (2008).

From Mercosur to UNASUR, one perceives the intent to integrate South America with the objective of bolstering the possibilities of regional development and also of working together to promote regional interests in international negotiations. At no time was any effort made to divide South America into Atlantic-facing and Pacific-facing countries, or along the lines of leftist or rightist governments, or between liberal models and models in which the state plays a regulatory role. It is thought that Brazil's option for South America was not (and is not) ideological. Since 1993, Brazil has advocated closer relations with CAN and has even endorsed Venezuela's membership in Mercosur.[15]

The fact that the region now features different models of economic development and different political regimes does not represent the rise of antagonistic blocs. That is certainly not the intent of the Pacific Alliance. At the Eleventh Ministerial Meeting of the Pacific Alliance (May 2014), it was decided that an informational meeting with the foreign ministers and trade ministers of the Mercosur countries would be held to begin a dialogue (for further discussion of the nascent ties between the two blocs, see the analysis by Alicia Frohmann and Manfred Wilhelmy in chapter 10). Similarly, different opportunities for dialogue between the Pacific Alliance and other parts of Latin America have been pursued.[16]

In recent years, Argentina and Brazil have come to see Asia as a strategic partner economically and politically. And, in keeping with its universalist approach and its aim to become a regional power, Brazil has emphasized the need for closer ties with "our potential peers in the international community"[17]—Russia, India, China, and South Africa (the other BRICS countries). Hence, Brazil's foreign policy strategy was twofold: to strengthen the South American region as the basis of global insertion and to expand relations with different regional poles. Distanced from Europe by the break in diplomatic ties with the United Kingdom after the Malvinas War, and politically distant from the United States, Argentina has found China to be an important trading ally.[18] Particularly in the context of Argentina's complicated post-default economic tribulations, China has become a key actor in the rebuilding of the Argentine economy.[19] In this way, and despite the more traditional relationship with the United States and Europe, Argentina came to prioritize its relationship with Asia as an instrument for negotiating with the other two poles. This initial political-economic interest in Asia also motivated strong expectations of the role that could be played by China; India later came to embrace this whole set of concerns.

THE PRESENCE OF CHINA AND INDIA IN THE SOUTHERN CONE

Today there is a relative consensus that the twenty-first century shows signs of becoming the "Asian" or "Pacific Century." When this expression began to be used in the 1990s as a counterpoint to the "Atlantic Century," it referred more specifically to the Asian economy led by Japan. Today, perhaps the "Chinese Century" would be more appropriate. In fact, the international affairs expert Richard Haass argues the following about what kind of Asian century we might expect in the twenty-first century:

> There can be two, very different Asian centuries, and the one that emerges will have profound consequences for the region's peoples and governments—and for the world. One future is an Asia that is relatively familiar: a region whose economies continue to enjoy robust levels of growth and manage to avoid conflict with one another. The second future could hardly be more different: and Asia of increased tensions, rising military budgets, and slower economic growth. . . . Some of what is needed can be modeled on what Europe has achieved [since World War II]. . . . The United States, an Atlantic power, was fully integrated into the region's economic and security arrangements. Something along these lines is likely to be no less critical for Asia, where the U.S., which is also a Pacific power, has vital interests and deep commitments. America's strategic "pivot" to Asia thus needs to be substantial and lasting. . . . The alternative is an Asia left to its own devices—and an Asian century that is dominated by China or characterized by frequent bouts of diplomatic tension or even conflict.[20]

China, the world's second-largest economy, has over time built a strong relationship with the developing world by promoting nonintervention in the internal affairs of the state, and a new international economic order through initiatives to reform global political institutions, such as the United Nations, or financial institutions, such as the International Monetary Fund and the World Bank.[21] China's strategy is evident in its presence in groups of emerging powers (such as the BRICS) and in policies seeking closer relations with Africa, Latin America, and Southeast Asia.[22]

India, though having relatively less capacity, is another Asian actor with a clear will to assume a greater share of power and one that is also seeking to forge partnerships with emerging or less-developed countries. Yet as India presents itself as the "world's largest democracy," it also seeks to pursue closer political ties with the United States and other Western powers. One clear example of this strategy is its participation in Asian negotiations, along with Australia and New Zealand, to counter the role of China. With their growing roles on the international stage, both India and China are expanding their potential influence, which will give them more power to intervene regionally and globally.

China's interest in LAC is also reflected in its presence in regional institutions, such as the Organization of American States (OAS), the Inter-American Development Bank (IDB), and the Caribbean Development Bank. Since 1990, China has been present at the meetings of the Rio Group, and it is an observer at meetings of the Community of Latin American and Caribbean States (CELAC), in addition to participating in the United Nations Stabilization Mission (MINUSTAH) in Haiti.[23] And India, in keeping with its multilateral strategy, under the banner of south-south cooperation signed trade agreements with Mercosur and grew closer to the Andean Community, the Caribbean Community (CARICOM), the Central American Integration System (SICA), and the Rio Group. A relatively new initiative is the India–Brazil–South Africa Dialogue Forum (IBSA), which seeks to strengthen relations and cooperation among these three countries on three continents.

The recent international financial crisis, as well as the impasses in the Doha Round of the World Trade Organization (WTO), made perfectly clear the fragility of the existing institutions (along with their rules) and the need for drastic changes to accommodate the interests of the different states, so as to bring about a more cooperative and stable environment internationally. In that regard, China and India, together with LAC, share a framework of political coordination and economic cooperation through "multilateralism of the south," conceived as an instrument to overcome the constraints imposed by the main power centers.[24]

The role played by China in the international economic recovery, as well as the consolidation of the G-20 in September 2009 as the decision-making council of the world economy, made it possible to strengthen ties and strategic partnerships among Argentina, Brazil, China, India, and even Mexico (all members of the G-20), thereby fostering an informal commitment to return to the prospects of adopting a common position in the international institutions. The pressure for China to assume an international leadership role is mitigated by the fact that China is not the only country facing such a demand. Rather, it is in a similar position as the set of countries currently called emerging powers, even though China is economically, politically, and strategically superior to these other countries in terms of its capabilities. Certain shared goals, however, stand out: a fairer distribution of power at the global level, a multipolar world order, and their own ascendant place in the international hierarchy.[25]

Although China's presence in LAC is geographically segmented—with Taiwan having maintained diplomatic relations with Central America and the Caribbean, the presence of Asia-Pacific Economic Cooperation (APEC) group members in the Pacific Alliance, and Brazil's importance not only as a trading partner but also as a political partner in the context of the BRICS—a supposed fragmentation along the lines of Atlantic and Pacific countries does not stand up when one considers China's presence in the region.[26] Such segmentation results precisely from the fact that LAC presents "a mosaic of countries" without the minimum unity required for a joint strategy for insertion into the international economy. Exclusionary proposals further weaken regional bargaining power. Moreover, that the LAC region is in the direct area of U.S. influence is relatively significant but is not the determining factor for Chinese insertion into the LAC regional economy.[27]

China's interests are pragmatic and focused on the search for reliable sources of commodities that are fundamental for the continuation of China's development.[28] At the same time, there is a political aspect to China's insertion into Latin America related to the effort to redefine the international order.[29] Left-leaning governments in LAC can be seen as ideologically compatible allies, yet a negative perception persists that they are volatile governments that may compromise the Chinese investment.[30] In this regard, it has been reaffirmed time and again that China's increasing presence in the region's economy is pragmatic and nonideological, so much so that China now describes its own economy as a "socialist market economy."

Overall, China's interests and presence in LAC are much more substantial than India's.[31] One could argue that the political dimension of a rebalancing of the international system is not of particular interest to the LAC countries—though it appears to be of interest to Brazil, as it is for other BRICS and the IBSA countries. Yet Argentina, Brazil, and Mexico were active participants in the G-77 and the Non-Aligned Movement, along with India and China. Today they are participants in the financial G-20, emblematic of the objectives of the reform of the international order. Argentina also points to China's fundamental role at the time of the Malvinas crisis and in the current post-default crisis.

China's first strategic partnership in LAC was with Brazil, in 1993. Since then, other Latin American countries have also become strategic partners: Bolivia in 2001, Mexico in 2003, Argentina in 2004, and Venezuela in 2005.[32] Brazil is thought to be an interesting partner for China in light of its tradition of autonomy; its respect for nonintervention in internal affairs; its relative political, economic, and technological weight; and its relatively continuous and consistent positions in the international organizations. And similarly for Brazil: China, with its new economic, commercial, financial, political, and strategic status, is a fundamental partner for entertaining Brazil's own claims in the current process of redefining the international order.

In any event, at no time was it considered that a "strategic partnership" meant a commitment to having no divergences or disputes, or, on the other hand, to providing unlimited support, as would be the case in a strategy of automatic alignment. The strategic partnership induces a consensus whereby each party maintains its own interests, but some of these interests are held in common, the partnership being a means for finding common ground, achieving greater cooperation on the matters in question, and possibly bringing about better political conditions for development. Hence, a strategic partnership is not an exclusively economic proposition, even if China is concerned primarily with its economic development, just as India, Argentina, and Brazil are concerned with theirs. The importance of scientific and technological cooperation in China's relationships with Argentina and Brazil should also be noted.[33]

Rengaraj Viswanathan considers that China's strategic presence in LAC attracted the attention of Indian entrepreneurs, who had not paid enough attention to this market. He adds that although India may not have the capacity to repeat on the same scale and with the same speed what China has done, it does have the potential to compete in areas in which it has comparative advantages (such as the pharmaceutical and IT sectors). Furthermore, he posits that India's insertion into the Latin American market could be aided by India's presenting itself as a strategic alternative to avoid LAC dependency on the Chinese market.[34]

The creation of the IBSA Dialogue Forum in 2003 reflected an effort not only to further south-south cooperation but also to facilitate a greater presence of each member on the other two continents. The objective of the IBSA, first, was to develop a more favorable environment for each member's respective strategies of international insertion,[35] and second, to expand economic-commercial and scientific-technological relations. This twin goal is partially confirmed if we consider that the India-Mercosur, the Mercosur-SACU (Southern African Customs Union), and the India-SACU trade preference agreements resulted from this strategy.

For Varun Sahni, however, Latin America was always on the periphery of India's interests.[36] It falls within the fifth priority of Indian foreign policy, encompassing multilateral arrangements aimed at defending the interests of developing countries in international negotiating processes. Despite this relatively negative view and India's clear interest in natural resources, India's investments and joint ventures in Argentina and Brazil have exhibited a strong emphasis on production and distribution in IT sectors (software) and pharmaceuticals. As Rengaraj Viswanathan notes, those are sectors in which India has comparative advantages and which are no doubt of interest to the Argentine and Brazilian business communities. One must not forget that the precedent for establishing the IBSA was precisely the joint effort of India, South Africa, and Brazil to break the patents for HIV/AIDS remedies and to stimulate the production of generic drugs.

TRADE RELATIONS

In 2009, China became Brazil's leading trading partner, surpassing, in the sum of exports and imports, a position held by the United States for eighty years. China's position as the leading destination of Brazilian exports appears relatively consolidated and was reinforced in 2012, when China also become the leading source of Brazilian imports. Table 12-1 highlights the importance of China for Brazilian exports, mainly in keeping surpluses constant ($35.72 billion from 2010 to 2014). Argentina already has China as its second leading export destination, but with continuing deficits ($23.16 billion in the same period). Exports to India and Japan continue to be relatively less, these markets being more important for Brazilian exports, and, to a lesser degree, for Argentine exports.

As a region, Asia is currently Brazil's leading trading partner. In 2014, 33 percent of all Brazilian exports went to Asia. As for Brazilian imports, Asia accounted for 31 percent in 2014. Of the ten leading destinations of Brazil's exports and sources of its imports, the three leading partners in 2012 and 2013, by total volume, were China, the United States, and Argentina. Among the ten leading destinations, Japan was

TABLE 12-1
Exports from Argentina and Brazil to Selected Markets
Percent unless otherwise indicated

	Total (US$ billions)	United States	Mercosur	China	Japan	India
Argentina						
2010	68.2	5.3	27.2	8.5	1.3	1.0
2011	84.1	5.1	26.9	7.4	1.0	0.8
2012	80.9	5.1	27.3	6.2	1.5	1.0
2013	76.6	5.6	28.0	7.2	1.8	1.1
2014	68.3	5.9	24.4	6.5	1.1	2.6
Brazil						
2010	197.4	9.6	13.3	15.6	3.5	2.3
2011	256.0	10.1	12.7	17.3	3.7	2.7
2012	242.6	11.1	11.5	17.0	3.3	2.3
2013	242.2	10.3	12.2	19.0	3.3	2.7
2014	225.1	12.1	9.1	18.0	3.0	2.1

Source: ECLAC (data from Comtrade database). Available at http://cepal.org/comercio/ecdata2/.

fifth in both years, India was seventh in 2012, and South Korea was seventh in 2013. Among the ten leading sources of Brazilian imports, South Korea was fifth in 2012 and sixth in 2013, Japan was seventh in both years, and India was tenth in 2013.

Compared to trade within the European Union, Mercosur intraregional exports are relatively low. Even so, Mercosur is the main destination for Argentine, Uruguayan, and Paraguayan exports, and for Brazil it is the third leading export market, after the European Union. When the total exports of the member countries of the Pacific Alliance and Mercosur to China or India are considered, Brazil accounted for approximately 50 percent of the total exported to China from 2010 to 2013, and Mercosur as a whole accounted for 60 percent (table 12-2). The only other country that figures relatively prominently is Chile, with 22 percent. Peru and Mexico, both APEC members, have had difficulty accessing the Chinese market. Exports to India, on the other hand, are very modest, reflecting the difficulties the different South American countries face in defining an export strategy, owing to the weight of China and to India's protections. Tariff preference agreements— Mercosur-India and Chile-India—came into force only in 2009 and 2007, respectively. Nonetheless, what stands out over the four years

TABLE 12-2
Share in Exports from Mercosur and Pacific Alliance Countries to China and India, 2010–13
Percent

	China			
	2010	2011	2012	2013
Argentina	8.8	7.4	6.1	6.1
Brazil	46.7	52.4	50.2	50.6
Paraguay	*	*	*	*
Uruguay	0.6	0.6	1.0	1.4
Mercosur	56.1	60.4	57.3	58.1
Chile	26.3	22.0	22.2	21.1
Colombia	3.0	2.4	4.0	5.6
Mexico	6.4	7.0	7.0	7.1
Peru	8.2	8.2	9.5	8.1
Pacific Alliance	43.9	39.6	42.7	41.9
Total in US$ billions	65.890	84.638	82.218	91.016

	India			
	2010	2011	2012	2013
Argentina	16.0	12.0	8.2	7.8
Brazil	42.2	35.2	38.6	22.4
Paraguay	0.9	0.5	0.1	0.3
Uruguay	0.2	0.2	0.1	0.1
Mercosur	59.3	47.9	47.1	30.6
Chile	21.2	21.5	17.9	16.5
Colombia	4.4	8.1	9.4	21.4
Mexico	12.5	19.8	22.9	27.3
Peru	2.7	2.7	2.7	4.2
Pacific Alliance	40.7	52.1	52.9	69.4
Total in US$ billions	8.248	9.083	14439	13.982

Source: ECLAC (Data from Comtrade Database). Available at http://cepal.org/comercio /ecdata2.

* Value is less than 1 percent.

from 2010 to 2013 is an upward trend in Mexico's exports to India (from 12.5 percent in 2010 to 27.3 percent in 2013) and in Colombia's exports to India (from 4.4 percent in 2010 to 21.4 percent in 2013), whereas Brazil and Argentina continuously lost their share—out of Mercosur members and the Pacific Alliance countries—of total exports to India.

TABLE 12-3
Brazil: Exports of Commodities to Selected Markets
Percent

Year	Asia	Japan	China	South Korea	European Union	United States	Latin America
1990	30.6	41.2	19.6	33.3	44.3	10.7	9.2
1995	25.8	34.8	15.9	28.7	43.8	9.9	6.4
2000	42.4	39.6	68.2	42.5	42.5	7.0	6.8
2005	53.0	58.0	68.4	55.5	48.1	9.2	11.6
2010	72.0	71.1	83.7	60.0	49.5	30.8	17.7
2011	75.5	74.7	85.0	66.5	51.7	33.7	19.6
2012	74.4	73.2	82.8	78.7	49.8	29.7	16.0
2013	77.6	74.9	84.7	80.6	49.7	24.3	13.7

Source: Elaborated from www.mdic.gov.br.

It is very striking that the share of the commodities sector of total Brazilian exports has doubled, climbing from 22.8 percent in 2000 to 46.7 percent in 2013, while the share of manufactured goods has fallen sharply (from 59.1 percent to 34.4 percent) (table 12-3). Up until 1996, China was absorbing mainly industrialized products. Beginning in 1997, commodities have gradually come to account for a larger share, to the point of representing more than 80 percent of Brazilian exports by the 2010s.

Although the trend in commodities exports from Brazil was already on firm ground, there has been a clear expansion, especially as of 2010, not only of purchases by China but also of purchases by Asia as a whole, particularly Japan and South Korea. In addition, in 2013, commodities accounted for 75–85 percent of these Asian countries' total imports. Also of note is a slight tendency toward a growing share of commodities in purchases by the European Union, as well as a higher share in the imports of the United States and Latin America, underscoring either Brazil's greater competitiveness in this sector or its reduced exports of manufactured goods. A growing share of natural resources can also be observed in Argentina's exports to China. In 2012, 57 percent of exports of Argentina's exports to China were commodities, 29 percent were manufactured goods of agricultural origin, 3 percent were manufactured goods of industrial origin, and 11 percent were fuels, lubricants, energy, and gas.[37]

According to data from Brazil, 83 percent of exports to LAC countries in 2013 were manufactured goods (up from 80 percent in 2012), and 55 percent of Brazilian exports to the United States were also

TABLE 12-4

Mercosur: Composition of Exports by Technology Content and Destination, 2013

Percent

Origin	Technology Content	Pacific Alliance	Mercosur	Rest of the World	Total
Mercosur (excluding Brazil)	Natural resources (primary and processed)	66.0	36.1	84.3	75.4
	Low-tech manufacturing	5.1	5.9	1.3	2.3
	Medium-tech manufacturing	22.9	41.7	4.6	11.6
	High-tech manufacturing	5.1	3.6	0.8	1.5
	Others	1.9	12.6	8.9	9.1
Brazil	Natural resources (primary and processed)	32.6	27.1	72.1	64.4
	Low-tech manufacturing	10.4	9.6	4.2	5.2
	Medium-tech manufacturing	49.7	53.8	14.3	21.1
	High-tech manufacturing	6.9	6.3	3.8	4.3
	Other	0.4	3.1	5.7	5.1

Source: INTAL Monthly Newsletter 215 (July 2014), p. 8.

manufactures (up from 51 percent in 2012), confirming that these two markets are the most important for Brazilian industry. IDB (INTAL) data for 2013 indicate that exports from Mercosur (excluding Brazil) to Pacific Alliance countries were mostly commodities (66.0 percent), whereas of exports from Mercosur countries (excluding Brazil) to Mercosur countries, manufactured goods accounted for 51.2 percent and medium-technology manufactures for 41.7 percent (table 12-4). In the case of Brazil, the share of manufactured goods (high-, medium- and low-tech) is more accentuated, accounting for 67.0 percent of exports to Pacific Alliance countries and 69.7 percent of exports to Mercosur countries.[38]

FOREIGN DIRECT INVESTMENT

In 2013, developing countries were the destination of 54 percent of foreign direct investment (FDI) flows, with Latin America receiving 20 percent of global investment. The United States is still the leading recipient; among the developing countries, China was second, Brazil fifth, Mexico tenth, India fourteenth, Chile seventeenth, and Colombia nineteenth. Before the 2008 financial crisis, Mercosur was receiving 2 percent of the total FDI; by 2013 it was the destination of 6 percent of FDI.[39]

A comparison of the data for Mercosur member countries and Pacific Alliance countries for the five years 2010–14 shows that Mercosur was the destination of 53.1 percent of FDI, and the Pacific Alliance, of 46.9 percent. When data for the two groups are pooled, Brazil received 41.4 percent of FDI, Mexico 18.3 percent, Chile 13.3 percent, Colombia 9.2 percent, and Argentina 7.5 percent (tables 12-5 and 12-6). The year-over-year trends show that FDI flows to Mercosur were relatively stable from 2011 to 2012, then moved downward in 2013 and 2014 (with Brazil between stable and suffering a slight loss, and Argentina experiencing a more accentuated loss). The Pacific Alliance appears to show an upward trend until 2013, then a decline in 2014; by member country, Colombia is most prominently characterized by the rising curve. Peru and Chile saw declines in 2013, while Mexico showed strong growth in 2013, with almost half (47 percent) stemming from the sale of Grupo Modelo to AB InBev.

At the end of the 2000s, two events made China's interest in Latin America evident. One was the launch in November 2008 of the first white paper for the region ("China's Policy Paper on Latin American and the Caribbean"); the other was China becoming a member of the IDB in 2009, after overcoming strong opposition from the United States and the countries of Central America.[40] At that moment, the Chinese Development Bank and China's Export-Import Bank entered into agreements with the IDB to participate in project financing in Latin America. The hope of the region's countries was that China's entry into the IDB would lead to increased investment by China in infrastructure and productive activities in the region.[41]

Enrique Dussel Peters has noted that in 2010–11, LAC became the second leading destination of Chinese investment and that 87 percent of it came from public enterprises.[42] The observation is extremely relevant when one realizes that Chinese investment goes forward only if approved by the main public institutions (that is, by the central government, the provincial governments, or the municipal governments) and

TABLE 12-5
FDI Inflows to Mercosur Countries, 2010–14
(US$ billions)

Year	Argentina	Brazil	Paraguay	Uruguay	Venezuela	Total
2010	11.3	48.5	0.2	2.3	1.6	63.9
2011	10.8	66.7	0.6	2.5	5.7	86.3
2012	15.3	65.3	0.7	2.5	6.0	89.8
2013	11.3	64.0	0.1	3.0	2.7	81.1
2014	6.6	62.5	0.2	2.8	0.3	72.4
Total	55.3	307.0	1.8	13.1	16.3	393.5

Source: UNCTAD, World Investment Report 2015 (2015), p. A5.

TABLE 12-6
FDI Inflows to Pacific Alliance Countries, 2010–14
(US$ billions)

Year	Chile	Colombia	Mexico	Peru	Total
2010	16.8	6.4	26.1	8.5	57.8
2011	16.9	14.6	23.4	7.7	62.6
2012	25.0	15.0	19.0	11.9	70.9
2013	16.6	16.2	44.6	9.3	86.7
2014	22.9	16.1	22.8	7.6	69.4
Total	98.2	68.3	135.9	45.0	347.4

Source: UNCTAD, World Investment Report 2015 (2015), p. A5.

only if the investment is in line with the "going global" policies. Data from the Heritage Foundation indicate that Brazil was the third leading destination of FDI up to 2011, and the fourth leading destination since 2012 (it was overtaken in 2012 by Canada as a result of the acquisition of Nexen by the China National Offshore Oil Corporation for $15.1 billion) (table 12-7).

The flows of Chinese FDI to Argentina are still very low, with a stock from 2005 to 2012 of approximately $500 million to $1.5 billion.[43]

André Luiz Oliveira considers that the short history of Chinese FDI flows to Brazil makes it possible to grasp differentiated interests in three distinct periods. In the first phase (1999–2009), there was a concentration of investments in manufacturing sectors, such as electronics, automotive, and telecommunications. These were market-seeking investments, guided by the companies' corporate strategies and not determined by the

TABLE 12-7
Chinese Outward Investment, 2005–14
(US$ billions)

Country	2005–10	2005–11	2005–12	2005–13	2005–14
United States	28.1	34.7	54.2	63.6	81.1
Australia	34.0	42.5	53.5	60.6	62.9
Canada	10.2	14.6	36.7	37.8	41.3
Brazil	14.9	24.6	27.5	32.1	33.2
Indonesia	9.8	19.9	25.0	27.0	30.9
Nigeria	15.4	18.1	15.6	20.5	28.8
Argentina	NA	11.7	NA	14.8	17.1

Source: Elaborated from http://report.heritage.org.

needs of the Chinese or Brazilian economy. The second period (2010) was characterized by high growth in the volume invested, which was highly correlated with the search for natural resources by Chinese companies. Finally, the investments announced in 2011 were aimed at a rearrangement in favor of industry and more advanced technology sectors. As noted by André Luiz Oliveira, "As of that year, we see an intensification of Chinese capital's interest in the search for markets with a view to forming platforms for export to Latin America."[44]

This perception is no different from others, such as the China-Brazil Business Council (Conselho Empresarial Brasil-China, or CEBC),[45] ECLAC, and UNCTAD. ECLAC states, "In South America (not including Brazil), natural resources receive more FDI than services, and manufacturing only small amounts."[46] UNCTAD has already highlighted the greater focus on the manufacturing sector in Brazil, noting its importance in industrial activities, especially in the automotive sector: "Brazil has taken new industrial policy measures aiming at greater development of its domestic industry and improved technological capabilities, which is encouraging investment by TNCs in industries such as automotives,"[47] highlighting that such investments are directed much more to the domestic market than to the external market.

There is a growing consensus that the increase in Chinese FDI is directly related to China's internationalization or "going out" strategy. In addition, and in keeping with that Asian nation's efforts to remove the perception of a "China threat," FDI can and does serve as proof that Chinese growth allows mutual benefits (the "win-win" rhetoric). Chinese investments in 2009, in addition to maintaining bilateral trade, were fundamental for keeping Latin America from feeling the impact of the global financial crisis more intensely.

THE MAIN IMPACTS OF CHINA'S PRESENCE: THE CASE OF BRAZIL

Data on Sino-Brazilian relations give rise to concerns and questions around Brazil's current international insertion, its strategy, and its partnerships, as well as its potential strengths and weaknesses. Some fundamental issues include the transformation of China into the "world's factory," its strong presence in the Brazilian market, the relative displacement of the space held by Brazil in the South American market, and considerations of deindustrialization and a return to a commodity-dependent economic structure, among others.[48]

Certain issues are fundamental for understanding Brazil's commercial positioning in relation to China. First, despite the strong asymmetry and the displacement effect, there is an awareness that the commercial relationship was and will continue to be extremely positive insofar as it makes up for cuts in imports from other countries, especially during global crises such as the one experienced in 2008–09. Objectively, China plays a fundamental role maintaining Brazil's balance-of-trade surpluses. Second, Brazil stands out not only for its endowment of natural resources but also for a complex and strong manufacturing sector and a system of science and technology with considerable potential. Accordingly, the country's agricultural capacity stems from a wide-ranging synergy of inputs, machinery, and equipment, such that agribusiness represents an intimate connection between agriculture and industry. Third, Brazil's imports from China are concentrated in electronics and machinery, which partially support renewed industrial development in Brazil.[49]

Ricardo Sennes and Alexandre Barbosa consider the Sino-Brazilian trade relationship to be characterized by the heterogeneity of impacts. In this regard, China is simultaneously depicted as (1) a supplier of cheap inputs that enhance the competitiveness of Brazilian goods (for both the domestic market and for export); (2) a competitor that uses aggressive strategies at times contrary to international trade rules, displacing major links from the national productive chain; (3) a competitor more efficient than Brazil in some sectors, within the rules governing international trade; (4) a major importer of some commodities (which helps maintain Brazil's trade surplus in these sectors); and (5) a growing investor in Brazil in consumer goods sectors (cars and motorcycles) and in the infrastructure, mining, and energy sectors, with a preponderance of the last.[50] As noted by Ricardo Sennes and Alexandre Barbosa, "this heterogeneity of bilateral economic relations—which goes beyond the predominant media one-liner that 'we export commodities to import industrial goods'—make China a special and different partner for Brazil."[51]

Although Brazil has been able to expand its exports so as to maintain constant surpluses, it has yet to reverse the loss of industrial competitiveness, leading to a wide array of analyses indicating that the country is undergoing a process of deindustrialization. And as China reached the milestone of becoming Brazil's leading trading partner, critics continued to lay blame on China for deindustrialization and the heavy focus on commodities in the Brazilian economy. If deindustrialization means a reduction in industry's share of GDP, there is no doubt that a process of deindustrialization is in fact occurring. Equally clear is China's interest in importing commodities, which account for most of Brazil's exports to China, as well as to Asia as a whole.[52] Alexandre Barbosa and others consider that the criticism regarding commodity dependence and deindustrialization may seem quite hasty. They emphasize market-seeking FDI, exemplified by the recent entry of Chinese companies in the automotive sector.[53]

There is a general consensus that manufactured goods show a downward trend in terms of their share of Brazilian exports. The difference of opinion is over whether this phenomenon can be characterized as a process of deindustrialization or whether it reflects a steady loss of competitiveness. Although there is no doubt it is a worrisome phenomenon, it does not originate from China's presence, even though the bilateral dynamics do have a magnifying effect. As several authors in this volume have suggested, the solution is not to demonize China but rather to look for a strategy to minimize or reverse the trend of diminishing Brazilian competitiveness.

FINAL CONSIDERATIONS

At its inception, Mercosur could have been interpreted as resulting from a dispute-resolution process between Argentina and Brazil with the objective of establishing a stable environment propitious for jointly tapping productive and commercial potential. In this regard, with the Argentine-Brazilian relationship at its core, Mercosur's constant crises, inconsistencies, and moments of questioning stem from short-term situations in both countries. In addition, since it was conceived as an instrument of international insertion, Mercosur moved to invest in the integration of South America in several areas: physical (infrastructure), political, economic, commercial, and strategic (regional security). Mercosur's intention was not to oppose the United States or to draw a divisive line between the South American countries of the Pacific and those of the Atlantic but rather to serve as a subregional organization that would facilitate playing a more effective role in the international system.

In the context of a nonexclusionary Mercosur, Argentina and Brazil have turned to Asia as another priority in their international insertion efforts. The global emergence of China and India over the last decade or so has to some extent displaced other Asian players, such as Japan and South Korea, as the main economic focus in LAC. Among the main considerations are (1) their economic and commercial capacity, (2) the availability of resources as a source of FDI, (3) the potential for scientific-technological cooperation, and (4) Asia's coinciding interest in reevaluating the current international order.

Despite the economic challenges faced by Brazil and Argentina, it is recognized that China has been and will continue to be an important buffer against external shocks, as well as a key player in fostering renewed development. China is a relatively new actor in the international system, with an even more recent role in the global economy, particularly since its accession to the WTO. In the initial phases of its "going out" policy, the focus was on placing labor-intensive, low-quality goods; in a later phase, China focused on higher-tech goods, followed by an avalanche of FDI, first in commodities, then in manufactures. Hence, if only recently, Chinese FDI indicates an intention to move to productive activities in situ so as to address internal or regional demands, or to deconcentrate productive activities in China. Such investments also facilitate gains in innovation and expansion of scientific-technological cooperation. Finally, South America certainly has the potential to move beyond China's emphasis on natural resources without resorting to exclusionary or divisive groupings along the lines of Pacific versus Atlantic strategies.

NOTES

1. This analysis is based on the assumption that the Free Trade Area of the Americas agreement *suggested* this proposal, yet it was never made clearly explicit. Can the abandonment of that proposal in 2006 be credited to Brazil's opposition, to Mercosur, or to the fact that the United States never made an objective proposal?

2. See Alcides Costa Vaz, "Parcerias estratégicas no contexto da política exterior brasileira: implicações para o Mercosul," *Revista Brasileira de Política Internacional* 42, no. 2 (1999), pp. 52–80; Henrique Altemani de Oliveira, *Política Externa Brasileira* (Editora Saraiva, 2005); Matias Spektor, "Ideias de ativismo regional: A transformação das leituras brasileiras da região," *Revista Brasileira de Política Internacional* 53, no. 1 (2010),

pp. 25–44; Maria Regina Soares de Lima and Monica Hirst, "Brazil as an Intermediate State and Regional Power," *International Affairs* 82, no. 1 (2006), pp. 21–40.

3. The objective of the Amazon Cooperation Treaty was to bring Brazil closer to the Andean countries and to define strategies for the regional joint development for the Amazon. Alcides Costa Vaz, "Parcerias estratégicas no contexto da política exterior brasileira," p. 61.

4. With the signing of the Tripartite Agreement in 1979, "a (Brazilian) dispute with Argentina was brought to a definitive close that had rankled bilateral relations for 11 years. Without eliminating this dispute it would not have been possible to develop relations with Argentina at the level of intimacy and trust as characterized them during the João Batista Figueiredo administration, and it laid the foundation for their successive improvement in successive administrations." Ramiro Saraiva Guerreiro, *Lembranças de um empregado do Itamaraty* (Siciliano, 1992), pp. 91–92.

5. The objective of the agreement was to build confidence between Argentina and Brazil, removing points of distrust stemming from the respective nuclear developments and ensuring a commitment to the peaceful use of nuclear resources.

6. The Rio Group (1986) had a Latin American political profile and sought to consolidate democratic processes throughout the region. Expanded in 1990 and taking in all the countries of the region, it became the interlocutor for Latin America and the Caribbean vis-à-vis other regions or countries. It also presented the emblematic sense of Brazil's acceptance as a "member" of the region. In addition, at the Unity Summit (2010) it was decided to create the Community of Latin American and Caribbean States (CELAC), based on the merger of the Rio Group and the Latin American and Caribbean Summit on Integration and Development.

7. In 1991, Brazil and Argentina established the Brazilian-Argentine Agency for Accounting and Control of Nuclear Materials (ABACC). They then signed the Quadripartite Agreement—bringing together Brazil, Argentina, ABACC, and the International Atomic Energy Agency (IAEA)—for the application of safeguards. With this Quadripartite Agreement, and the establishment of a set of safeguards with the IAEA, prior to accessing the Non-Proliferation Treaty the two countries gained international legitimacy and reaffirmed their commitments to nonproliferation. Everton Vieira Vargas, "Átomos na integração: A aproximação Brasil-Argentina no campo nuclear e a construção do Mercosul," *Revista Brasileira de Política Internacional* 40, no. 1 (1997), pp. 41–74.

8. "On signing the Treaty of Asunción, the four presidents take as the starting point the common perception that furthering the integration process may be the key for the more competitive insertion of their countries in a world in which large economic spaces are consolidating and where technological-industrial advancement is becoming ever more crucial for the national economies." Tullo Vigevani and others, "Parcerias estratégicas no

contexto da política exterior brasileira: Implicações para o Mercosul" *Revista Brasileira de Política Internacional* 51, no. 1 (2008), pp. 9–10.

9. "Many regionalist arrangements have been central to efforts to maximize bargaining power in a globalized world. Even if it is dressed up in other terms, a great deal of regionalist activity does have the character of an outwardly direct coalition." Andrew Hurrell, "One World? Many Worlds? The Place of Regions in the Study of International Society," *International Affairs* 83, no. 1 (2007), p. 139.

10. "Especially once the NAFTA negotiations had gone ahead, Brazilian policy-makers increasingly questioned the idea of a single region labeled 'Latin America.' Brazil's regional and international presence has been increasingly perceived as a process intimately connected to the emergence of 'South America' as a particular grouping within the international community." Maria Regina Soares Lima and Monica Hirst, "Brazil as an Intermediate State and Regional Power," *International Affairs* 82, no. 1 (2006), p. 29.

11. Spektor, "Ideias de ativismo regional," p. 42.

12. Ibid., 42.

13. See Luiz Alberto Moniz Bandeira, "O Brasil e a América do Sul," in *Relações Internacionais do Brasil: temas e agendas*, edited by Henrique Altemani and Antônio Carlos Lessa (São Paulo, Brazil: Editora Saraiva, 2005), pp. 267–97; Spektor, "Ideias de ativismo regional"; and Thiago Gehre Galvão, *Uma história de Parceria: As relações entre Brasil e Venezuela (1810–2012)* (Belo Horizonte, Brazil: Fino Traço Editora, 2012).

14. Leandro Couto, "Relações Brasil-América do Sul: a construção inacabada de parceria com o entorno estratégico," in *Parcerias estratégicas do Brasil: Os significados e as parcerias tradicionais,* edited by Henrique Altemani de Oliveira and Antônio Carlos Lessa (Belo Horizonte, Brazil: Fino Traço Editora, 2013), pp. 195–217.

15. Thiago Galvão, *Uma história de Parceria*, p. 146.

16. *INTAL Monthly Newsletter* 214, June 2014.

17. Mônica Hirst and Letícia Pinheiro, "A política externa do Brasil em dois tempos," *Revista Brasileira de Política Internacional* 38, no. 1 (1995), p. 11.

18. "China was an important political-commercial alternative for a country experiencing a tough stage of internal political transition." Sergio Cesarín, "China: Cooperación científico-tecnológica y alianzas empresarias, análisis del caso argentino," in *Las relaciones comerciales entre América Latina y Asia Pacífico: Desafíos y oportunidades,* edited by Ignacio Bartesaghi (Montevideo: Observatorio América Latina–Asia Pacífico, 2014), pp. 208–09.

19. Ibid., p. 212.

20. Richard N. Haass, "Which Asian Century?," *Project Syndicate*, October 28, 2013 (http://www.project-syndicate.org/commentary/richard-n—haass-on-asia-s-need-for-reconciliation-and integration#A1aYjtaejsqZommH.99).

21. Sergio Cesarín, "China: Restauración y capitalismo. Impactos en América del Sur," in *América Latina y el Caribe–China: Relaciones políticas e internacionales*, edited by José Ignacio Martínez Cortés (Mexico City: Unión de Universidades de América Latina y el Caribe, 2013), pp. 28–29.

22. Julia Strauss, evaluating the Chinese strategy of engaging with developing countries, emphasizes the positive effect of the consistency and continuity of China's rhetoric about the Five Principles, mutual benefits, political equality, as well as the feeling that they were "left behind" with the prescriptions and remedies applied by the North. Accordingly, while the discourse of many Western analysts analyzes the concerns, doubts, and alarms, the most relevant question in Africa, and even in Latin America, is how to maximize the opportunities and minimize the challenges stemming from the Chinese presence. Julia C. Strauss, "Framing and Claiming: Contemporary Globalization and 'Going Out' in China's Rhetoric towards Latin America," *China Quarterly* 209 (March 2012), pp. 134–56.

23. David Shambaugh, foreword to Adrian H. Hearn and José Luis León-Manríquez, *China Engages Latin America: Tracing the trajectory*, edited by Adrian H. Hearn and José Luis León-Manríquez (Boulder, CO: Lynne Rienner Publishers, 2011), pp. ix–xviii; Sergio Cesarín, "China: Restauración y capitalism."

24. Sergio Cesarín, "China e India en América Latina y el Caribe: Enfoques comparados de inserción regional," in *China e Índia na América Latina: Oportunidades e desafíos*, edited by Henrique Altemani de Oliveira (Curitiba, Brazil: Juruá, 2010), p. 21.

25. Henrique Altemani de Oliveira and Alexandre Leite, "Chinese Engagement for Global Governance: Aiming for a Better Room at the Table?," *Revista Brasileira de Política Internacional* 57, special issue (2014), pp. 265–85.

26. As for the geographically segmented Chinese strategy, see Sergio Cesarín, "China: Restauración y capitalism," pp. 37–41.

27. "China's goal and main challenge is to deepen its relations with the countries of Latin America without irritating Washington." Juan Gabriel Tokatlian. "A View from Latin America," in *China's Expansion into Western Hemisphere: Implications for Latin America and the United States*, edited by Riordan Roett and Guadalupe Paz (Brookings, 2008).

28. "Because of rapid economic growth, China needs to seek abroad overseas markets and raw material sources, which can be achieved in Latin America." Sun Hongbo. "China's Benefits in Latin America: American Scholars' Judgment and Anxiety," in *China–Latin America Relations: Review and Analysis*, edited by He Shuangrong (Reading, UK, and Beijing, China: Paths International Ltd. and Social Sciences Academic Press, 2012), p. 47.

29. "China and Latin America have the same or similar standpoints in multilateral domains including United Nations and international financial system reform, WTO Doha Round negotiations, and the United Nations climate change negotiations. They will also have more common interests as

multilateral contact channels increase, such as groups like the BRIC countries and the G20." Sun Hongbo. "China's Benefits in Latin America," p. 48.

30. "The negative is that some Latin-American left-wing governments' policy is volatile, and nationalization policies implemented could possibly damage Chinese enterprises' investment in these countries." Xu Shicheng "Analysis of Chinese Scholars on Latin America Left-Wing Government's Policies" in *China–Latin America Relations: Review and Analysis*, edited by He Shuangrong (Reading, UK, and Beijing, China: Paths International Ltd. and Social Sciences Academic Press, 2012), p. 44.

31. Atish Sinha, "Foreign Policy Considerations," in Foreign Service Institute, *Indian Foreign Policy: Challenges and Opportunities* (New Delhi: Academic Foundation, 2007), pp. 31–32.

32. Williams Gonçalves and Lana Bauab Brito, "Relações Brasil-China: Uma parceria estratégica?," *Século XXI* 1, no. 1 (2010), pp. 11–28.

33. Cesarín, "China: Cooperación científico-tecnológica y alianzas empresarias, análisis del caso argentino," p. 228.

34. Rengaraj Viswanathan, *Business with Latin America* (New Delhi: Exim Bank, January 2005), p. 114. "Our pharma companies have set successful examples of entry all over Latin America. The IT achievements of India have enhanced the image of India in Latin America. Medium and small countries and companies of LAC region provide greater opportunities for India since Chinese companies go for large markets and volumes. Some large importers of Latin America prefer to diversify their imports and not be overdependent on China."

35. "From the very beginning, it was clear that the IBSA forum would advance South-South cooperation. The main thrust behind the formation of IBSA appears to be on equalizing the political and economic architecture of the international system by developing a consolidated position of the South on issues related to global governance." Ruchita Beri, "IBSA Dialogue Forum: An Assessment," *Strategic Analysis* 32, no. 5 (2008), p. 816.

36. Varun Sahni, "India and Latin America," in *Indian Foreign Policy: Agenda for the 21st Century*, edited by Lalit Mansingh (New Delhi: Konark, 1997), p. 76; Jean-Luc Racine, "Quête de puissance: Multipolarité et multilatéralisme," in *New Delhi and Le Monde: Une puissance emergente entre realpolitik et soft power*, edited by Christophe Jaffrelot (Paris: Éditions Autrement, 2008), pp. 32–53.

37. Andrés López and Daniela Ramos, "Argentina y China: Nuevos encadenamientos mercantiles globales con empresas chinas. Los casos de Huawei, CNOOC y Sinpopec," in *China en América Latina: 10 casos de estudio*, edited by Enrique Dussel Peters (Mexico City: Unión de Unversidades de América Latina y el Caribe, 2014), p. 16.

38. Romina Gayá and Kathia Michalczewsky, "Pacific Alliance and MERCOSUR Trade Profiles," INTAL Monthly Newsletter, no. 215 (2014), pp. 7–14.

39. *World Investment Report 2014: Investing in the SDG's: An Action Plan*, edited by United Nations Conference on Trade and Development (Geneva: United Nations Publication, 2014).

40. China was the third Asian country to become a member of the IDB. Japan entered in 1976 and South Korea in 2005.

41. These notions were developed in part in Henrique Altemani de Oliveira, "Investimentos Externos Diretos Chineses no Brasil," in *Las relaciones comerciales entre América Latina y Asia Pacífico: Desafíos y oportunidades*, edited by Ignacio Bartesaghi (Montevideo: Observatorio América Latina–Asia Pacífico, 2014), pp. 181–207.

42. Enrique Dussel Peters, "Chinese FDI in Latin America: Does Ownership Matter?," Working Group on Development and Environment in the Americas, Discussion Paper 33 (November 2012), pp. 1–22.

43. Andrés López and Daniela Ramos, "Argentina y China," p.18; Sergio Cesarín, "China: Cooperación científico-tecnológica y alianzas empresarias, análisis del caso argentino," p. 210.

44. André Luiz Soares Oliveira, "O investimento direto das empresas chinesas no Brasil: Um estudo exploratório," master's thesis (Rio de Janeiro: UFRJ/COPPE, 2012), pp. 94–101.

45. For the China-Brazil Business Council (CEBC), Chinese investments in Brazil initially had the aim of "ensuring the supply of natural resources to address the demand provoked by the high rates of Chinese economic growth. It was the phase of the mining, oil, and gas projects, and the marketing of agricultural commodities." Next, China's expectations were directed to "infrastructure, in the areas of telecommunications, production and distribution of energy." And "more recently, investments sought to benefit from the appetite of the Brazilian consumer for vehicles, capital goods, and electro-electronics." CEBC, *Uma análise dos investimentos chineses no Brasil: 2007–2012* (São Paulo, Brazil, June 2013), p. 6.

46. ECLAC, *La Inversión Extranjera Directa en América Latina y el Caribe 2013* (Santiago, Chile: ECLAC, 2014), p. 10.

47. UNCTAD, *World Investment Report 2013—Global Value Chains: Investment and Trade for Development* (New York: United Nations, 2013), p. 58.

48. The term *primarização* of the Brazilian economy stems from the fact that manufactures have tended to show a loss in Brazil's balance of trade, while significant growth has been seen in natural resources.

49. Antonio Barros de Castro, "From Semi-stagnation to Growth in a Sino-centric Market," *Brazilian Journal of Political Economy* 28, no. 1 (January–March 2008), pp. 3–27. José Roberto Mendonça de Barros, *Crescer não é Fácil: A crise, a economia mundial e o crescimento brasileiro* (Rio de Janeiro: Campus, 2012), p. 266.

50. Ricardo Ubiraci Sennes and Alexandre de Freitas Barbosa, "China-Brasil: Uma relação multifacetada e dinâmica," in *Brasil e China no reorde-*

namento das relações internacionais: desafios e oportunidades (Brasília: FUNAG, 2011), p. 133.

51. Ibid.

52. Regis Bonelli and Samuel de Abreu Pessoa, "Desindustrialização no Brasil: Um resumo da evidência," Texto para Discussão 7 (Rio de Janeiro: FGV/IBRE, March 2010).

53. Alexandre de Freitas Barbosa and others, "Las relaciones económicas entre Brasil y China a partir del desempeño de las empresas State Grid y Lenovo," in *China–Latin America Relations: Review and Analysis,* edited by He Shuangrong (Reading, UK, and Beijing, China: Paths International Ltd. and Social Sciences Academic Press, 2012), p. 120.

Part IV

CONCLUSIONS

CHAPTER 13

Future Scenarios for Latin America's Relations with China and India

Mauricio Mesquita Moreira and Theodore Kahn

As the chapters in this volume attest, there is no one Latin America–China or Latin America–India relationship. Different countries in the region have engaged with China and India in different ways and to different degrees, with a correspondingly wide spectrum of results. In the case of China, the region's relationships are entering a new phase after the initial boom, with expectations and assessments on both sides adjusting to recent developments. In the case of India, the relationship still consists mainly of expectations: despite great potential, economic and diplomatic ties remain tentative, although India's new reform-minded government could give the relationship a decisive boost. In both cases the time is opportune to consider what the future holds for Latin America and the Caribbean (LAC) countries' relationships with Asia's two giants.

At least one thing can be said with near certainty about this future. Natural resource endowments, which have been the fundamental driver of the LAC-China relationship to date, will continue to shape the pattern of trade, investment, and diplomatic engagement between China and LAC in the future because of the overwhelming complementarities. In this regard, the region can be divided into two camps. In the first are resource-rich South American countries, which benefited enormously from the 2003–11 commodity boom generated by Chinese demand for minerals, fuel, and food. Even in a context of decelerating growth in China, this facet of the relationship offers a major opportunity for resource-rich countries to add value and sophistication to natural resource exports. Of course, China's reliance on external sources of basic commodities means that these sectors have also seen efforts by China to exert its asymmetric power to gain access to mineral, agricultural, and energy stocks under unfavorable terms for the region. The natural resource sector has also often been prone to environmental and social conflict, adding another dimension of risk.

The second group of countries consists of Mexico and Central America, which had the bad luck of having relatively similar productive structures to China during the LAC-China trade boom. These economies suffered from direct competition with China's low-wage manufacturing juggernaut while lacking the natural resource base to export to China on a large scale. They experienced heavy losses in the U.S. market, particularly in labor-intensive goods, but avoided a total economic disaster thanks to what is arguably their strongest comparative advantage: geography. Proximity to the United States gives them an edge on bulk, transport-intensive and time-sensitive goods.

The rapid wage increase in China also provided some respite, but when it comes to Chinese competition there is no room for complacency. With between 30 and 40 percent of the population still living in rural areas and internal migration restrictions that are just beginning to be lifted, China can still be a powerful competitor in labor-intensive goods and tasks for decades to come. Likewise, the heavy and growing concentration of highly skilled workers in the country's southeast has allowed China to make forceful inroads into sophisticated goods, which makes the usual call for "export upgrading" in LAC an uphill battle, particularly in light of Mexico's and Central America's weak human capital base. Geography is likely to remain their best bet, particularly if combined with a more sophisticated workforce, an advantage that could even attract the growing number of Chinese manufacturing firms going abroad. The fledgling Chinese car and consumer electronics industries are clear examples of opportunities in this direction.

It is worth pointing out, too, that these categorizations are not mutually exclusive, nor are they necessarily static. South American economies with large manufacturing sectors such as Argentina and Brazil have had to confront Chinese competition as well, and they face even more daunting challenges as geography is not so much on their side and the "Dutch disease" is a permanent threat. Mexico's recent energy sector reforms, in turn, mean that it is a likely investment target for China's state-owned energy companies.

In general, however, these structural characteristics determine the range of risks and rewards countries face in their relationships with China, where a clear pattern of trade and investment has emerged that is almost certain to persist. With India too, natural resource endowments are likely to be an important fault line in the relationship, as India also lacks sufficient energy and mineral resources to meet domestic demand. However, they do not in themselves determine outcomes. As the chapters in this volume emphasize, the modes of Chinese engagement with the region's resource-rich economies vary widely, even within individual sectors such as oil or agriculture. These differences are primarily the result of policy choices by governments on both sides, and it is these decisions that will shape the future trajectory, for better or worse.

The discussion in this concluding chapter lays out a set of policy choices that should help the region maximize the rewards and minimize the risks of these relationships. In the case of China, the contrast is quite clear, if one looks back over the past dozen years of rapidly increasing engagement, between the different paths countries have taken and their economic and political consequences. As the relationship matures, the region's ties with China could tend toward either of these routes, and governments need to realistically assess their engagement with China to make the right decisions. In advancing these arguments, the goal is not to speculate on the growth of China's economy in the coming years, a topic that is much discussed in the region and beyond. The assumptions here are that China's economy will continue to enjoy strong and consistent if somewhat decelerating growth for the foreseeable future, and that engagement with the region will remain on an upward trajectory, despite inevitable ups and downs.

Unlike in the case of China, the LAC-India relationship is still mostly waiting to happen. Despite encouraging signs of interest on both sides, trade and investment have yet to reach a critical mass. While there are obvious differences, particularly regarding the relative role of the state and private sector and the nature of comparative advantages, the Chinese experience holds important lessons for the region as LAC countries contemplate closer ties with India. Central among these lessons are the need for more pragmatism in diplomatic engagement and the importance of prioritizing open markets in trade and investment. To illustrate these points, the rest of the chapter lays out a "dream" scenario and "nightmare" scenario for the future of LAC-China and LAC-India relations. At the risk of sounding bleak, it begins with the downside.

CHINA: THE NIGHTMARE SCENARIOS

A worst-case scenario for the region would involve a pattern of interactions whereby China used its financial and geopolitical clout to dictate terms of economic and diplomatic relations, leading to the increasing subordination of Latin American countries to China's interests. In this nightmare situation, commercial ties would be increasingly conducted through exclusive deals that sought to cordon off China-LAC trade and investment from broader market forces. Regulatory frameworks would be watered down to accommodate Chinese projects—under implicit or explicit pressure—leading to environmental degradation and social conflict. Misguided economic policies that squandered natural resource rents and left governments desperate for cash would likely drive the nightmare scenario, making LAC governments easy targets for financing on China's terms. Such deals in turn would prolong unsustainable policies in the region, allowing LAC governments to put off necessary reforms. In the diplomatic realm, this reality would be obscured by the rhetoric of south-south cooperation that elevated an ill-defined ideology at the expense of the region's concrete economic interests.

Trade

China's voracious appetite for natural resources, channeled through international market forces, created a huge commodities boom and spurred export-led growth for most of South America in the 2000s. However, China's demand has slowed and commodity prices have been in decline since 2011, showing yet again the risks of an export basket highly concentrated in basic commodities. The problem is not the overriding pattern of trade between LAC and China. The strong complementarity in resource endowments between China's and South America's economies makes this inevitable. Instead, the region should focus on getting as much as possible from its natural resource–based comparative advantage with China. This means adding more value to natural resource exports by performing more processing and transformation of raw commodities at home.

In the nightmare scenario, the region would fail to take the steps necessary to export more sophisticated, higher-value-added natural resource–based products. Both the public and the private sectors have a role to play here. Governments in the region need to assertively advance a policy agenda that tackles the most important policy barriers to diversifying the region's natural resource exports. Key among these barriers are tariff escalation, a mechanism by which tariff rates increase in proportion to a product's level of processing and that is particularly prevalent in agricultural goods, and sanitary and phytosanitary barriers to trade, whereby what are ostensibly safety regulations on food and plant products become de facto trade barriers.

Part of the burden also falls on the private sector, which too often has lacked the initiative and vision to make a decisive move into China. Far too few firms in the region, for example, have followed the example of North American, European, and Japanese multinational corporations (MNCs) and established offices or production facilities in China. Instead of devoting the necessary resources to crack the Chinese market, the response of the private sector in this nightmare scenario would be to lobby governments for protectionist policies or simply to be content with the easy (if volatile) rents of raw commodity sales.

A further risk is that trade would veer in the direction of exclusive contracts that undermined competition and cordoned off LAC-China exchange from the broader global trade flows. In agriculture, for example, Mariano Turzi explained in chapter 6 how China's commercial strategy in the sector is determined by state policy that seeks to maintain national control of the supply chain "from soil to shop." This raises the likelihood that China will seek to control agricultural trade with the region, negotiating particular nonmarket terms for its purchases and foreclosing opportunities for LAC firms to add value through their own production processes. In the energy sector, China has in some cases gained access to oil production at below-market prices through loans-for-resources deals, a straightforward example of how such exclusive arrangements can deprive the region of gains that would have come through selling their resources in open markets.

Another tool that China could deploy in this regard is the nascent "renminbi diplomacy," driven by China's desire to see its currency widely used in international trade. China's currency swap agreement with Argentina in 2009—the first of its kind with a Latin American government—could serve as an additional lever for China to exercise control over trade flows. It is worth emphasizing that long-term purchase contracts in and of themselves are not problematic. In fact, such deals are par for the course in commodities markets. The troubling prospect is that LAC governments with dire financing needs and no other options might expose themselves to arrangements that served China's state policy interests. Such deals, often transacted at below-market rates, would likely be bad ones for the region.

The trade dimension of this nightmare scenario would not be complete without some discussion of the possibility of misguided actions on the import side compounding the inaction and submission on the export side. In this case, we would see the region's largest economies increasingly resorting to protectionism and government intervention to stave off Chinese competition and the perceived threat of deindustrialization. The motivation would come from a mix of nostalgia over the failed import substitution policies of the past and an admiration for the Chinese state-led "model." Even though this would hurt China's manufacturing exports, China would look the other way, as it has done in the past, as long as its access to natural resources remained open and Chinese manufacturing firms were able to tap these markets by "tariff jumping" foreign direct investment (FDI). This protectionist turn would be more of hindrance than a help, as it would delay an inevitable adjustment toward the region's comparative advantages while hurting local firms' incentives to increase productivity and innovate. The stagnation of productivity would be compound by a fiscal crisis as rent seeking turned rampant. A rerun of the debt crisis of the 1980s would be likely, but this time the bailout would probably be funded by China or by Chinese-sponsored multilateral institutions.

Investment and Financing

With more than $4 trillion in reserves, financing is China's trump card in the region (all currency figures are in U.S. dollars unless otherwise noted). In a troubling preview of what a nightmare scenario in the investment and financing sector would entail, LAC governments with acute financing needs and few alternatives have racked up considerable debts with China. Chinese loans are increasingly concentrated in Ecuador and Venezuela, two countries that are effectively shut out of international capital markets. Venezuela alone has borrowed an estimated $65 billion since the mid-2000s. Again, it is not the simple fact of these loans that is potentially problematic for the region but the terms laid out by the Chinese. Though often opaque, common mechanisms are loans-for-resources deals that require countries to repay debts with oil (sometimes at below-market rates) and tied loans for projects contingent on hiring Chinese firms and equipment.

Chinese financing for infrastructure projects in the Caribbean has often required the use of Chinese labor, mirroring China's pattern of engagement in Africa, whereby communities of Chinese workers are transplanted to host countries, with all the predictable social conflicts, as discussed by Jacqueline Mazza in chapter 8. Nor are larger economies necessarily immune. Argentina recently passed legislation, following a raft of cooperation agreements with the Chinese government and state-owned enterprises (SOEs), which gives China rights to infrastructure deals without competitive bidding and loosens visa requirements for Chinese workers, potentially opening the door to temporary Chinese labor forces. In a nightmare scenario, this type of deal would proliferate, as governments with dire financing needs would be compelled to part with natural resources at low prices, sacrifice opportunities for domestic firms and workers, and accept worse terms on infrastructure projects than they would have received through competitive bidding.

The same concerns surround Chinese FDI, which has largely been concentrated in natural resources. This FDI has been carried out by SOEs and has targeted the same countries that have built up large debts with China. Not coincidentally, these countries generally have policy frameworks that effectively exclude foreign private investment, allowing China, with its preference for state-to-state negotiations, to step in and fill the investment gap. The combination of loans and direct investment can lead down a path of near total Chinese control of natural resource sectors: in Ecuador, Chinese energy companies currently control around 90 percent of total production (see chapter 5). While most of this oil is sold by Chinese SOEs on world markets, this type of arrangement undoubtedly gives the Chinese enormous leverage over the development of the country's energy sector. The combination of growing financial reliance on China and increasing direct investment from Chinese firms raises the possibility that governments in the region might fail to enforce robust regulatory frameworks on environmental and social issues. In a doomsday scenario, FDI flows would reinforce Chinese influence in natural resource sectors, while investments in the region's manufacturing sector, which would serve to diversify the relationship, would fail to materialize owing to LAC governments' lack of persistence or vision in attracting them.

Cooperation and Diplomacy

The common denominator of this nightmare scenario is that countries with acute financing needs are vulnerable to China imposing conditions for trade, investment, and loans. Why would LAC governments sign on to such deals? One clear reason is that cash-strapped governments with no recourse to international financial markets have few other options. A second reason is that they find it politically expedient to do business with China, where arrangements that may otherwise be viewed with skepticism are couched in the triumphant language of "south-south cooperation." Diplomatic engagement and cooperation, in a worst-case scenario, would see China successfully use bilateral, regional, and inter-regional forums to advance its particular interests through the exclusive, quasi-mercantilist relations described above, while LAC governments would either fail to recognize or lack the leverage and strategic capacity to advance their own concrete interests, such as ensuring that China conducted its trade practices according to established multilateral rules. To the extent that governments could make political hay by flouting close relations with a rising non-Western power, they would be more inclined to sacrifice economic interests. A region beholden to China would be compelled to promote Chinese positions on global governance and international issues, whether or not they corresponded with its own.

CHINA: THE DREAM SCENARIOS

Fortunately, none of the above need come to pass. China's enormous economy, even if growing at slower rates, will still deliver an unrivaled market for exactly the type of products that the region produces in abundance. If LAC governments and the private sector make a different set of choices, ties with China could open up increasing opportunities to diversify and add value to exports and attract investment from a range of Chinese firms that are channeled into sustainable growth and help bind the region closer to Asia's fast-growing economies. In this dream scenario, diplomatic cooperation would support these objectives in pragmatic ways while also advancing common interests, where they exist, in global institutions.

Trade

Market-based trade has been the foundation of the LAC-China relationship and has delivered great benefits to both sides. While Chinese demand for commodities has fallen off, China remains a major market and therefore a top trading partner for countries in the region. In an ideal world, the region would diversify its export basket to China, taking advantage of the evolution of Chinese import demand as its economy shifted toward a more consumption-driven growth model.

A number of possible and plausible options exist to expand and diversify exports to China. The first place to start would be to build on existing comparative advantages to add value to natural resources.

Natural resource–based products have increasing capacity to incorporate sophisticated technology, and the region boasts strong capabilities in biotechnology and a well-established agribusiness infrastructure, as Turzi discusses in chapter 6. These advantages mean LAC is well positioned to produce products such as processed and packaged meats, prepared meals, and even genetically modified foods that will increasingly be in demand by China's middle class.

Services are another area in which the region could expand exports to China, whose domestic capacity is expected to fall short of burgeoning demand in the coming years, leading to increased imports. A handful of LAC firms in information technology (IT), financial, and other business services have established successful operations in China, and others could follow suit. Tourism represents one clear example where the region could diversify service exports to China, as newly affluent Chinese begin to travel abroad in large numbers and awareness of Latin America's natural and cultural assets increases.

Of course, exports of the so-called "traditional" natural resources—minerals, oil, and agricultural commodities—will continue to make up the bulk of the region's exports to China. As Robert Devlin and Theodore Kahn suggest (chapter 7), the idea that the region will become a major exporter of manufactured products to China, in light of the formidable challenges of integrating into East Asia's dense and well-developed value chains, ventures beyond the realm of a dream scenario into pure fantasy. The pull of complementarity between the two economies will ensure that the overarching pattern of trade continues to be defined by the commodities-for-manufactures exchange. This is not something to fight against. While these exports would be subject to inevitable price fluctuations based on Chinese and global demand, natural resource revenues, if well managed, could boost foreign exchange earnings, support public finances, and promote export-led growth. They could provide critical financing for the investments in human capital and infrastructure the region needs to improve its competitiveness, whether in China or anywhere else.

The dream scenario would naturally have to contemplate Chinese imports, as the presence of China as a major manufacturing powerhouse that presents a competitive challenge to the region is not going away any time soon. In an ideal world the region would avoid reverting to protectionist responses, while China itself refrained from unfair subsidies and support for its domestic firms that skew the playing field of global trade. Policymakers and firms in LAC should understand that low-cost manufacturing imports from China can offer key inputs to the region's own production processes, and these trade flows need not be in conflict with the region developing dynamic comparative advantages in manufacturing sectors of its own.

Investment and Financing

Diversified exports would be complemented with diversified FDI from the Chinese, driven not by the need to jump tariffs but by the advantages of proximity, access to resource-intensive inputs, and the quality of the labor force. As the Chinese economy developed more sophisticated private companies, these firms could become increasingly important players in China's outward direct investment alongside the large SOEs in energy, mining, and agriculture that have accounted for most of the FDI in LAC to date. Ideally, Chinese FDI would branch out to include manufacturers, helping diversify the relationship and generate more employment in the region.

This is not to say that there is no place for natural resource sector FDI in the dream scenario. Assuming it was done under competitive bidding procedures and with appropriate environmental safeguards and regulatory frameworks, Chinese investment could help develop the region's natural resource sectors and provide an important source of financing as many countries contemplate ambitious investment plans. The energy sector is especially promising in light of LAC's large potential for unconventional energy resources in shale and deep-water sites, as discussed by Francisco E. González (chapter 5), and Chinese energy firms' keen interest in developing expertise in that area. The key in all sectors is that Chinese firms adhere to a competitive, stable, and transparent framework for foreign investment, alongside MNCs from the United States, Europe, and the rest of Asia. Making this a reality would require, first and foremost, responsible economic and sector management in the region, so as not to be at the mercy of Chinese and only Chinese investment, which would inevitably result in less than optimal arrangements for the LAC side. Likewise, Chinese loans, whether for general budget support or tied to specific infrastructure projects carried out by Chinese contractors, should be just one among many options governments in the region consider to finance their infrastructure needs.

Cooperation and Diplomacy

What political and institutional arrangements would best support the dream scenario? The last decade has seen a proliferation of cooperation initiatives, spanning the new Community of Latin American and Caribbean States (CELAC)–China regional forum to new bilateral and sector agreements. While a clear indicator of interest on both sides, these initiatives do not necessarily translate into substantive cooperation that promotes sustainable and mutually beneficial ties. On the positive side of the ledger, free trade agreements (FTAs) between China and Chile, Peru, and most recently Costa Rica have resulted in important gains for LAC exporters in terms of access to these markets, but unfortunately the politics are not auspicious for further FTAs, as discussed in chapter 7. On the other hand, the strategic partnership and strategic alliance agreements signed between China and various LAC countries have generally been vaguely defined and have not consistently provided the basis for progress on the many issues they encompass.

Regardless of the format, the priority for the region should be to use diplomatic engagement and cooperation to address in a pragmatic and coherent way the main obstacles to trade and investment that stand in the way of realizing the "dream scenario" outlined here. Examples include tariffs, especially the issue of tariff escalation discussed above, and nontariff barriers to trade such as sanitary and phytosanitary measures and other regulatory bottlenecks that impede LAC exports' entry into the Chinese market. However, there is a range of additional policies not part of the traditional trade agenda, such as transportation services agreements to improve connectivity, that would also go a long way toward boosting trade.

While certain issues might be best handled bilaterally, the region can clearly muster greater leverage vis-à-vis China by using regional and subregional groupings to advance common interests, which certainly exist despite the great diversity among the region's economies. In an ideal world, therefore, LAC governments would identify areas where interests align and promote them assertively in forums such as the new CELAC-China meetings. In general, countries in the region need to instill more pragmatism into their relations with China, recognizing that close engagement on trade and commercial issues does not demand that they subscribe to all of China's positions in the international realm.

INDIA: THE NIGHTMARE SCENARIO

To see the worst-case scenario with respect to the LAC-India relationship does not take much imagination. Unlike China, India does not control massive foreign reserves with which it can spread its influence across the region. Nor does its economic structure support internationally oriented SOEs under whose aegis foreign policy and commercial interests converge. For these reasons and others, there is little danger that the relationship devolves toward LAC's subordination and Indian control.

In fact, the nightmare scenario would look a lot like the present: protectionism by governments on both sides, but especially India's, and lack of resolve and initiative by the private sector would prevent the commercial relationship from really taking off, despite the presence of considerable complementarities. As chapter 7 shows, trade between the two economies totaled $43 billion in 2013, a mere 15 percent of LAC-China trade. Meanwhile, FDI has been limited to Indian pharmaceutical, IT, and biofuels firms investing in LAC. This is certainly a good start, and Indian IT firms already employ 25,000 Latin Americans, according to Rengaraj Viswanathan (chapter 4). Still, Indian FDI in the region totaled only $16 billion between 2000 and 2012. The potential exists for far deeper linkages, with Indian firms taking advantage of relatively high-skilled and bilingual workers to provide services both to the region and the United States, with its increasingly large Spanish-speaking population.

On the other side, multilatinas have almost completely ignored India, with LAC firms' announced investments totaling only $722 million over the past decade. While there are clearly challenges to operating in such a geographically and culturally distant environment (although governments can take steps to bridge this gap), LAC firms are potentially missing an opportunity to get in "on the ground floor" of India's growth takeoff. Owing to its size and demographic characteristics, projections of India growing at China's rates of 7 percent or higher over the next couple of decades have been common.

In terms of diplomatic engagement, important initiatives to address concrete barriers to trade have been few and far between, despite stirrings of interest in closer cooperation. India has preferential trade agreements with Chile and Mercosur, but these agreements fall well short of FTAs in their coverage and depth of liberalization. Brazil and India have attempted to forge deeper cooperation in the context of the BRICS and IBSA forums, the latter being a trilateral grouping with South Africa. The former has arguably been undermined by lack of agreement and divergence of interests among its very different members and by attempts by China to steer its agenda. In the case of IBSA, there have been a number of agreements in areas ranging from agriculture to the information society, but the forum does not seem poised to tackle the immediately relevant barriers to trade and investment. The present situation thus shows the limitations of diplomacy and cooperation based on lofty yet often nebulous notions of south-south cooperation, which are subject to the ebbs and flows of political support and can serve to obscure rather than resolve the key issues.

INDIA: THE DREAM SCENARIO

In laying out the dream scenario for LAC and India, it is instructive to reflect on the experience of the last dozen years of LAC-China relations. Naturally, fundamental differences exist, and these serve to highlight the great potential for LAC-India ties. Unlike in the case of China, India's outwardly oriented firms are mostly private, meaning that commercial ties are likely to progress through market-based terms without foreign policy objectives influencing firms' trade and investment decisions. Second, India does not marshal the overwhelming financial arsenal that has allowed China to enjoy an unquestionable advantage in bargaining power in its relations with LAC; by contrast, LAC and India can approach each other on a more equal footing. Finally, India as a trading partner presents a different set of comparative advantages than does China. As discussed by Jorge Heine and Hari Seshasayee (chapter 3) and by Viswanathan (chapter 4), India has forged its international competitiveness on the basis of services such as IT and business processes and pharmaceuticals, which offer more complementarity than competition with the region.

Notwithstanding these differences, there are clear lessons emanating from LAC's relations with China about how to manage the India relationship. Most important, engagement should be pragmatic and geared toward advancing a concrete policy agenda to promote commercial ties and advance the development prospects of both sides, rather than emphasizing quixotic and ill-defined efforts at all-compassing and globally oriented cooperation. A second warning, related to the first, is that the commercial relationship should be based on the premise of open markets and competition, not on exclusive deals negotiated on opaque terms.

A dream scenario would therefore see a steady increase in bilateral trade and foreign investment as governments pragmatically addressed high tariffs and connectivity issues and the private sectors on both sides proactively pursued existing complementarities. Indian pharmaceutical and IT/outsourcing firms would build on their initial presence in the region, exploring opportunities to set up more production facilities, research labs, and call center operations in the region. While not without the potential for competition, these sectors provide considerable complementarities, as LAC offers Indian IT and outsourcing firms a strategic base of operations to serve both the region and the United States, owing to the time zone advantages and LAC's supply of educated, bilingual workers. India's pharmaceutical firms, meanwhile, do not pose the same direct competitive threat as China's to LAC's core manufacturing strengths. On the other hand, LAC would ideally be able to find a large and growing market for its natural resources, where it could not only expand the trade in basic commodities—which India, like China, does not possess in sufficient quantities to meet domestic demand—but also leverage its advanced capabilities in biotechnology to export more sophisticated and higher-value-added products.

TURNING DREAM SCENARIOS INTO REALITY

The actions needed to steer the relationships with China and India in the direction of the dream scenarios are by no means out of reach or far-fetched. While effective cooperation with Chinese and Indian counterparts is undoubtedly part of the equation, much of the work can and in fact must be done by the region itself. As described, the greatest risks for LAC in relations with China arise when governments become dependent on Chinese financing because of poor economic policies. In such contexts, LAC governments can hardly be expected to resist Chinese efforts to secure for China's own firms (and, increasingly likely, its workers too) privileged access to contracts, natural resources, and employment opportunities or to advocate aggressively for greater access to China's market.

An obvious starting point is therefore to make the necessary reforms at home in order to engage with China from a position of strength rather than desperation. Beyond that, governments in the region should identify and work on the key issues to address to make the most of the opportunities provided by China's enormous economy while minimizing negative externalities in the environmental and social realms. The goal should be to expand trade and investment on market-based terms by improving access for more sophisticated natural resource–based products and to actively promote investment by Chinese firms in a variety of sectors, subject, of course, to competitive terms and under robust environmental and social protections.

What is important is to pragmatically identify specific, concrete barriers—for example, long delays in winning approval for agricultural exports or the lack of air connections between LAC and Chinese cities—and to advance these issues in a coordinated and persistent way in the rapidly growing bilateral and multilateral LAC-China forums. Where common interests exist across LAC countries, governments should leverage regional and subregional groupings to enhance their bargaining power on such issues.

The private sector, too, has a key role to play by making a decisive commitment to succeeding in China. In this regard, firms need to devote the resources and develop the expertise necessary to operate in China, including hiring staff with the requisite language and country knowledge and, when the scale and nature of the industry merit it, to set up more direct operations in China, which relatively few LAC firms have done but which provides major advantages, based on the experiences of the firms that have taken this approach.

In the case of India, all of the above also apply. The tasks are similar, but there are arguably more immediate obstacles in the form of high tariffs and information barriers owing to lack of familiarity that governments need to address first. India's economy remains relatively closed to trade and foreign investment. As discussed throughout the volume, the government of Narendra Modi, which came to power in May 2014, could undertake major reforms and expand on existing trade agreements, putting India on a more open and integrated path. If this turns out to be the case, governments in the region have an opportunity to make important progress on dismantling the major barriers needed to kick-start LAC-India relations.

ABOUT THE AUTHORS

HENRIQUE ALTEMANI DE OLIVEIRA is a professor of International Relations at the State University of Paraiba (Brazil) as well as director of the Asia-Pacific Studies Center.

DEEPAK BHOJWANI is a retired Indian Foreign Service (IFS) Officer and the founder of the consultancy Latindia. From 2000–2012, he served as India's Ambassador in seven Latin American countries.

ANTHONY BOADLE is a senior political correspondent in Brazil for Thomson Reuters. Prior to that, he held a variety of journalistic posts throughout the Western Hemisphere, including news editor in Washington, D.C., and bureau chief in Havana, Cuba.

ROBERT DEVLIN is an adjunct professor of Latin American Studies at Johns Hopkins-SAIS and an associate director at the Dublin consulting firm Communiqué International.

ENRIQUE DUSSEL PETERS is a professor at the Graduate School of Economics of the Universidad Nacional Autónoma de México (UNAM). He is also the coordinator of the Center for Chinese-Mexican Studies at UNAM and the coordinator of the Academic Network of Latin America and the Caribbean on China (RED ALC-CHINA).

R. EVAN ELLIS is a research professor of Latin American Studies at the U.S. Army War College Strategic Studies Institute. He is also a nonresident senior fellow with the Center for Strategic and International Studies in Washington, D.C.

ALICIA FROHMANN is a professor at the Universidad de Chile and an international trade consultant with the United Nations Economic Commission for Latin America and the Caribbean (ECLAC). Previously, she served as director of ProChile, the Trade Promotion Agency for the Chilean Government's Ministry of Foreign Relations.

KEVIN P. GALLAGHER is a professor of Global Development Policy at Boston University's Pardee School for Global Studies, where he co-directs the Global Economic Governance Initiative (GEGI).

FRANCISCO E. GONZÁLEZ is the Riordan Roett Senior Associate Professor of Latin American Studies at Johns Hopkins-SAIS.

JORGE GUAJARDO is a senior director at McLarty Associates in Washington, D.C. From 2007–2013, he served as Mexico's Ambassador to China.

JORGE HEINE is a professor of Political Science at the Balsillie School of International Affairs, Wilfrid Laurier University. From 2003–2007, he served as Chile's Ambassador to India, Bangladesh, and Sri Lanka.

THEODORE KAHN is a PhD candidate in the Latin American Studies program at Johns Hopkins–SAI and a consultant in the Integration and Trade Sector of the Inter-American Development Bank (IDB).

JACQUELINE MAZZA is an adjunct professor of Latin American Studies at Johns Hopkins-SAIS, teaching at both the Washington, D.C. and Bologna, Italy campuses. She is the former principal labor markets specialist at the Inter-American Development Bank.

MAURICIO MESQUITA MOREIRA is the principal economic advisor and research coordinator of the Integration and Trade Sector at the Inter-American Development Bank (IDB).

GUADALUPE PAZ is the associate director of the Latin American Studies Program at Johns Hopkins-SAIS. She is also the director of faculty affairs and planning in the SAIS Office of Academic and Faculty Affairs.

REBECCA RAY is a fellow at Boston University's Global Economic Governance Initiative (GEGI).

RIORDAN ROETT is a professor of Latin American Studies and the director of the Latin American Studies Program at Johns Hopkins-SAIS.

HARI SESHASAYEE is a Latin America specialist at the Confederation of Indian Industry. He previously worked as a Senior Researcher at the Gateway House (Indian Council on Global Relations).

SUN HONGBO is an associate professor at the Institute of Latin American Studies (ILAS) of the Chinese Academy of Social Sciences (CASS).

MARIANO TURZI is a professor of International Relations at the Universidad Torcuato Di Tella (UTDT) and New York University in Buenos Aires.

RENGARAJ VISWANATHAN is a distinguished fellow of Latin American Studies at the Gateway House (Indian Council on Global Relations) and a retired Indian Foreign Service (IFS) Officer. From 2007–2012, he served as India's Ambassador to Argentina, Uruguay, and Paraguay and prior to that as Ambassador to Venezuela and Consul General in So Paulo, Brazil.

MANFRED WILHELMY is a professor at the Institute of International Studies at the Universidad de Chile.

XIANG LANXIN is a professor of International History and Politics at the Graduate Institute of International and Development Studies in Geneva.

INDEX